SPEAKING *with* NATURE

Also by Ramachandra Guha

History

The Unquiet Woods: Ecological Change and Peasant Resistance in the Himalaya

Environmentalism: A Global History

A Corner of a Foreign Field: The Indian History of a British Sport

India after Gandhi: A History

Biography

Savaging the Civilized: Verrier Elwin, His Tribals, and India

Gandhi before India

Gandhi: The Years that Changed the World, 1914–1948

Rebels against the Raj: Western Fighters for India's Freedom

Memoir

The Commonwealth of Cricket

The Cooking of Books

Essays

An Anthropologist among the Marxists and Other Essays

The Last Liberal and Other Essays

Patriots and Partisans

Democrats and Dissenters

Edited Works

Social Ecology

The Picador Book of Cricket

Makers of Modern India

Makers of Modern Asia

SPEAKING *with* NATURE

THE ORIGINS OF INDIAN ENVIRONMENTALISM

RAMACHANDRA GUHA

FOURTH ESTATE · *New Delhi*

First published in India by Fourth Estate 2024
An imprint of HarperCollins *Publishers*
4th Floor, Tower A, Building No. 10, DLF Cyber City,
DLF Phase II, Gurugram, Haryana – 122002
www.harpercollins.co.in

2 4 6 8 10 9 7 5 3 1

P-ISBN: 978-93-6213-490-5
E-ISBN: 978-93-6213-890-3

Typeset in 11.5/15.8 Sabon LT Std at
Manipal Technologies Limited, Manipal

Printed and bound at
Thomson Press (India) Ltd.

MIX
Paper | Supporting responsible forestry
FSC® C010615

This book is produced from independently certified FSC® paper
to ensure responsible forest management.

For Joan Martinez-Alier, friend and fellow traveller on the road from Red to Green

And for my daughter, Ira, an accidental environmentalist

God forbid that India should ever take to industrialization after the manner of the West. The economic imperialism of a single tiny island kingdom is today keeping the world in chains. If an entire nation of 300 million took to similar economic exploitation, it would strip the world bare like locusts.

—Mahatma Gandhi, writing in December 1928

Contents

Introduction

Shades of Green

THE GREAT BRITISH HISTORIAN E.P. Thompson once remarked that 'India is not an important country, but perhaps the most important country for the future of the world. Here is a country that merits no one's condescension. All the convergent influences of the world run through this society: Hindu, Moslem, Christian, secular; Stalinist, liberal, Maoist, democratic socialist, Gandhian. There is not a thought that is being thought in the West or East which is not active in some Indian mind.'[1]

Some may cavil at E.P. Thompson's assertion that India is (or ever was) the most 'important' country for the future of the world. But I want rather to focus on his other claim—namely, that there has been an astonishing diversity of intellectual opinion in India. This is a product of the country's size, its cultural heterogeneity, and its daring (if admittedly imperfect) attempt to construct a democratic political system in a deeply hierarchical society. Indeed, among the countries of the so-called 'Global South', India is notable for the vigour, sophistication and self-confidence of its intellectual traditions. In this respect it stands out; to be contrasted not only with the smaller countries of Asia and Africa, but also with its even larger neighbour, China, where the scholarly traditions of the past have been brutally crushed by a totalitarian state.

This book explores a significant yet somewhat neglected strand of Indian intellectual life—that pertaining to the past, present and possible future of human relations with the natural world. By the canons of orthodox social science, countries like India are not supposed to have an environmental consciousness. They are, as it were, 'too poor to be green'. As the MIT economist Lester Thurow famously (or notoriously) remarked in 1980: 'If you look at the countries that are interested in environmentalism, or at the individuals who support environmentalism within each country, one is struck by the extent to which environmentalism is an interest of the upper middle class. *Poor countries and poor individuals simply aren't interested.*'[2]

This magisterial dismissal of any possibility of poor countries being interested in environmentalism was, at least with regard to India, several years out of date. In the spring of 1973, a popular peasant movement in the Himalaya, known as Chipko, threatened to hug the hill forests to stop them from being felled by commercial loggers. Many of the participants were unlettered; however, the leaders, though themselves from peasant backgrounds, were informed and articulate about wider issues. They wrote essays and tracts (usually in Hindi) tracing the direct link between industrial forestry, soil erosion, landslides and floods. These showed that what at one level was an economic conflict—between the subsistence demands of peasants for fuel, fodder, etc., and the commercial motivations of paper and plywood companies—had deeper ecological implications as well.

Chipko was followed by a series of other grassroots initiatives around community access to forests, pasture and water. They likewise posited subsistence versus commerce, the village versus the city, the peasant versus the state, the subaltern versus the elite. Studying and reflecting on these conflicts, scholars argued that they showed the way to reconfiguring India's development path. Given the country's population densities and the fragility of tropical ecologies, India had erred in following the energy-intensive, capital-intensive, resource-intensive model of economic development pioneered by the West. When the country got its freedom from British rule in 1947, it should have instead adopted a more bottom-up, community-oriented and environmentally prudent pattern of development. However, the argument further proceeded, it was not too late to make amends. The state and the citizen should both heed the lesson of Chipko and modify public policies and social behaviour accordingly.

The environmental debate in India was at its most vigorous in the decade of the 1980s. Scientists, social scientists, journalists and grassroots activists all contributed to it. The debate operated at many levels: philosophical, political, social, technological. It touched on the moral and cultural aspects of humanity's relations with nature; on the changes required in the distribution of power to promote environmental sustainability; on the design of appropriate technologies that could simultaneously meet economic as well as ecological objectives. The debate embraced all resource sectors—forests, water, soil, transport, energy, biodiversity, pollution and industrial safety.

The post-Chipko environmental upsurge led to some institutional changes within India. New laws seeking to conserve forests, protect wildlife and control pollution were enacted. In 1980 the Government of India started a new Department of Environment, upgraded later into a full-fledged Ministry of Environment and Forests. New centres of ecological research were set up in Indian universities. Terms such as 'ecological history', 'environmental sociology' and 'ecological economics' began entering the teaching curriculum and research agendas of the academy. A new breed of 'environmental journalists' came into existence; their reports on forests, pollution, biodiversity and grassroots struggles featured in newspapers and magazines.

In those years, thinkers and activists in India played a profound role in shaping global conversations about humanity's relationship with nature as well. Indian scholars posited the idea of 'livelihood environmentalism' in contrast to the 'full-stomach environmentalism' of the affluent world. Some of the most pungent criticisms of overconsumption in the West came from Indian writers. Scientists like Madhav Gadgil and A.K.N. Reddy, journalists like Anil Agarwal and Sunita Narain, and activists like Medha Patkar and Ashish Kothari acquired international reputations. Ideas originally developed in India were discussed and debated in other countries and continents.[3]

I cut my scholarly teeth studying (and occasionally participating in) those debates. My first book was a social history of the Chipko movement. Then, prompted by the experience of living for several years in the United States, I widened my lens, geographically speaking, by exploring the articulation of environmental concerns in a comparative context. Some of this latter work was done in collaboration with the Catalan scholar Joan Martinez-Alier, whose extensive knowledge of Latin America and Europe complemented my own understanding of India and North America.[4]

Social movements have their origin myths. They exalt and elevate a foundational event which serves both as a source of inspiration and as a point of departure. I knew only too well that Chipko, which began in the last week of March 1973, had that very special place in the hearts and minds of Indian environmentalists. Looking beyond my own country, I now found that most American environmentalists dated the beginning of their movement to the publication, in the fall of 1962, of Rachel Carson's book *Silent Spring*. One might even say that this was the proverbial spark that lit the prairie fire—but perhaps the metaphor (evoking destruction) is inappropriate in the present context.

The controversy generated by *Silent Spring* played a crucial part in fuelling popular mobilization in America around the question of environmental degradation. Through the 1960s and beyond, the 'environmental' movement joined the civil rights movement, the feminist movement and the anti-war movement as a major vehicle of social mobilization. Like those other movements, the environmental movement raised public consciousness through marches and demonstrations and the publication of books and pamphlets. And it simultaneously urged politicians to reform their laws and policies in favour of their own special concerns—namely, the protection of endangered species and wilderness areas, and the provision of clean air and water, rather than equal rights for women and African Americans or an end to American adventurism abroad.

The impact of the environmental movement on the political and economic structures of the United States was decidedly uneven. On the other hand, its impact on the American academy was substantial. *Silent Spring* and its aftermath gave birth to a brand-new field of scholarship known as 'environmental history'. The term was first used by the American scholar Roderick Nash in 1972, and given formal shape by the founding in 1976 of the American Society for Environmental History (ASEH). The European Society for Environmental History came into existence only two decades later, in 1999. In 2005, a Society for Latin American and Caribbean Environmental History was established. (There is as yet no Indian or South Asian or even pan-Asian equivalent of these bodies).

British and European historians had previously set new standards in economic and social history, in the study of agriculture, industry and commerce on the one hand, and in the study of social inequality and peasant and working class struggles on the other. Cultural history and intellectual history were also most highly developed on the Continent. However, the field of environmental history, the study of human relations with the natural world, has found its fullest expression in the American academy. There are now more than a thousand members of the ASEH, more than a thousand published scholars in America who self-identify as 'environmental historians'.[5]

The American historian Alfred Crosby, himself one of the pioneers of the field, has remarked that 'the environmentalist movement of the 1960s and after was the engine that drove environmental history. What had been a discontinuous mutter of complaint rose to a continuous shout audible even in the halls of academe.'[6] Paying back their dues to the social movement that inspired them, scholars went on to excavate what I shall call a 'prehistory' of environmentalism, showcasing American thinkers who, from a century (and more) before the publication of *Silent Spring*, wrote with passion and insight about the destruction of the wilderness by commercial and industrial interests.

The term 'environmentalist' came into common currency only in the 1970s; yet, as these American historians persuasively showed, individuals like John Muir and Aldo Leopold (among others) certainly qualified, in terms of what they said and how they said it, as environmentalists. The works by these historians in turn fed back into the movement, with late twentieth century activists inspired and nourished by the example of long-dead precursors such as Muir and Leopold.[7]

I remarked earlier that it was American scholars who were in the forefront of the discipline—or sub-discipline—of environmental history. It is also Americans who have contributed most prolifically to the history of environmentalism. Now, in a spirit of (mostly friendly) competition, historians of other countries set to work. So, for example, we have had important works published in English of environmentalism in the United Kingdom, Germany, France,

Russia and Norway. These emulate their American counterparts in seeking to demonstrate that, though as a popular *movement* environmentalism is a phenomenon of the latter decades of the twentieth century, many of its themes were anticipated by prescient men (more rarely women) writing in earlier times, and in countries other than the United States.[8]

As the first movers in the field, American environmental historians had constructed a pantheon of prophets, among whom three were perhaps pre-eminent—the naturalist John Muir and the wildlife biologist Aldo Leopold, whom I have already mentioned, and their distinguished forebear Henry David Thoreau, long hailed as an iconic figure in the history of American individualism and American dissent, now (with reason) seen as an early environmentalist as well. While this trinity attracted the most attention—and admiration—other American thinkers such as the geographer-diplomat George Perkins Marsh and the utilitarian forester Gifford Pinchot were also hailed as environmental pioneers.[9] A stream of biographical and critical studies appeared around these men, locating their work against the background of the rapacious exploitation of natural resources in nineteenth- and early twentieth-century America. Through their writing and campaigning, Muir, Marsh and company sought to tame and reverse this process of destruction, albeit in their different, distinctive, and occasionally clashing ways.

While based on primary research, in their presentation these works were lyrical and triumphalist, presenting their subjects as environmental teachers and guides not just to their fellow Americans, but to the world. The work of these historians was picked up by popular writers, who likewise conveyed their nation's precedence and priority in this field. The editor of a recent anthology that starts with Thoreau and features Marsh, Muir and Leopold, argues that 'environmental writing is America's single most distinctive contribution to the world's literature', and that out of this writing 'emerged the *first modern environmentalists*'. The anthologist further adds that these American environmental writers were 'doing the necessary work of seeking out ideas and images that will help America, *and then the world*, to confront the very much deeper problem we now face'.[10]

This 'Americans were there first' narrative has been complicated by European historians, who have argued that other countries had produced their own environmental pioneers, and sometimes earlier than in the United States. Henry Thoreau, the oldest of the Holy Trinity of American environmentalists, was born in 1817; by which time the German explorer Alexander von Humboldt had already produced an impressive body of work that, in so minutely describing nature as an interconnected web of living beings, showed him to be 'a prescient proto-environmentalist'[11] who anticipated not just Thoreau and John Muir, but also Charles Darwin. Historians of empire made the case that French and British scientists working in Asia, Africa and Australia had written of deforestation and desiccation prior to the early environmentalists celebrated in America.[12]

Meanwhile, the original template of environmental history had been challenged within the United States itself. This was because in the classic, trendsetting books and essays, the heroic pioneers were all men, and all white. These narratives, wrote one critic, 'elided the diverse roots of environmental reform, ignored key constituencies, narrowed the scope of issues involved, and failed to identify key participants'.[13] Among the groups largely ignored by the early histories of American environmentalism were women, people of colour, and indigenous groups. More recent works have sought to focus on these hitherto excluded groups, exploring their attitudes to nature and the natural world through the nineteenth and twentieth centuries. Thus, while it may have been supposed that the brutal experience of slavery would permanently alienate black Americans from the American landscape, in fact writers like W.E.B. Du Bois wrote with great empathy and appreciation about mountains, parks, gardens and forests.[14]

Notwithstanding its richness and scholarly sophistication, this burgeoning literature on the history of environmentalism has been characterized by one major defect. This is its narrow geographical focus. The challenge to American intellectual hegemony in this field first came from Europe, and what took place there was noticed in America. The traffic of ideas across the Atlantic was intense. Yet the conversation was conducted as if environmental movements and environmental thinkers could not exist outside Europe and North America. I hasten to add that this bias did not originate in any sort of colonialist condescension or feelings of racial superiority. Rather, it most likely had its roots in conventional social science wisdom which still held—notwithstanding Chipko and the like—that environmentalism was 'a full stomach' phenomenon, possible and conceivable only in societies where a certain level of material prosperity had been reached.

To show how persistent and widely shared this conventional wisdom was, consider these remarks from a book by Eric Hobsbawm published in 1994: 'It is no accident that the main support for ecological policies comes from the rich countries and from the comfortable rich and middle classes (except for businessmen, who hope to make money by polluting activity). The poor, multiplying and under-employed, wanted more "development", not less.'[15]

These remarks mimic those of Lester Thurow from a decade and a half previously. Nonetheless, they are deeply disappointing. Unlike Thurow, Hobsbawm was a historian, not an economist, and therefore we must presume, more attentive to the messiness of social life, more interested in exploring hidden details than in postulating grand generalizations. Unlike Thurow, whose life was lived largely within the North American academy, Hobsbawm had a keen interest in Latin America, a continent he had travelled widely in. He kept himself abreast of current events in Africa and Asia. He had friends, students and colleagues in countries around the world. One would have thought a scholar as learned and well informed as Hobsbawm would have heard of the Chipko movement in the Himalaya or the Green Belt movement in Kenya. Or at least, given his strong connections with Latin America, of the movement of Chico Mendes and the rubber tappers in Brazil—another example of the environmentalism of the poor.[16] Surely, he had read of the brutal murder of Mendes in 1988? Or was it that the conventional wisdom was so seductive that it continued to be upheld regardless of an inconvenient fact or two? Or perhaps Hobsbawm's Marxist faith did not allow him to see environmentalism as anything other than a bourgeois deviation from the class struggle?

Some writers have looked for the origins of environmentalism in the distant past, in religious scriptures that allegedly mandated a profound respect for nature, or in folk traditions that promoted prudent resource use.[17] This search, I believe, is somewhat anachronistic. For environmentalism is a distinctively modern phenomenon, made feasible and possible only in the past two (at most, two and a half) centuries. This is because the speed and intensity of environmental change that came in the wake of the Industrial Revolution was unprecedented in human history. The factory system was accompanied by the easy availability of fossil fuels, new forms of transport and communication, increasing urbanization, the invention of synthetic chemicals, industrial-scale mining and rapid increases in human population. These transformative developments aided economic growth in the short and medium term, yet without taking account of the future costs they would impose on the earth and all its inhabitants.

All through history, humans have affected, and been affected by, the natural environments they live and labour in. Nonetheless, as John McNeill points out, 'modern history seems a case apart. The scale, scope, pace, and intensity of anthropogenic environmental change since the emergence of fossil fuels around 1800, and especially since 1945, eclipse that which went before.' In past times, notes McNeill, 'humans lacked the power to disturb global ecology'.[18] The key word here is 'global'. Previously, there were many examples of localized environmental disturbance due to human intervention, instances of modest areas of forests being cut, soils in particular fields being depleted, or the odd river or two being polluted through small-scale mining using hand tools. However, such instances of environmental abuse were never so serious as to impact an entire country, let alone the world as a whole. It is only with the Industrial Revolution that air and water pollution, chemical contamination of the soil, deforestation and biodiversity loss began occurring on a massive scale, affecting hundreds of millions of people. It was only after the Industrial Revolution that there arose the perception of a possible *global* environmental crisis, the realization that the new technologies and ways of living now being crafted by humans could, if unchecked, undermine their own future on earth.

Some Hindu religious texts spoke lovingly of trees; others (as in a famous passage in the Mahabharata) celebrated the destruction of forests. Some peasant communities had designed social institutions regulating the use of water and forests in their locality; others had not.[19] Humans have engaged with nature in varied and often contradictory ways throughout history. However, it is only in modern times that humans have reshaped and degraded nature so dramatically as to make the state and fate of the earth a matter of moral (and political) concern.

My early work on environmentalism sought to challenge the idea that the poorer countries of the Global South, and especially the poorer individuals within it, would not be interested in treating nature and natural resources with care, understanding and respect. Its temporal focus was the decades of the 1970s and 1980s, when debates about environmentalism were at their most intense in my home country, India.

The present book takes a longer view, by rehabilitating thinkers who wrote about these themes before the Chipko movement itself began. It originated—as historical projects so often do—in serendipitous discoveries in a library, of pamphlets and tracts written in the 1930s and 1940s by two Indian thinkers speaking in what seemed to be a recognizably environmentalist idiom. These individuals were named Radhakamal Mukerjee and J.C. Kumarappa. Mukerjee worked (and wrote) from within the interstices of a university position, while Kumarappa was a social activist and a close associate of Mahatma Gandhi. At the time I first stumbled across their works—in the late 1980s—neither were anywhere close to being a 'household name' in India. Mukerjee, who died in 1968, was known to some within the academy; Kumarappa, who died in 1960, was known to those who had worked directly with him. And both, of course, were entirely unknown outside India—though, as it happens, I myself discovered their writings in the stacks of the Sterling Memorial Library at Yale University.

My work on grassroots struggles such as Chipko had challenged the prejudice, so common in North American and West European scholarly circles, that individuals and societies needed to achieve a certain degree of economic prosperity before they developed any sort of environmental sensibility. It also took issue with the claim made by many Indians themselves that environmentalism was a Western fad which had no place in our country. In the mainstream press, environmentalists were widely derided as backward-looking reactionaries who wished to keep India from joining the march to modernity. Those who led campaigns in defence of forest rights or stood alongside those displaced by large infrastructure projects, were accused by politicians and industrialists of being funded from overseas and even sometimes of being CIA agents in disguise. I sought to counter these arguments in two ways: first by demonstrating that this was an environmentalism of the *poor*, with peasants, tribals, pastoralists and fisherfolk forming its core constituency; and second, by arguing that given India's higher population densities, fragile ecologies and lack of access to colonies, it had to forge a more environmentally responsible economic path than the West had.[20]

Popular struggles like Chipko, I argued, were endogenous to India and resonated with the concerns of Indians. They were not a pernicious first world export. Their voices and concerns needed to be heard and even acted upon, if my country was to assure for itself a more contented future. Now, coming across the writings of these forgotten pioneers, I hoped to consolidate my case, by showing how Indians had debated questions of sustainability and prudent use well before Chipko. From Radhakamal Mukerjee and J.C. Kumarappa, I went in search of other such figures who might credibly qualify as 'early environmentalists'. I found some who preceded even Mukerjee and Kumarappa, writing about how colonialism and industrialism had ravaged rural landscapes and undermined community life from the late nineteenth century onwards.

By the early 1990s, I had several notebooks filled with material on what I now thought of as India's 'first wave' environmentalists. I also had a shelf of out-of-print books and pamphlets to go with them. In the year 1992, I published a scholarly article based on my research. It featured four thinkers—the aforementioned Mukerjee and Kumarappa, and two individuals of British extraction who had worked in India, the town planner Patrick Geddes and the anthropologist Verrier Elwin. Though I did not say so explicitly, my aim was to provide contemporary Indian environmentalism with a credible intellectual genealogy. I hoped to do for my country what American environmental historians had done for theirs—namely, recover and rehabilitate hidden or little-known voices from the past who had, in different ways, anticipated the concerns of the present.[21]

The essay attracted some notice, and I planned to expand it into a full-length book, a study of Indian environmental ideas to complement the study of Indian environmental activism I had already published. Even as I was planning this book's narrative arc and identifying archives to visit, I was contacted by a publisher who made me an offer I could not refuse. This was to write a one-volume political and social history of India. My country had just completed fifty years of freedom, a period fraught with conflict and controversy but through which we had nonetheless maintained our territorial unity and at least some semblance of democratic functioning. That project took several years to complete, whereupon I began work on a biography of Mahatma Gandhi, which took even longer to finish.

By the time these deviations had run their course two decades had passed. I was now ready to once more pick up the threads of that as yet unwritten book on the origins of Indian environmentalism. In retrospect, the delays were fortuitous, for two reasons. First, they deepened my understanding of the broader historical context in which the thinkers featured in this book lived and worked. Second, in the course of visiting archives across the world I found material on other thinkers apart from the quartet I had first written about—thinkers who, in what they said and how they said it, could likewise be considered to be environmentalists before the age of environmentalism. These inadvertent or at least unplanned detours into political history thus gave me the time and opportunity to expand my cast of characters as well as deepen the vein of primary materials on which a work of this kind must be based.

In publishing the book now, thirty years after the project first took shape in my head, I have been encouraged by a remark of the historian A.P. Thornton: 'A writer has to make do with what ideas come to him; but he can always send them out again in better shape.'[22]

When I began my career, in the 1980s, the discipline of environmental history was in its infancy in India. As for Indian activists, they were monumentally ahistorical, obsessed as they were (perhaps inevitably) with reshaping the present so as to ensure a more sustainable future. Though they nodded respectfully to Chipko as marking the beginning of their movement, they looked no further back.

In the decades since, while environmental history has developed into a robust field of research in India, it has resolutely focused on the material side of things—on how Indians have, over the decades and centuries, used and abused forests, water, land and other resources.[23] However, ideas matter too. That is the presumption of this book, which offers a history of environmental ideas in India through profiles of ten thinkers who wrote insightfully and often provocatively about human attitudes towards nature. Four have already been named—Mukerjee, Kumarappa, Geddes and Elwin. The others are the writer and institution-builder Rabindranath Tagore, the Gandhian activist Madeleine Slade/Mira Behn, the scientists Albert and Gabrielle Howard, the Hindu ideologue K.M. Munshi, and the roving naturalist M. Krishnan.

These thinkers came from widely varying social and intellectual backgrounds and lived in different parts of India. Some had human relations with nature as the principal focus of their work; some were better known for their contributions in other fields. Yet, as this book shows, all, without being anachronistic, can be considered to be environmental pioneers, if we accept John McNeill's definition of environmentalism 'as the view that humankind ought to seek peaceful coexistence with, rather than mastery of, nature'.[24] Likewise, though the term 'sustainable development' came into currency only in the 1980s, we can see the thinkers featured here as clearly anticipating that concept, if, following Paul Warde, we understand sustainability as 'the idea that to endure, a society must not undermine the ecological underpinnings on which it is dependent'.[25]

In India, environmentalism as I define it was made possible only after the subcontinent came under the control of British imperialists. Colonial rule constituted an ecological watershed, in that it brought with it new technologies of controlling, manipulating, reshaping and destroying nature. In pre-British times, the state had occasionally participated in natural resource management, as with the elephant forests maintained by the Mauryan kings, or horse pastures maintained by medieval chiefdoms. However, under the British the state became a far more active player in human–nature interactions, by, among other things, taking over the subcontinent's vast woodlands under government control, and constructing large-scale irrigation projects. The British also brought the railway and modern factories to India, both of which were fuelled by coal and hence productive of major transformations in the environment. The pace of urbanization also greatly accelerated after the advent of the British Raj.

My narrative begins in the second half of the nineteenth century, when the profound environmental implications of colonialism first became apparent, provoking the variety of responses by the thinkers profiled in the book. The first person featured in the book, Rabindranath Tagore, was born in 1861;

the last, M. Krishnan, died as recently as 1996. The narrative thus spans more than a century of Indian history, for the first part of which the country was under British rule and for the latter part an independent nation.

The ten thinkers featured here practised many different vocations or callings. Three were principally writers, four others principally scholars. Two were activists in the Indian freedom struggle. One had no 'principal' profession, partaking in equal measure of the law, literature and politics. However, they are united for our purposes in that they all addressed human–nature relationships, and that they did so in writing.

This introductory chapter is followed by nine others, eight devoted to a single individual, one to a husband-and-wife pairing whom for intellectual reasons I have chosen to treat together. Each chapter provides a brief biographical sketch but focuses on the ideas articulated by each individual. My narrative draws from many fugitive sources and is often interspersed with direct quotations, since it is important to hear these pioneers in their own voice(s). The book ends with an epilogue where I tease out how these long-dead thinkers, individually and collectively, speak to the environmental concerns of our own time.

In the academy, literary scholars are trained to disparage nonfiction, 'to treat it as at best supplementary to "real literature" like the novel or poetry'. The words quoted are those of the South African scholar Rob Nixon, who notes that he himself, going against the grain, is 'drawn to nonfiction's robust adaptability, imaginative and political, as well as to its information-carrying capacity and its aura of the real'. Nixon further observes that 'a particular joy of teaching transnational environmental literatures is the vigorous, varied writing on offer from within nonfiction's broad domain—memoirs, essays, public science writing, polemics, travel literature, graphic memoirs, manifestos, and investigative journalism'.[26]

This book utilizes and draws on all these genres (except graphic memoirs), while adding some new ones, such as letters, plans, educational treatises and public social science writing. Conventional literary scholars may see my underplaying of poems, plays and novels as a weakness—and even as a disqualification. I myself do not regret focusing here on these varied forms of non-fiction writing, while accepting that there is perhaps a complementary book to be written (by someone else) on the ways in which environmental change has been represented and understood by Indian poets, novelists and playwrights in the nineteenth and twentieth centuries.[27]

However, I do regret another and perhaps more telling weakness of this book—that its protagonists are, with only two exceptions, all male. I might quote in extenuation the words of Paul Warde, who, in the preface to his book *The Invention of Sustainability*, notes ruefully and factually that its pages are 'overwhelmingly filled with the voices of men, and by and large rich men, not because they had any intrinsically greater significance than women, but because they were able to participate in debates and have a record of them in a way that women, and poorer men, were not'.[28] What was true of early modern Europe was truer of early modern India, where the social, economic, political and legal mores of the time excluded women even more forcibly from public debates. Notably, the two women featured in this book were both of European origin. (On the other hand, five of the eight male characters are Indian.) The barriers and burdens of patriarchy, harsh enough in the West, were infinitely harsher here. Though India remains a country largely dominated by men, freedom and democracy have opened up more possibilities for women. Now, in the third decade of the twenty-first century, many of India's most admired environmental scientists and environmental activists are women. However, in the times in which this book is set, a career in science or social activism was very nearly impossible for them.

Despite its exclusions—forced or inevitable—the writers featured here do represent a wide diversity of approaches and perspectives. Some were extremely peripatetic, travelling widely across India and the world in the course of their work. The others, even when living for long periods in one place, journeyed to other parts of the country. The geographical range covered by their lives (and, more crucially, by their writings) is immense—from the mountains in the far North to the flat Tamil country in the deep South, from the deltaic regions of Bengal in the East to semi-arid Gujarat in the West, with Central India also adequately represented. Mountains, deserts, alluvial floodplain, plateau, tropical forests, pastures, wetlands, rivers, the coasts, the village, the town, the city—all these distinctive ecological regimes find their place in the narrative. Through these thinkers this book thus pays proper respect to the unparalleled natural and social diversity of the Indian subcontinent.

Though set in India, this is a book with a decidedly transnational and even global frame of reference. Five of these thinkers were born and raised overseas. Their work was informed by their personal and philosophical formation in their country of origin, and by their experiences and journeys within India as well. Of those born in India, one studied in the United Kingdom and North America, while two others extensively travelled in other countries. They each brought their overseas experience to bear on their interpretations of social and environmental conditions in their homeland. One of my subjects spent little time outside India and another never left the country at all, yet both were widely read in Western literature and well aware of what was happening in the rest of the world.

As I have noted, the conventional social science wisdom holds that environmentalism is a 'postmaterialist' phenomenon, which manifests itself only after a country has reached a certain degree of material prosperity. This theory assumes that societies or nations in different parts of the world, as they 'progress' at different speeds, are unaware of one another. The flow of individuals and ideas between East and West exemplified by this book shows how specious this assumption is. Indeed, the environmentalism of all our protagonists was, to a lesser or greater degree, motivated and informed by their knowledge of other countries. Several among my subjects saw the West as a cautionary tale. They argued that India must not imitate the resource-intensive and environmentally profligate models of industrial development that had been pioneered in Europe and North America, and whose destructive impact on nature and human life was already visible to those who cared to see.

Histories of environmentalism have been largely dominated by a national frame of reference. However, in writing this history of Indian environmental ideas I do not hope merely to fill a geographical lacuna—namely, to have a book on my country placed in a shelf that already has books on this subject that deal with the United States, Germany, France, Holland, Norway, Australia, etc. Rather, I believe that the historical and intellectual experience of India offers something different and distinctive to the global environmental debate. This is for at least four reasons: *demographic*, *political*, *economic* and *ecological*.

At the time the narrative of this book begins, India's population was second only to China's; now no other country has more people than India. For roughly half the period covered by this book India was the largest colony of the greatest empire; for the other half, the largest electoral democracy in the world. The study of environmentalism thus reveals how intellectual life was articulated in conditions of colonialism as well as in conditions of (relative) political freedom. Third, since India was desperately poor when the narrative of this book begins and remained substantially poor when it ends, we have here a perhaps decisive rejection of the belief, still widely prevalent in some quarters (including among Indians too) that one can afford to be green only after a certain level of material prosperity has been reached. Finally, in ecological terms India may be the most diverse nation on earth, containing within its borders the high Himalaya and the Thar desert, rich tropical forests and thousands of miles of coastline, muddy deltas and arid plateaus, and much else besides. The plant, bird and animal life are comparably diverse, and so also are forms of human endeavour. India may be the only nation to boast both of hunter-gatherers and nuclear weapons.

When E.P. Thompson called India 'perhaps the most important country for the future of the world', he had its cultural and intellectual pluralism principally in mind. Its demographic distinctiveness and its astonishing ecological diversity lend even more credence to the claim. I hope therefore that this book may bring back its precocious subjects into conversations in India itself; and perhaps inform environmental debates in other lands as well.

Environmentalism in Western (and especially American) contexts has often assumed a markedly individualist character, of a man, by himself, seeking communion with nature. The figures of John Muir and Henry Thoreau are emblematic in this regard. It is not given to twenty-first century man to spend as much time alone in the woods as Muir and Thoreau, so he seeks to emulate them episodically, through short treks in the wilderness or excursions into the ocean, sometimes by himself, at other times with just a few others, friends or family.

Close encounters with redwood forests and rare, cherished sightings of tigers or whales do indubitably enhance a person's love for, and understanding of, nature. But they just as often serve to separate them from their fellow human beings, who—unless they are friends or family—are viewed as interlopers, who violate the sacred space that the nature worshipper seeks to make his own.

On the other hand, the spirit of community, of human community, underlay these early Indian environmentalists. They wished to work with their compatriots in creating a more caring world, in which respect for nature and respect for humans would have an equal and mutually reinforcing place.

This book profiles ten thinkers, each with their distinctive personal biography and intellectual trajectory. One cannot, must not, collapse them all into a unifying 'Indian' environmentalism. Nonetheless, there may be ways in which they represent a collective ethos somewhat different and distinct from environmental pioneers elsewhere. This lies in their comparatively greater alertness to questions of social justice. That is to say, while they were deeply attentive to nature and natural processes—thus qualifying as 'environmentalists'—they were also, for the most part, acutely conscious of social and political processes. Living in a time of colonialism, they could not but be keenly aware of discrimination on lines of race and nation; or of the sharp cleavages within Indian society itself, of caste and class particularly (they were less alert to the question of gender).

The late Anil Agarwal liked to say that Indian environmentalism thought 'beyond pretty trees and tigers'.[29] He had movements such as Chipko in mind, yet his characterization entirely applies to most of the thinkers featured here, who lived many decades earlier. They admired beautiful woods and appreciated the need to protect the tiger and the elephant, yet they had a larger, more capacious, vision of human–nature relations. They were not so much speaking *for* nature—in the manner of the redwood-loving John Muir or modern-day Earth Firsters—but speaking *with* nature. With just one or perhaps two exceptions, these individuals combined a love for and close observation of the natural world with a simultaneous desire to build a more caring society, a more sustainable economy and a more democratic political order.

My original entry into environmental research was shaped by the debates generated by the Chipko movement. In the decades I was away, professionally speaking, from the field, such local and national concerns had been largely, if not comprehensively, displaced by the global debate on human-induced climate change. When I first began work on this book, I saw it as an elaboration of a forgotten first wave of Indian environmentalism, to be read and discussed (I hoped) by those currently active in the second wave that Chipko had sparked. While residues of that second wave still remain, perhaps the book's main audience shall now be constituted by those who are aware of or participate in environmentalism's third wave, that provoked and stimulated by the challenge of climate change.

In an essay on the climate crisis published in 2020, the marine ecologist Callum Roberts remarked that 'the question of the age is whether we can adapt from fulfilling our own selfish interests to fulfilling the self-interest of humanity before it is too late'.[30] This was precisely the question that the individuals profiled in this book were asking, a century previously, before human-induced climate change became a topic of concern. The nuanced and differentiated answers these thinkers provide us may be worth attending to still, whether our own focus is local, national or global.

CHAPTER ONE

The Myriad-Minded Environmentalist

RABINDRANATH TAGORE

THE BEST-KNOWN BIOGRAPHY OF Rabindranath Tagore in English carries the subtitle 'The Myriad-Minded Man'.[1] This is entirely merited. For Tagore was a poet, novelist, playwright and essayist; a man who transformed the Bengali language through his prose; a composer who wrote hundreds of songs and set them to music, many of which are still sung decades after his death, among them the national anthems of Bangladesh and of India; the first Asian to win a Nobel Prize and the founder of a major university; a friend of Mahatma Gandhi and a mentor of the nationalist icons Jawaharlal Nehru and Subhas Chandra Bose; an artist who took up his brush in his late sixties, his sketches and paintings since commanding high prices at auction; a restless traveller who made three trips to Japan and five to the United States, and spent time in

Europe, Latin America, China, Indonesia and Iran as well, winning friends, admirers and the occasional critic in all these places.

This list of the things Tagore did and the fields he contributed to is staggeringly rich and diverse. Yet it is not comprehensive. It does not, for instance, mention the impact of nature on his work. This is a theme neglected by numerous biographies and critical studies of Tagore, which, while they may fleetingly mention an odd poem about nature or landscape, rarely give this aspect of Tagore's thought close or careful attention. To be sure, this may only be because, exercising the privilege of authorial selection, these writers have focused on the many other aspects of Tagore's life and work that they thought (not unreasonably) deserved close and careful attention.[2]

This chapter seeks to demonstrate that Tagore was a precocious environmentalist, whose thoughts on how nature shaped human life, and how humans reshaped nature in turn, bear recovery in their own right. Tagore's writings on the use and abuse of nature by humans were more important to his worldview and literary oeuvre than has generally been acknowledged. Yet this rehabilitation of Tagore's environmental thought is not merely of academic interest alone. For his words and warnings speak directly and often compellingly to the environmental challenges that confront India and the world today. In making my case, I draw on a wide range of Tagore's writings, in different genres, written or published at different phases in his very long life.

Indian environmentalists often claim Mahatma Gandhi as one of their forebears. However, they seem not to know of the relevance to their struggle of the one Indian whom Gandhi recognized as his moral equal, namely, Tagore. From Gandhi's writings on restraint and a simple lifestyle one can possibly infer some broad lessons on how humans should relate to nature. On the other hand, Tagore's environmentalism was more direct as well as multifaceted. As the following discussion shall show, he advocated an ethic of respect for nature on aesthetic, educational, political and civilizational grounds.

Tagore was born in 1861, into a family of wealth and privilege. In his memoirs, he recalls that from the Bengali children's primer which gave him the first elements of an education, the 'two literary delights that still linger' in his memory were, strikingly, both images of nature, these being lines which (in English translation) read: 'The rain patters, the leaf quivers', and 'The rain falls pit-a-pat, the tide comes up the river'.[3]

Tagore grew up in the family home in the north Calcutta locality of Jorasanko. This was a three-storeyed mass of buildings built around several courtyards, in which lived several generations of family members—babies, children, married couples, elderly parents, grandparents—as well as their maids, cooks and bearers. A room that Rabindranath frequented as a little boy had a window from which he often looked out. Some forty-five years later, this is how he recalled the scene: 'A tank with a flight of masonry steps leading down into the water; on the west bank, along the garden wall, an immense banyan tree; to the south a fringe of cocoa-nut plants. Ringed round as I was near this window, I would spend the whole day peering through the drawn venetian shutters, gazing and gazing on this scene as on a picture-book.'

In this pool adjacent to the Tagores' house, their poorer neighbours came to bathe. The child watched them with fascination, noting their individual idiosyncrasies—one man 'who would never step into the water himself but be content with only squeezing his wet towel repeatedly over his head', another 'who jumped in from the top steps without any preliminaries at all', a third who 'would walk slowly in, step by step, muttering his morning prayers the while'. As the morning progressed the line of bathers grew thinner, until the 'bathing-place would be deserted and become silent. Only the ducks remained, paddling about after water snails, or busy preening their feathers...'

Once the humans had departed, the boy's attention wandered to the birds, and then, to a large tree that lay at the tank's edge. He was fascinated by the 'dark complication of coils at its base'. It was of this tree that many years later the poet wrote:

> With tangled roots hanging down from your branches, O ancient banyan tree,
> You stand still day and night, like an ascetic at his penances,
> Do you ever remember the child whose fancy played with your shadows?

Of his childhood encounters with nature Tagore was to remark: 'How intimately did the life of the world throb for us in those days! Earth, water, foliage and sky, they all spoke to us and would not be disregarded.'[4]

Tagore's memoirs were written when he was approaching the age of fifty. Towards the end of the book, he reflected on what nature had meant to him over the course of his life:

> From my earliest years I enjoyed a simple and intimate communion with Nature. Each one of the cocoa-nut trees in our garden had for me a distinct personality. When, on coming home from [school], I saw behind the sky-line of our roof-terrace blue-grey, water-laden clouds thickly banked up, the immense depth of gladness which filled me, all in a moment, I can recall clearly even now. On opening my eyes every morning, the blithely awakening world used to call me to join it like a playmate; the perfervid noonday sky, during the long silent watches of the siesta hours, would spirit me away from the workaday world into the recesses of its hermit cell; and the darkness of night would open the door to its phantom

> paths, and take me over all the seven seas and thirteen rivers, past all possibilities and impossibilities, right into its wonderland.[5]

Other critics, seeking other sorts of clues in Tagore's memoirs, have not mined them for what they say about his early consciousness of earth, sky and water, for their acute (and minute) observations of birds, plants and trees in the world of nature.

Tagore's family owned vast estates in the eastern part of the Bengal Presidency. When he was in his twenties, his father commanded him to go there to oversee their holdings and their management. He went reluctantly, loath to leave his family and the city, but once there he fell in love with the landscape of deltaic Bengal. His letters to his family are redolent with natural imagery, as he delicately describes the interplay of land, water, plants and animals.

Here, then, is an excerpt from a letter written by Tagore to his niece Indira Debi sometime in the 1890s, from an unnamed place in eastern Bengal:

> Our boat is moored off a lonely grass-covered island in the river. The world is at rest. What a glorious day it is, today! Such loveliness all around! After many days I am really meeting Mother Earth again, and it is as if she says 'Here he is', and I reply 'Here is she'. We sit side by side without stir or speech. The water gurgles, the sunlight sparkles, the sand crunches. Tiny wild shrubs crane their heads to watch. A stray bird gets up calling *chik-chik*. It's all like a dream, and I feel like writing on and on, just about that and nothing else—the gurgle of the water, the glitter and shimmer of the sunshine, and all the dreaminess of this island. I want to wander day after day along these sandy banks, and write about nothing but this—oh, how badly I want to![6]

And here is an excerpt from another letter by Tagore to his niece Indira, written in 1895 from the family estate in Shelidah in eastern Bengal:

> We can draw a deep and secret joy from nature only because we feel a profound kinship with it. These green, fresh, ever-renewing trees, creepers, grasses and lichens, these flowing streams, these winds, the ceaseless play of light and shade, the cycle of the seasons, the stream of heavenly bodies filling the limitless sky, the countless orders of life—we are related to all this through the blood-beat in our pulse—we are bound by the same rhythm as the entire universe.[7]

These letters were written of course in Bengali, yet even in English translation they are evocative enough. They bear comparison to the writings of American naturalists in the nineteenth century, exploring new landscapes with wonder and excitement, capturing their diversities of species and habitats in their prose. The 'profound kinship' that Tagore felt with nature makes him, as it were, akin to John Muir. Yet though we know Muir as a pioneering American environmentalist, this label has thus far been denied to the Indian writer, perhaps because his attention to nature, though impressive enough, was merely one part of his personal and professional journey.

Tagore was born into a family which liked to expansively travel, both within India and to lands abroad. In these journeys outside his hometown Calcutta and his native province Bengal, he encountered landscapes and natural elements very different from what he had grown up with, responding to them with joy and wonder (and occasionally, with disgust).

When he was about thirteen, Tagore was taken by his father for a long holiday in the Himalaya. Above the town of Dalhousie (in present-day Himachal Pradesh) the family had rented a bungalow. As they climbed up from the plains—father and son being carried on a palanquin by bearers—the terraced hillsides 'were all aflame with the beauty of the flowering spring crops'. The boy's eyes

> had no rest the livelong day, so great was my fear lest anything should escape them. Wherever, at a turn of the road into a gorge, the great forest trees were found clustering closer, and from underneath their shade a waterfall trickling out, like a little daughter of the hermitage playing at the feet of hoary sages rapt in meditation, babbling its way over the black moss-covered rocks, there the *jhampan* bearers would put down their burden, and take a rest. Why, oh why, had we to leave such spots behind, cried my thirsting heart, why could we not stay on there for ever?[8]

When he was sixteen, Tagore was sent to England for a spell. He first lived in London, where he tried, unsuccessfully, to learn Latin from a tutor. He went for an excursion to the Devon countryside and was charmed by what he saw. 'I cannot tell you how happy I was,' he wrote later, 'with the hills there, the sea, the flower-covered meadows, the shade of the pine woods…' One day he walked down to the coast, where he found a 'flat bit of overhanging rock reaching out as with a perpetual eagerness over the waters; rocked on the foam-flecked waves of the liquid blue in front, the sunny sky slept smilingly to its lullaby; behind, the shade of the pines lay spread like the slipped-off garment of some languorous wood-nymph'.[9]

Tagore had been travelling in Europe from the time he was a young boy. It was in 1916, when he was in his early fifties, that he visited Japan for the first time. It was a long, leisurely journey by ship, from Calcutta to the capital of British Burma, Rangoon, from there to the town of Penang in British Malaya, from there on to the Chinese city of Hong Kong, also a British protectorate, and from Hong Kong to his final destination, the island nation of Japan, a country that had never been ruled by Europeans (and which thereby added to Tagore's fascination for it). En route the poet kept a diary, where he recorded his impressions of the ever-changing human and natural world that he and his travelling companions were to encounter.

Tagore's first impressions of the premier port of Malaya were altogether pleasant. He wrote:

> Our ship reached the port of Penang just as the sun was setting. Seeing the water and land clasp each other in a bond of love, I had a deep sense of the earth's beauty. The earth, stretching both its arms, was embracing the sea. The faint rays of light that pierced the clouds and fell on the bluish mountains were like the thin vein of gold that covers the face of a bride without completely hiding her features. Water, land and sky played together a divine tune from the gates of heaven as the evening approached. [10]

As the great steamship he was on prepared to dock, Tagore's mood grew darker. He wrote:

> As our ship slowly drew near the wharves, the full horror of the great effort of man to overcome nature became conspicuous: the machine was cutting with its sharp, angular claws into the soft curves of nature. What ugliness the enemies of man within him can create! On every beach, in every port, the greed of man is making grotesque faces at the sky—and thereby banishing itself from the kingdom of heaven.[11]

In 1927, a decade after his journey to Japan via various British-ruled ports, Tagore chose to visit the Dutch East Indies. This time, the poet does not appear to have kept a detailed diary on board ship. Fortunately, we do have a letter he wrote to his niece Pratima describing his first impressions of the little and predominantly Hindu island of Bali. This read:

> When we crossed over to Bali we saw the Earth in all the freshness of its eternal youth. The old centuries here have their ever new incarnation. The habitations of its people nestle in the lap of shaded woodlands, lulled in a limpid leisure—a leisure decorated with preparations for frequent festivity. In this secluded little island there are no railroads. The railway train is the vehicle of modernity. The modern age is miserly, and reluctant to make provision for any kind of surplus; time is money, says the modern man and, in order to avoid any waste of it, the panting locomotive perspires smokily as it thunders on from country to country. But in this island of Bali the modern time has spread itself over the past centuries and become one with them. It has no need to shorten time, for everything belongs here to all time, as much to the past as to the present. Just as its seasons flow along, opening out flowers of many a colour, ripening fruits of many a flavour, so also do its people live on from generation to generation, sustaining the superfluity of their traditional ceremonials, rich in form and colour, song and dance.

Tagore's evocation of the rural–ecological idyll of Bali continues:

> But if railways are not, there is the modern globe-trotter, and for him there are motor cars. What if this child of a constricted age has come into the land of unbounded leisure—he must all the same get through his sight-seeing and his enjoyment within the minimum time. For myself, as I was being whirled along by hills and woods and villages, raising clouds of dust, I felt all the while that this was above all the place where one should walk. There is not much of a loss if one's eyes are raced over rows of buildings

> lining a street, but where, on either side of the road, feasts of beauty offer their regalement, this steed of emergency should be kept interned in its garage.[12]

After a week driving and walking across the island, Tagore wrote to his son: 'The island of Bali is so well-ordered in its completeness because it is small. It is one with its woods and hills and waterfalls, its temples and sculptures, its cottages, cornfields and market places. Nothing strikes the eye as out of place.'[13]

In the 1920s, the motor car was widely admired as a sign of progress and human achievement, though from our own perspective a hundred years later one cannot but see it as having contributed rather substantially to global warming. Tagore was not prophetic enough to recognize this, of course. Nonetheless, it would be a mistake to portray him, as some of his contemporaries did, as an anti-modern Luddite. Rather, he was working his way towards a vision where technological innovation would serve humans and harmonize with nature, rather than dominate them both utterly. He appreciated Bali because its inhabitants did not seek to conquer time or space in the manner of the residents of New York or London. In this little island, the fields, the houses, the modes of transport, all reflected a way of life that sought to blend and merge culture with nature.

Tagore valorized technological innovations on the human scale, where man was a partner rather than a servant of the machine. This passage, written as his ship was entering Penang, is suggestive:

> In the harbour we saw many small boats. There are few things created by man as beautiful as these small sailing boats that skim over the surface of the water to the rhythm of the wind. Indeed, when men have to move in tune with nature their creations cannot be anything but beautiful. The boat has to make friends with the

> winds and the waves, and so it comes to partake of their beauty; whereas a machine, pretending to look down upon nature from the pinnacle of its power, only displays by this vanity its own ugliness. A steamship has many advantages over a sailing vessel, but the beauty has been lost.[14]

In this exploration of the role of nature and landscape in Tagore's work, I have thus far raided a range of his non-fiction writings—his essays, letters, memoirs and travelogues. Let me now briefly turn to the place of nature and landscape in his more creative work.

The historian Niharranjan Ray, one of the few scholars to recognize and stress Tagore's ecological sensibilities, wrote of his early verse collection, *Manasi* (1892), that it contained some poems 'which are full of the still beauty and sweetness of nature', while in other poems he is 'equally responsive to her [nature's] wild, relentless and destructive moods', as in a poem about the fury of a cyclonic storm.[15]

Decent English translations of Tagore's early nature poetry are hard to come by. Among the exceptions is a sonnet by Tagore entitled 'Sabhyatar Prati' (To Civilization) and originally published in his 1896 collection, *Chaitali*. The poem sharply contrasts the soulless, denaturalized and concretized city of Calcutta with the verdant beauties of the rural landscape of eastern Bengal. As translated by the Bangladeshi scholar Fakrul Alam, the sonnet reads:

> Give back the wilderness; take back the city—
> Embrace if you will your steel, brick and stone walls
> O newfangled civilization! Cruel all-consuming one,
> Return all sylvan, secluded, shaded and sacred spots

And traditions of innocence. Come back evenings
When herds returned suffused in evening light,
Serene hymns were sung, paddy accepted as alms
And bark-clothes worn. Rapt in devotion,
One meditated on eternal truths then single-mindedly.
No more stone-hearted security or food fit for kings—
We'd rather breathe freely and discourse openly!
We'd rather get back the strength that we had,
Burst through all barriers that hem us in and feel
This boundless universe's pulsating heartbeat.[16]

Tagore's most famous book of poems is the verse sequence, *Gitanjali*, which won him the Nobel Prize for Literature in 1913. The previous year, the poet was in London, where, at the home of the painter William Rothenstein, he read some of his early poems in his own English translations. In attendance was his friend C.F. Andrews, who later provided a report of the soirée for readers back in India. Here Andrews remarked: 'At every verse the Bengal scenery—the Monsoon storm clouds, the surging seas, the pure white mountains, the flowers and fields, the lotus on the lake, the village children at play, the market throng, the pilgrim shrine—came before the eyes, moulded into melodies of exquisite sweetness.'[17]

Twenty years after the publication of *Gitanjali*, Tagore composed a volume of poems called *Banabani* (The Voice of the Forest), which approached trees and the forest in a mystical, religious spirit. The verses in *Banabani*, writes Niharranjan Ray, 'are inspired by the poet's old love of nature, but now this love is enriched by a mature culture and a deeper understanding of tradition'.[18]

The opening poem of the collection, 'Vrikshavandana' (A Prayer to the Tree), reads, in translation:

> O Tree, you are the adi-prana [first or original breath], you were the first to hear the call of the sun and to liberate life from the prison-house of the rock. You represent the first awakening of consciousness. You brought to the earth beauty and peace. Before you the earth was speechless; you filled her breath with music.[19]

This was published when Tagore was in his seventies. His poems thus display a lifelong engagement with nature, with what plants, trees, birds and animals, as well as land, sky and water, meant to him and the human world to which he belonged.

In 1914, a year after Tagore won the Nobel Prize, he published his first extended piece of writing in English. This provided an outline of his thinking on morality, aesthetics and faith. The tract, called *Sadhana*, began by speaking of the role of forests in Indian culture. It 'was in the forests that our civilization had its birth', wrote the poet, 'and it took a distinct character from this origin and environment. It was surrounded by the vast life of nature, was fed and clothed by her, and had the closest and most constant intercourse with her varying aspects.'

'To realize this great harmony between man's spirit and the spirit of the world,' continued Tagore, 'was the endeavour of the forest-dwelling sages of ancient India.' Even after the forests had given way to cultivated fields and cities and kingdoms had emerged, Indians continued to look back with 'adoration upon the early ideal of strenuous self-realization, and the dignity of the simple life of the forest hermitage, and drew its best inspiration from the wisdom stored there'.

Tagore contrasted this attitude with that of the West, which 'seems to take pride in thinking that it is subduing nature; as if we are living in a hostile world where we have to wrest everything we want from an unwilling and alien arrangement of things'. Tagore argued that 'in the west the prevalent feeling is that nature belonged exclusively to inanimate things and to beasts, that there is a sudden unaccountable break' between humans and nature. On the other hand, he claimed, 'the Indian mind never has any hesitation in acknowledging its kinship with nature, its unbroken relation with all'.[20]

In another essay, published five years later, Tagore called the forests 'the one great inheritance' of India and Indians. He offered an intriguing contrast between how forests shaped Indian history and how the sea had shaped the history of northern Europe. 'In the sea,' wrote Tagore, 'Nature presented itself to these [European] men in her aspect of a danger, of a barrier, which seemed to be at constant war with the land and its children. The sea was the challenge of untamed Nature to the indomitable human soul. And man did not flinch; he fought and won...'

Tagore contrasted the European conquest of the sea with the level tracts of peninsular India, where 'men found no barrier between their lives and the Grand Life that permeates the Universe. The forest gave them shelter and shade, fruit and flower, fodder and fuel; it entered into a close living relation with their work and leisure and necessity, and in this way made it easy for them to know their own lives as associated with the larger life.' Thus the 'view of Truth, which these men found, was distinctly different from that of those [the Northern Europeans] whom we have spoken above; and their relationship with this world also took a different turn, as they came to realize that the gifts of light and air, of food and drink, did not come from either sky or tree or soil, but had their fount in the all-pervading consciousness and joy of universal life'.[21]

This essay of 1919 was called 'The Message of the Forest', the title mirroring that of Tagore's early volume of poems. Three years later, he published a sequel, which he titled 'The Religion of the Forest'. Here he spoke of how in ancient India, 'the forest entered into a close living relationship' with the work and leisure of humans. They did not therefore think of their natural surroundings as 'separate or inimical'. So 'the view of truth, which these men found, did not manifest the difference, but the unity of all things'.[22]

This view of a primordial attachment of Indians to forests was perhaps somewhat rose-tinted. The texts and scriptures of ancient India by no means speak in one voice on this matter. While the Upanishads do talk of the unity of all creation, and Sanskrit drama does contain moving evocations of nature, on the other side there is the episode in the Mahabharata where the burning of the Khandava forest and the killing of its animals is celebrated as proof of the advance of civilization, the necessary and even mandatory conquest of primitive hunters and gatherers by a sophisticated agrarian civilization.[23] And surely Tagore saw that many, perhaps most, Indians of his day treated forests in severely utilitarian terms, as a source of raw materials rather than of pleasure or spiritual upliftment. Perhaps the writer wanted to believe that his own love for nature, and for forests in particular, was not an idiosyncratic individual taste, but borne rather of a deep and enduring civilizational inheritance.[24]

Let me now move from the aesthetic perceptions of nature in Tagore's work to the role of nature and natural resources in the everyday life of the two major institutions he founded. These institutions were Santiniketan, which began as a school for boys in 1901 and grew into a full-fledged university; and Sriniketan, an accompanying experiment in the renewal of village life, that was started in the 1920s. Both were based in rural Bengal, in what is now the district of Birbhum, about a three-hour train ride from Calcutta. They were located originally on a property owned by the Tagore family, with more lands being acquired over the years, as the institutions expanded in size and grew in numbers.

Krishna Kripalani, a scholar who worked closely with Tagore, summarized his educational ideals in terms of ten maxims, of which the first is: 'The child should be brought up in such environments as would provide him with opportunities of direct and close contact with Nature. Civilised existence in society imposes, in any case, such severe restraints on the first, fresh and vital impulses of life that human nature tends to be perverted unless its impulses are renewed and revitalised with constant reference to Nature.'

Other maxims include learning through the mother tongue, an equal emphasis on individual initiative and group action, an appreciation of cultural heritage, etc. Nature makes a reappearance in the sixth maxim, which Kripalani glosses as: 'When the child's senses have been trained to a proper awareness of his surroundings and he has learnt to observe and love Nature, his experiences should then be made intelligible to him, at a later stage, in terms of scientific categories.'[25]

In July 1927, by which time the school he started, Patha Bhavan, had been in existence for a quarter of a century, Tagore found himself speaking at the Indian Association in Singapore, to an audience of parents whose own children were educated in a resolutely metropolitan environment. He told them of his own school, where 'boys are taught amidst natural surroundings. They grow up in the midst of the sights and sounds of Nature, among trees, birds, in the open air. This school seeks to enable my boys to realize their bond of unity with Nature.'

In another speech in Singapore, to a gathering of children and teachers in the city's Victoria Theatre, Tagore expanded on his method of learning in and with nature. He told his audience about how and where the children in his school had their lessons:

> We have a mango grove. It is full of shade, and in summer, full of the beautiful perfume of the mango blossoms and there are innumerable birds and moths and all kinds of insects living on them. This you may think might distract their attention. But that is not so. I allow them sometimes to have their lessons and to look more closely at some of the things which attract their eyes. Very often they call my attention to some strange birds that have come and perched on the bough—'Sir look at the bird? What bird is that?'—right in the middle of their lesson. And then I talk to them about that bird. ... They should observe that bird. It would have been wrong were their minds absolutely dull to these impressions, and I would much rather be interrupted in my lessons than force them to keep their minds only on what has been placed before them. Often, again, they would speak to me of their admiration for something unusual—such as an especially fine bunch of mango leaves. I find that helps them, and that this constant movement of their mind is necessary for them. It is the method which nature has adopted in her own school for the young.

Tagore continued:

> Well, we are in the heart of nature—the open sunlight, the open sky; our children have for their neighbours the chirping birds and the blossoming trees. They are where they were born, where they have been sent by their God, having the companionship of the whole living world round them. This is necessary for them because it is their natural environment, where their mind has its true delight, where it can taste true knowledge, its food, with a joy, a relish that is necessary for its assimilation.[26]

In 1921, Santiniketan (the Abode of Peace) became home to a new and more advanced educational experiment, a university which carried the name Visva-Bharati, indicating its ambition to bring the world (Visva) to India (Bharat), as well as to take India to the world. The university went on to establish departments dedicated to the study of Japan and China, to the study of classical and contemporary Indian languages, as well as a celebrated art school.[27]

The land acquired for the university's construction was dry and bare. So, to make the place more appealing to the eye as well as more conducive to the sort of learning he desired to impart, in 1928 Tagore inaugurated what was to become an annual festival. This Briksharopan (tree-planting) ceremony was held in July, shortly after the onset of the monsoon. In a play staged on the occasion, the five basic elements of nature—earth, water, sunlight, air and sky—were represented by five students playing these roles. Saplings of carefully chosen (and mostly indigenous) species were planted by boys and girls with loving care, the ceremony accompanied by music and poetry. Over the decades, these saplings, now full grown, helped transform a barren landscape into one dotted with trees and groves.[28]

In a lecture to the Santiniketan community, Tagore explained his idea behind Briksharopan thus:

> Man's greed grew as he received Mother Earth's bounty. ... Men cut down trees to meet their endless needs and stripped the Earth of shade. As a result, the air became increasingly hotter, while the fertility of the soil increasingly diminished. That is how northern India, deprived of its shelter of forests, now lies scorched by the harsh rays of the sun. With all this in our minds, we initiated a tree-planting ceremony to teach the children to replenish the plundered stores of Mother Earth.[29]

The tree-planting ceremony was one of several festivals begun in Santiniketan by Tagore, with a view to nurturing among students an affectionate and caring relationship with nature, so that they could seek to harmonize their own lives with its rhythms and variations. The other festivals he introduced included Vasantha Utsav (Spring Festival), Varsha Mangal (Welcoming the Monsoon), Sharad Utsav (Autumn Festival), Ploughing Ceremony (Halakarshana) and Nabanna Utsav (Harvest Festival).[30]

Tagore took great care in choosing the shrubs and trees that surrounded his homes in Santiniketan, making sure that there were flowering plants throughout the year. In the campus as a whole, there were groves dedicated to specific species: one for the stately sal trees; another for the trees bearing the most delicious of all fruits, the mango; and so on.

When he was away from Santiniketan, Tagore's letters home often asked about the plants and trees he had left behind or hoped would flourish in his absence. In the summer of 1933, he wrote to his daughter Mira: 'Ask them [the staff] to plant neem, shirish, and other trees on the street that leads to my room this monsoon. It's not a bad idea to plant a few jackfruit trees either.' Seven years later, while in the hill station of Darjeeling, he wrote to a colleague in Santiniketan:

> Pay attention to the garden. ... I love tall trees, but they shouldn't be very close to the house. Keep in mind the drumstick tree—it flowers in winter but is quick to grow tall. Mahaneem, shimool, these take root in the soil there quite easily. ... The fragrance of lemon flowers is a favourite, keep some provision for that. The flowers of the chalta tree have great flamboyance, shirish, jamrool, roses I like for their flowers. ... The gardens will need watering all through the month of Jaistho. A line might be cut to incorporate kurchi and kanchan trees later. A few gawndhoraaj wouldn't be

> bad either. The trees that I don't like are the chhatim and kadam. Find out why shirish trees do not grow sturdy in my land.

In translating and quoting this passage, the critic Sumana Roy writes: 'This letter was written in April, almost exactly a year before his death. It is an extraordinary letter for two reasons: the poet's overwhelming concern for the trees of Santiniketan and his greed for more of the same.'[31]

In these efforts to plant up Santiniketan with trees and flowers, Tagore was surely inspired by the verdant landscape of eastern Bengal in which he had spent so much time in his youth. With an arid, sandy soil, and with far less water available, the place where the university was located could never remotely parallel the natural beauty of the river Padma and its surroundings. But it could still be made green and pleasant and welcomingly habitable. And so, under the poet's guidance and instruction, it became.[32]

Tagore grew up in the city, but grew increasingly disenchanted with urban lifestyles. As the writer Aseem Shrivastava observes, Tagore believed that 'the ecological alienation of metropolitan life profoundly cripples our sensibility, leaving humanity in a self-destructive state of spiritual destitution'. The poet was thus encouraged to locate his educational experiment, Santiniketan, deep in the countryside rather than anywhere near the city of Calcutta. For Tagore, 'open skies, planted fields, and swaying palms [were] more essential to untrammelled learning and the formation of the mind than the hectic cultural exchanges a modern metropolis affords (and a village denies)'.[33] Or, as Tagore himself remarked: 'When I am in close touch with Nature in the country the Indian in me asserts itself and I cannot remain coldly indifferent to the abounding joy of life throbbing within the soft down-covered breast of a single tiny bird.[34]

A century before Tagore, English writers had responded in a similar fashion to the radical alterations in the natural landscape that the expansion of cities like London represented. In his classic book on the subject, Raymond Williams explains why, for poets in particular, the country conveyed a more appealing ecological aesthetic than the city: 'The means of agricultural production—the fields, the woods, the growing crops, the animals—are attractive to the observer and in many ways and in the good seasons, to the men working in and among them. They can then be effectively contrasted with the exchanges and counting-houses of mercantilism, or with the mines, quarries, mills and manufactories of industrial production.'[35]

Like his English forebears, Tagore saw modern cities as being parasitic on the natural resources of the countryside. At the same time, he was not unduly romantic about the village life he had witnessed at first-hand. His family owned large tracts of agricultural land in eastern Bengal. He and his brothers were sent by turn to manage them. Rabindranath was assigned this responsibility in the early 1890s, by which time he was an established poet, admired and much feted in Calcutta. In a lecture given many years later, Tagore wrote of how in this first extended experience of the countryside, 'gradually the sorrow and poverty of the villagers became clear to me, and I began to grow restless to do something about it. It seemed to me a very shameful thing that I should spend my days as a landlord, concerned only with money-making and engrossed with my own profit and loss.'[35]

Over the next decade, as Tagore spent more time in his estates, these feelings of guilt intensified. He wished to ameliorate the poverty of the peasants through constructive social work. In 1906, he sent his son, his son-in-law and a friend's son to the

University of Illinois at Urbana-Champaign, to study modern methods of agriculture and dairying, with a view to implementing them in India.

Inspired by the poet, a young schoolteacher named Atul Sen organized a group to work on improving the living conditions of villagers in the Tagore estates in eastern Bengal. They concentrated on medical relief, primary education, forest conservation and settlement of disputes by arbitration. More than a hundred primary schools were opened.[37]

Tagore's philosophy was anti-industrial but not anti-modern. He wished to renew village life, using the principles and techniques of modern science. That is why he sent his son Rathindranath to study agricultural technology in the University of Illinois. The son did not prove entirely worthy of his father, however, so Tagore went looking for someone else who could scientifically supervise programmes of rural uplift in the villages around Santiniketan. He found him in the person of an idealistic young Englishman named Leonard Elmhirst, whom he had met in New York in 1920.

Born in 1893, the son of a Yorkshire curate, Elmhirst had studied history at Cambridge before enlisting in the army during the First World War. He fell sick in Mesopotamia, and came to India to recuperate. Here he got interested in agriculture, through meeting the British missionary Sam Higginbottom, who ran an experimental farm outside the northern Indian city of Allahabad. This encouraged Elmhirst to go to Cornell University in upstate New York to study agricultural science. In November 1920, when Tagore was in New York, he heard of the young Englishman and arranged to meet him. This is how, years later, Elmhirst recalled Tagore's words to him at that meeting:

> I have started an educational enterprise in India which is almost wholly academic. It is situated well out in the countryside of West Bengal at Santiniketan. We are surrounded by villages, Hindu,

> Muslim, Santali. Except that we employ a number of these village folk for various menial tasks in my school, we have no intimate contact with them at all outside their own communities. For some reason these villages appear to be in a state of steady decline. ... Some years ago I bought from the Sinha family a farm just outside the village of Surul, a little over a mile from my school. I hear that you might be interested in going to live and work on such a farm in order to find out more clearly the causes of this decay.[38]

Elmhirst came out to Santiniketan in November 1921, a year after meeting Tagore in New York. The experiment in Surul originally went under the name 'Institute for Rural Reconstruction', before Tagore came up with the crisper and more elegant 'Sriniketan'.

Tagore asked Elmhirst to find better methods for villagers to grow their crops and vegetables, to help them gain access to credit and get a fair price for their produce. He also hoped to augment their farm income with cottage industries such as rice milling and umbrella making.[39]

In Sriniketan, Elmhirst began taking Bengali lessons, for several hours each day. In January 1922 Tagore told him that ten Santiniketan students had come to him and were keen to do work in villages after graduating. Since they knew both Bengali and English, they could assist the foreign-born expert in his activities. Tagore now instructed Elmhirst:

> Stop your Bengali lessons. If you learn too much Bengali yourself you'll want to go on your own to the village to ask questions. You will then make the great mistake of trying to become indispensable to this enterprise like any foreign missionary. I want you never to go alone to any village but always to take with you either a student or a member of your staff to act as interpreter. Only in this way will they learn what kind of questions you ask and just how the farmers and villagers frame their answers. These answers

> they will then have to interpret back to you. In this way they will never forget the experience.[40]

After Elmhirst had been in Sriniketan for a couple of years, Tagore told him it was time to move on, 'to give the Indian staff of the young Institute a chance to find their own feet'.[41] Elmhirst travelled with Tagore to China and Japan in 1924, and from there to Latin America. The following year, with the poet's blessings, Elmhirst married the American heiress Dorothy Straight, and the couple now set up home in a medieval manor in rural England, Dartington Hall, which they refurbished and made the centre of an experimental farm. Straight helped support Sriniketan financially, while her husband remained in close touch with Tagore.

Tagore was a keen observer of the natural world, yet what we might term his 'nature aesthetic' was merely one element of a wider ecological consciousness. He was, for example, sharply critical of the environmental devastation caused by unbridled industrialization. When the poet was growing up, the river Hooghly had homes and farms all along it; now, the banks were dotted with factories. Writing in 1916, he wrote that he was

> fortunate in having been born before the iron flood of ugliness began clinging to the river banks near Calcutta. At that time the embankments of the Ganges, like the arms of the villages on the banks, embraced their people and kept them close to their bosom. In the evenings people would go for boat-rides on the river. The current of the people's hearts and the flow of the river—between these was no hard and ugly demarcation. Then the real beauty of the Bengali countryside could be seen even in the immediate

> vicinity of Calcutta. Although Calcutta was always an up-to-date city, it didn't take over the nest from its foster parents entirely, like the young of the cuckoo. But afterwards, as commercial civilization began to spread, the beauty of the countryside too was slowly covered up to the point where now Calcutta has segregated all of Bengal from the lands surrounding it. The vernal beauty of the country has succumbed to the hideous form of Time, showing its iron teeth, belching smoke and fire.[42]

The following year, in a lecture in America, he warned thus against the dehumanizing and destructive cult of the machine:

> Take man from his natural surroundings, from the fulness of his communal life, with all its living associations of beauty and love and social obligations, and you will be able to turn him into so many fragments of a machine for the production of wealth on a gigantic scale. Turn a tree into a log and it will burn for you, but it will never bear living flowers and fruit.[43]

During the course of Tagore's life the city of his birth had become a bustling industrial powerhouse. In the second half of the nineteenth century jute mills proliferated in and around Calcutta, processing the raw fibre grown in eastern Bengal into packing material sent all around the world. The first jute mill was established on the river Hooghly in 1855, six years before Tagore was born. In 1869, when he was a little boy, there were a mere five mills with 950 looms operating. By 1910, when Tagore was approaching the age of fifty, there were a staggering 30,000 looms in operation, exporting more than a billion yards of cloth.[44]

The waterways around Tagore's native city, whose banks once featured little hamlets and fishing boats, were now lined with the large chimneys of the ever-proliferating jute factories, emitting tonnes of smoke. This transformation repelled him, finding expression in his writings.

In 1880, when he was in his late teens, Tagore went for a boat ride up the Hooghly, from Calcutta to the French enclave of Chandannagar, where his brother Jyotindra had a riverside home. Tagore had just returned from a spell in England, and this re-immersion in the Bengal countryside was for him a joyous experience. Of the boat journey and the stay on the river's banks in Chandannagar he wrote:

> The Ganges again! Again those ineffable days and nights, languid with joy, sad with longing, attuned to the plaintive babbling of the river along the cool shade of the wooded banks. This Bengal sky full of light, this south breeze, this flow of the river, this right royal laziness, this broad leisure stretching from horizon to horizon and from green earth to blue sky, all these were to me as food and drink to the hungry and thirsty. Here it felt indeed like home, and in these I recognised the ministrations of a Mother.

Such was the Ganges near Chandannagar back in 1880. By the time Tagore came to pen his reminiscences thirty years later, much had changed. As he wrote there:

> That was not so very long ago, and yet time has wrought many changes. Our little river-side nests, clustering under their surrounding greenery, have been replaced by mills which now, dragon-like, everywhere rear their hissing heads, belching forth black smoke. In the midday glare of modern life even our hours of mental siesta have been narrowed down to the lowest limit, and hydra-headed unrest has invaded every department of life. Maybe this is for the better, but I, for one, cannot account it wholly to the good.[45]

The visual transformation of the river landscape in and around his native city dismayed Tagore. In an essay of 1922, he wrote in disgust that

> Calcutta is an upstart town with no depth of sentiment in her face and in her manners. ... The only thing which gave her the sacred baptism of beauty was the river. I was fortunate enough to be born before the smoke-belching iron dragon had devoured the greater part of the life of its banks; when the landing-stairs descending into its waters, caressed by its tides, appeared to me like the loving arms of the villages clinging to it; when Calcutta, with her up-tilted nose and stony stare, had not completely disowned her foster-mother, rural Bengal, and had not surrendered body and soul to her wealthy paramour, the spirit of the ledger, bound in dead leather.[46]

These passages inevitably recall the great British poets of the eighteenth and nineteenth centuries, who were likewise repelled by the outrage done to nature by the expansion of cities and factories, and who wrote so movingly (as well as so despairingly) about it. The names of William Blake, William Wordsworth and John Clare come to mind, though perhaps most akin to Tagore's thinking was William Morris, who, while by no means in the same league as the other three as a versifier, had, like Tagore, many interests in life outside his poetry, being an activist and a builder of institutions (as well as being engaged in socialist politics). For example, one can immediately see a kinship between some of Tagore's writings quoted in this chapter, and this paragraph from Morris's long narrative poem 'The Earthly Paradise', which begins by asking the reader to

> Forget six counties overhung with smoke,
> Forget the snorting steam and piston stroke

> Forget the spreading of the hideous town;
> Think rather of the pack-horse on the down,
> And dream of London, small, and white, and clean,
> The clear Thames bordered by its garden green...[47]

Morris wished for a harmonious relationship between the city and the countryside, and between humanity and nature. So did Tagore. However, his writings were not derivative but born out of his own experience and expressed in his own words. The parallels owe themselves to these writers living through a similar historical process—the radical transformation of landscapes and social relations that modern industrialization brought with it, first in England and then, with a certain lag, in India.

However, unlike those British poets, whose thought and experiences were confined to (and confined by) their island nation or at most to a few culturally (and ecologically) akin countries of the Continent, Tagore had a capaciously global vision. He had travelled all over the world, encountering many different landscapes, cultures, religions and ways of life other than those of his native Bengal. And, as an Indian living under British rule, he had an understanding of what Britain had wrought in its colonies, something denied to those (otherwise so gifted and acutely sensitive writers) who lived in Britain itself. This wider, as well as deeper, understanding of the modern world is strikingly manifest in some passages of Tagore's famous tract, *Nationalism*, which have a profoundly ecological message that has unfortunately escaped most commentators on that work. Because the book was originally written in English, it has been far more widely read than his poems, plays and stories that first appeared in Bengali. And yet, perhaps naturally and inevitably, its readers and commentators have focused on its political message, on its warnings against xenophobia and nationalist hubris, while ignoring its powerful ecological critique of industrialism and imperialism.

Here, for example, is the poet-turned-prophet analysing the environmental consequences of European imperialism, while speaking of the devastation caused by the rampant greed and new technologies of the new industrial age:

> The political civilisation which has sprung up from the soil of Europe [and] is overrunning the whole world, like some prolific weed, is based on exclusiveness. It is always watchful to keep at bay the aliens or to exterminate them. It is carnivorous and cannibalistic in its tendencies, it feeds upon the resources of other peoples and tries to swallow their whole future. It is always afraid of other races achieving eminence, naming it as a peril, and tries to thwart all symptoms of greatness outside its own boundaries, forcing down races of men who are weaker, to be eternally fixed in their weakness. Before this political civilisation came to its power and opened its hungry jaws wide enough to gulp down great continents of the earth, we had wars, pillages, changes of monarchy and consequent miseries, but never such a sight of fearful and hopeless voracity, such wholesale feeding of nation upon nation, such huge machines for turning great portions of the earth into mince-meat, never such terrible jealousies with all their ugly teeth and claws ready for tearing into each other's vitals.[48]

These words were spoken at a public event in Japan in 1916. That Asian nation was far more advanced, economically and industrially, than Tagore's native India, yet he nonetheless hoped that Japan would restrain itself from going all the way down the route mapped by Europe. He reminded his hosts that too eagerly embracing the urban–industrial way of life would be a denial, even a repudiation, of their own culture, of 'the spiritual bond of love she [Japan] has established with the hills of her country, with the sea and the streams, with the forests in all their flowery moods and varied physiognomy of branches...'

Tagore urged Japan to offer the world a vision of humanity's relations with nature rather different from that being envisioned and put into practice in modern Europe. For, as he wrote, Japan 'has taken into her heart all the rustling whispers and sighing of the woodlands and sobbing of the waves; the sun and the moon she has studied in all the modulations of their lights and shades, and she is glad to close her shops to greet the seasons in her orchards and gardens and cornfields'.

The visiting poet reminded the Japanese that 'the ideal of *maitri* [friendship] is at the bottom of your culture—*maitri* with men and *maitri* with Nature'.[49] That ideal had to be renewed and reaffirmed, even if it might seem like 'an anachronism, when the sound that drowns all voices is the noise of the market-place'. He defiantly stated his own belief 'that the sky and the earth and the lyrics of the dawn and the dayfall are with the poets and the idealists, and not with the marketmen robustly contemptuous of all sentiment—that, after all the forgetfulness of his divinity, man will remember again that heaven is always in touch with his world, which can never be abandoned for good to the hounding wolves of the modern era, scenting human blood and howling to the skies'.[50]

From lectures delivered in Japan in 1916 let me move to a lecture delivered six years later by Tagore on his home turf. In 1922 Leonard Elmhirst, the newly appointed director of the Institute of Rural Reconstruction in Sriniketan, gave a lecture on the renewal of village life. Elmhirst's talk was prefaced by some introductory remarks by his mentor and employer.

In his remarks, Tagore warmed to one of his pet themes, the exploitative characteristics of urban–industrial civilization. 'Civilisation today,' he remarked, 'caters for a whole population of gluttons. An intemperance, which could safely have been tolerated in a few, has spread its contagion to the multitude.' 'The city,' he continued, 'represents energy and materials concentrated for the satisfaction of an exaggerated appetite, and this concentration is considered to be a symptom of civilization.'

Tagore then offered a parable of environmental destruction, imagining that on the moon a new race of beings was born, 'that began greedily to devour its own surroundings'. His parable continued:

> Through machinery of tremendous power this race made such an addition to their natural capacity that their career of plunder entirely outstripped nature's power for recuperation. Their profit makers dug big holes in the stored capital of the planet. They created wants which were unnatural and provision for these wants was forcibly extracted from nature. When they had reduced the limited store of material in their immediate surroundings they proceeded to wage furious wars among their different sections, each wanting his own special allotment of the lion's share. In their scramble for the right of self-indulgence they laughed at moral law and took it as a sign of superiority to be ruthless in the satisfaction each of his own desire. They exhausted the water, cut down the trees, reduced the surface of the planet to a desert, riddled with enormous pits, and made its interior a rifled pocket, emptied of its valuables.

This parable of what might happen on the moon, of course, resonated with what Tagore was witnessing on earth in his own time, where the age of industrialism and colonialism had led to an unprecedented assault on the earth and its resources. This imaginary race of rapacious beings on the moon, he continued,

> behaved exactly in the way human beings of today are behaving upon this earth, fast exhausting their store of sustenance, not

> because they must begin their normal life, but because they wish to live at a pitch of monstrous excess. Mother Earth had enough for the healthy appetite of her children and something extra for rare cases of abnormality. But she has not nearly sufficient for the sudden growth of a whole world of spoiled and pampered children.[51]

These extracts from Tagore's writings make it clear that, among other things, he understood the devastating environmental consequences of industrialism and of imperialism, and that, in his own way and in his own words, he anticipated by many decades the now (justly) influential idea of the ecological footprint, the vast and unsustainable demands that the production and consumption patterns of a particular nation or social strata makes upon the earth. In this lecture at Sriniketan, Tagore offered in passing an aphorism that can serve, a century and more later, as a maxim of environmental responsibility for our times. It reads: 'When our wants are moderate, the rations we each claim do not exhaust the common store of nature and the pace of their restoration does not fall hopelessly behind that of our consumption.'[52]

I began this chapter by remarking that most biographers of Tagore have not paid proper attention to his responses to the natural world. Being Bengalis themselves, these biographers had both an insider's perspective as well as a proprietorial attitude to the poet. They thus focused on how Tagore had transformed their language, their literature, their music, their public and cultural life, without quite seeing how nature had transformed him.

Among the few exceptions to this trend have been Niharranjan Ray, who was a historian rather than a literary scholar per se; and G.D. Khanolkar, who, because he was not from Bengal at all, could see more clearly what Tagore had that poets in his own part of the world (Maharashtra) perhaps largely lacked.

Interestingly, Niharranjan Ray's book on Tagore is based on lectures he delivered in the southern state of Kerala, far away from the native province of both author and subject. Here, Ray summarized the place of nature in Tagore's poetry thus:

> We know that from early youth Tagore used to see nature as permeated with the same life of emotion as that of man. This belief that nature is alive in all the senses in which man is, he never gives up or forgets, rather the years only enrich this belief, deepen it, until, in a deep spiritual synthesis, the poet creates and discovers a new significance in the world of nature. This synthesis and this significance we find clearly in *Vanavani*. In early youth he wrote simple descriptions of nature, but in *Sonar Tari* there is a deeper communion with it which crystallises into an absorbed self-identification in *Chitra*. In *Balaka* and *Puravi* there is yet further development, and further penetration; at the final stage which is revealed in *Vanavani*, he achieves an integration of his personal attitude with that of the forest-dwelling sages of the Upanishads. And in superb poetry the poet recaptures all the wonder, all the unfathomed mystery which must have belonged to life's first language in which the trees and forests speak, to the world's oldest history as recorded in them.[53]

This resonant summary comes deep into Ray's book. On the other hand, in his preface itself, Khanolkar writes:

> In the life of any poet we can detect a basic melody, with which he harmonizes a number of contrasting tunes, to evolve a theme of freshness and glory. ... What was Tagore's basic melody? It was a passionate love of Nature, a yearning to live close to her. Other poets have loved Nature, but they did not feel Tagore's utter

> oneness with her, his sense that all her creatures were as members of his own family. He discovered the key to life's riddle in the one spirit which, for him, informed earth and sky and water, man and beast and tree.[54]

G.D. Khanolkar's *The Lute and the Plough: A Life of Rabindranath Tagore* appeared in English translation in 1963 (the Marathi original had appeared two years earlier, on the occasion of Tagore's birth centenary). Niharranjan Ray's *An Artist in Life: A Commentary on the Life and Works of Rabindranath Tagore* was published four years later, in 1967. It is only fair and proper that I acknowledge these scholars who saw, far earlier than I did, the deeply ecological element in Tagore's journey.

My own narrative, drawing on a wide range of Tagore's oeuvre, and from his earliest writings to some of his last, does, I believe, demonstrate that even though the term 'environmentalist' had not acquired its present meaning in his lifetime, Tagore was indeed a pioneering environmentalist. Like his work in general, Tagore's ecological thinking was many-sided rather than narrowly focused—he was, as it were, a myriad-minded environmentalist.

In the first instance, Tagore had a lifelong engagement with the beauty and variety of nature. He paid attention to plants, birds, animals; to trees, mountains, rivers. While immersing himself so thoroughly in the countryside of his native Bengal, he yet wrote insightfully about landscapes as different as the majestic Himalaya, the tropical island nation of Bali, the forests and mountains of continental Europe. Nature was for him a constant and caring companion wherever he travelled. He had a love for, and felt a kinship with, all of nature's elements.

Tagore's aesthetic appreciation of nature was so deep and profound that in this respect he can certainly rank alongside the celebrated nature poets of early modern Europe and the wilderness romantics of the United States. What marks him out is that he combined this love of the natural world with a sharp awareness of the political and economic forces which threatened it. Tagore had an aesthetic aversion to large cities and to factory production; underlying his opposition to those modern forms of living and working was also an awareness of the environmental destruction they brought in their wake. This awareness he shared with some British thinkers of the time—the names of William Morris and Edward Carpenter come to mind—but where Tagore went further than his European contemporaries was in his linking industrialism with imperialism, by showing how European nations restlessly searched, and then invaded, other parts of the globe for plunder and for profit.

To be sure, the deleterious economic consequences of European imperialism had, even before Tagore, been a staple of nationalist narratives in India. There had been much talk of the drain of financial resources away from British rule, and of the destruction of indigenous artisanal enterprise. But Tagore gave this critique of industrialism and imperialism a distinctive ecological twist. He saw early that while modern technologies could enormously expand productive capacity and economic opportunity, they also came with an unprecedented ability to destroy and lay waste the earth. To quote again those remarkable lines from his lecture of 1922 to the students and staff of Santiniketan, modern machinery had encouraged humans to embark on a 'career of plunder [that] entirely outstripped nature's power for recuperation. Their profit makers dug big holes in the stored capital of the planet. They created wants which were unnatural and provision for these wants was forcibly extracted from nature.' If these tendencies continued unchecked, Tagore foresaw a future where humans had 'exhausted the water, cut down the trees, reduced the surface of the planet to a desert, riddled with enormous pits, and made its interior a rifled pocket, emptied of its valuables.'

With these words I rest my case. Apart from being the greatest Bengali (and probably Indian) writer of his day, apart from being the first Indian (indeed Asian) to win a Nobel Prize, apart from inspiring some of the most influential leaders of the Indian national movement, apart from writing songs that are still sung and painting sketches that are still discussed, apart from founding a university which is still in existence a century later—apart from all these things, Rabindranath Tagore was an unacknowledged founder of the modern Indian environmental movement.

CHAPTER TWO

Ecological Sociologist

THE WORK AND LEGACY OF RADHAKAMAL MUKERJEE

SOCIOLOGISTS HAVE A WELL-DESERVED reputation for writing clunky prose. I was myself trained in sociology but in time began to identify myself as a historian, in part because I preferred archival research to fieldwork, in part because I found the language of historians to be (by and large) so much more appealing than the language of sociologists.

This chapter is focused on the legacy of an economist-turned-sociologist, and may therefore be somewhat less 'readable' than the others in this book. Rabindranath Tagore, of course, was above all a writer, and his prose was eloquent and evocative. The chapters that follow deal with individuals who took some care with their writing, seeking to make it clear and accessible. The sociologist I now turn to had none of these attributes. One of his students described his prose style as 'rather hurried, repetitive, verbose, and replete with cross-disciplinary citations'.[1] Yet it may be worth attending to what he had to say nonetheless.

Radhakamal Mukerjee (to give our prolix sociologist his name)[2] was born almost three decades after Rabindranath Tagore, on 7 December 1889. He was raised in the town of Murshidabad, once the capital of the Bengal subah (province) of the Mughal empire. His father was a prominent lawyer. An autobiography, published after Mukerjee's death and edited by his students, speaks of the powerful influence that nature had on his childhood. The Mukerjees lived in a large house in Murshidabad with a well-tended garden and orchard, whose 'songs, colours and scents' were an 'integral part' of his growing-up years. In old age, Mukerjee recalled the different moods of nature as he had experienced them in his childhood, benign as well as dangerous, welcoming as well as forbidding. Each season in Bengal, he wrote,

> forged new links with nature, full of joys, memories and imaginings. The plaintive songs of the common hawk-cuckoo in the moon-lit nights every summer and spring, and of the bright orange-pekoe during the heavy downpour of the rainy season aroused vague yearnings. The mango and lemon blossoms announced, together with the notes of the *koel*, the advent of spring and set as it were the scene for it. The arrival of the monsoon was heralded by the serried flight of the cranes and the massing of the dark, rumbling rain-clouds that would suddenly overcast the sky. ... The whole landscape would be obliterated as the shower came nearer and became heavier ... A sense of utter loneliness and sadness then became overwhelming. With the lightning flash and thunder one's mind would be wafted to

> the near and dear ones separated from us. Or one would ponder about Life itself.[3]

Sixty years after he left Murshidabad, Mukerjee remembered the 'dear, old banyan tree' in the garden that 'overlooked the daily activities inside the house' and was 'the most enduring link between one season and another and between the past and the present'. Fresh in his memory too was the river 'not far distant from the home', this being the great Ganges, 'with its boats of different sizes and shapes, carrying merchandise and tidings from distant unfamiliar lands'.[4]

In 1905, when Mukerjee was in high school, Bengal was partitioned by its British rulers into two separate provinces, sparking a widespread popular movement against the division. He found himself enveloped in the 'intellectual and social climate of patriotism' of the Swadeshi movement, which emphasized Indian pride, advocating the boycott of foreign goods and the promotion of indigenous industries.[5] The following year he moved to the city of Calcutta, to join the prestigious Presidency College, where he took a BA in English and History, before shifting to Economics for his MA. Mukerjee spent much time in the well-stocked college library, and also wrote for the college magazine. It was as a student in Presidency College that, as he recalled, he chose to see the disciplines of Economics, Political Science, Sociology and History as complementary rather than distinct. Meanwhile, he was also reading the great Bengali writers of the late nineteenth century, such as the novelist Bankim Chandra Chatterjee, the historian Romesh Chandra Dutt, the social reformer Ishwar Chandra Vidyasagar, and the poet Rabindranath Tagore. His studies in the classroom and in the library had stimulated in him 'the desire and striving to envisage man, society and civilization as wholes that defeat any compartmentalization and its aims'.[6]

In 1914 Mukerjee met Patrick Geddes in Calcutta. Geddes, who is the subject of a later chapter in this book, was a Scottish polymath who had come to India to lecture about his work on town planning in Europe. Speaking with Geddes, recalled Mukerjee, was a transformative experience, with the 'encyclopaedic mind and generous heart' of the Scotsman 'greatly stimulating' the Bengali's 'intellectual outlook and imagination'.

Geddes introduced Mukerjee to the writings of the French geographer Frédéric Le Play and the American conservation pioneer George Perkins Marsh, author of the 1864 classic *Man and Nature: Or, Physical Geography as Modified by Human Action*. Recalling their conversations fifty years later, Mukerjee wrote of Geddes that he remained 'certainly one of the greatest minds I have encountered, marked by a remarkable quickness, vitality and comprehensiveness of thinking'. The influence of Geddes was personal as well as intellectual; when the Scotsman came to the Mukerjee family home, 'everybody was struck as much by his massive head, his reddish-gray hair and his flowing beard as by his acceptance of Indian manners, etiquette and food'.

In later years, Mukerjee came to regard Geddes's approach as 'in some measure mechanical and over-tidy, underrating the complex and often unpredictable social and psychological factors'. However, at the time they met, Geddes played a catalytic role in consolidating Mukerjee's incipient inter-disciplinary approach, and, more importantly, in making him alive to the geographical and ecological influences on social life and social organization.[7]

By the time he met Patrick Geddes, Mukerjee had begun writing essays in both Bengali and English on social and economic affairs.

Inspired by his conversations with the Scotsman, he now wrote a book setting out what he had learned about his country's past and its possible future. He called the book *The Foundation of Indian Economics*.

Mukerjee prevailed upon Geddes to write the foreword to his book. Geddes did so, noting here that India was experiencing the breakdown of its village order at the hands of the Industrial Revolution, something which had already occurred in Europe. There were, in the West as in India, two familiar responses to this process—the 'regretful', as in the Romantics like John Ruskin and William Morris, and the 'triumphalist', exemplified by the politicians and economists. But Mukerjee, remarked Geddes approvingly, avoided both extremes by seeking to rebuild the old with the help of the new, displaying in the process a 'cheering faith in the survival capacity of his old village as well as in the value of its villagers'.[8]

In this, his first book, Mukerjee himself deplored the tendency of European thinkers to 'judge the progress of different peoples by an abstract and arbitrary standard deduced from the evolution of western civilisation'. The 'idea that western humanity represents the culmination of the idea of humanity', he observed, 'is based on the narrowness and prejudices of the western sociologists'.[9] Indeed, even in the West that abstract ideal was coming under criticism, from dissenters such as Geddes himself. Western industrialism was now being seen as flawed on three counts: (i) its elevation of production over distribution, so that massive increases in wealth had not led to a decline in poverty; (ii) its elevation of the economic motivation in humans, leading to cultural and spiritual impoverishment; (iii) its drive towards homogeneity, by the crushing of individuality and the flattening out of all local customs and idioms to one uniform standard. Mukerjee also noted in passing the massive dependence of Western living standards on access to raw materials from overseas colonies.[10]

It was as yet early days for industrial development in India, and Mukerjee hopefully charted out a radically different path from the West. Indian industrialization, he wrote in 1916, would

> tend to establish a solidarity between the villager and the city, the labourer and the employer, the specialist and the layman, the multitude and the genius, the brain worker and the manual labourer. ... India will not allow the city to exploit the village, she will retain the vitality of life and culture of the village. She will not suck out the blood of one part of society to feed another part ... but she will feel the pulsations of life deep and strong in her throbbing veins in every part of her social system.[11]

Mukerjee's scepticism of Western models rested on, among other things, a deeply conservative view of the place of women in Indian society. Thus he wrote that 'the woman of the West is becoming more and more economically independent. Not supported by her own family and unable to find a husband or deserted by him she has to earn her own living. Thrown into the hard struggle and competition for wealth, she gradually loses the idealism that is natural to her. She asks for votes in order to shield herself from the individualistic economic system regulated in the interests of men, but the feverish excitement, the constant fever and fret of modern industrialism, gradually renders her unfit for motherhood—the essential and incontestable right of every normal woman.'[12]

In 1915, Mukerjee took a job teaching Economics in Punjab University in Lahore. A couple of years later he moved back to Calcutta, teaching in his alma mater, Presidency College, while completing a PhD dissertation entitled 'Socio-Economic Change in the Indian Rural Community'. In 1921, he was appointed to a professorship in Lucknow University, where he spent the rest of his working life.

Over the next two decades, Mukerjee wrote a series of books that reflected his deepening interest in the ecological basis of social and economic life. The first to appear in print was *Principles of Comparative Economics*, published in 1922. This exalted the 'communalism' of the East over the 'individualism' of the West. The term 'communalism' later came to refer to conflict and rivalry between India's two largest religious groupings, Hindus and Muslims, but Mukerjee's use is more akin to what philosophers now call 'communitarianism', namely, to act on behalf of the community or social group to which one belongs. Most of his examples in this book came from India, though occasionally he drew on Chinese and Japanese illustrations to further his case.

In the early pages of *Principles of Comparative Economics*, its author contrasted 'Eastern Co-operation versus Western Compulsion', baldly stating: 'Throughout the East group-interests correspond to public welfare.'[13] In describing the Indian caste system Mukerjee recognized the principle of hierarchy that defines it, yet he tended to minimize its baleful effects. For instance, in a book of 400 pages, there were only a few fleeting references to the pernicious practice of untouchability. Mukerjee even suggested, perhaps somewhat patronizingly, that castes could rise up the social ladder by adopting less degrading occupations.

Western nations excessively strengthened the powers of the state, wrote Mukerjee, while Western societies excessively valorized the individual. India, on the other hand, he said, 'stands for communalism. The basis and support of communalism as a social framework and a social ideal is her profound and conscious realization of a cosmic humanism, according to which the individual governs all his subjective and objective experiences in terms of the one and all-sufficient relation with God as manifest in the pulsating life of nature and humanity.'[14]

While its basis may lie in religious or spiritual tradition, this communal spirit, claimed the sociologist, had salutary practical effects on social life. 'In India,' wrote Mukerjee, 'communalism implies the mutual recognition of rights and duties among classes, and mutual respect and esteem. The village commonwealth has cultivated a communal conscience which punishes an attack on public rights and public property whether by individuals or classes.'[15]

Mukerjee's book is, among other things, an exaltation of a village-centric social order. He saw industrialization on the Western model as destructive of family and community life, and as compelling migrants to the city to live in inhuman conditions, where several families were cooped together in one-room tenements with no access to clean air, clean water, or a visually attractive landscape. 'In comparison with the slum,' he remarked, 'the peasant's dwelling is much more comfortable and accommodating.' There were more rooms, and the house often had a courtyard too. He further claimed that 'in the countryside the moral standard is much higher than in cities', with less crime and a more integrated and hence happier family life.

Mukerjee went so far as to write that 'farm life in the country is educative, morally and intellectually. That is an essentially artificial and faulty system of education which separates the people from nature and the soil. And if the love for the soil tends to disappear, a nation ought to cultivate it assiduously. The "feline attachment to the soil" is a useful racial trait.'[16]

Written in the early 1920s, this was an unfortunate echo of the 'blood and soil' rhetoric used to define national identity in some parts of nineteenth-century Europe, indeed, an idea vigorously embraced by Nazi Germany within a decade of the publication of Mukerjee's book.

The sociologist's evocation of the collective spirit of Indian village life was more convincing when he talked of the community's relationship to gifts of nature such as water, forests and pasture. He may have been the first Indian economist to recognize the vital importance of common property resources to the sustenance of peasant agriculture. While cultivated land was owned by individuals or families, wells and canals were traditionally held and managed by the village as a whole, as were woods and grasslands. Here, 'where private ownership might confer a privilege against the rest of the community, their use has never been allowed to be exclusive', he wrote.

In the precolonial Indian village, it was the collective ownership and use of irrigation channels that was most significant. The management of irrigation, observed Mukerjee, 'compels men to give up an anti-social individualism, or suffer in consequence; as a condition of general prosperity it forces men to enter into closer economic relations with other men...' Thus, 'in the Indian village communities there are minute communal relations of the supply of water to prevent the mutual rights of the cultivators. To prevent a tyrannical use of property, India has sought to establish a kind of communal ownership of tanks and the distributary channels of irrigation—the most important instruments of agricultural production.'[17]

Likewise, forests and pasturelands were also open to all members of the village, who could graze their cattle and collect fuelwood from these areas held in common, while limiting themselves to what they needed for their own household use without any commercial exploitation for personal financial gain.

Mukerjee argued (accurately) that these indigenous systems of common property management had been grievously undermined by colonial rule—as indeed, they had been previously undermined in Britain itself, as part of what was called the 'enclosure' movement. Now, in colonial India, a freshly formed State Forest

Department had taken over the wooded areas, working them for commercial purposes and criminalizing villagers who sought to use them for subsistence. The village 'tanks' (as small, manmade lakes are called in India) had also been placed under a government department, with officials appointed by and paid by the state put in charge of their upkeep. This change, wrote the sociologist, 'has brought about a complete loss of initiative of the people as regards ... public works, which were formerly maintained by the indigenous machinery, but which have fallen into desuetude and disrepair in the absence of all responsibility and all authority, customary or positive'.[18]

Previously an official appointed by the panchayat or village council was in charge of allocating water fairly and equitably, while at periodic intervals the village as a whole engaged in desilting the tanks and keeping them going in perpetuity. Now, with the colonial state having usurped ownership and management, apathy and decline had set in.

Unlike Tagore, who saw the city as essentially parasitic, avariciously feeding on the resources of the countryside, Mukerjee argued that in premodern and precolonial times the village and the town had complementary and co-operative relations. 'In India,' he claimed,

> the village has existed and has thrived independently by the side of the city, each supporting the other. The settled habits of the population, the instincts of attachment to the soil and the family altar, the love for a life in nature in a scheme of humanised and socialised industry, have determined the specific type of Indian agrarian economy, and the prosperity and political power of towns and cities have never been able to eclipse the self-government of the village, the foundation of Indian polity and the self-direction of industry and agriculture within the village, the foundation of Indian economics.[19]

Mukerjee's book was reflective and analytical rather than programmatic or prescriptive. However, towards the end, and perhaps influenced by Geddes, he recommended the creation of 'garden villages for Indian workers'. Millowners could pool together to buy land to create these model villages, featuring 'cottages with good-sized gardens, and roads, wide and tree-lined, and tanks and temples'. Those currently living in crowded, unsanitary, polluted slums in cities like Bombay, Bangalore and Calcutta could thus be resettled in the countryside, travelling by suburban railway to the factories where they worked.

In 'such garden villages', wrote Mukerjee hopefully,

> with mentality enlivened by contact with something of rural beauty and growth, cottage industry will reappear, and also artistic industries from lapidary work down to the manufacture of buttons and wearing embroidery. Communal ethics and traditions, communal festivals and amusements will again assert themselves, and in these new mill villages of electricity and art, hygiene and initiative, new enterprises of our work-people will be seen ...[20]

Radhakamal Mukerjee's *Principles of Comparative Economics* drew on a wide range of reading and to some extent on his own field research. Many of the examples were drawn from secondary sources; but quite a few came from his own experiences, from his visits to slums in Calcutta and Bombay and his conversations with peasants in Bengal and the Punjab. This book was written in the wake of Gandhi's movement of non-co-operation with British rule, which seems to have reawakened the sociologist's youthful patriotism, which in turn might explain the exaltation of Indian traditions that the quotes above demonstrate. This evocation, even glorification, of communal life and communal associations in premodern India was also surely influenced by his brother, the distinguished historian Radha Kumud Mookerji, also a professor at Lucknow University and the author of, among other books, one entitled *Local Government in Ancient India*.

Four years after *Principles of Comparative Economics*, Mukerjee published a book entitled *The Rural Economy of India*. The preface noted that economics as a discipline had its origins in the study of the nineteenth-century West, and 'does not easily fit into our [Indian] rural environment'. Challenging this bias of Western scholars, Mukerjee argued that the rural economy was 'an independent, worthy subject of investigation, and not [merely] as an adjunct of a set of doctrines derived from city and industrial conditions'. While Western economic historians seemed to regard industrialism 'as far more interesting and important than ... agricultural history', this Indian scholar hoped to show through this book that 'a study of economics which neglects the history of agriculture and the transformation of rural economy cannot but be partial and incomplete: it treats primitive and less advanced peoples as beneath its consideration and tends to view humanity exclusively from the standpoint of the [West in the] nineteenth century'.[21]

Offered as an alternative to Eurocentric social theory, Mukerjee's *The Rural Economy of India* covered a wide range of topics, such as the economics of smallholdings, the institutional organization of agriculture, the impact of population density on agrarian life, the lack of rural credit and the exploitation of peasants by moneylenders. Perhaps the most interesting chapter, certainly from the point of view of the present book, was entitled 'Crime Against Tree and Water'. It began with a discussion of 'the protective and conservative functions of forests', and the consequences of the human neglect of these functions. Mukerjee pointed towards the history of Persia and the Middle East, 'where formerly rich vegetation used to flourish', before 'the careless hand of man destroyed trees so prodigally that the natural conditions of countries suffered disastrous reversion; thus these countries became dry and sometimes uninhabitable.'[22]

Much of the chapter was spent providing examples of forest denudation in different parts of India, and how this had variously led to an increase in the incidence of floods, a decrease in rainfall and scarcities of materials vital to rural subsistence. Unusually for an economist, Mukerjee had read widely in the scientific literature, with citations to such journals as *Indian Forester* and the *Agricultural Journal of India* appearing in the footnotes.

In arresting the decline of forests, Mukerjee offered to India not a Western but an Eastern example—that of Korea under Japanese occupation. Here, the extensive schemes of forest restoration had helped prevent floods and the silting of rivers, improved the availability and quality of water for irrigation, enhanced the supply of fish in rivers, provided fodder and pasture for sheep and cattle, and probably increased rainfall too. Reforestation had thus provided an 'immense gain to agriculture' and cottage industry, apart of course from enhancing the beauty and attractiveness of the landscape.[23]

This chapter on crimes against trees and water ended with another positive example—taken from the hill tribes of northeastern India, who practised jhum or swidden agriculture, cultivating a series of plots in turn. Swidden was demonized by foresters as destructive and by agronomists as primitive. However, the sociologist showed that jhum was both rational as well as sustainable. In burning vegetation to make way for a field, the tribes always spared the large trees while felling bamboo clumps. The 'natural features of the hill tracts', Mukerjee pointed out, 'are such that *jhumming* must be the principal method of cultivation. The absence of stone, the light nature of the soil and the steepness of the hillsides make cultivation by terraces an impossibility.' He continued: 'And as tree forest is not jhummed, which would cause irreparable damage and make recovery as tree forest practically impossible, such a method of cultivation, though it encourages nomadic habits, is a suitable method of settlement for these hill tribes.'[24]

Mukerjee's arguments in favour of jhum found few takers within the scientific and bureaucratic establishment of British India. Foresters continued to work energetically to ban jhum all across India, while agronomists sought to nudge or cajole the tribes towards settled cultivation. However, later anthropological work confirmed Mukerjee's early defence by showing in painstaking detail how swidden rested on a rich and deep knowledge of the natural environment. In the hills of monsoonal tropical South and South-East Asia it was often the most productive as well as the only sustainable form of agriculture.[25]

Mukerjee also wrote about the importance of the Indian village community in a series of articles in the widely read Calcutta monthly, *The Modern Review*. He wrote here that, unlike in Europe, common property continued to be an important aspect of agrarian life in India and other parts of Asia. Thus 'meadows, forests, pastures, irrigation channels do not pass through the stage of individual property but evolve on account of social necessities from an absolutely free use directly to elaborate forms of [community] regulation'. He spoke of how, in Java, 'woods and wastes are common property, cultivated fields, private property'. In Japan, 'tunnels for conducting rice-field water through considerable hills, aqueducts, reservoirs, etc., represent a vast amount of communal labour hardly to be met with anywhere'.

Then, speaking of India specifically, Mukerjee remarked that

> judged from an agricultural standpoint the village community in India has shown the highest skill in the demarcation of rights in land so as to injure as little as possible the interest of every man in intensive cultivation. If we consider the density of the Indian

> population, and the complication of the open-field system due to manuring, and to co-operative irrigation as well as the differences in topographical conditions, we have to admit the wonders worked by the careful and discriminate intervention of the village community, guided neither by tribal traditions nor by idealistic principles, but by the necessities of agricultural communal life.[26]

In 1925, Mukerjee published a book that was more methodological in nature. Called *Borderlands of Economics*, it advanced the case for economists to creatively interact with scholars of other disciplinary backgrounds. Mukerjee argued for a 'system of economics revivified at its foundations and renewed in its methods by a broad-minded co-operation of the sciences of life, mind and society'. There were separate chapters on what anthropology, geography, sociology, physics, biology and psychology—though intriguingly, not history—could contribute to the economist's understanding of human life and behaviour.

The chapter on biology and economics stressed the importance of the then relatively new science of ecology. 'Economics hitherto has tried to understand man apart from his environment,' observed Mukerjee, 'and neglected the materials and methods of plant and animal ecology.'[27] The vital role played by different natural environments in enabling or constraining different forms of economic activity, remarked the scholar, awaited serious study.

'Interdisciplinarity' is a term much bruited about in the Indian (and global) academy of the twenty-first century. Scholars are urged to get out of their disciplinary silos, to speak to, learn from, and adopt the methods and frameworks of scholars who work in other academic fields and other university departments. In this search for an integrative framework to study society, Radhakamal

Mukerjee was a real pioneer. His books and essays consistently ventured beyond the discipline of economics in which he was trained. As he grew older, he himself preferred to be called a 'sociologist', in the belief that this academic discipline was not so narrowly focused as the one (economics) to which he originally owed his allegiance.[28]

In 1930, Mukerjee published an essay in an American academic journal, to which he gave the title 'An Ecological Approach to Sociology'. There had recently arisen, within American sociology, a school of research which gave itself the name 'human ecology'. Many of its adherents were based at the University of Chicago, then emerging as an intellectual powerhouse to rival the East Coast 'Ivy League', a cohort of Harvard, Yale, Princeton and Columbia. These scholars wrote about the social organization of urban life, and in speaking of how different ethnic groups distributed themselves across the city and related to each other, they saw analogies with how different species of animals and plants interacted. Hence their use of the term 'human ecology'.[29]

However, the name these Chicago sociologists gave their school was a misnomer. Ecology was to these American scholars merely a metaphor. Their work had nothing to do with ecology as we understand it. That is to say, it had no connection to the animal and plant world, no connection to the world of nature and natural processes.

In his essay 'An Ecological Approach to Sociology', published in the *Sociological Review*, Radhakamal Mukerjee sought to shift his fellow sociologists from metaphor to reality. The school of scholarship that called itself 'human ecology', he noted, 'has been concerned almost entirely with ... the effects of man upon man, disregarding often enough the trees and animals, land and water'. An 'undue prominence has been given in history and economics', he added, 'to these purely human influences'. On the other hand, said Mukerjee, the works of geographers and ecologists 'clearly emphasize the importance of the physical environment in its relation to society, and especially in its effects upon occupation and family life'.

Mukerjee had been reading the works of scientists like Charles Elton and A.G. Tansley, and was keen to pass on what he had learned to sociologists who probably had not heard of these scholars or even perhaps of the new scientific discipline, ecology, that they were giving concrete shape to. The Indian thus told the largely American readers of the *Sociological Review* about 'ecology, the science of the balance of species, the comprehensive physiology of life in all its forms', which 'not only throws light on social origins but also gives the clue to an understanding of the regional balance of population'.

In this landmark essay of 1930, Mukerjee broke new methodological ground, by orienting sociologists towards what they could learn from a science, ecology, that was just then emerging. However, his concern was not merely to expand the intellectual horizons of his fellow academics. Like everyone else featured in this book, Mukerjee had a keen interest in practical social reform. He wished to use his knowledge of ecology to urge his fellow humans to build for themselves a more caring and sustainable world.

The science of ecology studied the factors that made for a natural balance, as well as those factors that made for an unnatural imbalance.[30] Thus, as Mukerjee now told his fellow sociologists, 'an important section of plant and animal ecology deals with the disturbances which human and animal populations bring about in the natural ordering of the array of different plants and animals formed in a given region at a particular time'. Speaking then of his native country, Mukerjee described how 'overgrazing and trampling by man's domestic stocks result in the complete destruction of the vegetable cover and the appearance of perennial or seasonal weeds in the river-plains of India'.

Humans had an unprecedented ability to modify and reshape the order of nature. Their methods of forest clearance, farming, stock-raising and the import of exotics had, in India and elsewhere, set up 'a train of primary or secondary sequences in which an entire series of plant species and communities are implicated'. These disturbances, if not unchecked, could lead to the disappearance of important, even vital, plant and animal species, to a decline in soil fertility, to deforestation, desertification and drought, thereby imperilling the possibilities of human life flourishing in the region.

The last paragraph of Mukerjee's essay is at once exhortative and meditative. It reads:

> Human, animal and plant communities are subject to similar rules, though shifting ones, which maintain a balance and rhythm of growth for all. Each community cannot appropriate more than its due place in the general ordering of life, from which nothing can be obtained without influencing everything else. Working symbiotically, they represent inter-woven threads of a complex web of life. No one thread can be isolated. None can be snapped or removed without the whole garment of the life of nature and human society being disfigured. The warp and the woof of the garment have become increasingly coherent as organic evolution has advanced. The inter-linkages of a fig-tree, an earth-worm, a rat and a bird are many, but the threads make much more intricate patterns as we reach the social economy of man. Though man often tears asunder the fabric through ignorance or selfishness, social progress no doubt consists in consciously weaving the forces of nature and society into finer and finer patterns of correlation and solidarity. It is the knowledge of and respect for the intricacy of the web of life which will guide man to its highest destiny.[31]

This paragraph is no doubt wordy, its construction characteristic of the sociologist tone deaf to the rhythms of the language he is writing in. The ideas that animate it, of the interdependence of humans and the natural world, of the web of life and how dangerous it can be to wantonly tamper with it, are now commonplace among environmental scientists and activists. But back in the 1930s they were precocious and even pioneering. Mukerjee was advocating an ethic of restraint and responsibility that ran counter to the ethos of a rapidly urbanizing and industrializing society, which recognized no natural constraints to its growth and expansion.

In the same year, 1930, Mukerjee published an article in the *American Journal of Sociology* (*AJS*), the flagship journal of the discipline. This too advocated a closer alliance between the social and the natural sciences, often using similar phrases and examples as those advanced in his *Sociological Review* essay. Here, however, he more explicitly offered to American sociologists the analytical category of the 'region', which to him was the 'most important contribution' of the new science of ecology. It was by identifying distinctive regions and the linkages within them of plant, animal and human communities that sociologists could forge a necessary and productive alliance with ecologists.

In his *AJS* essay, Mukerjee wrote that 'many of the industrial countries of the West have adopted a scale of social and industrial living which has little reference to the resources and possibilities of the regions themselves'. This 'lack of balance between the standard of consumption and the production of food and raw materials', he continued, 'has been the chief cause of the present spendthrift use and unfair distribution of the world's resources'. Himself living under British colonial rule, the Indian sociologist believed that 'industrial civilization cannot thrive for long on an unstable balance between man's demands and the region's yields, which is maintained by improvident use of resources in men and materials in other parts of the world'.[32]

Like Tagore, Mukerjee recognized that imperialism was more than a system of political and economic domination. It was also a system of intensive resource extraction. The high living standards of one part of the world were in part enabled by its control of other parts of the world. Imperialism, the domination of one country or people over another, was therefore not just immoral, but also, in an environmental and ecological sense, unsustainable.

In the year 1930, Mukerjee published two separate articles in American academic journals, seeking to alert his fellow sociologists to the importance of the emerging science of ecology to their work. Four years later, he published an article in an Indian journal seeking to alert his fellow economists to the constraints that ecology placed on forms of livelihood. Trifling with nature, he argued, could have dangerous consequences for economic activity.

This article carried the telling title 'The Broken Balance of Population, Land and Water'. It focused on the denudation of forests and grasslands in the Indo-Gangetic plains, which had led to the formation of extensive areas of ravine, unfit for cultivation or habitation, and also made rainfall scarce and more erratic. The resultant shortages of water and of fodder had told particularly severely on the cattle, which were now smaller and weaker, yielding less milk and were less willing to work in the fields. 'It is not improbable,' he wrote, 'that in some distant future the Ganges valley may share the fate of the Indus valley, where once there was smiling plenty. The traces of ancient river beds and sand-buried cities extended over a vast space in the desert country east of the Indus testify to the gradual desiccation of a once fertile region.'[33]

In the 1930s, Mukerjee began to spend a considerable amount of time in his native Bengal. The partition of Bengal had been undone, but the province was now convulsed by a rising tide of Hindu–Muslim conflict. Mukerjee thought this conflict had ecological roots, in the shifting of the river system of Bengal eastwards. The decimation of forests in the Chota Nagpur plateau had led to a drying up of the rivers of western Bengal, while carelessly constructed canals and railway lines had led to an increase in waterlogging and hence of malaria. Meanwhile, agriculture was prospering in the Muslim-dominated districts of the east, where population growth was also more robust.

For all his scholarly training, Mukerjee was not above a parochial identification with the Hindu upper castes, and with the cities and towns where he had been born and raised, these being (in his words) 'the seats of ancient learning, culture and prosperity in Bengal'. He feared that in time Chittagong would displace Calcutta as the pre-eminent port of eastern India, and feared, even more, that the culture and demography of his native province would tilt in favour of Bengali Muslims. He therefore urged Hindus to have larger families, and to actively encourage widows to marry and have children. Otherwise, he warned, Hindu Bengalis would become the 'Athenians of the East', decaying and destroying themselves by their complacency'.[34]

Back in the 1920s, Mukerjee had been a vigorous advocate of communitarianism, of decentralization and village-centred economics. However, after an extended foreign trip in the late 1930s that took in the Soviet Union, the United States (of the New Deal) and the industrial countries of Western Europe, Mukerjee became an enthusiast for planning by the state. In October 1937, on his return to India from a six-month lecture tour overseas, he told a reporter in Bombay that 'economic planning has been the chief implement in different countries in Europe for recovery from the depression'. He also spoke in admiring terms of 'the far-reaching and comprehensive measures of soil conservation, flood control and rural rehabilitation of the New Deal in America', which 'forces the conclusion that India must immediately launch far-sighted agricultural, industrial and social planning projects under the new regime of Provincial Autonomy if she wants to take advantage of the tide of world recovery'.[35]

Mukerjee's enthusiasm for planning intensified after the Indian National Congress constituted a National Planning Committee under Jawaharlal Nehru's chairmanship in 1938. In an essay published three years later, he praised the Tennessee Valley Authority as 'the most interesting regional planning agency for the co-ordinated development of agriculture, forestry, navigation, soil-erosion and flood control'. India, he argued, should likewise prepare plans 'for a complete river watershed as a great natural territorial unit', and create, among others, a Ganges and an Indus River Commission, and a Godavari Board and a Kaveri Board too. At the same time, Mukerjee recommended the renewal of local institutions, writing that 'without the co-operation of village panchayats in the control of grazing and improvement of natural grasslands, many fertile areas of India would share the fate of the *Brajabhumi*, once flowing with milk and honey, but now stripped entirely of the vegetative covering, a cattle-made desert extending over several hundreds of square miles in the heart of the world's most fertile plain'.[36]

In 1945, when the Second World War ended, the Maharaja of Gwalior appointed Mukerjee as economic adviser to his princely state. Mukerjee spent several months travelling through the territory, afterwards publishing a pamphlet with the title 'Planning the Countryside'. Its tone and tenor were noticeably different from that of his *Principles of Comparative Economics*, published two decades previously. For one thing, he was now far more alert to, and far more critical of, the practice of untouchability, which reformers like Mahatma Gandhi and the great scholar-activist B.R. Ambedkar had made a matter of public debate in the intervening years.

The first chapter, entitled 'Planning for the People', began with this line: 'Planning is the utilization of modern technological science and social knowledge for the improvement of the life of [the] individual and society.' This was worlds removed from Mukerjee's social philosophy of the 1920s, which held that community wisdom and tradition would on their own regulate the life of individual and society. The next page of the pamphlet contained these remarks about the Indian village whose virtues he had once so exalted: 'The village is still in the medieval age. Caste restrictions, untouchability, bondage and servility of the agricultural labouring classes have combined to smother initiative and the desire for improvement'.[37]

Perhaps because independence was now imminent, Mukerjee did not have to resort to a defensive patriotism. He could be frankly and openly critical of the deficiencies of Indian society, with a view to helping to correct them when political power passed to Indian hands, as it soon would. However, there was both continuity as well as change in his intellectual approach. In this book, he retained, and indeed reinforced, his deeply ecological approach to social and economic life.

This is particularly manifest in a chapter on erosion control, which begins: 'Soil erosion under the peculiar conditions of topography and climate of Gwalior is the greatest single menace to its prosperity.' Travelling through Gwalior, Mukerjee found that the state's major rivers, such as the Chambal, the Kunwari and the Betwa, had in recent decades witnessed the rapid growth of ravines, 'scouring valuable cultivable lands and rendering the life and toil of the farmers ever more and more difficult'. In districts like Morena and Bhind, 'the aching scene of desolation of hundreds of miles of ravines that looks like a barren wavy sea has its counterpart in a marked and quick deterioration of fertility and standard of living and farming in the entire tract bordering the ravines and in the more or less complete destruction of pasturage'.[38]

To check and reverse the process of erosion, Mukerjee recommended a comprehensive programme of 'bunding, terracing, contour terracing, channelling and seasonal planting of defensive grasses such as common muni and bhabar that can bund the soil and fix even steep slopes'. This would build the soil on which trees could later grow. While these areas were being restored, villagers should be persuaded to abandon their traditional practice of free-range grazing, since 'excessive grazing by flocks and herds is one of the significant factors in speeding up soil erosion and destruction'. Henceforth, 'steep slopes should be reserved for grass and forest under proper management that must include complete closure to grazing or rotational grazing according to the condition of the slope, soil and vegetation'. In this manner, 'pasture management, afforestation and regulation of agricultural practice—all should aid one another in soil conservation in the critical areas'.[39]

In this 'planned strategy against erosion', wrote Mukerjee, 'steady team-work is essential.' Thus the economist would work out the best mix of food, cash and fodder crops to serve the needs of the community; the agricultural scientist introduce contour bunding and trenching; the ecologist select suitable, nutritive and drought-resistant crops; the forester choose the most appropriate tree species for the landscape and climate. Finally, the administrator would elicit the co-operation of the peasantry, aiding them in organizing 'Ravine Reclamation Panchayats', village councils with a mandate to restore a ravaged landscape. Having outlined his visionary scheme, Mukerjee ended the chapter with these words of exhortation: 'The conservation of soil and the conservation of water which are intimately associated with each other, together touch the entire field of man's exploitation of the earth and thus a rational programme involves the highest amount of co-operation of man's uses of trees, grasses, soils and waters in the background of his population pressure and standard of living.'[40]

The Gwalior report dealt with one, moderately sized, princely state. Meanwhile, Mukerjee had also applied his ecological lens to the most pressing political problem of the day: whether, when the British finally departed from the subcontinent, they would leave behind one independent nation or two. In 1940 the Muslim League had declared itself against the free and united India that Gandhi and his Congress Party had struggled for, insisting that when—or whenever—the British left they would fight for the creation of a Muslim homeland to be called 'Pakistan', which, apart from Sind and the Baloch and Pashtun areas bordering Afghanistan, would include the western portion of Punjab and the eastern portion of Bengal.

After the Congress leaders were jailed following the 'Quit India' movement of 1942, the Muslim League was free to propagandize its scheme without any opposition, and did so quite successfully. Among the most eager proponents of the idea of Pakistan were sections of the Muslim intelligentsia of Lucknow, the city where Mukerjee himself lived and worked.

In 1944, Mukerjee published a pamphlet that bore the provocative title *An Economist Looks at Pakistan*. This argued that the geographical and ecological realities of the subcontinent made an independent Pakistan economically unviable. The upper reaches of the Ganges had an organic connection with the river's delta, which would be sundered by the creation of Pakistan's proposed Eastern wing. If Pakistan was to be created, then only rapid industrialization could ameliorate the poverty of the masses, but with the coal and iron reserves existing on the other side of the border, 'Pakistan would be in constant desperate need of the mineral resources of Hindustan'. Therefore, 'the inexorable logic of Economics even more demand a united India in the coming post-war epoch of Asian industrialization'.

Mukerjee insisted that it was 'soils, rivers, raw materials and minerals', and not religion, that 'represent the physical framework largely regulating the features of economic ... planning'. If 'religion drives a wedge through the natural groupings of a modern economic structure through the preaching of itinerant Muslim or Hindu Mullahs, Priests and other separatists,' then 'we have to bid adieu to all hopes of fashioning the social and economic democracy of the future'. His own hope was that 'Hindus and Muslims with more food, clothing and other necessaries and decencies of a civilized existence, will become more understanding towards each other. The surer and safer road to Indian unity is through Economics and not through Politics.'[41]

Unfortunately, the logic of economics and of ecology failed to prevail over the emotional appeal of religion and culture. Three years after Mukerjee's pamphlet was published, the British left the subcontinent, and the separate and opposed nations of Pakistan and India came into existence.

In the 1920s, Mukerjee had begun corresponding with the American sociologist Howard Odum, who was based at the University of North Carolina, and wrote about the American South and its distinctive ecological, cultural, demographic and historical features. (Howard Odum's children, Eugene and H.T. Odum, would become two of the most influential ecologists in postwar America.) The intellectual frameworks of Odum and Mukerjee resonated with one another. Both focused on a regionalist approach to economic and social planning, drawing heavily on their personal and practical experience of their own region, the Indo-Gangetic plain in the case of Mukerjee and the American South in the case of Odum.

A scholar of Odum's work describes its key theoretical concept in terms that entirely apply to Mukerjee:

> Regionalism is a means of synthesis of all the social sciences and, to some extent, of the humanities. It is the method whereby one can study society and see it whole, and not in bits and snatches from the viewpoint of some narrow specialty. Yet, it is more than that. It is a program of action. It is an approach whereby the regions may be integrated into the national whole without losing their differentiation. It is a practical basis on which to pursue social planning. ... Regionalism is a grandiose concept that must be grasped whole or not at all, else it degenerates into a kind of 'sectional-local' provincialism.[42]

The American sociologist invited his Indian counterpart to write for a book series he was editing, being brought out by the Century Company in New York. Mukerjee accepted the invitation. His book, *Regional Sociology*, was published in 1925. Here he wrote that any human group must be considered in relation 'not merely to temperature, humidity, sunshine, altitude, etc., but also to their indirect effects, the interwoven chain of biotic communities to which it is inextricably linked, the plants it cultivates, the animals it breeds and even the insects which are indigenous to the region'.[43]

In *Regional Sociology*, Mukerjee studied the impress of the natural region on economic institutions, property structures, culture, character and diet. In this framework, differences (and similarities) between different societies could often be explained with reference to ecological factors. Thus the community-oriented cultures of China and India, centred on the village, were interpreted as an adaptive response to rice cultivation, where the activities of field preparation, transplanting, irrigation, etc., all required a great deal of collective action. Indeed, in almost all long-settled peasant cultures, the ecological imperatives of water and land management worked with cultural factors to foster community solidarity. In contrast, wheat cultivation, particularly in the cold northern hemisphere, was typically an activity of pioneers and hence, productive of individualism. Again, unlike rice, the ecology of wheat cultivation made it amenable to a socio-technical organization that approximated the factory. Thus, as Mukerjee remarked, 'the great [wheat] fields in Canada may be said to be populated by machines rather than men'.[44]

A decade after the publication of *Regional Sociology*, Mukerjee gave a series of lectures at the University of Madras, where he re-emphasized the importance of viewing humans in their regional and ecological context. He remarked:

> Man's skill and efficiency too often have been displayed without regard to the essential biological fact of his solidarity with nature. With better appreciation of this solidarity, the conservation of natural resources will be raised from an economic creed to a biological faith. The permanence of civilization depends chiefly on man's intimate understanding of and co-operation with the totality of the region's forces, including not merely climate, soil, and topography, but also the associated vegetable and animal life. In a new country man can with impunity disobey the order of nature, mainly because of the large margin and variety of nature's reserve; but, when man has become established in his adopted region, his security and well-being will be found to rest on maintaining the balance and rhythm in the organic nature that forms his environment.[45]

There is here an implied contrast between India and the United States. In the former, a long-settled civilization, humans had to work within the limits that nature set for them. In the latter, a scantily populated continent, European migrants could, at least for a time, 'with impunity disobey the order of nature'.

In the book of his Madras lectures, Mukerjee presented a chart drawing on his readings and his studies. It is reproduced in slightly modified fashion below:[46]

SOCIAL REGRESSION	SOCIAL EVOLUTION
Deforestation	Protection and plantation of forests
Mountain denudation and field erosion	Tree-cropping in the hillsides
Single and continual cropping	Scientific pasturage and permanent agriculture
Silting up of rivers and loss of natural and flush irrigation	Conservation of rain, river and subsoil water supply
Surface tillage, defective soil aeration drainage	Plant and animal breeding and introduction of new strains
Soil exhaustion	Selection and use of micro-organisms in cropping
Destruction of crops and herds by insects	Ecological control of plant and animal pests
Destruction of too large a number of animals and birds for food and materials	Preservation of animals and birds from extinction
Deficiency diseases of animals and humans	Conservation of the environment suitable for animal and human habitation
Spread of bacterial and protozoal infection	
Contamination of the region by wastes and sewage	
Growth of jungle in human settlement and of weeds in streams	Economic balance between the forest, meadow-land, field and factory
Depopulation in the countryside and congestion in the big cities and manufacturing regions	Regional planning of villages, cities and industries

This is a veritable Green Charter for India, many of its details still entirely relevant and applicable eighty and more years after it was first drafted. It beautifully illustrates Mukerjee's dicta that humanity has no option but to 'some extent imitate Nature's extraordinarily slow methods', and that applied human ecology is the 'only guarantee of a permanent civilisation'.[47] The sociologist himself looked forward to the day when 'ecological adjustment [would] be raised from an instinctive to an ethical plane'.[48] His programmatic wish was for humans to forge an 'alliance with the entire range of ecological forces', for humans to curb their 'quick and [far] reaching exploitative activities by importing new values—the thought for tomorrow, the sacrifice for inhabitants of the region yet unborn'.[49]

Radhakamal Mukerjee was prolific as well as prolix. A list of publications compiled after his death has forty-seven books written by him, on an extraordinarily wide range of subjects, from his first book *The Foundations of Indian Economics* (1916) through *Regional Sociology* (1926) on to *The Changing Face of Bengal* (1938) and *Social Ecology* (1942), and then further to *The Indian Working Class* (1945), *The Social Function of Art* (1948), *The Social Structure of Values* (1949) and *The Dynamics of Morals* (1951), and still further to *The History of Indian Civilization* (two volumes, 1956), *The Philosophy of Social Science* (1960) and *The Flowering of Indian Art* (1964). In the year Mukerjee died, 1968, was published his *The Way of Humanism: East and West*, with four further books published posthumously, assembled by his students from the manuscripts he had left behind.[50]

A lot of what Mukerjee wrote was superficial and ephemeral. No one now remembers his contributions to Indian art history, for example. He is scarcely read any more by professional economists, or by professional sociologists either. However, in the field of human ecology he was a true pioneer, and much of what he wrote on or around this subject is of real and enduring worth.

As noted earlier, Mukerjee owed his early interest in ecological studies to his encounters with Patrick Geddes. He acknowledged the influence of Geddes, but apparently not enough—that, at least, was the view of Geddes's great American disciple, Lewis Mumford. In March 1925, Mumford wrote to Geddes saying: 'Have you seen Radhakamal Mukerjee's new book on Regional Sociology? I have just glanced at it; enough to see that he has been assimilating you lustily, albeit it would seem unconsciously, since he mentions your work only at one point, and makes no acknowledgement at all. That sort of thing enrages me. It is good, however, that however anonymously your thoughts are getting into circulation; and one of these days I shall sit down and add a little bibliography to works like Mukerjee's, which will balance accounts.'[51]

There appears to be an element of sibling rivalry here. The young American who had attached himself to Geddes is judgemental about the young Indian who has done likewise. One supposes that Mumford in time outgrew these feelings of rivalry, since the international reputation he went on to achieve far exceeded Mukerjee's. Mumford's magisterial works on the history of technology and on the history of the city, published in 1934 and 1938 respectively, went on to achieve canonical status. Both books were inspired by Geddes's writings and by what Geddes had taught the author in person. This debt Mumford himself generously acknowledged in his work, and in his life, naming his only son 'Geddes'.[52]

Mukerjee himself was influenced by Geddes, but also by Rabindranath Tagore. Growing up in Bengal when Tagore was at the height of his fame, he would have surely steeped himself in Tagore's poetry, plays, novels, essays and songs. Mukerjee's interest in rural reconstruction also perhaps owed something to the founder of Sriniketan.

Contrary to what Mumford suggested, in his published writings Mukerjee does in fact mention Geddes quite regularly. Tagore features far less often, perhaps because sociologists do not generally wish to cite poets (lest they seem not solemn enough). However, when in 1961 Tagore's birth centenary was being observed, at a time when Mukerjee knew he was himself in the last stages of his own life, the sociologist wrote an essay on the poet's social philosophy. Here, he summarized the message of Tagore for contemporary India as follows:

> We have neither the right nor the power, he [Tagore] warns us, to exclude any people from building up the future destiny of India. To an urban-industrial India neglecting the village and the villager his message is that of self-sufficiency in the hamlets and co-operation of the villagers for the purposes of agricultural reconstruction, education, improvement of communications and water supply and the provision of all cultural amenities for the rural folks. The conception of a peasant democracy growing out of the union of self-conscious and independent rural communes has permanent lessons for an agricultural country like ours in which parliamentar[ian]ism is likely to develop into a class rule, the supremacy of the new rich and middle classes.[53]

The vision Mukerjee attributed to Tagore was of course not dissimilar to that held by Mahatma Gandhi as well. The sociologist himself had consistently advocated a healthy, balanced, non-exploitative relationship between the city and the countryside. He would do so in the 1920s when India was under colonial rule, and he would do so again in the 1960s, when the government of independent India was so fiercely committed to promoting urbanization and industrialization above all else.

The reservations that Tagore had about the urban-industrial way of life were perhaps as much moral and cultural as they were ecological. Mukerjee's reservations were more centrally ecological. His own studies had inculcated in him a deep knowledge of, as well as a profound respect for, the intricacies of the web of life, of which humans were only one, albeit the most dominant, element. These interconnections, argued Mukerjee, made it obligatory for humans to act responsibly and with restraint if they wished not to undermine the prospects of life on earth. Mukerjee was thus an environmentalist before the birth of environmentalism, as well as an 'environmental sociologist' and an 'ecological economist' long before those branches of scholarly enquiry had been thought of or invented.

As proof of this precociousness, let me conclude this chapter by offering one last Mukerjee quote, which comes from a book he wrote in the 1930s on the riverine ecology of his native province, Bengal. After documenting humanity's crimes against land, water, pasture and trees, he remarked:

> Co-operation in the conservation of land, in the use of water, in forest management, in the training and management of rivers, and, finally, in the reciprocal relations of village and city must be the keynote of the future. Throughout the ages man has despoiled the earth, and sinned in ignorance against waters, trees, and animals, thereby releasing destructive forces, which have impoverished and ultimately ruined his civilisation even in the most favoured regions. Man's future advance lies, indeed, in a bio-economic co-operation, based on scientific study and comprehension of the complex web of life that comprises both the animate and the inanimate realms; and this is deeper and more far-reaching than co-operation merely within the human community.[54]

CHAPTER THREE

Gandhi's Economist

J.C. KUMARAPPA AND RURAL RENEWAL

IN THE LAST WEEK of May 1929, a letter arrived at the Sabarmati ashram in Ahmedabad, intended for the place's founder and moving spirit. Written on the letterhead of 'Cornelius and Davar, Incorporated Accountants and Auditors, Bombay', it addressed its recipient, south Indian style, as 'Mahathma Gandhi'. The correspondent enclosed an essay he had written, which analysed how the British colonial government's policy of taxation had lessened the productivity of the Indian masses in the last hundred years. He wanted Gandhi's advice on whether to publish it, and wished also to consult him 'as to the way in which I can best serve our country'. The letter ended by asking Gandhi to grant the writer 'an appointment at your convenience'.[1]

The writer of this letter was a Christian from the Tamil country called J.C. Cornelius. Born in 1892, he grew up in a devout Bible-reading home, being educated in institutions run by Christians in Madras before going off to study accountancy in the United Kingdom. On being articled he returned to India, where he set up a commercial practice in Bombay. The practice, established with a Parsi partner named Dorab Davar, attracted a steady stream of colleagues, but it left Cornelius somewhat dissatisfied. Seeking further academic qualifications, in 1927 he went off to the United States, where he did a BSc in business administration at Syracuse University before moving to Columbia University to do a master's in economics.

In New York, J.C. Cornelius got to know the city's Gandhi-admiring priest, John Haynes Holmes. He spoke several times at the Community Church on Park Avenue where Holmes was the minister. In their conversations they must surely have spoken about the Mahatma, whom the priest had in his sermons anointed 'The Greatest Man in the World'. [2] Holmes, who at this stage had neither met Gandhi nor visited India, was much taken with this alert young Tamil from Gandhi's homeland. He wrote to Cornelius commending his 'exceptionally clear and very musical voice', his 'perfect command of English', his 'precision and charm of presentation', adding: 'You should have fine success on the American platform, and if there is anything I can do to help please let me know.'[3]

At Columbia, Cornelius came under the influence of the economist E.R.A. Seligman, who, some years previously, had also supervised the doctoral dissertation of B.R. Ambedkar, who went on to make a considerable mark as a scholar and social reformer and, in time, oversaw the drafting of the Indian Constitution. Living in the United States and interacting with radicals like Holmes and Seligman made Cornelius increasingly sceptical of the claims—then accepted by most Indian Christians—that the British were a civilizing and beneficial influence on India. Seligman himself was an authority on taxation and finance, which led

Cornelius to write his own master's thesis on public finance in British India.

On returning to Bombay in the spring of 1929, Cornelius rejoined his practice, but his heart was not in it. He thought that he could, and should, contribute to the nationalist cause rather than make more money for himself. In this he was influenced also by his elder brother, a professor at the Tata Institute of Social Sciences. On 10 May 1929, in a striking affirmation of their new identification, the brothers filed an affidavit in a court in Bombay asking that their surname be changed from 'Cornelius' to 'Kumarappa'.[4]

Ten days later, J.C. Kumarappa, previously known as J.C. Cornelius, wrote to the leader of his country's freedom struggle, asking to meet him. Now Gandhi got more unsolicited letters than any Indian who ever lived. However, he had at hand a splendid secretarial staff, which adroitly sifted out the wheat from the chaff, the significant from the unimportant. Kumarappa's letter fell squarely in the first category. Hence a reply was swiftly sent, asking the America-returned Indian economist to present himself at the Sabarmati ashram.

On 29 May—exactly a week after his first letter to Gandhi—J.C. Kumarappa took the night train from Bombay to Ahmedabad. The next day he met Gandhi, who, after a brief conversation, directed him to his colleague D.B. (Kaka) Kalelkar, who was the vice chancellor of the Gujarat Vidyapeeth, a nationalist university set up as an alternative to the colonial education system. The two men did not at first hit it off, with the Tamilian offended at Kalelkar's suggestion that he rapidly learn Hindi. However, Gandhi himself quickly recognized the potential in the Columbia-returned scholar and got the Gujarat Vidyapeeth to offer him a post as professor of economics. He was to be paid Rs 75 pay per month plus Rs 15 for house rent.[5]

At least one of Kumarappa's brothers tried to dissuade him from joining Gandhi. He was advised to further build up his practice in accountancy, and 'strive towards professional success'.[6] The family's reservations came in part from the traditionally pro-Raj outlook of Indian Christians, and in part from the sense that after such laboriously acquired advanced degrees from the United States, Kumarappa should not throw it all away for the uncertain life of a Gandhian nationalist.

Kumarappa, however, would not be dissuaded. That day in Ahmedabad had made him a convert to the Mahatma's credo—for life. He had already adopted an Indian-sounding surname, and now, to confirm the transition—or transformation—he would abandon European dress too, henceforth wearing a kurta and dhoti made of khadi, homespun cloth, in the best nationalist style.

Shortly after moving to Ahmedabad, and assuming the post of professor of economics at the Gujarat Vidyapeeth, Kumarappa was asked by Gandhi to supervise the study of living and working conditions in a taluka (subdistrict) not far from Ahmedabad known as Matar. The students of the Vidyapeeth were at his service to assist him.

Till he was assigned to study the villages of the Matar taluka, Kumarappa had probably never visited a village. He epitomized a remark of his vice chancellor, Kaka Kalelkar, that 'if there is one thing that characterises the educated man in India and distinguishes him from his *confrere* elsewhere, it is his abysmal ignorance of the actual rural conditions in his own country'.[7] Now, with the aid of his students, the Vidyapeeth's new professor of economics resolutely sought to correct this. From December 1929, Kumarappa and his wards began touring the villages of

Matar, collecting data on land, housing, cropping patterns, taxes and much else. They worked in the field uninterruptedly for three months, but then their analysis of the data was interrupted by the onset of Gandhi's Salt March of 1930, and the large-scale arrests of nationalists that followed. It took almost two years for the report on the research of Kumarappa and his team to be made public.

A Survey of Matar Taluka, published by the Gujarat Vidyapeeth in December 1931, begins with an epigraph from the Mahabharata, which exhorts the king thus:

> Are large tanks dug in your kingdom at proper distances by which agriculture has not to depend entirely on rain? Are the agriculturists in your kingdom in want of food or seed? Do you advance them loan (of seed grain) taking only a fourth part of every hundred?

The data presented in Kumarappa's report suggested that the rulers of British India had grievously dishonoured the Mahabharata's maxims. Their rates of land revenue increased steadily every year, placing unbearable burdens on the peasantry, leading to periodic protests, these asking, not always successfully, for the reduction or remission of taxes levied by the state on agriculturists. 'The land revenue code as it stands today,' remarked Kumarappa, 'is an ordinance of the worst type giving unlimited power into the hands of the executives.'[8]

The state's indifference towards the peasantry was also manifest in the lack of any assistance or advice in the selection of seeds. The Government of the Bombay Presidency had a well-staffed and moderately well-funded Agricultural Department, yet 'most of the village people were not cognizant of even the existence of such a department'. Again, despite having a grandly named Registrar of Co-operative Societies, the state had done virtually nothing to aid peasants in getting access to credit, or with marketing their produce, leaving them at the mercy of the local moneylender.[9]

A chapter on irrigation, dealing with that resource most vital to agriculture, water, began with another epigraph from the Mahabharata:

> He [the ruler] should multiply the number of tanks and wells containing large quantities of water, and should protect all shady trees.

Unfortunately, this injunction had been honoured mostly in the breach, for many of the tanks in the Matar taluka were 'in bad repair and little attention had been paid to directing water into these tanks from their catchment areas'. Villagers told the Vidyapeeth's survey team that if the bunds (embankments) of the tanks were raised, then their capacity would be greatly enhanced, allowing the villagers to cultivate a crop that would get them good returns, such as rice. Their pleas to the state had gone unheeded. 'If the Irrigation Department has at heart the good of the farmers,' commented Kumarappa, 'it should leave no stone unturned in exploring ways and means of increasing the productivity of these villages, more especially as the possibility of raising rice, which is [a] valuable food crop, seems to be within reach.' The economist also faulted the state for allowing grazing on common land without the payment of a fee, the consequent shortages of fodder adversely affecting the health of village cattle.[10]

Kumarappa's survey found that even the most diligent peasant families were underemployed or even unemployed for large parts of the year. In between tilling, sowing, weeding, watering and harvesting there were long stretches of time when peasants did no work at all. In these weeks and months, it would be ideal 'for the farmer to be engaged in a subsidiary occupation, such as spinning'. This would reduce expenditure on expensive mill-made cloth imported from outside the village. The economist calculated that if the villagers were to supply themselves with their own clothing, this would lead to a 70 per cent increase in per capita income.[11]

While asking for a more enlightened and caring state, Kumarappa also urged the villagers to scrutinize their own failures, their own inability to rise above the interests of family and caste and work co-operatively for the good of the community as a whole. Scattered through *A Survey of Matar Taluka* are remarks on the ways in which nature and natural resources could be used wisely and well by the peasants of the region. Cattle dung was a valuable source of agricultural fertilizer, yet the surveys done by Kumarappa and his students concluded that 'even where so used, such manure is not of high quality, as urine and farmyard waste is not collected properly, and the manure is often allowed to dry up'. Further, caste prejudices meant that, unlike in other agricultural civilizations like China, human waste was not used by farmers as manure, despite its great value in this regard.

Kumarappa called for 'a certain amount of sustained propaganda' to aid Indian peasants in overcoming this unfortunate prejudice. He urged that villagers be persuaded to go out into their own fields to answer the call of nature, covering up their refuse with mud afterwards, and allowing the material to compost before it was ready to use as manure. He suggested portable privies, made of matting, which would provide privacy, and which in his estimate would cost only five rupees each. For those who did not own land there could be community toilets, where human waste would likewise be made into manure, this sold to the agriculturists, with the proceeds going to a community fund.[12]

In this, his first extended exposure to the Indian village, Kumarappa was dismayed to find that the best drinking water sources had been monopolized by the upper castes. While the water was sometimes brackish and surrounded by muddy environments, he found that 'on the whole it may be said that in this taluka the caste people are fairly well provided with drinking water ... But the facilities for the untouchables are in a deplorable condition. ... In many of these villages, Dheds, Chamara and Bhangis [all "Untouchable" castes] have to get what water they can from pits dug in tank-beds. They are put to a great deal of hardship, especially during the summer months.'[13]

The drinking water available to lower castes was of shockingly poor quality. However, in the case of that other gift of nature, clean air, this was not always available even to the top strata of rural society, and particularly their women. The homes of the upper castes, while sturdily built of brick and wood, had 'practically, no arrangement for ventilation except the open doors'. And 'the kitchen, being right in the interior and having insufficient outlet for the smoke, adds to the discomfort of the house'. Adding to 'impurities in the air within the house' were lamps which burnt kerosene oil yet lacked the glass chimneys needed to complete the process of combustion, further polluting the atmosphere. The report asked families which lacked the money for these glass chimneys to shift to castor oil for their lamps, which would be cleaner without being more expensive.[14]

An interesting aspect of Kumarappa's report was that it noticed conflicts over nature between humans and other species. A large hunting preserve was maintained by the Nawab of Cambay from which wild animals often trespassed into farmlands, damaging crops and causing financial loss to villagers.[15] In some villages, the common fund was maintained by merchants of the Jain faith, who saw salvation in feeding food to birds. In these hands, wrote Kumarappa, resources that could have alleviated human suffering were instead 'used for repairing temples, feeding birds, dogs, and for entertaining visitors. Even when people are starving maunds of grain are being thrown away to the birds. One fails to see any rational action in such sentimental provisions for the exhibition of kindness to dumb creatures.'[16]

As a Gandhian who believed in the virtues of work and 'bread-labour', Kumarappa was scathing in his criticisms of the so-called holy men who wore saffron robes to blackmail villagers into supporting them. 'An imperceptible burden is thrown on the community,' he wrote, 'by the maintenance of fakirs, sadhus and bavas. These people are not producers in the economic sense of the word. They have abandoned the old function assigned to them of teaching the people and helping them in the practice of their religion. Today, their position is parasitic as they are purely consumers.'[17]

In the conclusion to his report, Kumarappa came down hard on the failures of the British Raj. Drawing no doubt on his experience of life in the independent countries of the West, he wrote: 'In other parts of the world when people labour with such low production the Government support the sufferers with doles to keep them from starvation. But in India, the Government taxes them more heavily and drives them into the quick-sands of indebtedness.' The arrogance of the state and its apathy towards the people was epitomized by the Irrigation Department, in whose functioning 'the one idea seems to be to increase the [user] rates and charge people for water they have not received. One may almost call this department a "Dry Irrigation" Department as many of the tanks it possesses are but dry fields rented out for cultivation.'[18]

For all the harsh things it says about the British Raj, Kumarappa's Matar report is also an indictment of peasant society—of its failure to rise above caste distinctions and speak and act for the community as a whole, of its careless and suboptimal use of natural resources. This principled even-handedness is reflected in the report's penultimate paragraph, which states:

> If Matar taluka is to progress, the people will have to make a determined effort to get rid of their idle moments, to improve

> their methods of cultivation by avoiding all waste, and utilizing all forms of manure and preserving their seeds with care, and to refrain from unproductive expenditures until they have means to educate their children and live decently. The Government, on its part, should cease to attempt to draw blood out of stone and turn its attention to finding ways and means of helping the people out of the 'slough of despond' in which we find them today.[19]

Between 1931 and 1933 Kumarappa was in and out of jail. He was one of the few Christians in the country to take an active part in the freedom struggle. His open identification with Gandhi led him to publicly quarrel with the Church establishment in India, which had sided with the Raj. In the summer of 1930, Kumarappa engaged in a sharp exchange of letters with Bishop Foss Westcott, the head of the Anglican Church in India. On the British bishop's acquiescence to colonial repression, the Indian Christian wrote:

> At present the inhuman methods used by the Government towards the Satyagrahis is unworthy of an opponent like Gandhiji, and no gentleman can countenance it, leave alone one who professes to follow the Prince of Peace, without a word of protest while such brutalities and tortures are being used. This attitude of callousness is tantamount to a denial of our Lord...[20]

In 1933 Gandhi put on hold his political struggle against the Raj and decided to devote himself to constructive work. The next year, at the Bombay session of the Congress, Gandhi promoted a new organization to put into practice the idea of swadeshi, or self-reliance. It was called the All India Village Industries Association (AIVIA). The resolution creating the AIVIA said, among other things, that 'village reorganization and reconstruction necessarily implies revival and encouragement of dead or dying village industries...'

Kumarappa was put in charge of the AIVIA. Gandhi had now moved his home base from Ahmedabad to central India, and it was here, near the town of Wardha, that the AIVIA established its headquarters, in a campus named Maganvadi, after one of Gandhi's close associates who had died prematurely.

The work of the AIVIA fell into five parts: research, production, training, extension and publication. The Association's Management Board was chaired by a nationalist lawyer and had other freedom fighters as members; while its Board of Advisers included, among others, the great scientists J.C. Bose and C.V. Raman. Kumarappa himself served as the Association's general secretary.

Constructive workers from across India came to Maganvadi to be trained by Kumarappa and his team. To set an example, Kumarappa built his own hut in Maganvadi entirely from local materials. Its walls were made of bamboo and plastered with mud, and its roof was tiled. It consisted of a single room, 12 feet by 14 feet, which served as his bedroom dining room, study and bath, with a simple privy constructed over a trench outside, on open ground. It had cost all of Rs 150 to construct, and was his abode for the next two decades.[21]

In 1938, after he became president of the Congress, Subhas Chandra Bose set up a National Planning Committee (NPC), with Jawaharlal Nehru as its chairman. They asked Kumarappa, as the general secretary of the AIVIA, to serve on the committee. He was hesitant to join, since he knew that both Bose and Nehru were great admirers of the Soviet model of planned industrial development. He communicated his reservations to Gandhi, who prevailed upon him to set them aside and put the AIVIA's point of view before Nehru, Bose and company. In the event Kumarappa lasted just a year, resigning when he found his own views on the most suitable development path for India much at odds with the fervent modernizers who had captured the imagination of the Congress.[22]

Ignored by the intellectual leaders of his own party, Kumarappa took his ideas to the public. In 1941, he organized a khadi exhibition in Bombay, aimed at persuading urban consumers to buy handmade products. In an article in the *Bombay Chronicle*, Kumarappa argued that centralized industry destroyed the initiative and spirit of the worker, 'while cottage and village industries release the personality of the producer and make him a lover of liberty and freedom. A nation made up of such persons will be independent and resourceful. Therefore, it behooves us to patronise goods produced under such conditions.' In a follow-up article, published on Gandhi's birthday, he specifically addressed urban women, asking them to buy khadi products instead of expensive silks from Belgium or Paris. 'Every sister who buys a foreign article,' he wrote, 'takes the bread out of the mouth of our artisans by causing unemployment in our own land ... In Tamil we have a saying that a crow regards its own little ones as the most precious. But we have become foster parents to foreign and mill products, forgetting our own people.' Kumarappa ended his article by insisting that 'we have to develop a burning religious zeal for the welfare of our villagers'.[23]

For Kumarappa, the nurturing of village industries was important for generating local employment and local income, but also for the sustainable use of natural resources. He thus unfavourably compared machine-driven paper factories, which used freshly cut bamboo from the forests, with small handmade paper units, which recycled bamboo already used as baskets and mats and discarded by homes and offices once they were worn or torn. By leading to the decimation rather than conservation of forests, 'the mill process of making paper', he wrote, was 'thoroughly unscientific and wasteful in the utilization of natural resources'.

Kumarappa likewise contrasted the process of obtaining jaggery from palm trees with sugar made in mills from the produce of heavily irrigated sugarcane fields. The latter used more land and much more water and was less nutritious to boot. These sugar mills, he remarked, existed 'only to satisfy the greed for accumulation of wealth by individuals, at the cost of nutritious food products found in Nature'.[24] Writing in Gandhi's newspaper, *Harijan*, Kumarappa commended to its readers an experiment in Morvi state, where the AIVIA had planted a forest of date palms covering an area of six square miles. He hoped this could be replicated widely, as the production of jaggery and sugar from palm juice released fertile land currently under sugarcane for the cultivation of essential food crops. Further, apart from providing healthy and nutritious jaggery and sugar, date palms had other uses, such as providing timber for homes, leaves for mat-making, etc., thus helping villagers become more self-sufficient in their primary needs.[25]

Among the resource-conserving innovations designed by Kumarappa in Maganvadi was a lamp he named Magan Deep (the Light of Magan), which used vegetable oil rather than kerosene, and was thus less polluting as well as more attractive to the eye. In a well-attended meeting of Gandhians from all over India held in Indore, he got the AIVIA to light up the premises at night with hundreds of such lamps. Another innovation, developed by his colleagues under his instruction, was a smokeless stove called Magan Choola. Whereas the traditional Indian stove, which used firewood, emitted a huge amount of smoke, this newly designed stove burnt biomass more cleanly, making it much healthier to use for the housewife.[26]

In November 1947, shortly after the British had left, Kumarappa wrote an essay outlining three possible paths for rural development in independent India. The first looked to the village as a source of raw materials for urban industry; the second saw the village as a market for goods produced in towns; the third viewed the village as 'an entity in itself affording complete facilities for the development of the individuals composing the population of the village'. Kumarappa strongly advocated the last path, arguing that only through it could the villager become 'a worthy citizen of a democratic State'. He urged that village panchayats (councils) be given the responsibility for water supply, health, hygiene, education and vocational training. He asked that the cultivated land available in the village be used to meet local needs, growing cereals, pulses, vegetables, oilseeds and dairy products for local consumption, with surpluses being traded with neighbouring villages for essentials they could provide. 'Such a scheme of rural development,' he remarked, 'will not be a patchwork made by government officials according to the whims of the various departments, but being based on self-help and local contribution in labour and in kind it will be an ideal training ground in the art of living...'[27]

Through the 1930s and 1940s, even while he was supervising the practical work of the AIVIA, Kumarappa was writing books and pamphlets setting out the intellectual—or perhaps one should say ideological—basis of a village-centred economic order. Kumarappa's economic and ethical defence of agrarian civilization hinged on a novel distinction he made between 'pack type' and 'herd type' societies. He developed this contrast from the non-human world, between animals like the wolf which were predatory, aggressive and carnivorous, and animals like the sheep which were peaceable, non-violent and vegetarian. In the human world, the starkest example of the 'pack type' was of course the modern West. According to Kumarappa, after only a relatively short period as an agricultural civilization, the West was overtaken by the Industrial Revolution; consequently, its societal features were heavily marked by the hunter, nomad and industrial stages of human evolution—all predatory pack-type societies. By contrast, long-settled, stable, agrarian cultures like China, India and Japan (before the last named began its forced march to industrialization) were held up as exemplars of gentler herd-type societies.[28]

Kumarappa, following Gandhi, believed that 'there can be no industrialisation without predation', while agriculture is, and ought to be, 'the greatest among occupations', in which 'man attempts to control nature and his own environment in such a way as to produce the best results'. He expressed this contrast between agriculture and industry in terms of their attempted modifications of the natural world. In the former, he wrote, 'the system ordained by nature is not interfered with to any great extent. If there is a variation at all, it follows a natural mutation. The agriculturist only aids nature or intensifies in a short time what takes place in nature in a long period.' On the other hand, in industrial society the 'variations from nature are very violent in that a large supply of goods is produced, irrespective of demand, and then a demand is artificially created for goods by means of clever advertisements'.[29]

In this analytical scheme, the task of humans was to co-operate intelligently and lovingly with what Kumarappa called nature's Economy of Permanence. However, like most Gandhians of his generation Kumarappa was an immensely practical man, primarily interested not in theoretical reflection but in ameliorating the lot of the Indian peasant and artisan. An acute set of observations thus emerge from his own field experience and constructive work, on how to more carefully husband the natural resources of the agrarian economy. As already noted, he stressed the need to use nightsoil as manure, asking for subsidies to be given to individuals, as a means of overcoming caste prohibitions, for converting human excreta and village waste into compost manure. He viewed the substitution of chemical fertilizer for organic manure as an example of the Economy of Permanence yielding to the manmade Economy of Transience. He commented on the poor maintenance of irrigation tanks, urging the conservation of water to augment the water table and reduce brackishness. He did not fail to observe, either, that in villages where clean drinking water was available for upper castes, Untouchables were not similarly privileged.[30]

Water was by no means the only natural resource whose conservation Kumarappa was concerned with. He dwelt on the importance of maintaining soil quality by checking erosion and waterlogging. And in a pithy comment on actual and preferred models of forest management, he said:

> The government will have to radically revise its policy of maintaining forests. Forest management should be guided, not by considerations of revenue but by the needs of the people ... Forest planning must be based on the requirements of the villagers around. Forests should be divided into two main classes: (1) those supplying timber to be planned from the long range point of view, and (2) those supplying fuel and grasses, to be made available to the public either free of cost or at nominal rates. There are village industries such as palm gur, paper making, pottery, etc., which can flourish only if fuel and grass can be supplied to them at cheap rates.[31]

In an article carrying the telling title 'What is Progress?', Kumarappa argued that 'in the measure in which we are able to pull alongside nature's dictates, we shall be progressing in the right direction. But in so far as we are pulling against the course of nature, we shall be creating violence and destruction...'[32] Strewn through Kumarappa's writings are observations with profound ecological consequences. This remark, for instance, could well serve as a basic condition for environmental responsibility: 'If we produce everything we want from within a limited area, we are in a position to supervise the methods of production; while if we draw our requirements from the ends of the earth it becomes impossible for us to guarantee the conditions of production in such places.'[33]

Kumarappa distinguished between two kinds of natural resources, which he termed Current Economy and Reservoir Economy (corresponding to what we now conventionally know as renewable and non-renewable resources respectively). An excessive reliance on the latter led to violence. 'If we desire to promote non-violence in society,' he wrote, 'more percentage of wood, which belongs to current economy, must be used and less of iron. Petrol falls into our reservoir economy. As it becomes less and less, its use leads to conflict. The increasing violence in our society today is due to the nations running into reservoir economy abandoning current economy.'[34]

Like Gandhi, Kumarappa was a critic of both Western capitalism and Soviet communism, holding them to be but two variants of a centralizing, destructive and violent system of production.[35] The Second World War, with its massive loss of life and livelihood, confirmed Kumarappa in his view that agrarian economies, powered by animal power, were less prone to deadly wars than industrial economies powered by fossil fuels. In an essay published in 1947 he remarked:

> In the cow-and-horse-centred economies we have unlimited sources, for we could breed as many bullocks and horses as we needed; and there being no restriction on the amount available, it does not arouse anybody's greed or envy. But coal and petrol, being limited in their supply and quantity; the use of such sources of power leads to friction amongst nations as the sources of supply

> dry up. It is now well recognised that these global wars are in no small measure due to different nations seeking to get control over oil fields. Hence the coal and oil economies lead to conflict among nations. Unlike them the cow and horse economies are comparatively peaceful economies.[36]

I suppose the operative word here is *comparatively*. There had been, as Kumarappa surely knew, a succession of wars both in medieval India and in medieval Europe, but none had remotely exacted the toll of human life that the wars of the industrial age would.

After India became independent in August 1947, many Congressmen joined the government, either at the Centre or in the states. However, Kumarappa refused to become a minister or even a member of the Constituent Assembly of India. For he saw a crucial role for social activists in India's new and evolving democracy. Their job was to keep the politicians on their toes. 'As the waters of a river are kept in their course by its banks,' he wrote, 'so also the government of a country has to be directed by forces which lie outside the official sector of the Government.'

Kumarappa told his fellow Gandhians that 'what we should aim at is not to replace the ministers, but to hold up models that they should follow. The constructive workers should direct them into proper channels by the beacon light of their example.' A well-organized group of social workers would, argued Kumarappa, provide a 'directive force' to the government. He wrote: 'Their service to the people will be their sanction and the merit of their work will be their charter. The ministers will draw their inspiration from such a body which will advise and guide the [central and state] Governments.'

In older democracies such as the United Kingdom, there existed a robust Opposition in Parliament itself. But in India, with a single party, the Congress, so dominant, this political check did not exist. Therefore, said Kumarappa, 'the body of constructive workers will form the bulwark of safety for the people against exploitation'. By its scrutiny and its example it could keep the government honest, forcing it to provide 'the needed emphasis to the affairs of the people and ensure their welfare, bringing in Swaraj [freedom] to the masses'.[37] Kumarappa's article was carried in Gandhi's weekly, *Harijan*, with a short postscript by Gandhi himself, dated 24 January 1948, which read: 'This is very attractive. But it has to be confessed that we have not the requisite number of selfless workers capable of giving a good account of themselves.'

Five days later, possibly with Kumarappa's article in mind, Gandhi suggested that the Congress be disbanded and reconstituted as a body of constructive workers named the Lok Sevak Sangh, with units in different parts of India. The members of this body would work for the abolition of untouchability, the promotion of inter-faith harmony, the renewal of rural economic life, education and sanitation, etc.[38] The very next day, before the idea could be debated or taken forward, Gandhi was assassinated.

In an article published a year after Gandhi's death, Kumarappa sharply criticized his former colleagues in the freedom movement who were now living luxurious lives as ministers and members of Parliament in the old imperial capital, New Delhi. He did not even spare Nehru, who had recently shifted from a comfortable bungalow to the second grandest home in the city, once occupied by the chief of the British Indian Army. He wrote: 'The mansion in York Road was not good enough for the Prime Minister, who is always talking of increasing our standard of living, and he had to move into the palace of the Commander-in-Chief! The Ministers are vying with each other and giving garden parties, but when we look at the sum total of benefit that they have conferred on poor John citizen, we could almost say nil...'[39]

Gandhi's secretary, Mahadev Desai, would jokingly refer to Kumarappa as 'the violent exponent of non-violence'.[40] Desai had in mind here the polemical, no-nonsense tone of the essays and editorials Kumarappa wrote in the bulletin of the AIVIA and in the house journal of the Gandhians, *Harijan*. This uncompromising, all-or-nothing approach characterized Kumarappa's personal correspondence as well. In October 1947, a Gandhian from Assam, who had been jailed during the freedom movement, wrote to Kumarappa asking him, as 'one who is a close student of the subject and has dedicated his life for a principle and a cause', to write the foreword for a book manuscript he had prepared on 'Industrial Decentralization'. Kumarappa read the manuscript and wrote back saying:

> Your scheme of decentralisation is only a form of splitting up factories and unwieldly units of production. No doubt this will lessen the evils of industrial cities and their slums. This, however, is not our view of decentralisation. We aim at producing goods for the consumption of the villagers where the towns will not call the tune. We hope to produce village organisations which will be training grounds for democracy. Under such a scheme the villagers will be masters of [their] lives in which economics is only one aspect of life. Just decentralisation is not everything. We do not want to make man a means of production. Man is an entity. Any system that ignores this fact is not worthy of our consideration.

In returning the manuscript, Kumarappa told the writer that 'as your line of attack is fundamentally different, you will agree, it would not be proper to write a Foreword with many reservations'.[41]

Kumarappa's bluntness alienated many of his old colleagues in the Gandhian movement. One such, the scholar and long-term follower of the Mahatma, K.G. Mashruwala, wrote to him six months after Gandhi's death that 'even those who respect you and believe with you to a great extent have begun to disregard your criticism as having become habitual'.[42]

In 1951, Kumarappa was asked to serve on the advisory board of the newly established Planning Commission. Nehru and his economic experts had committed themselves to a path of centralized industrial development; the inclusion of the dissenter was a nod to Gandhi, common mentor of Nehru and Kumarappa.

For the first meeting of this advisory board, Kumarappa took a train from Wardha to Delhi, travelling third class as was his wont. From Delhi station he went in a horse-driven tonga to the venue, the South Block offices of the Government of India, located on Raisina Hill, next to the Viceroy's Palace, now renamed Rashtrapati Bhavan. A furlong short of its destination the vehicle was flagged down by a policeman, who said it could not proceed further, since the prime minister was soon to pass that way for an important meeting, that of the Planning Commission. Kumarappa told the policeman that he was to attend the same meeting and would like to reach before the prime minister did, so that he could stand up and greet the great man when he entered the room. He was allowed to pass.

The Gandhian and the tonga were once more stopped, outside South Block, by a military man this time. Kumarappa once more engaged in and won the argument. Later, at the meeting itself, he told Nehru of his troubles in entering the building, expressing his dismay at a public sign on New Delhi's roads saying 'Bullock Carts Not Allowed'. This, said the Gandhian, ill-befitted a democracy where everyone was considered to be equal. He now joked that the next time he would seek to come to the meeting in a bullock cart.

The prime minister artfully replied that the sign was intended to save the drivers of bullock- and horse-drawn carts from being hit by speeding cars or lorries. To this Kumarappa responded: 'Sir, you are a lawyer and used to special pleading, but to a simple man like me your argument looks upside down. When there are two persons in public and the presence of one is likely to be a menace to the other, my common sense would lead me to restrain the source of danger rather than the possible victim. Accordingly, I would put up a notice, "Motor cars and lorries not allowed", and thus protect the bullock cart drivers.' The repartee evoked laughter all around, but of course the original (and offending) sign stayed.[43]

Notwithstanding the years they had spent together in the Congress and the freedom struggle, notwithstanding the deep bond each shared with Gandhi, Nehru and Kumarappa had radically different ideas about economic development in free India. Sensing this, Kumarappa soon dropped out of the Planning Commission's advisory panel. However, when in August 1951 the government issued a draft outline of the First Five Year Plan, the Gandhian economist subjected the text to critical scrutiny in print. He wrote that while the plan had put forward 'grandiose schemes' for constructing large dams, 'hardly anything has been suggested to meet the ever present problem of soil erosion, top-soil washing off, and other local problems connected with wasting of our land resources'. He thought the plan should instead have allocated money for many small schemes 'for building *nallas* [small canals] on hill streams at short intervals'. These, he said, 'will not only break up the speed of the current but will also gather the silt at short intervals and conserve water and raise the water level'.

Kumarappa also complained that the chapter on forestry had retained the commercial-mindedness of colonial systems of forest management. He thought that the Forest Department in independent India should be regarded not as a revenue-generating body, but as a department to serve the people. It must move away from focusing on the timber species that large industry desired, and instead focus on non-timber forest produce more useful to smaller units.

Kumarappa also deplored the excessive emphasis given to the promotion of fertilizer factories. The precondition for the widespread use of chemical manure, he noted, was a large number of scientists who could 'prescribe the proper dosage for every particular piece of land. Applying fertilizers without such precautions will land us in a tremendous catastrophe by ruining our soil'.

Finally, Kumarappa thought that the Plan document was 'rather academic and verbose' in its presentation, and that it suffered 'from the lack of a philosophy of life'.[44]

Two years later, Kumarappa wrote a short but pungent critique of the Nehru government's approach to economic development. He thought it excessively influenced by Western models. It was top-down rather than bottom-up, he said, and disregarded ecological constraints. In this it departed from the ideals of Gandhi, who would have wished that in independent India's development plans, 'the needs of our people and the resources at our disposal should be co-ordinated with restrictions under which nature has placed us'.

Kumarappa's article appears to have been provoked by Prime Minister Nehru's decision to invite an American expert, Albert Mayer, to advise on the government's new 'Community Development' programmes. Kumarappa worried that these schemes, based on foreign models, would disregard rather than build upon the respect for nature and natural limits that (in his view) had characterized agrarian life in India. As he put it:

> Our method has been a co-ordinated cycle of the earth, animal and man; our needs were produced by these means and such industries as we had were based on these foundations for processing and finishing the products. For instance, when the earth yields her corn bountifully, we eat the grain, the animal eats the leaves and the stalks, and we and the animals return to the earth our refuse in the form of manure to start the cycle all over again. If we build a road, we sink along with it a well or dig a tank to provide the road material. Thus our plans are well-coordinated. On the other hand, when a tractor run on crude oil is used there is no complementary cycle. The waste gases go into the air to pollute it. The tractor is not connected organically with the earth or with man. It stands apart. This is patchwork and does not form a cycle.

Kumarappa insisted afresh that agrarian society was prudent in its use of natural resources, whereas industrial society was profligate. His article ended with this tirade against the wasteful lifestyle of Americans who had come to advise Indians:

> Such American guides live in the most luxurious style and import from their own country all their requirements including food. They house themselves in air-conditioned buildings with 'deep freeze' equipment, which is considered the height of luxury even in luxurious America. So whatever goodwill there may be behind the efforts, I fear these will lead to no purpose, as their ways and our ways are poles apart. It is not possible in this short note to give examples of the extravagant ways of the Americans, which they have followed in the past in building up their country; how they have burnt forests and built roads and wasted their lands with short-term agricultural methods, and passed on from place to place to seek pastures new. It is impossible for us to use such persons as our guides and yet hope to succeed! ... The sooner India turns to her own genius and relies on her own strength and

> resources for development, the better it will be for herself and her message of peace to the world.[45]

Lurking behind this critique was perhaps a sense of personal disappointment, that instead of approaching Gandhians like himself, who had worked for decades in rural India and who lived in villages, Nehru's government had asked an American to design flagship projects in rural India. The critique was perceptive nonetheless; particularly with regard to the varying attitudes to resource consumption of the West and India. Kumarappa, we might note, had lived in America before the onset of the Great Depression, during the boom years of its wealth and luxury, the 1920s. He knew that country far better than Nehru; indeed, he also knew his own country (particularly its villages) far better than the prime minister.

As a last illustration of Kumarappa's ecological thinking, let me quote from an unpublished article he wrote in 1955. This was a response to the recently published report of the States Reorganisation Commission, which mandated that the provincial boundaries of India be redrawn on linguistic lines. In his essay, Kumarappa argued that instead of using language as the principle of provincial reorganization,

> We should lay our States along the river valleys, build canals and tanks, organise water transport and village and agro-industries to provide occupation. ... The hills, where the sources are, abound in waterfalls. A fall of a few feet will generate enough electric power to run cottage industries. We could organise small industries run by carpenters and blacksmiths. Wood, timber and other raw materials will be available in the forests, when properly planned and exploited. Some minerals can also be obtained here. Conservation of forests along the river valleys can come under unified control ensuring a co-ordinated policy.

In offering this alternative, Kumarappa invoked both the example of ancient south India and of modern Japan. 'The Pandyan kings had done much on these lines in utilizing the waters of the Cauvery,' he remarked, adding: 'The Japanese also follow the rivers from their mountain sources in this fashion. This scheme will raise the level of the subsoil water also and fill the wells in the neighbourhood. By this method we can grow two or three canals a year wherever even one is in uncertainty.'

Kumarappa urged a network of canals to facilitate transportation by boats, which would be cheaper and use fewer resources than railways and trucks. This could lead to a revival of the once flourishing boat industry, which would also provide rural employment outside of the farming season. He envisaged a network of provinces named after rivers, having harmonious relations with one another. There would, in his scheme, be a Kaveri state, a Godavari state, a Krishna state, a Mahanadi state and so on. He claimed that while the creation of linguistic provinces would lead to bickering, 'river valley provinces will lead to plenty, prosperity, and to the peaceful living together of various peoples'.[46]

This was a bio-regional approach, with some parallels to the sort of arguments that Radhakamal Mukerjee had made in the 1930s. There is no evidence that these two heretical thinkers ever met (or indeed read each other's work). One was a university scholar, the other an activist with Gandhi. Yet there are striking parallels in their work. In different but arguably complementary ways, they each challenged the dominant intellectual consensus of the time, which asked that India emulate without question Western models of centralized industrialization. Kumarappa and Mukerjee were two notable dissenters, who warned of the ecological and social disruptions that might ensue as a result of such imitative thinking. It has been a pleasure, and a privilege, to set them side by side in the present book, as writers who may have been before their time but whose legacies speak directly and compellingly to us today.

After Gandhi's death in 1948, a group of his followers met in his ashram in central India, and formed an organization called the Sarva Seva Sangh (Society for the Service of All). This sought to dedicate itself to the tasks of rural renewal and village self-sufficiency that Gandhi had so vigorously advocated.

Nehru was Gandhi's appointed political heir, so chosen and nominated by the Mahatma in the late 1930s itself. However, to carry on his legacy in constructive work Gandhi had not anointed a specific successor. He perhaps thought he had some (or perhaps even many) years to live, and would himself lead attempts to transform society on the ground, while non-violently mobilizing the forces of popular opinion to keep the excesses of the state in check. In the event, one of his oldest followers, the ascetic Maharashtrian scholar Vinoba Bhave, emerged as the successor to Gandhi in the sphere of social work. In 1948, when a Communist insurgency broke out in Hyderabad, Bhave took up a campaign of land donation (Bhoodan) to blunt its edge. He marched from village to village, district to district, state to state, urging large landlords to donate part of their holdings for cultivation by the poor and the landless. His marches and the attention they attracted propelled Bhave to the head of the constructive work movement. He became to the Sarva Seva Sangh what Nehru was to the Government of India.[47]

In March 1951, Kumarappa suggested that the Sarva Seva Sangh work actively to demonstrate the potential and promise of village self-sufficiency. In the present economic system, noted Kumarappa, farmers, the real producers, faced privation while the higher strata of society in cities prospered. He therefore proposed that the Sarvodaya (Gandhian) workers promote a balanced system of cultivation in land acquired for the purpose. 'To carry out this experiment,' he wrote, 'it will be necessary for us to get a fairly compact area free from modern complications of high finance, the intrigues of big commerce and the wrong leads of interested parties.' The experiment could include, apart from balanced cultivation, schools, hospitals and improved sanitation. This experiment, wrote Kumarappa, would in time 'provide the basis for a countrywide self-sufficient programme of rural reconstruction ... This has not been done yet nor is it capable of being done through present governmental agencies. Hence it is imperative that the Sarva Seva Sangh should take up the scheme and give a lead to the country in this particular department of life which has till now been sorely neglected.'[48]

To take the idea forward, Kumarappa himself established an ashram in the village of Seldoh in the Wardha district, some twenty-five miles from his own base in the AIVIA headquarters in Maganvadi. Seldoh was chosen because some of its participants had been jailed in the satyagrahas against the Raj, 'and so had a taste of the political struggle'. The village had 120 households. This Gandhian experiment aimed to balance cultivation with animal husbandry, and to promote composting, basic education, health and hygiene.

The ashram in Seldoh was inaugurated on 17 May 1951 by J.B. Kripalani, one of Gandhi's closest disciples, who had recently emerged as a fierce critic of Nehru's policies as prime minister (which may have endeared him to Kumarappa). With a group of children from the Untouchable castes, Kumarappa served food at the first collective meal. Kumarappa, who had a talent for water divining, also helped dig the first well. In a brief speech he said that

> while working everyone should judge his work from the lasting nature of values flowing from it and its being of common good.

> For instance, planting a mango tree will provide shade and shelter to man and animals equally and for long long years. The planter will also receive the blessings of all at the same time. They will deliberate as to who planted this tree and with what good motive. Against this a tomato plant grows and finishes quickly and the only one to draw any benefit from it will be its planter or his family ... It stands no comparison with the mango tree for being of any common benefit.

Over the next few months, Kumarappa travelled regularly between this new ashram and his home base with the AIVIA in Maganvadi. In Seldoh he stayed in a hut made in the traditional style, of thatch and wood.

The ashram workers had put up a trench latrine but villagers at first objected to it. Kumarappa explained to them the virtue and value of nightsoil as manure. Compost pits were created, mixing human waste, cow dung and forest leaves. The ashram also started a school for sixty village children, and a health clinic. Kumarappa helped mediate in property disputes, saving villagers from going to court. An ashram goshala (cow shelter) was started at the foot of a hill where cattle grazed. This was inaugurated by Gandhi's English disciple, Mira Behn (formerly Madeleine Slade), whose own environmental legacy is the subject of a later chapter of this book.[49]

Kumarappa had hoped that the experiment at Seldoh would be replicated more widely by his colleagues in the Sarva Seva Sangh. He was particularly keen that Vinoba Bhave himself endorse the idea. However, while Bhave's tireless energy and charismatic personality encouraged landlords to donate some of their property to his Bhoodan campaign, unlike Kumarappa this Gandhian was not of a practical bent of mind. Having acquired land, Bhave did little to organize people to work it productively and sustainably. This disappointed Kumarappa, who wrote him several letters urging him to take up rural development in a more focused manner. One letter of April 1955 saw Kumarappa writing to Bhave thus:

> You have spared no pains in collecting land for the landless. Lands have been gifted much faster than we can handle them—either distributing them or utilising them. I strongly hold that it is stealing when we hold more property than we need, even if it be gathered with the owners' full consent. Our purpose in getting the lands is to put them to such use and under such conditions as we advocate for a Sarvodaya Order. In so far as our possessions are far more extensive than we could handle we stand guilty of stealing. ... To prepare them it takes time. Should we not slow down collections to get our equilibrium?
>
> On the other hand, you are appealing to constructive workers to close down running institutions and plunge into Bhoodan work. This will make the whole thing lopsided. To my mind, this is wholly wrong. Sarvodaya Order consists of several phases of which Bhoodan distribution and utilisation of land form only a part, however important it may be. Without consolidating our position, why should we rush forward? Our zeal for one item on our programme should not destroy the work so far built up at the cost of tremendous pain and infinite human work over decades. ... As I had pointed out, this short sightedness comes of fixing targets ... What is the great hurry? Simply because we had fixed a certain time within which to get a certain quota, should we rush forward at all costs?[50]

In his reply, which was in Hindi, Bhave said that many new workers were joining the Bhoodan movement and thus there was no question of his relying on old workers. He did not address Kumarappa's concerns about fixing targets and closing down existing institutions, saying loftily that four years ago when

Bhoodan started there was a spirit of pessimism (nirasha) among constructive workers but now they had gathered strength and courage. Bhave ended by patronizingly telling Kumarappa to take physical as well as mental rest.[51]

Kumarappa wrote back, in English, repeating his warnings about setting numerical targets, arguing that proper utilization of land was more important than its distribution. He said that when entire villages were received as gifts, they could be developed into demonstration centres.[52]

In the India of the 1950s, there was an aura around the heads of Jawaharlal Nehru and Vinoba Bhave, the former regarded as the country's pre-eminent political leader, making India a force in world affairs, the latter through his saintliness and sacrifice being hailed as the spiritual heir of Gandhi. To take on both required courage. As one Gandhian who himself stayed scrupulously clear of controversy remarked: 'Kumarappa is one of the very few in India to-day, who through a life of unbroken dedication to a cause, has earned the right to speak with moral authority to many of those who are already weakening and faltering as they try to walk in the way indicated by Gandhiji. He can challenge the economics of exploitation because his life is without exploitation of anybody.'[53]

Back in the 1920s, when India was still a colony, Kumarappa had spent time both in England and in the United States, to acquire academic qualifications. In the 1950s, by which time India was an independent country, Kumarappa had the opportunity to visit several large non-Western countries, to study their methods of economic development.

In September–October 1951, Kumarappa visited China as part of an Indian Goodwill Mission to attend the second anniversary celebrations of the Peoples' Republic of China. In his travels, Kumarappa saw in many places what he termed 'the spirit of New China', as manifest in the absence of beggary, in the friendliness towards strangers, in the lack of a purdah system for women, in the cleanliness of the streets, above all in the superbly organized anniversary celebrations, in which more than a million people participated with 'perfect order and discipline' in Tiananmen Square. Of this last demonstration the visitor remarked: 'A people with this spirit will never be slaves. It seems presumptuous on our part to think that India leads the East; China is miles ahead of us.'[54]

Writing to his fellow Gandhian G. Ramachandran, Kumarappa conveyed his appreciation of the progress made by Chinese agriculture since the revolution. The Russian revolution, he noted, 'was pivoted on the proletariat while China is rebuilding on Agrarian Reforms'. Unlike in the Soviet Union there were no collective farms in China. Though this was to change, and quite radically, at the time of Kumarappa's visit to China in 1951, 'private property is the rule of the day but the use is strictly controlled by the state. Private profit, though strictly limited, is still the motive force and the incentive.' Landlordism had been abolished, yet rich peasants who cultivated their own land were left untouched. Previously, tenants paid more than 50 per cent of their produce to the landlord, now they paid only 13 per cent to the state, this collected in kind.[55]

From China, Kumarappa proceeded to Japan, where he spent a further six weeks, studying the agriculture of the Japanese and their cottage industries. He was impressed by Japanese co-operatives, which had sprung up organically from below rather than being artificial creations of the government. He saw the great value they placed on handmade products, unlike in India where there had developed a craze for machine-made stuff. He witnessed many different forms of handicraft production at work, including paddy husking, oil pressing, soap making, glazed pottery, mats, bamboo products and handmade paper.

In Japan, Kumarappa was struck by the 'form, beauty and orderliness' of everyday life, and by the fact that, like in China, nightsoil was widely used, collected 'in a perfectly clean way' and then mixed with water and used as manure. He approvingly noted that the Japanese state worked in a decentralized fashion, with local prefectures having far more financial and administrative authority than in India. A full 50 per cent of the prefectural taxes in Japan were spent on education.

Kumarappa's report on his trip summarized the lessons that India could learn from Japan, the most important of which were that 'there should not be the wide gulf prevailing between the officials and administrators and the people', that 'like the Japanese we should learn to value our own products', that Indians should strive towards 'a standard of life set up by the leaders based on our own culture' (rather than merely ape the West).[56]

In March 1952 Kumarappa visited the Soviet Union, as a delegate to the International Conference of Economists. A report of the conference has this striking paragraph: 'Dwelling on the question of irrigation, Dr Kumarappa said that approximately 97 per cent of the rainfall in India escapes into the sea and only a small portion is absorbed by the soil. What India needs therefore is not big dams on the rivers, but small dams on the streams which accumulate rainfall to be absorbed by the soil. Unfortunately, India lacks this kind of irrigation.'[57] This was a subtle—or not so subtle—dig at Nehru, who was an enthusiastic advocate of large dams, once going so far as to call them the 'temples of modern India'.

Much of what he saw in Russia impressed Kumarappa. He thought there was far less official hierarchy than in India, a far smaller gap between the leaders and the people. He admired their spirit of self-reliance, their emphasis on education and health, and the fact that so many of the doctors were women. He was moved that the palaces of princes and nobles had been converted into museums of art and culture to which all had access. However, he was critical of the regimentation of thought and action, which rested on overt control and a hidden threat of violence.[58]

In poor health and disenchanted with the turn the Gandhians had taken post-Gandhi, in March 1955 Kumarappa left Wardha for his native Tamil country. He retreated to an ashram in T. Kallupatti, in the Madurai district, that had been established by a social worker named G. Venkatachalapathy. Kumarappa had meanwhile begun an interesting correspondence with a politician named S.K. Dey. An engineer trained in the United States, Dey had left a well-paying job in the private sector to join as an adviser on the government's Community Development scheme. 'Community Development' was one-half of the price paid by the Government of India (the Khadi and Village Industries Commission being the other half), committed as it was to rapid industrialization, to calm its conscience for having named Gandhi, that certified rural romantic, the 'Father of the Nation'.

Dey and Kumarappa had been in correspondence since the summer of 1952. Dey wrote to Kumarappa for advice shortly after joining as an adviser on the Community Development programme. The Gandhian wrote back saying 'the whole scheme reflects an amazing lack of confidence on the part of the Prime Minister in the ability of his colleagues that he should bow so low to invite foreigners to rebuild the countryside'. He saw the scheme as the 'thin edge of the wedge of the era of American Financial Imperialism'.[59]

Three years later, by which time Dey was a minister in Nehru's Cabinet, he wrote to Kumarappa again, asking him to assess the progress (or otherwise) of community development in Madurai district. 'Criticisms coming from a person of your stature,' said Dey, 'will help materially to give a shake-up to our workers who, I am beginning to feel, stand in need of a progressively increasing dose of it because of the complacency we are all tending to develop based on the spot compliments we receive from foreign visitors after their casual observation of our work.'[60]

Despite his age and ill health, in the first months of 1956 Kumarappa agreed to tour the villages of Madurai that came under the Community Development scheme. Dey was touched, telling Kumarappa that 'we have very few people left today with the baptismal fire still intact in them. You have succeeded in remaining still, a member of that rare tribe.'[61]

The old Gandhian indeed came out firing. At Dey's suggestion, he undertook a survey of rural development work in twenty-seven villages of Madurai district, taking himself from place to place by bus and bullock-cart. In the report Kumarappa wrote afterwards, his criticisms of the Community Development programme were unforgiving. Most of its funds, he pointed out, were taken up in unproductive schemes like road-building. Moreover, the 'persons who have co-operated [with the government] belong to a small section of the public, though moneyed and influential'. But the Harijans or lower castes 'are notoriously neglected', the 'poor are still standing apart suspiciously'.

Kumarappa spoke of the penchant of officials for taking bribes, for acting arrogantly towards villagers because they had themselves been educated in cities. 'Generally speaking,' he summed up, 'the atmosphere around officials and gram sevaks [village workers] is not one of love for rural people and their life but one of their own employment and advancement.' The insensitivity of the public officials was compounded by their brief, handed down from above, which was completely at odds with the physical realities of Indian agriculture.

In his report, Kumarappa made a series of sharp criticisms, highlighting the ecological unwisdom of what passed for rural development in independent India:

1. (on water conservation)

    The irrigation tanks are as a rule silted up and eroded ... If these tanks are desilted four or five feet, much of the cry for water will cease and the farmers can get two or three crops a year where even getting one is a gamble today. Attention to these tanks will give us control over floods and reduce erosion. If properly advised and guided, I am sure, the villagers will gladly extend their co-operation in such schemes ... This is a programme that will quickly raise the production of food several-fold and thereby better village conditions in a very short time.

2. (on fertilizer overuse)

    There are no facilities [in the agricultural demonstration centres] for soil and water analysis. In the absence of these no artificial or chemical manures should be used. Now such fertilizers are being supplied at favourable rates. They may prove ruinous in the end. At present the Government seems more anxious to dispose of their fertilizers than to observe the evil effects of their use in the course of years of indiscriminate use on all kinds of fields.

3. (on forest protection)

    Water supply depends on an efficient forest policy. The Government is overanxious on the revenue production of forests rather than their being a conserving ground for water. Every village should have its common lands properly taken care of.

4. (on the protection of artisans)

> Welfare of villagers rests on the occupations open to those who are not fully employed on the land. (Village) industries provide the necessary complement to work on land. A few stray attempts are being made to help with the Ghani [oil press], Khadi work, bee-keeping etc. But these are not considered an essential feature of the development [work] and suffer from a lack of emphasis ... All village industries will have to be resuscitated to put life into rural parts.[62]

S.K. Dey, to his great credit, had copies of the report made and circulated to senior officials. Kumarappa was touched. 'I appreciate the willingness you evince to take the stick from me! It is a healthy sign,' he told the minister, before adding this characteristic caveat: 'Why not start by using hand made paper for your stationery?'[63]

In November 1956, Dey wrote Kumarappa a long ruminative letter. He was, he told the Gandhian, born in a farming household but then 'built myself into an Engineer and got naturally biased towards industrialization in a big way in the first flush of my contact with the civilization of the West'. In time he realized that large-scale industrialization was not appropriate for India, and 'the immediate solution of our problems cannot be had through anything other than village and small industries planned within certain limits on the basis of regional self-sufficiency. ... I am trying as best I can to propagate the spirit of khadi and Village Industries wherever I go.'

Although he was now a Cabinet minister, said Dey to Kumarappa, 'I have struggled to continue [as] the farmer's son I was born. I will continue struggling. It is friendly critics such as you that can keep a leaf of grass such as I am from being blown the wrong way under the prevailing wind.'

The minister's letter to the Gandhian ended thus: 'I do hope and trust that you will take care of yourself and not allow the depression around to get the better of your spirit. Even if you cannot do anything physically, your thoughts which are prompted by purity of love and affection and well-being of our common people, will serve to add to the common stock which is so low now and which is yet so vital if others are to draw on it invisibly for their own nourishment in the growing struggle.'[64]

This was all deeply moving. Tragically, the prevailing wind, of large-scale industrialization on the Soviet model, was now officially endorsed by the Nehru government's Second Five Year Plan, which relegated both community development and Gandhian ideals of rural reconstruction to the margins of Indian political and economic life.

Kumarappa had eleven siblings. Of these he was particularly close to two: his elder brother J.M. Kumarappa, a widely respected professor at the Tata Institute of Social Sciences in Bombay; and his younger brother Bharatan Kumarappa, a scholar of comparative religion who, after taking doctoral degrees in Edinburgh and London, joined his brother in Maganvadi and, after Independence, was appointed by the Government of India's Publication Division as the first chief editor of the *Collected Works of Mahatma Gandhi*.

In the last week of June 1957, Bharatan Kumarappa died of a heart attack in New Delhi. He was barely sixty. J.C. Kumarappa was devastated by the news and suffered a heart attack himself. The doctor who attended to him thought he would not survive. But he did, though he never after recovered his health, the death in October 1957 of his elder brother J.M. Kumarappa shattering him further. He was in and out of hospital for the next two and a half years. He died on the evening of 30 January 1960, twelve years to the day after Gandhi. As per Kumarappa's wishes, his body was cremated using cow dung cakes (he had expressly forbidden the use of the expensive but ritually preferred sandalwood).[65]

In hospital in Madras, J.C. Kumarappa would sit in the veranda every morning and evening to take advantage of the sea breeze. As one colleague recalled, when passers-by stopped to say hello, Kumarappa's eyes 'would always scrutinize whether their clothes were of khadi; whether the articles they used were products of village industries or whether they wore large quantities of jewellery which he wanted them to part with, when occasions arose. To his utter frustration, he would find that only two out of a hundred wore khadi and much less had adopted simple ways of living, and would exclaim, "Bapu [Gandhi] is better dead than alive", for there is no trace of him within a decade after his death.'[66]

In December 1957, the prime minister was in Madras on official business, and on hearing of his old comrade-turned-critic's ill health turned up at the hospital to see him. We do not know what they talked about, but I think that even the gruff and unsentimental Kumarappa would have been touched by Nehru's gesture.

Kumarappa's first biographer, M. Vinaik, tells a story about his mentor's visit to the Soviet Union in 1952 to attend an international conference of economists. While in Leningrad, Kumarappa was driving with a Russian economist in a car. They passed a canal, and the Russian remarked: 'When Rasputin's body was thrown into this canal, it was picked up about two furlongs down the stream. But I was thinking just now that if your body was ever thrown into this canal, we shall have to look for it two furlongs up the river, because your economic thought runs contrary to the current prevalent today!'[67]

In his valorization of rural life, Kumarappa, like his mentor Gandhi, was going radically against the grain of economic thought in the twentieth century, which insisted that rapid industrialization was the only way forward for all countries. In challenging this consensus, Kumarappa—like Gandhi again—sometimes presented a somewhat idealized picture of village India. Nonetheless, his analysis of the environmental profligacy of industrial society was prescient. Notably, he was not content with critique, seeking to renew Indian village life by making it more harmonious with its natural setting.

Kumarappa began the task of building an ecological programme on Gandhian lines. Hence his focus on soil maintenance, water conservation, recycling, village forest rights, and protection of the artisan—an agenda of rural reconstruction that, all these decades later, still has a direct relevance to India today.[68]

For all his originality as a thinker, Kumarappa was a complex, difficult man. He could be dogmatic in his views, and rude in his manner of expressing them. He alienated many people, among them many erstwhile friends and colleagues in the Indian freedom movement. These included Jawaharlal Nehru, the prime minister of India, and Vinoba Bhave, the acknowledged head of the constructive work stream of the Gandhian movement. Both Nehru and Bhave had known Gandhi longer than Kumarappa had. Each bristled at the thought of being lectured about what was Gandhi's 'real' legacy by this truculent Tamilian who had joined the struggle for independence many years after they had done. Nonetheless, it must be counted a great pity, for India and the world, that there was to be no meeting ground between Kumarappa on the one side and Nehru and Bhave on the other.

Kumarappa's counsel, if accepted by the prime minister, could have acted as a check on the centralizing and anti-ecological tendencies of planned industrial development. Kumarappa's advice, if accepted by Vinoba Bhave and the Sarva Seva Sangh, might have prevented Bhoodan from becoming a utopian ideal that failed because no attention was given to the question of how the land gifted would be managed productively and sustainably. But it was not to be, and both people and nature suffered as a result.

CHAPTER FOUR

Scottish Internationalist

PATRICK GEDDES AND ECOLOGICAL TOWN PLANNING IN INDIA

MAHATMA GANDHI LIKED TO say that 'India lives in her villages'. This was true, in a demographic sense—the majority of the population of the subcontinent were indeed based in the countryside and depended on agriculture and animal husbandry for a livelihood. However, for many nationalists the village was also the centre of Indian culture and civilization. They were hostile to the idea that their country should follow the path of the West, where, in recent decades, a greater number of people had migrated to the cities and worked in factories. While modernizing intellectuals thought this urban-industrial future was inevitable as well as desirable for India, thinker-activists such as Tagore and Kumarappa dissented. They saw the modern industrial city as parasitic and exploitative. The renewal of rural life and making it compatible with its natural surroundings was the main thrust of their work.

Radhakamal Mukerjee had slightly more time for the city. He did not think it possible to reject urban life altogether. However, his focus remained on the village too. From his early writings celebrating communitarian living in rural India to his later works on planning the countryside, it was peasants, pastoralists and rural artisans whose well-being he was most concerned about. The ecological problems he wrote about were quintessentially agrarian in their character—deforestation, soil erosion, the scarcity of water, and the like.

Tagore and Kumarappa were thoroughgoing agrarians. Mukerjee was a qualified agrarian—but an agrarian nonetheless. There will be other agrarians we will meet later in the book, who, in their varied, distinctive and original ways, sought to make rural life in India more compatible with nature. However, in this chapter we shall take temporary leave of the countryside, by profiling a thinker who worked in and for the city. He recognized that cities were a central feature of premodern India, and that urban living would acquire greater importance in the industrial age. India under British rule was increasingly turning towards modern forms of factory production, which necessitated a shift in population from the countryside to urban centres. One could not turn one's back on the city. One had, rather, to make it more habitable.

In the summer of 1900, a great World Fair was to be held in Paris. Among those who participated in the exhibition was a Scottish ecologist and town planner named Patrick Geddes. To raise money for his stall, Geddes went on a speaking tour in the United

States, where, at the home of a mutual friend, he met the Indian spiritualist Swami Vivekananda and his Irish disciple Margaret Noble (who had taken the name Sister Nivedita). They got along famously, and Vivekananda and his disciple both came and visited Geddes's stall in Paris later in the year.[1]

Soon afterwards, Nivedita went to see Geddes in Edinburgh, where, as he recalled, she settled 'above our house into an attic cell which suited at once her love of wide and lofty outlooks and her ascetic care of material simplicity'. The plan was that they would write a book together on East–West relations. Each wrote draft chapters, but then, remembered Geddes, 'within our own limits of time, necessarily narrow, we failed to satisfy our own and each other's critical scrutiny, or to meet standards of science and idealism we had fixed beyond our reach'.[2]

After her return to India Nivedita wrote a book of her own, called *The Web of Indian Life*, which she dedicated to Geddes.[3] She also asked her Scottish friend to advise on a new scientific university which the industrialist Jamsetji Tata was planning to establish. Geddes wrote her a series of letters, later published as a booklet, where he insisted on the 'necessary and increasing internationalism of science. Science which like ours in England too often loses touch with the Continent and with America, is not wide enough to inspire India, which must in this respect be as free and eclectic as Japan.'[4]

His developing friendship with Nivedita, an Irishwoman-turned-Indian, inculcated in Geddes a deep desire to come to the subcontinent. However, his commitments in Scotland and Europe prevented that from happening, and in 1911 Nivedita passed away, just short of her forty-fourth birthday. Three years later, Geddes was finally able to visit the subcontinent, where he was to spend an extended period of time, writing a series of mostly forgotten plans about the towns and cities of India. Those plans, what they say and how they say it, are the focus of this chapter.

But first we must introduce the reader to Geddes's life and work before India.

Patrick Geddes was born on 2 October 1854, the same day as Gandhi, fifteen years before him. He studied first at the Perth Academy, and then found his way to London where he attended the lectures at the Royal School of Mines of the scientist known as 'Darwin's bulldog', Thomas Henry Huxley. Patrick Geddes said of his teacher that Huxley 'had no use either for loafers or for the subject-a-period method of instruction which kept students in other departments running all day from one fragment of knowledge to another. ... What Huxley succeeded in giving so supremely well to his students was a feeling for unity, yet the infinite variety, of all the series of related organic forms.'[5]

After his studies in London Geddes spent several months in Paris, where he exposed himself to an array of intellectual and cultural influences a typical Scottish (or English) scholar of the time would not have ever known of. Among these were the works of Frédéric Le Play, who explored the connections between geography and social structure. From France, Geddes went to Mexico on a botanical expedition, further expanding his mind and his knowledge of life forms. On his return to Scotland he was appointed lecturer in zoology at the University of Edinburgh. In his seven years in the city he immersed himself in teaching and in civic activism. He was one of the founders of an Edinburgh Social Union which worked, among other things, on affordable housing for workers and students, and on making the city's older parts compatible with modern living without destroying their architectural or cultural heritage. Meanwhile, he published his first essays and research papers, on subjects as varied as zoology and art. He preached what we now call inter-disciplinarity, polemicizing against 'that separation of the school of industry from the school of science which produces pedants in the University and philistines in the work-shop'.[6] He started a Summer School of Arts and Science in Edinburgh, to which he brought over distinguished scholars from the Continent.

In 1888, Geddes took up a chair in botany at the University of Dundee. He continued to be based in Edinburgh, commuting by train. He had acquired an old building at the head of Edinburgh's famous Royal Mile, which he refurbished and made into a museum, naming it the 'Outlook Tower'. The rooms of the buildings had maps, charts and pictures, depicting different aspects of the natural and social history of Edinburgh, Scotland and the world. Many distinguished lecturers came and spoke here, among them the anarchist geographers Elisée Reclus and Peter Kropotkin.

In a fascinating essay of 1895 called 'Life and Its Science', Geddes wrote of the bond that did, and should, exist between humans and the natural world. 'As the simplest greetings of "good morning" and "good day" remind us,' he wrote, 'some sympathy with Nature, some interest in our fellows, are instinctive and universal.' Whether child or adult, a human being could not but be 'a Nature-lover and a Season-observer; Spring with her buds and lambs and lovers, Autumn amid her fruits and sheaves, Summer in her green, and Winter with her holly, are all themes as unfailing as human life'.[7] In another essay published the same year, Geddes called nature 'the ultimate teacher and examiner'. He saw his own scientific role as being 'the exponent not of any special science of nature, nor of any tradition of culture, but the concrete synthetician of all these'.[8]

The words 'ecology' and 'environment' were not in common use in the late nineteenth century, but, as the historian Murdo Macdonald observes, 'Geddes must be seen as an ecologist of the mind as well as of the planet.' His interest in the diversity of life-forms and his worries that modern industrial society would leave behind a landscape at once homogenized and degraded, were strikingly ahead of his time. So was his capaciously interdisciplinary approach to learning: thus, as Macdonald further writes, 'throughout his life he resisted the fragmentation of knowledge consequent on misguided notions of specialization in education, that took as their model the production-line rather than the person'.[9]

The main intellectual influences on Patrick Geddes were three-fold:

1. English craft socialism, especially the works of John Ruskin and William Morris. Through them he learnt to view industrialism with a critical eye.
2. French historical geography, notably the works of Elisée Reclus and Frédéric Le Play. From them he learnt to view culture and economy in their ecological context.
3. The geographical anarchism of Peter Kropotkin, which reinforced the ecological analysis while promoting a scepticism of centralization.

Geddes made important contributions to scientific debates on economics, sociology, zoology, botany and geography. He even wrote a famous essay on art criticism. However, his most enduring work was in the theory and practice of town planning. Here he took a historical and ecological approach, studying the rise of the modern city and its impact on the natural environment.

In 1903, Geddes was asked to prepare a plan for the renewal of Dunfermline. This was the hometown of the fabulously wealthy American entrepreneur Andrew Carnegie, who had promised to put in $2.5 million (then a colossal sum) for a plan to improve the surroundings of his former fellow townsmen. The trustees of the scheme had to choose between Geddes, a botanist by profession, and a trained architect. They chose Geddes, giving him the first of what were to be many contracts to draw up plans for towns large and small. His Dunfermline report was published under the title *City Development: A Study of Parks, Gardens, and Culture Institutes*.

In October 1910, the Royal Institute of British Architects organized a major conference on town planning, to which scholars and practitioners from all over Europe were invited. The idea that cities could be carefully and artfully planned was relatively new to the modern imagination, and this conference was an attempt to make architects, accustomed to building discrete structures, more aware of how what they did fit into the landscape as a whole.

This conference had special presentations on ancient Greek and Roman cities, on medieval French towns, and on cities of the present. There was a panel on specific town plans, in which Patrick Geddes presented his ideas for the renewal of Edinburgh. In a lecture profusely illustrated with maps, charts and photographs, Geddes deplored the fact that modern Edinburgh was disfigured by class distinctions in settlement patterns, and by pollution. He urged for a harmonious integration of nature and work, so that the Edinburgh of the future would become, as he put it, 'an industrial city and a garden city in one'.[10]

In his writings of this period, Geddes coined many neologisms, which broadly fall into three categories; those which are deservedly forgotten (such as 'politography' and 'politogenics'); those that are deservedly remembered and which have entered the English vocabulary (such as metropolis, megalopolis and conurbation, all to do with modern cities and their scale); and those which are now largely forgotten but may need to be rehabilitated. In the last category fall his distinction between two phases of technological culture, which he called 'paleotechnic' and 'neotechnic'. The first, which drove the Industrial Revolution, used coal and oil as sources of energy, and was wealth-creating yet enormously polluting; the second, which Geddes hoped to help usher in, would use clean energy and resource-conserving technologies while maintaining (and distributing more fairly) the wealth created by earlier ages.

By now Geddes had assembled an impressive collection of materials on urban history and town planning. He was increasingly seeing himself as a scholar of cities and a practitioner of urban renewal. His key ideas are summarized in his book *Cities in Evolution*, published in 1915. Here, in a memorable phrase, he termed the late nineteenth century an age of 'carboniferous capitalism', based on non-renewable resources and polluting in its impacts. Produced out of the exploitation of nature, the paleotechnic age had, Geddes remarked, seen the dominance of man by machine, by finance and by militarism. Geddes hoped for a new, neotechnic age based on solar energy and on long-lasting alloys, marked by 'its better use of resources and population towards the betterment of man and his environment together'.

Although respectful of tradition, Geddes was not a backward-looking reactionary. He was neither a nostalgic romantic nor a fervent modernizer. There is a fine passage in *Cities in Evolution* that sums up his philosophy:

> Beauty, whether of Nature or art, has too long been without effective defense against the ever-advancing smoke-cloud and machine-blast and slum-progress of paleotechnic industry. Not but that her defenders have been of the very noblest, witness notably Carlyle, Ruskin, Morris, with their many disciples; yet they were too largely romantics—right in their treasuring of the world's heritage of the past, yet wrong in their reluctance, sometimes even passionate refusal, to admit the claims and needs of the present to live and labour in its turn, and according to its lights. So that they in too great measure but brought upon themselves that savage retort and war-cry of 'Yah! Sentiment!' with which the would-be utilitarian has so often increased his recklessness towards Nature,

> and coarsened his callousness to art. The romantics have too often been as blind in their righteous anger as were the mechanical utilitarians in their strenuous labour, their dull contentment with it. Both have failed to see, beyond the rude present, the better future now dawning—in which the applied physical sciences are advancing beyond their clumsy and noisy first apprenticeship, with its wasteful and dirty beginnings, towards a finer skill, a more subtle and more economic mastery of natural energies and in which these, moreover, are increasingly supplemented by a corresponding advance of the organic sciences, with their new valuations of life, organic as well as human.[11]

Geddes completed the manuscript of *Cities and Evolution* in the spring of 1914. Later that year he visited India for the first time. The governor of Madras, Lord Pentland, a Liberal Party politician who was a native of Edinburgh, asked Geddes to come and show his carefully curated exhibition on the history of cities. This would first be put on display in Madras, and then travel to Bombay, Calcutta and other cities of the British Raj. Writing to a friend about his plans to take his cities exhibition to India, Geddes remarked: 'I am anxious to make something better of it—both as regards the British official and the Indian student.'[12]

Geddes sailed for Bombay in the autumn of 1914 by the P&O liner S.S. *Nore*. The materials for his exhibition were being sent separately to Madras by a cargo ship. The ship carrying the scholar docked safely in Bombay; but the ship carrying his life's work was sunk by a German destroyer named the *Emden* (the First World War had just broken out). The vessel went down into the Indian Ocean and, with it, the work of half a lifetime. Geddes was stranded in the subcontinent with no exhibition to show. Characteristically, he turned his mind instead on gathering new material, on studying the rise, decline and transformation of the cities and towns of India. As he stoically wrote to his wife, while conveying that his exhibition now lay at the bottom of the sea: 'This difficulty shall be made an opportunity...'[13]

Geddes's first trip to India stimulated the desire to work more intensively in the subcontinent. Writing to the historian of Indian art and crafts E.B. Havell, Geddes listed the twenty towns and cities he had visited. He hoped to return soon and design plans for some of them, advocating 'conservative surgery instead of wholesale and heroic operations'. Geddes told Havell that his plans for Indian cities would be drafted 'generally with endeavour to maintain something of rural character and abate excessive urbanism'.[14]

Between 1915 and 1924 Geddes spent the winter and spring in India, going back to Scotland and Europe during the summer. He travelled very widely across the subcontinent, studying its cities ancient as well as colonial. He was impressed with the holy city of Banaras, whose riverfront was, as he wrote to his wife, 'a medley of architecture and life, of colour and verdure, of palace and ruin, of temples and shrines, of life—and death—the like of which is nowhere else to be seen!' And he was moved by the great Meenakshi Temple in Madurai, 'by its vastness—two cathedrals would go inside its walls and far more—by its extraordinary cloisters surpassing in magnitude and in richness of effect, in wonder of lighting, all else in the world, in length those of all the Oxford Colleges put together.'[15]

Geddes was to be based in India for almost a decade, from 1915 to 1924. Here, he first worked as a freelance town planner and then as the first professor of sociology and civics of the University of Bombay. He travelled widely and interacted with Indians of all classes. He briefly met Mahatma Gandhi, knew Annie Besant, and befriended the great Bengali thinkers Rabindranath Tagore and Jagadish Chandra Bose. In his years in

India he also wrote nearly fifty town plans, some commissioned by native princes (maharajas), some written at the behest of colonial administrators. The towns he wrote about range from Dacca in the east to Ahmedabad in the west, from Lahore in the north to Tanjore in the south.

Geddes carried on working despite great personal tragedy—the death of a son on the battlefield in France, and the death of his wife through illness in Calcutta. Through his work and travels in the subcontinent, Geddes had, as he told an English friend, become 'an Indian-Educated European'.[16]

Geddes's methodological contributions to the art of town planning were his concepts of 'diagnostic survey'—an intensive walking tour to acquaint oneself with the growth, development and existing status of the city being planned for—and 'conservative surgery', the practice of gentle improvements with minimal disruption of people and their habitat. These ground rules were meticulously observed in his Indian town plans. However, his town plans are far from being dry-as-dust technocratic reports. Wonderfully idiosyncratic, they are shot through with throwaway lines and bon mots, while his philosophy emerges in the most unexpected places.

Running through Geddes's Indian town plans are three central themes, which I call, respectively, Respect for Nature, Respect for Democracy and Respect for Tradition. Let me now take these three themes in turn.

Geddes's town plans are deeply ecological, and in at least four respects:

First, he sees the Indian city as defined by its relationship to water. Traditional India viewed rivers as sacred. In this it merely anticipated the science of geography, which also stressed what Geddes called 'the fundamental and central River-factor of human environments'. While writing a plan for the central Indian city of Indore, Geddes wished to redesign it around its rivers. Elsewhere,

where there were no rivers, he recommended the renewal and revitalization of tanks.

Second, Geddes was always alert to spaces, however small, that could be claimed by trees. As a skilled botanist, he had a keen eye for which species went with which aspect. His plans are filled with meticulously specific recommendations, a line of cypresses here, a grove of mangoes there, pipal planted in one place, banyan in another.

Third, he stressed the conservation of resources, to minimize the city's dependence on the hinterland. Therefore, he strongly recommended the preservation and maintenance of tanks and reservoirs; simultaneously a protection against flooding after heavy rain, a beneficial influence on climate, and of course an assured source of water (Geddes scoffed at the fear of sanitary engineers that these water bodies would be a malarial hazard, pointing out that they could easily be stocked 'with sufficient fish and duck to keep down the Anopheles').[17] Particularly noteworthy here is what he says about wells. These, he remarked, should 'be regarded as a valuable reserve to the existing water supplies, even if these be efficient'. For 'any and every water system occasionally goes out of order, and is open to accidents and injuries of very many kinds; and in these old wells we inherit an ancient policy, of life insurance, of a very real kind, and one far too valuable to be abandoned'.[18]

Fourth, Geddes emphasized the importance of recycling. Sewage could be fruitfully used to manure gardens; thus, as he so beautifully put it, converting 'a fetid and poisonous nuisance into a scene of order and beauty'. This might even lead to an elevation in the status of the sweepers, who would be put in charge of using nightsoil to raise and cultivate gardens. One would thus redeem what Geddes termed 'one of the main historic disasters of India', namely, that Indic religions regarded human waste as defiling, whereas other cultures such as China and ancient

Rome had 'fully and frankly appreciated and even idealized the manuring process'.[19]

The centrality of nature in Geddes's plans was a means to an end, the harmonizing of city and country. To enhance the beauty of the city and the health of its inhabitants, he strongly stated the 'case for the Conservation of Nature and for the increase of our accesses to her'. He thus prescribed the careful preservation of upland watersheds outside cities as well as forestry and park-making within them.[20] Speaking of 'that "return to Nature" which every adequate plan involves, with pure air and water, and cleanliness in surroundings again rural', he said that 'the problem is how to accomplish this return to the health of village life, with its beauty of surroundings and its contact with nature, upon a new spiral turning beyond the old one which, at the same time, frankly and fully incorporates the best advantages of town-life'.[21]

Respect for Nature, in all these varied aspects, is then the first major theme of Geddes's work. The second theme is that of Democracy. This too has several distinct aspects. The first is that of participation. Let me quote from his best-known and most exhaustive Indian plan, that written for Indore. 'As the physician must make a diagnosis of the patient's case before prescribing treatment,' remarked Geddes,

> so with the planner for the city. He looks closely into the city as it is, and enquires into how it has grown, and suffered. And as the physician associates the patient with his own cure, so must the planner appeal to the citizen. Hence the Indore reader should go round and look at the City for himself; and with its Plan for partial guide, he may check, and amplify, the diagnosis; and perhaps accelerate the treatment.[22]

The democratic town planner, he said, must pay special attention to the needs of less privileged groups. I have already mentioned

Geddes's concern for the status of the Untouchables. But he also emphasized the rights and needs of women and children, which tend to be ignored in most plans. Hence his appreciation of courtyards and balconies, where women had their own private space, and his stress on the creation of parks for children to play in. In Bharuch he was deeply impressed by the fact that the wells had eight or even sixteen wheels on a fixed overhead pulley, whereas in other places there was generally only a single wheel. The ordinary or common method of stooping down to lift water put enormous pressure on the abdominal and pelvic organs. But the Bharuch method, where one stayed erect and only used the arms, was much gentler on women. As Geddes said, 'I know of no simple labour and health-saving appliance which better deserves wide popularisation among Indian Municipalities'.[23]

Another aspect of Geddes's democratic instincts was his opposition to the mindless destruction of buildings to 'improve' the town or to build highways for cars to drive through. In the Changar Mohalla of Lahore, he was appalled by a scheme for redevelopment which planned to destroy five mosques, two dharamsalas, several tombs and temples, and shops and dwellings. It spared only one building: the police station. Geddes condemned the scheme as an 'indiscriminate destruction of the whole past labour and industry of men, of all buildings good, bad and indifferent, and with these, of all their human values and associations, profane and sacred, Police Office only excepted!'[24]

Geddes urged the planner 'not to coerce people into new places against their associations, wishes and interest...'[25] His ground rule for clearance and eviction was that 'these must in any and every case be deprecated until and unless new and adequate location is provided'.[26] Not surprisingly, Geddes repeatedly clashed with engineers and civic officials who wished to destroy poor neighbourhoods to spruce up the city and build broad avenues.[27]

This leads me to Geddes's third theme, the Respect for Tradition, the promotion of what is now called heritage preservation. After a visit to the town of Nadiad (in present-day Gujarat), he said the town planner must have an 'appreciation of all that is best in the old domestic architecture of Indian cities and of renewing this where it has fallen away'. It was absurd to destroy, as being 'out of date, fine old carven housefronts, which Western museums would treasure and Western artists be proud to emulate'. He urged the impatiently modernizing Indian town planner to pause and consider 'where domestic architecture is so good, and often so rightly wrought and adorned, that it is well worth their while to cultivate a wise conservatism, and so to meet the modern requirements of the present without losing the constructive traditions of the past.'[28]

On a trip to the port city of Surat Geddes spied a beautiful mosque whose view was obscured; this led him to recommend something he usually abhorred, the straight line, at the end of which would lie this mosque, now visible to all. Then, after visiting the greatest of Gujarat's cities, Ahmedabad, he was inspired to recommend a civic museum that would have several distinct rooms:

First, a display of archaeological materials, shards of temples from the Hindu past; second, the showcasing of 'the rise and flower of that marvellous [Muslim] architecture to which Ahmedabad owes its special eminence and attractiveness'; third, panels demonstrating how these monuments, now decaying, would be restored and placed once again amidst tree-filled parks; fourth, panels on the ancient city walls with suggestions on how to conserve them (at this time these walls were being threatened by a new Ring Boulevard; Geddes lobbied, in the end unsuccessfully, against the new road); fifth, moving from the grand to the everyday, a display of the domestic architecture of the old neighbourhoods, the pols, this paying special attention to the development and detail of their carvings; last, and definitely the least, a room showing what Geddes called 'the intensifying deterioration and squalor of the ruder industrial age'.

In passing, Geddes offered a five-word motto that those interested in heritage preservation might urge on every architect and town planner, namely: 'To Postpone Is to Conserve'.[29]

Having outlined the main elements of Geddes's theory of town planning, let me move on to an analysis of two specific plans that he wrote in India. Both were commissioned by native princes rather than the colonial administration.

The first plan was the most ambitious of all the reports Geddes wrote in India. This was for the city of Indore, the capital of the princely state of Holkar in central India. Now in the state of Madhya Pradesh, Holkar was a fairly large princely state (approximately 24,000 square kilometres in area), and Indore was, by the standards of the day, more a city than a town, its population then around 100,000. Geddes spent almost a whole year in Indore, his research eventuating in a two-volume report extending over several hundred pages.

Geddes began his report by digging deep into the settlement history of Indore, his analysis driven by both knowledge and speculation, the details of extant buildings and their layout used to draw a larger picture of how the town grew and evolved. The fact that one of the oldest streets was along the river and had a temple at one end and bathing ghats at the other, was, he argued, evidence that this was originally a resting point for pilgrims en route to the holy city of Ujjain. As the town grew, through trade and warfare, ramparts were built around it; these were no longer intact, since much of the basalt had been taken away for building homes.

Given the sacred origins of Indore, Geddes wanted a new shrine to be built on the river, 'a white temple with graceful spire' which 'would be seen from far and near, and doubled by its reflection mirrored in the stream'. He even identified the site best suited for this. From such elegant new buildings 'may be gradually developed the beauty of these river landscapes', and if these were interspersed with trees and parks, they would make Indore 'into one of the most beautiful cities of India, and one sacred accordingly'.[30]

In the first decades of the twentieth century, Indore emerged as a centre of the cotton industry. One chapter of Geddes's plan allowed for the creation of a new factory district, with space enough for workers' houses and gardens for their children to play in as well. The factories themselves should, he said, have higher ceilings than those preferred in Indian mills, to reduce heat and allow the circulation of air, and thus lead to 'the improved vigour and health of the workers'. He wanted an end to the disposal of untreated effluents into nearby rivers; if this was done, he said, 'bathing ghats and fisheries will thus alike prosper, instead of being destroyed'.[31]

Geddes also argued that silk production could emerge as an important supplement to the cotton industry in Indore. He recommended that mulberry trees be grown in the municipal gardens, and women encouraged to rear silkworms in their homes. As he put it:

> For silk is specially a woman's industry. Her instinct is above all that of tending life, while a man's labour and thought is too much limited by his tools. ... In Cyprus the woman hatches the silkworms, like a bird its eggs, carrying the egg-box under her armpit; and as the eggs hatch, she gently lifts each little silkworm as it grasps the mulberry-leaf she offers, and puts it on her mat or tray. She gathers fresh leaves daily or oftener, and she and

> her children watch and tend them as no ordinary men would do, throughout their whole development.

Geddes argued that through silk production 'the status of women is notably increased, and in various ways—witness the cleaner and healthier household, and her personal earnings too'.[32]

A chapter on Indore's water supply called this liquid 'the first necessity, alike of rural and urban location and existence'. To assure a better and more sustainable supply, Geddes recommended the desilting and linking of existing tanks, the removal of polluting activities such as gravel collection and the revival and renewal of wells. He termed two large reservoirs built recently 'unnecessarily and extravagantly vast'. He further noted that the plans sanctioning 'this gigantic expense, amounting, I am told, to something like twenty lacs' were 'mostly all unsigned, with consequent evasion of responsibility for their practical failure: for, after all this labour and outlay, no extra water has been available'.[33]

Geddes's hope was that the administrators of Indore would set to work at cleaning up the city's two rivers, planting up their banks with trees, and making them the centrepiece of the city. 'The main beauty and glory of Indore is already in its river landscapes,' he remarked. Premodern societies in East and West had an abiding reverence for water and water bodies, but, noted Geddes, 'amid our modern development of roads and railways, our concentration upon machines, we have for the time largely lost sight of the rivers'. Note the caveat 'for the time'; Geddes, in tune with his broader futuristic vision of humanity's move from a mechanical and polluted present to an organic and unpolluted future, spoke hopefully of how 'thought is again emancipating itself, from this and other limitations of our age of mechanical progress, and entering upon a new period, of deeper re-interpretation of nature and life, in terms of vital process'. Geddes thought he saw a 'return to the old-world conceptions of nature and religion', in which the material and spiritual significance of rivers was

> becoming more fully understood than of old, and again not felt not less deeply. Again we see the Rivers in their panoramic beauty and sublimity, and in their social significance. And the dependence of all forms of life, together with our own, upon these uniting waters, is becoming realized, as not only the widest conception of physiology and economics, but also as of psychological and emotional significance, for each and all.

It was Geddes's admirable yet perhaps naïve desire to see this new-old love and reverence for rivers awaken (or reawaken) among Indore's elite, who would (he hoped) then change their ways accordingly.[34]

Geddes's Indore report also contained an interesting chapter on 'garden designs'. This drew on his walks through the city, identifying spots that could be filled with trees and plants. Near one temple he found a vacant plot which he thought could be made into a 'bright little flower garden' for Hindu women and children to spend time in. A mohalla (locality) of the Muslim trading community, the Bohras, was dominated by the house of their spiritual leader, set in an unused open space where Geddes envisaged a nice little garden, its paths planted up with trees and its margins with flowers, making it 'a Zenana Park', in which Muslim women, otherwise homebound and in purdah, 'can walk and sit, with their children at play'. The ecologist hopefully thought that a creation of such a recreation space 'should practically put an end to the tuberculosis which is the perpetually recurring tragedy of Zenana life'. Such parks and gardens, set near temples, mosques and other shrines, would serve as 'centres in which the needs of health and of idealism meet and mingle, combined in life and crystalized in beauty'.[35]

There was a large tract of land all around the Indore palace, absolutely free of homes and habitations, in which Geddes, his imagination running riot, thought of establishing a series of gardens: a rock garden, a herb garden, a sacred garden, a Japanese garden, a vegetable garden, a fruit garden, a pleasure garden. These would all bear, to lesser or greater degree, the hand of man, with regard to the selection of flowers, shrubs and tree species to be planted and their layout. However, there would be one very special garden entirely untouched by humans. For Geddes believed that it was the duty of all governments to preserve characteristic stretches of 'wild nature', setting aside from the human hand 'a true "Nature Reservation", a "Nature Park" in every natural region'. In the countryside such patches of wild nature could of course be very extensive. Yet, there was a need for them in the cities too, even if on an altogether modest scale. Thus of Indore Geddes remarked that

> to have some such reserve, even on a small area, as near as may be to this City as it increases towards its educational, intellectual and cultural future, is a real need. ... As a beginning and permanent reminder of these needs, at least, let us find a corner somewhere, besides these gardens, to run wild year after year as it will. Not that this can ever or at least within any ordinary time, become really wild; but it will none the less be suggestive to the naturalist.

To this special untouched space Geddes gave the name 'Evolution Garden'.[36]

Towards the end of his report, Geddes turns lyrical and even utopian, offering a renewed and revitalized Indore as a model for how India (and the world) could reimagine city life. 'The fuller one's familiarity with the great Capitals,' he wrote, 'whether of West or East, the more must the student of cities turn with new hope to the small ones.' He continued:

> Great and rich and grand though may be the cities whose population is now reckoned by the million, their best achievements date from smaller days. ... Civilisation, alike in its higher movements and achievements and on its comparatively permanent levels, has flourished best in smaller aggregates; and—despite the megalomania of every Megalopolis, and the deep and manifold depression of every minor city accordingly—it tends do so still; and so may again, more fully.[37]

For Geddes, among the great advantages of smaller cities was that in them humans were still within easy reach of nature, that family and neighbourly life was richer, that administrators were less impersonal, and that there was a deeper sense of local patriotism. He was writing here, of course, as a partisan of Edinburgh over London, and one who sometimes saw more hope and possibility even in Dundee than in Edinburgh. Indore could, in this reimagining, become a much more liveable and attractive city than Delhi, Bombay or Calcutta.[38]

The second report by Geddes I shall highlight was on the small town of Balrampur in the United Provinces. In 1917, Geddes was asked by the Maharaja of Balrampur to advise on the remaking of the town in which he resided. The planner spent but a few weeks in the place, writing a report which, though short in length, was replete with specific recommendations. Geddes began with the palace and its grounds, suggesting that the shrubberies be made less shabby by planting up gaps, with the naturalist in Geddes paying attention to species, recommending the short- and large-leaved loquat in front of the tall and small-leaved shisham. The west lawn would be given dignity and character by the planting of a banyan, in time to be 'a great and monumental tree'. The approach to the palace would be a stately avenue planted with tamarind or a species of ficus.

Coming to public buildings, Geddes suggested the creation of a brand-new library which, apart from regular periodical and reference services and reading rooms, would also have a juvenile reading room 'and some day even a Ladies room'.

Next, Geddes considered the improvement of the old town of Balrampur, mohalla by mohalla, suggesting thinning of houses here, clearing of tanks there, protection and planting up of open spaces someplace else. Clearly Geddes had walked over the entire area, taking notes as he did. His scheme revolved around the renewal of the town's once extensive but now decayed tank system. These had once linked the mohallas, culminating in a grand lake in front of the palace. Geddes wished to clean the tanks and plant up their sides and embankments, so that, as he said, 'each neighbourhood and mohalla may thus speedily be brought to take pleasure and pride in its local portion of the Park System, and to protect it accordingly'.[39]

Geddes thus hoped to convert Balrampur's disused water tanks from being 'fetid ponds and [a] civic disgrace' to becoming 'pure lakes and the main ornaments of their city'. This, he argued, would be a way to recover the finest aspects of Balrampur's and India's past. 'It cannot be too often and clearly affirmed,' he claimed,

> that the old Tank Parks of so many Indian Cities are not only the glory of India, but are without rivals in Europe, since often surpassing in their beauty of mingled land and waterscapes, the glories of Versailles and Potsdam, as of Dutch and Canal Cities.[40]

Geddes ended with a stirring invocation of what a carelessly modernizing India appeared to have lost but what it might, with skilled guidance, yet reclaim. He remarked that of

> all unfavourable impressions of contemporary life and culture in India, none is more obvious and insistent than the general decline of esthetic sense and productiveness, which till the Industrial Age was possessed by both Indian and European, but is now eclipsed in both alike—witness their fallen taste in arts and crafts, in gardening and decoration, and above all in the general deterioration of architecture, [and] the indifference to landscape appreciation.

Geddes said this in 1917; but it remains painfully true to this day. But like him we must hope, as he insisted, that 'this blindness is neither historic or permanent in either of us [Indian or European]', and that 'the sense of beauty is returning in nature in cities alike', whether in Balrampur or in a hundred other places spread across our land.[41]

This report on Balrampur, eighty pages long, is written with love and learning. It is an encrusted little gem, but alas, a gem cast before swine. One cannot believe the Maharaja of Balrampur ever read it. Meanwhile the professor himself had moved on to the next town, and the next plan.

In his early years in India, Geddes got a few commissions from the British Raj, writing short plans on towns as diverse as Thane in the west, Dacca in the east and Lahore in the north. However, there soon arose a mutual antipathy between the rule- and hierarchy-bound colonial bureaucracy and the maverick Scottish professor, and these official commissions dried up. A senior officer of the Bombay government complained that Geddes's ideas were 'impaired by the strong element of vague idealism, by lack of familiarity with local conditions and requirements, by a tendency to evade recognition of practical difficulties, and by a general avoidance of points relating to the technique of town planning'.[42]

Geddes also crossed swords with Edwin Lutyens, then planning the imperial city of New Delhi. He thought Lutyens insufficiently aware of the circumstances of Indian lives, and deplored his disregard for Indian artistic and aesthetic traditions. Word of Geddes's reservations got to Lutyens, who wrote angrily to a friend about 'a certain Professor Geddes' who 'seems to have talked rot in an insulting way and I hear is going to tackle me!' Lutyens described Geddes as 'a crank who does not know his subject. He talks a lot, gives himself away then loses his temper.'[43]

In March 1918, his friend the Bengali biologist Jagadish Chandra Bose wrote to Geddes saying: 'My belief is that they [the British officials] won't give you any more Town-planning—the mischief you have done to the exploiters is already great! ... The Anglo-Indians are organised against you, and your notoriety [in dress and manner, or in combativeness?] will precede you everywhere.' Bose suggested that Geddes work with him in his research institute in Calcutta instead. However, a desk- and laboratory-based job did not appeal to Geddes. So Bose now generously lobbied on his behalf with the Indian princes, and a stream of commissions from them then followed.[44]

Geddes thus turned his back on the white man's Raj and sought to place his talents at the service of Indian maharajas instead. The most substantial of these princely commissions came from the ruler of Holkar, this the proposed redesign of his state's capital Indore, which has been discussed earlier in the chapter. In the winter of 1919, after finishing his Indore report, Geddes was appointed to a new chair of Sociology and Civics at Bombay University. He had recently lost both his wife and his son, and was therefore, as he wrote to his American disciple Lewis Mumford, 'too full of sorrows' to return to Edinburgh.[45]

The new professor of sociology and civics was much admired by his students in Bombay. As one of them recalled years later, Geddes

> just set you on fire with love of this earth and with desire to cleanse it, to beautify and rebeautify it, to build and rebuild it. That he taught us to look at life with eyes of love and reverence and wonder is to put it rather coldly. He opened up a new vision of life altogether, one which we are not accustomed to behold. A walk with him in a garden filled one with the sense of the entrancing miracle that Life is. It was not mere emotion which cools off and passes away. ... He set you on fire for practical endeavour and spoke of the futility of dreams that did not rouse the dreamer to action.[46]

Sadly, however, while Bombay itself was a large and rapidly growing city urgently in need of more harmonious development, the officials of the government continued to cold-shoulder the professor. And Geddes was looking to influence more than the minds of his students; he wished to reshape the lives of citizens on the ground.

In April 1921, on a ship bound back from Europe (where he had gone for a brief vacation), Geddes found that among his fellow passengers on the S.S. *China* was the Maharaja of Patiala. They got talking, and soon he had a fresh commission, to write a plan for the capital of this Sikh princely state in the Punjab.

In April 1922, his teaching for the academic year concluded, Geddes left Bombay for Patiala. He was put up in the Maharaja's guest house, from where he wrote excitedly to Lewis Mumford that he was immersed in

> a very interesting set of problems of town planning practice. An old Indian city grown up very irregularly within its fortifications

> round palace-citadel, & extending at various times with growth, up to 50,000, but not yet adjusted to railway & other modern conditions: & strongly mingled of wealth & poverty, magnificence & squalor, chaos & confusion!

Outside the palace complex, wrote Geddes, 'was a stately ellipse of irrigation canal-boulevards', while inside it were 'labyrinths of lanes between a few main thoroughfares—among these a multitude of old tanks filled up & drained off by engineers, now available towards three or more miles of park system, & so on'. There was much that could be done 'to carry out improvements', the question being whether the palace treasury would allocate the money, currently

> being swallowed between urgent needs of government & magnificence of H.H.'s policies & equipment on all sides from ancient elephants & modern cavalry to Rolls Royce staff as well of [garage] of motors (fifty and more!).[47]

Along with a garage of fifty motor cars also went a harem of more than one hundred concubines. Even by the standards of Indian princes Maharaja Bhupendra Singh of Patiala led a very sybaritic life indeed.[48] Having momentarily interested himself in the Scottish professor on ship, now, back in his palace, caught between cars and concubines on the one side and cricket and polo on the other, the Maharaja had no time at all for Geddes. Taking their cues from the ruler, the officials of the palace gave him short shrift as well. After experiencing months of stalling and prevarication, Geddes wrote exasperatedly to the Maharaja:

> But pray pardon me—as the old man of his profession in India (and in Europe) for saying, plainly, that your Highness—despite that encouraging interest in Improvements expressed on 'China'—

> is in danger in this Improvement campaign—like a General without the trained officers, and the enthusiastic and devoted army of citizens I had looked forward to organise, as in so many other cities in past years.

The letter ended with the professor beseechingly asking the Maharaja for an appointment:

> Can your Highness kindly fix an appointment when next in Patiala? ... Best of all, if your Highness would allow me to accompany him on a short motor drive to the main areas planned for improvement between Moti Bagh and Baradari ... so as to realise them clearly upon the actual ground? (This will only take an hour or so ...)[49]

The Maharaja would not spare even that hour, so Geddes, as a last resort, tried to get the Dewan (chief minister) of Patiala state interested in his scheme. The Dewan was apparently 'under the (too commonly acquired) impression of such Town Planning as all expense to State, and City, and possibly great—or at least too much expense'. Geddes hoped to meet the Dewan to disabuse him of this misconception, to demonstrate that 'my scheme and ideas are essentially those of an advisor to the trustees of a (partly seriously) depreciated property, and towards the improvement of its value and productivity'. Geddes told the Dewan that his plans would act as 'an impulse to citizens to build or repair, and improve, where they are, and with only minimum aid from the state (and that made up by its moral encouragement)'. Pressing the case, his letter concluded: 'There are finer architects than I and bolder planners too: but none so economical, in India or in Europe. ... Pray then grant me the opportunity which I have as yet missed—alike with yourself, with your Ministers, and with the Municipality, as well as with your Highness.'[50]

An appointment with the Dewan was not forthcoming either. The Patiala fiasco, coming on top of the others that had preceded it, led to a deep sense of disenchantment with India for Geddes. In December 1922 he wrote to Mumford complaining that

> I can't do much with so few students & these spoiled in a sub-London cram-shop like an Indian University, & especially this, the most bureaucratized. ... Nor is working for British Bureaucrats or Indian Maharajahs satisfactory, for different reasons, both so far fairly obvious. You have a freer & more open atmosphere to work in, by far. So while working powers last, I may be good for several seasons in States, & perhaps flee to California instead of Europe for winters.[51]

Having failed in India, the ageing Scottish internationalist now hoped to make a fresh start on the other side of the globe, in America.

Geddes's greatest contribution to urban ecological thinking was his deep recognition of the interrelationship of the human and natural environments. Geddes insisted that a training in sociology was indispensable for the would-be planner.[52] While his professional colleagues were 'plainly accustomed to think of town planning as an art of compass and rule, a matter to be worked out between engineers and architects almost alone', Geddes himself believed that 'the true town plan, the only one worth having, is the outcome and flower of the whole civilisation of a community and of an age'.[53]

At a more philosophical level, Geddes was a harbinger of what he termed 'the general revolution in science now in rapid progress, the change from a mechanocentric view and treatment of nature and her processes to a more and more fully *biocentric* one'.[54] 'Biocentric' is of course a term now much favoured by radical environmentalists to describe their own worldview. But unlike the radical socialists of his day and the radical ecologists of ours, Geddes's interest lay not in dreaming of new communities but in studying and improving the habitats of existing cities.

Geddes's overall philosophy of town planning can be captured in three quotes from his Indian reports.

First, from a plan for Dacca, where he says that

> the Town Planning movement is on this side a revolt of the peasant and the gardener, as on the other of the citizen, and these united by the geographer, from their domination by the engineer.[55]

Second, from a plan for Balrampur, where he remarks that for the town planner,

> the problem is not simply, as for municipalities and their engineers, today the removal of sewage, or tomorrow the supply of water, at one time the removal of congestion, or supply of communications; and at some other the problems of housing, or again of suburban extension. Our problem is to make the best of all these specialisms and their advocates. ... Our attitude differs from that of the specialist intent upon perfection in his own department, whatever be the outlays, whatever the delays to others accordingly; it is rather that of the housewife, the agriculturist or the steward, who has to make the best of a limited budget, and not sacrifice resources enough for general wellbeing to the elaboration of a single improvement.[56]

Third, from his great two-volume plan for Indore, where he argues that

> to be effective, action is not simply a matter of diffused science, of intellectual knowledge, as too many still think, since we were all trained at College to be intellect-idolaters. An idea has to be emotionalised to bring forth action. Emotion is the vital spark, which ignites the cold potentiality of knowledge into the flame and energy of desire, will and resolve, of purpose and deed.[57]

The sociologist Shiv Visvanathan has argued that, in mediating between the local and the universal, the parochial and the cosmopolitan, Geddes saw himself as a sort of urban gardener. 'The gardener was the peasant in the city, and Geddes wanted city planning to incorporate a "peasant" view of science.' Visvanathan continues: 'Life to a gardener is capable of repair, rebirth and revival. Like the gardener, one pruned only certain selected parts, the dilapidated sections, but only to encourage life processes. This whole act of conservative surgery should be achieved through co-operation and persuasion.'[58]

Visvanathan also writes that Geddes's career was a 'magnificent list of interesting failures'. Certainly, the Indian period of his life was a series of disappointments. As a university man himself, he was keen to get the commission to design the campus of the Banaras Hindu University; however, after initially encouraging him, the university's prime mover, Madan Mohan Malaviya, chose to entrust the job to someone else instead.[59] He also hoped to design the campus of the new university at Santiniketan, encouraged by Rabindranath Tagore writing to him in May 1922 that 'I have often wished for my mission the help of men like yourself who not only have a most comprehensive sympathy and imagination but a wide range of knowledge and critical acumen.

It was with a bewilderment of admiration that I have so often followed the architectural immensity of your vision.'[60] In the event, this too did not come to pass.

Meanwhile, the imaginatively conceived and carefully constructed plans Geddes did write, for towns in British India and in the princely states, were not realized in practice. While they lay gathering dust in offices and libraries, his compatriots Edwin Lutyens and Herbert Baker were being commissioned to design the great new imperial capital in Delhi. His closest Indian friend, the scientist Jagadish Chandra Bose, thought that Geddes had not got the recognition he deserved because his life and work were too diffused. The 'very fact of your versatile intellect', wrote Bose to Geddes, 'has made it hopeless for any one to see the thing as a whole and to understand fully your contributions'. Bose told Geddes that, in spite of his 'curious idioms', 'a great portion' of his Indian town plans was 'fine literature, original thought and adequate expression'. The scientist urged his Scottish friend to take a year off and set down his thoughts in a book where the reader could follow 'you in your development things step by step'.[61]

Tragically Geddes did not follow Bose's advice and write a systematic treatise on the past and future of Indian cities. Yet my reconstruction of what he wrote in so many scattered places does, I trust, demonstrate the enduring relevance of his work. Indian towns and cities have expanded enormously in size and scope in the century since Geddes wrote his unfulfilled plans for them. This expansion raises a series of portentous questions for citizens and planners alike. How can we provide safe, secure and pleasant housing for the different social classes in the city? What forms of transport will city residents use to commute to and from their workplace? Where will the water and energy to sustain them come from? Can one reconcile growth and development with environmental sustainability? And with aesthetics? Can we, in the dense and ever more crowded cities and towns of India, provide for small parks, gardens and water bodies to provide a sense of beauty and community? In sum, how can we make the lives of city residents more habitable, in all senses of the word? Any attempt to answer these questions must surely mandate a turn, or re-turn, to Geddes and his work, if not for actionable ideas for implementation, at least for moral and ecological inspiration.

CHAPTER FIVE

Dissenting Scientists

ALBERT AND GABRIELLE HOWARD AND THE QUEST FOR AN ECOLOGICAL AGRICULTURE

IN THE MID-1980S, WHILE teaching in the United States, I was introduced by a student of mine to the work of the poet and critic Wendell Berry. I read his book *The Unsettling of America*, a searing critique of agro-business and its destruction of human community and of the land itself. I found that, unlike most writers or ideologues before or since, Berry sought to put his ideas into practice, by cultivating a small farm in Kentucky on ecological principles.

In India, where I had come from and where I would return, most farms were smallholdings of the sort that the Kentucky poet himself lived and worked on. Unlike in the United States, there were no massive, single-owner farms of many thousands of acres each. However, other elements of the American model of commercialized agriculture had entered the Indian landscape. These included chemical fertilizers and pesticides, whose use had become ubiquitous in many parts of India, under the rubric of what came to be known as the 'Green Revolution'.

Wendell Berry was very much a dissident voice in the American landscape. Could his ideas have any resonance in my country? India had turned to chemical farming out of desperation. It was a series of monsoon failures and a near-famine situation in several states in the early 1960s that compelled the government to promote high-yielding hybrid varieties of wheat and rice, which required large infusions of water and of chemical fertilizers to deliver the best results. Areas where water was readily available, and which had a history of commercial agriculture, were identified; in these districts, seeds, chemicals, loans and marketing facilities were made readily available.

By the mid-1970s, the new strategy had begun bearing fruit. Production of wheat and rice had increased, and an improved public distribution system was able to transport food from grain-surplus to grain-deficit areas of the country. Though there remained substantial inequalities of access, and malnutrition was still widely prevalent, the threat of famine had been averted. India was no longer dependent on imports of American, Canadian or Australian grain to feed its own people.

Within its own terms, the new agricultural strategy was a success. India was now on the way to becoming self-sufficient in food. This economic security would also assure its political independence; for, had my country continued to rely on Western food aid, we may have had to abandon our traditional position of 'non-alignment' between rival superpowers and become an ally, perhaps even a client state, of America.

By the early 1980s, however, there were visible signs that this economic and political benefit had come at an ecological cost. In areas where chemical agriculture was intensively tried, observers noticed both an increasing contamination of the soil and a growing depletion of groundwater aquifers. Was this really a 'Green' Revolution? For all the gains to the country, economic as well as political, in the short run, would the strategy be sustainable in the long run?

These questions were being debated in environmental circles before I left India, and reading *The Unsettling of America* brought them once more to the fore. In his book, Berry had praised the work of an agricultural scientist named Albert Howard for departing from laboratory research and immersing himself in the social, cultural and environmental context in which farming was practised. The American radical wrote admiringly that the British scientist 'sought to establish agriculture upon the same unifying cycle that preserves health, fertility and renewal in nature'. Berry provided this arresting quote from Howard himself: 'Instead of sending the experimenter into the fields and meadows to question the farmer and the land worker so as to understand how important quality is, and above all to take up a piece of land himself, the new authoritarian doctrine demands that he [the agricultural scientist] shut himself up in a study...'[1]

Soon after reading *The Unsettling of America*, I came across, in a Boston bookshop, another book which had Wendell Berry listed on its cover and title page, this time as one of the editors. The book was called *Meeting the Expectations of the Land: Essays in Sustainable Agriculture and Stewardship*. It made the case for practising agriculture without the use of chemicals, for a form of land management which (to quote Berry) 'does not deplete soils or people'. The book was dedicated to three individuals no longer alive: Thomas Jefferson, Aldo Leopold and Albert Howard.[2]

Even while growing up in India, I knew of Thomas Jefferson's status in the history of the United States, of his contributions to American independence, his deep interest in science and scholarship, and—what was of most relevance to the book at hand—his belief that national renewal was best brought about by yeoman farmers who owned the land they cultivated and gave it their caring attention. Through my students at Yale, I had got to know of Aldo Leopold, his life and work, and his iconic book *A Sand County Almanac*, which had inspired generations of American environmentalists. However, I had never heard of Albert Howard until I found him mentioned in these two books that had Wendell Berry as author or editor. Going to the university library, I found a book of Howard's, which—to my interest and embarrassment—informed me that he had spent several decades conducting scientific research in my homeland. Much of this research was done in collaboration with his wife, Gabrielle, who was perhaps as original a scientist as her far better-known husband.

It is to Albert and Gabrielle Howard's work in India that I now turn.

Albert Howard was born in 1873 to a farming family in Shropshire. His father owned a farm of 550 acres, where he practised mixed farming, raising cereals, fruits and vegetables, while also maintaining a herd of cows. The countryside also had ample woodlands, giving Howard an early appreciation of the mutually beneficial interactions between field and forest.

After studying in a local primary school, Howard was sent by his parents to a moderately prestigious private school, Wellington College. From there he proceeded to St John's College in Cambridge, where he took a Tripos in Natural Science. His first employment was in the Caribbean, teaching agricultural science to college students in Barbados. After a couple of years there he returned to his homeland, studying hop farming in Kent before departing once more overseas, this time to India. He reached the subcontinent towards the end of 1905. Early in the new year, he joined the newly established Imperial Agricultural Research Institute (IARI), located at a place called Pusa in the eastern province of Bihar, as its 'Imperial Economic Botanist'.[3]

Shortly before coming out to India Howard had met and fallen in love with a student in Cambridge named Gabrielle Matthaei. Three years younger than him, she was a product of the progressive North London Collegiate School. From a German family and described as 'quiet and reserved', at Cambridge she found inspiration in the teaching of the chemist Ida Freund. Born and raised in Vienna, Freund moved to England in 1881, joined Girton College, took a first in Natural Science and later became the first woman to gain a university lectureship in chemistry. Despite losing a leg she remained focused on her teaching and her research, mentoring many female students and publishing a series of research papers as well as two chemistry textbooks. A recent assessment of her life and work describes Freund as 'a committed feminist', deeply interested in promoting 'education for girls, particularly in science', while simultaneously expressing a desire 'for scientific accuracy, individual effort and examination success'.[4]

Gabrielle Matthaei admired Ida Freund enormously; nonetheless, she found herself gravitating from chemistry to botany, and chose that subject for Part II of the Tripos. She carried out research under F.H. Blackman, a Fellow of the Royal Society and arguably the leading plant physiologist of his day. Her research results formed a vital part of what has become known as 'Blackman's Law'—this described by one commentator as an example of the 'Matilda Effect', namely, 'the celebration of a man's but not a woman's contribution to a joint endeavour'.[5]

Had Matthaei continued at Cambridge she could have joined the faculty, and perhaps even become one of the first women to be appointed to a professorship. Instead, she moved to India to marry Albert Howard and work with him, because of their shared interests in science, and because she seems to have found him less patriarchal than Englishmen of his class and generation generally were. Their relationship was, from the first, of intellectual equals. In July, when the Howards were engaged and not yet married, Albert sent Gabrielle (then still at Cambridge) a paper to comment on. In her reply she remarked, among other things, that 'the part on plant disease could be vastly improved'. While the paper's 'ending was quite good', she added, Albert should more clearly 'bring out the point that the plant knows no division of science, in growing and carrying out its functions it uses all'.[6] This was an early, and striking, illustration of the holistic approach that was to distinguish the science of the Howards from their professional peers.

Albert and Gabrielle Howard were married in a Bombay church towards the end of 1905. However, the structure of the British Raj would not permit women to be employed as scientists. So, for their first few years in India, Gabrielle ran the household while helping her husband in his science, without position or reward. In 1910 Albert was able to persuade his bosses to have her appointed as 'Personal Assistant to the Imperial Economic Botanist'. Three years later, she was upgraded to the rank of 'Second Imperial Economic Botanist'.

After two decades working in the employ of the colonial state, the Howards moved to Indore, the capital of the princely state of Holkar. They jointly established and ran an Institute of Plant Industry, which, among other things, developed an 'Indore Method of Composting', still practised in India and around the world. While Albert was the Institute's director, Gabrielle played an active part in designing the building and the laboratories. When they held seminars she was often a featured speaker, this attracting some hostility, for, as she wrote to her mother in England, the audience in a princely state—which was even more conservative than in British India—'had not heard a woman speak before'.[7]

In the second half of 1929, Gabrielle Howard was stricken by cancer. The Howards returned to Europe for her treatment, which was unsuccessful in saving her life. She died in August 1930 in Geneva, a city where her younger sister Louise then lived, working with the International Labour Organization (ILO). Prior to joining the ILO, Louise Matthaei had studied classics at Newnham, taught briefly at Cambridge, and also worked for a spell with Virginia and Leonard Woolf at the Hogarth Press.[8]

After Gabrielle's death, Louise and Albert began spending time together, fell in love and married. With his first wife's passing Albert had no heart to stay on in India. He and his second wife now made their home in England. After Howard died in 1947, Louise wrote a biography of her husband, and, in further burnishing of his memory and legacy, formed an Albert Howard Foundation of Organic Husbandry as well as the *Albert Howard News Sheet*. She republished several of his books as well. Louise Howard died in 1969, outliving her sister by almost four decades, and her husband by more than two.

In India, Albert and Gabrielle Howard travelled a great deal and experimented on a wide variety of crops. They were first based at Pusa, in the Indo-Gangetic plains, but they also spent much time in Kashmir and in Balochistan. The crops they worked on included wheat, tobacco, sugarcane, cotton, tomatoes and gram. With these (and other crops) the Howards sought to develop new strains and have them tested in varying soil and water conditions. They then took these results from the laboratory to the field, urging Indian peasants to adopt the strains that seemed best suited to the social and natural conditions in which they laboured.

Like J.C. Kumarappa and Radhakamal Mukerjee, Albert and Gabrielle Howard saw India as a land of villages. Like them again, they sought to ameliorate the living conditions of the farmers who lived there. However, while Mukerjee approached the matter as an analytical sociologist and Kumarappa as a Gandhian constructive worker, the Howards saw themselves as scientists, taking the fruits of their research to the people they wished to serve.

Albert and Gabrielle Howard began their professional career just as agricultural research was becoming a distinct scientific discipline, being taught for the first time in universities, establishing its research journals and scientific societies. In this situation, seeking to 'prove its position as a branch of learning', agricultural science almost wilfully ignored the world of practical knowledge that peasants themselves possessed. This gap was particularly acute in the colonies, where British-trained scientists almost automatically assumed that the local population 'would be ignorant, obstinate, and averse to knowledge'.[9]

Albert Howard, on the other hand, was from the first disinclined to set himself up as a scientific expert sent from the metropole to guide and lead the illiterate masses who lived in the colonies. Thus, as his second wife and biographer remarks, Howard was

> adamant in opposing the fashionable complaint that the peasant must be 'educated' or even bullied into acceptance of Experiment Station results. He believed fundamentally in peasant shrewdness or perhaps he would have called it peasant wisdom, but was almost equally determined that from the other side only very clear improvements should be popularized for adoption, and entirely opposed to the stupidity of launching a stream of small Experiment Station successes, following rapidly on each other, all very much of the same kind, and confusing to the average recipient. In this, as always, he showed great common sense and above all stood for a genuine and sincere relationship between experimenter and cultivator; nothing irritated him so much as

> the professional vanity which sacrificed this essential position to the temptation of publishing small temporary research results.[10]

A crop on which the Howards worked extensively was wheat, a staple grain across much of northern and western India. They were impressed by the system of mixed cropping in place, where wheat was grown with leguminous crops such as chickpea and mustard, thereby maintaining the fertility of the soil, restoring to it the nitrogen which the wheat had extracted for its own growth. This practice was absent in the Punjab, where nonetheless the cultivators retained three different kinds of indigenous weeds in their wheat fields. These weeds, Howard found, performed the same function that leguminous plants did elsewhere. In such matters, he wrote, 'the Indian ryot has nothing to learn from Western practice'.[11]

Howard was impressed by the knowledge of their natural surroundings that the peasants of the subcontinent possessed. He found, notes his biographer, that 'the Indian vernacular vocabularies for describing the state of the soil are far richer than anything we have evolved in our Western languages'. As he himself wrote of the farmers of the Punjab:

> Many terms are used to describe the physical character of the soils: thus *nyai* is rich land round the homestead. Heavy clay soils are termed *dakar*, *chamb*, and the heaviest clays on which rice only can be grown are termed *rakar*. The best soils of the Punjab are well-drained loams known as *rohi*. The lighter loams are called *rausli* and the sandy soils which grow only millets are known as *bhur* or *maira*. *Tibba* is almost pure sand and *reti* is a soil with wind-blown hillocks of sand.[12]

In their research with peasants, Albert and Gabrielle Howard came to understand the vital importance of soil aeration. In some parts of India, 'want of air causes much more damage than want of water'.[13] The farmers often understood this better than scientists; thus, in parts of Bihar, there was prevalent a practice, which involved gently breaking up the crust (locally known as papri) which formed on these alluvial soils after the rains. Once the papri was broken, oxygen was released to nourish the plant, making it grow once again.

This attention to, and respect for, farmers' knowledge ran counter to the views of imperialist ideologues such as the colonial civil servant F.L. Brayne, who saw the Indian peasant as ignorant and backward in all respects. A younger contemporary of the Howards, Brayne was a fanatical Evangelical who sought to 'teach' the peasants of the Punjab the virtues of thrift, hard work and self-help, which (in his view) they altogether lacked. Brayne forced peasants to go in for wells rather than canals; he instructed them to divert cow dung from their hearths to their fields when in the sandy soils it actually reduced yields; he urged them to use the English iron plough in place of the traditional wooden plough better suited to the local ecology; and he promoted, over the hardy local cows, the pedigree Hissar bulls, magnificent to look at but far too costly to maintain.[14]

Unlike Brayne and his ilk, the Howards appreciated the depth of local knowledge. However, they did not make the mistake that some contemporary agrarian romantics do—which is to believe that peasants have all the answers to their own predicaments. Unlike their colleagues, they would not patronize and talk down to farmers. Nonetheless, they would not abandon their commitment to scientific reason and experiment. The peasants of India were for them neither subjects nor teachers, but collaborators.

In a fascinating essay, the sociologists Alyssa M. Kinker and Thomas F. Gieryn argue that in their bottom-up approach to science, the Howards inverted the orthodox approach of their fellow agronomists—which was 'pursuing better agriculture through research'—towards pursuing 'better research through agriculture'. As the Howards saw it, 'not only are peasant practices amenable to scientific investigation, they also can be evaluated fairly within a quantitative analytical frame'. This approach involved leaving the comfort and safety of the research laboratory for work in the field. Notably, the Howards recognized the importance of market signals, observing how alert farmers were to opportunities to switch crops or crop strains depending on what gained them better returns. Their science involved studying the choices cultivators made and exploring ways of making them more economically viable as well as sustainable in the long run. Kinker and Gieryn summarize the Howards' approach as follows: 'Local cultivators' knowledge remains implicit and unorganized: it wants direction, mobilization and practicalization—translation into viable technologies, enhanced crop production and profit.'[15]

Their fellow scientists at the IARI focused sharply, or narrowly, on the growth of individual plants, seeking to increase the proportion of grain to stalk. The Howards followed a different approach; as the geographer Bret Wallach observes, 'the Howards were more than plant breeders ... they were exponents of the grandest kind of holistic research, and it was this that would eventually set them at odds with the research community within which they worked.'[16]

Albert and Gabrielle Howard opposed 'the vicious principle of departmentalism' in the IARI, where those who worked on the growth of plants conducted their research in isolation from those who studied its chemical components, those who studied water regimes, and those who investigated soil types. The Howards, on the other hand, advocated and practised what, many decades later, was to be accorded the approving label 'interdisciplinary research'. One initiative, led by Gabrielle Howard, was the holding of an unprecedented joint session of the Agriculture and Botany sessions of the Indian Science Congress, on a subject of vital importance to farmers across the subcontinent, the improvement of fodder and forage. Papers were canvassed from botanists, agronomists and livestock specialists, these examining the problem from many different angles and as manifested in all the provinces of British India.[17]

Sceptical of those they mocked as 'laboratory hermits', Albert and Gabrielle Howard actively interacted with farmers of all classes growing all sorts of crops. However, while appreciative of the empirical knowledge of the cultivators, the Howards did not unduly romanticize them. Noting the carelessness with which farmers in the Punjab used water, they remarked that 'crops like wheat ... are watered periodically largely because the water is there' rather than because the plants needed the water. They were speaking here of water from newly dug canals; now, a century later, farmers all across India use tubewells to over-irrigate fields, leading both to excessive soil salinity as well as the alarming depletion of groundwater aquifers.

In 1921, the Howards published a monograph significantly titled 'The Saving of Irrigation Water in Wheat Growing', whose first sentences read: 'One of the main directions in which Indian agriculture can be improved is in the proper use of irrigation water. Overwatering is the rule throughout the Continent, particularly on the alluvium of the Indo-Gangetic plain and in many of the deltaic areas of Peninsular India.' Of wheat growing in Balochistan they wrote that 'the local practices are wasteful and unscientific in the extreme. Water is thrown away in all directions; there is no effort to conserve the soil moisture and to make the best use of what is, to the wheat crop, a most timely and well-distributed rainfall.' Their report contained a series of recommendations to farmers on how to use water more wisely, by spreading it over a wider area rather than intensively irrigating select tracts, as well as providing periodic fallow periods where crops were not watered at all.[18]

The Howards insisted that farmers would use water more prudently if wastefulness on their part was penalized. As they put it: 'If the cultivators paid for water by volume they would learn to improve their methods and use less.'[19] (This remains a viable, but alas infrequently implemented solution in India, where, to win votes at election time, political parties of all persuasions promise farmers free water and electricity.)

Working with peasants in the many different agro-climatic regions of India led Albert Howard to turn 'from a contemplation of the plant into a contemplation of the medium in which it grew—the soil'. Thus, as his biographer remarks, Howard developed 'a point of view infinitely wider than that given to the systematic or even economic botanist'. Unlike the narrow specialist, Howard was 'altogether unable to separate plant from soil; the soil came into his vision as the great originator of all things growing or alive, as "Mother Earth", the nurse of life and mistress of decay'.[20]

Like Patrick Geddes, Albert Howard had trained as a scientist, with a proper respect for research, experimentation and data collection. Like Geddes again, Howard nonetheless departed from the growing tendency towards specialization by taking a holistic rather than fragmentary approach. Howard spoke disparagingly of 'that disease of civilization—fragmentation—by which such intimately related subjects as agriculture, food, nutrition, and health have become split up into innumerable rigid and self-contained little units, each in the hands of some group of specialists'. In centres of teaching and research across the world, knowledge was increasing at the expense of understanding. 'The remedy,' wrote Howard, 'is to look at the whole field covered by crop production, animal husbandry, food, nutrition, and health as one related subject and then to realize the great principle that the birthright of every crop, every animal, and every human being is health.'[21]

This broader, more all-encompassing view of agricultural science led the Howards to incur the displeasure of their fellow scientists at the IARI. They were accused of treading on the turf of colleagues in other disciplines, and of consorting too readily with the 'natives'. While grateful for all that their years working for the Government of India had taught them, the Howards eventually found another assignment in India outside the formal purview of the colonial state. In 1924 the ruler of Holkar state offered the scientist couple 300 acres of land just outside the town of Indore to start a research station. The Indian Cotton Committee, a representative body of cotton growers and traders, agreed to help fund the institute on an experimental basis. Twenty other princely states of the cotton belt of central India promised to provide additional monetary support.

Albert and Gabrielle Howard now moved from Bihar to central India, where they supervised the building of laboratories and a library and put in place a 'model village' of peasants to work with on their fields. In Indore, they established a research programme of which 'the key notes were two: the study of the whole crop within its environment, and the care and attention paid to the duty of conveying results to those to be served'.[22]

The Howards moved to Indore a few years after Patrick Geddes's own stint in the city. One supposes they would have been aware of him, though they do not mention his work. Nor does their biographer, Louise Howard. This may have been because Geddes's domain of research and action was the city, whereas that of Albert and Gabrielle Howard was the village. Nonetheless, the historian can see a distinct parallel. Like the Scotsman, the Howards went in search of princely patrons after falling foul of the scientific and administrative straitjacket of the British colonial state in India.

In their first years in India, Albert and Gabrielle Howard conveyed the fruits of their research through publications in scientific journals and the technical bulletins issued by the IARI. However, from the mid-1920s, they began writing for a wider audience as well.

In 1924 Albert Howard wrote a book on crop production in India, published by Oxford University Press (OUP). The book was divided into three parts. In Part I, Howard elaborated on some of his pet themes, such as the loss of fertile land in many parts of India for want of adequate attention to drainage; the importance of adequate ventilation of the soil; the need to use irrigation water carefully and responsibly ('the first thing that strikes the traveller in the canal-irrigated tracts of Northern India,' he remarked, 'is the waste of water which goes on all sides');[23] and the significance of leguminous crops in increasing the supply of nitrogen in the soil.

In Part II, Howard expressed scepticism about the value of introducing exotic crops, advocating the improvement of indigenous varieties instead. A series of chapters on individual crops (cotton, wheat, rice, sugarcane and pulses among them) packed in an impressive amount of information in a matter of a few pages each, such as their distribution across India, variations in yield, the role of soil and climate and results of research into improved strains. Apart from drawing on the author's own research and travel, each chapter synthesized a vast amount of secondary literature; a nine-page chapter on cotton lists almost sixty references to papers written by colleagues, both British and Indian.

Part III presented Howard's view of agricultural science as it was and as it should be practised. The 'ideal investigator', he wrote, would be 'well trained in all branches of botanical science, including morphology, anatomy, physiology, pathology, systematic botany, ecology, and genetics. In addition, he must have a sound knowledge of general science, in which chemistry and physics should be included. Such knowledge is essential because, in crop-production, it is not the plant alone that has to be studied but *the plant in relation to its environment*.'[24]

Albert Howard's *Crop Production in India* was reviewed by a professor of plant ecology at the University of Nebraska. His name was John Weaver, and he was a close associate of the distinguished ecologist Frederic Clements.[25] The review was published in *Ecology*, the journal of the newly founded Ecological Society of America. It praised what the writer saw as Howard's fundamentally ecological approach. Weaver wrote of the agronomist's book that 'in every chapter numerous problems of plant growth in relation to environment are brought before the reader in such a stimulating manner that one can scarcely conclude but that ecology will reach its greatest usefulness in the field of general agriculture. It is a book to which every student of environment should have ready access.'

Later, the reviewer observed that in the book, 'chief attention is given to soils as a source of sufficient water, air and organic matter for the crop, and to soil structure. If these environmental factors are made favorable, abundant crops can be produced, for the soils of India are exceedingly fertile.'[26]

Howard himself infrequently used the term 'ecology'. It is nonetheless significant that his work was recognized as 'ecological' by the American scientists pioneering this new discipline. It is also noteworthy that the reviewer highlighted the attention paid by the author to soil fertility. In Indore, as we shall later see, this became the principal focus of the Howards' work.

The Howards' second major effort at popular outreach was a book called *The Development of Indian Agriculture*, this time carrying the names of both Albert and Gabrielle on the cover. Commissioned in 1924, while they were still in the employ of the colonial state, it was published three years later, after the couple had moved to Indore. The preface noted that agricultural research in India over the past twenty years had 'removed two misconceptions which were current at the beginning of this century, namely (1) that science can teach the cultivator nothing and (2) that even if the villager can be helped, he will never alter his present practices'.[27]

The book presented a wide-ranging survey of agricultural practices in India. It presented details of the crops grown in different parts, whether for subsistence or for the market. It spoke of the importance of natural factors of production (such as soil and water), of the role of agricultural research, and of the significance of the 'human factor' (namely, the mental attitudes of the vast bulk of the Indian population who lived in villages). The book drew substantially on the Howards' research and publications over the years, but also on the work of other agronomists, economists and foresters.

Early in the book, the Howards highlighted the problem of soil erosion, prevalent in many parts of the subcontinent. 'The annual loss of soil,' they wrote, 'which takes place in India by erosion is immense and is an important factor in reducing the annual harvest.' They then outlined the ways in which this could be arrested, such as afforestation and the construction of embankments.[28]

While stemming soil erosion was one important endeavour, improving the quality of the soil already under cultivation was another vital aspect of agricultural renewal in India. The Howards were sceptical of the benefits of chemical fertilizers, placing their faith in natural methods instead. They believed that 'artificial manures do not supply what Indian soils really need, namely fermented organic manure in a finely divided condition'. Nonetheless, they believed that 'the solution of India's manurial problem is now in sight. What is needed is the concentration of all the available resources of the Agricultural Department on the proper utilization of every form of crop residue.'[29]

In this book written for a general audience, the Howards returned to a theme of their scientific papers: namely, the wastage of water by the Indian peasantry. The 'discovery of the most effective method of using irrigation water', they remarked, 'has been greatly neglected in India'. Cultivators were prone to overuse irrigation water, leading to the diminution of the natural fertility of the land. The Howards advocated the adoption of a system 'in which the cultivator can be encouraged to use as little water as possible, and also to give the land a periodical irrigation-fallow'.[30]

In a chapter on 'the human factor', the Howards expressed their disappointment with the lack of initiative taken by Indian cultivators to organize themselves for the more productive use of their lands. As they wrote, 'it is not sufficient to apply science to Indian agriculture and to bring the results to the notice of the people. This is only half the battle. The people themselves must desire to make effective use of the results and to improve their general condition. In other words, they must be educated and must be taught to think for themselves, how to read for themselves and how to act as an intelligent and progressive community.'[31]

In a context of widespread illiteracy (an estimated 92 per cent of Indians could not read or write), education was key—the education both of adults as well as children. The Howards expressed their admiration for the American public school system, where, through community initiative, schools with dedicated teachers were set up in many rural areas, transforming the lives of the people. Something similar was needed in India. The Howards thus called for 'a resolute and well-sustained effort on the part of the State to assist local bodies in the solution of Indian rural education in a practical and efficient fashion'.[32]

These recommendations were well intentioned but naïve—naïve both about the operations of colonialism, and about the social dynamics of the Indian countryside. The British Raj had no real interest in providing high-quality school education for the Indian masses, seeing it as too costly, an unnecessary diversion of resources. At the same time, the existence of a sharply stratified caste system in Indian villages greatly inhibited the manifestation, whether symbolic or substantive, of any sort of 'community' spirit. The absence of any mention of caste in the work of the Howards is quite striking. It is possible that they never learnt to fluently speak Hindustani or any other Indian language, yet they had travelled very widely in rural India, and worked (albeit probably with the aid of interpreters) with farmers in different districts growing different crops. Surely they knew that Brahmins would not eat with Rajputs, Rajputs would not eat with Banias, and no Brahmin or Rajput or Bania would even countenance being in the same room as someone from a backward or Untouchable caste. How, then, could there be a concerted, bottom-up effort to construct a school system open to all?

There does not appear to be a single mention of caste in *The Development of Indian Agriculture*, or, so far as one can tell, anywhere else in Albert Howard's writings either. Could he really have been so ignorant about this essential aspect of Indian life? Or did he just think it more convenient to ignore it? It may have been that as a scientist and as an Englishman Howard did not think it his business to advocate radical social reform to Indians. Hence perhaps his decision to avoid the caste question altogether.

The Howards had hoped for 'the concentration of all the available resources of the Agricultural Department on the proper utilization of every form of crop residue'. When this was not forthcoming, they decided to make it the focus of their own work in Indore, where they were free of the bureaucratic constraints of the colonial state. Here, at the newly founded Institute of Plant Industry, they took inspiration from the work of an American scientist and social reformer, F.H. King. Born in 1848 on a farm in Wisconsin, King had done a doctorate from Cornell, and taught for a decade in a university in his home state before joining the United States Department of Agriculture. In the course of his career, he had travelled to China, Japan and Korea and made his acquaintance with the traditional farming practices in those countries. He had been deeply impressed by how the fertility of the soil had been sustained over millennia through the use of organic manures.

King summarized his findings in his book *Farmers of Forty Centuries*, first published in 1911.[33] Reading King, the Howards sought the application in India of these East Asian methods: namely, the creation of compost heaps where plant and animal residues would be allowed to slowly decompose, becoming rich in nitrogen, before being taken to fields ready for cultivation.

Working with Indian associates in Indore, the Howards advocated the fermenting of animal and vegetable wastes in a plot of land specially reserved for the purpose. At the base would be a variant of calcium carbonate (to reduce acidity); on top of this were to be placed successive layers of animal and vegetable wastes. Vents were created to allow aeration. The heap was turned over at intervals of several weeks. It took a few months for the wastes to convert themselves into organic manure which could then be applied to the cultivators' fields.

What became known as the 'Indore Method of Composting' was described in detail in a monograph that Albert Howard co-authored with his colleague Yeshwant Wad, a chemist at the Institute of Plant Industry.[34] Howard and Wad claimed that the techniques for the manufacture of humus that they had developed could be adopted 'throughout the tropics and sub-tropics, and also on the small holdings and allotments of the temperate zone'. They added, 'How rapidly the method can be incorporated into the large-scale agriculture of the west is a question which experience alone can answer.'[35]

As two scholars of their work remark, 'to legitimate composting as scientifically sound, when most conventional science had devalued it as nonprogressive or inefficient, Albert and Gabrielle selectively remade science: the organization of knowledge-making, and its relationship to Nature and the indigenous expertise of Indian cultivators, was refashioned. ... Composting became for Albert an arena for negotiating relationships between and among ancient wisdom and modern science; soil fertility and human health; agricultural productivity and politico-economic integrity.'[36]

Eventually, as many as a thousand carts of compost were being produced annually at the Institute of Plant Industry in Indore, adding greatly to the fertility of the cotton farms in and around the town. However, since the Howards were now working outside the colonial administrative system, their work was not actively taken up by their colleagues in British India, nor, it appears, in other princely states either. As Albert Howard was to recall, among his former colleagues in the IARI the reception

> was, with few exceptions, definitely hostile and even obstructive, largely because the method called in question the soundness of the two main lines of work on cotton—the improvement of the yield and quantity of the fibre by plant breeding methods alone, and the control of cotton diseases by direct assault. If the claims of humus and of soil fertility proved to be well founded, it was obvious that this factor would influence the yield much more than a new variety or anything an entomologist or a mycologist could achieve.

The production and application of compost on a large scale, wrote Howard sardonically, might 'prove to be revolutionary and a positive danger to the structure and perhaps to the very existence of a research organization based on the piecemeal application of the separate sciences to a complex and many-sided biological problem like the production of cotton'.[37]

The Institute of Plant Industry in Indore aimed to practise a new kind of agricultural science as well as a new style of labour management. In their years in the service of the British Raj, the Howards were dismayed at the harsh treatment of Indian workers. So, when Albert found himself in charge of his new institute, Gabrielle and he radically reduced the hours of work (particularly in the hot season) for their staff, sought to provide housing and medical facilities, and adequate leave as well.[38] The staff responded to this more empathetic approach by working harder and with greater focus. Many years later, one of their Indian colleagues feelingly wrote that

> the deep attachment of Mr. and Mrs. Howard to their work, their colleagues, their staff, students and field workers, not forgetting their cattle, fields, and crops, was so marvellous that it inspired each and all voluntarily to respect, admire and enthusiastically co-operate with them in all their activities. It was a happy sight to see them on their rounds of inspection meet each worker at his duties, inquiring, encouraging, discussing as the case might be, caressing bullocks and gratified to find crops and land in condition. Wherever they moved, all was life.[39]

As noted earlier, in 1929 Gabrielle Howard was stricken by cancer, dying the following year. In 1931, Albert Howard gave up the directorship of the Institute of Plant Industry in Indore, and came back to England. Living with his second wife Louise, he involved himself in the affairs of his native country, where he became, in the words of one chronicler, 'the most influential figure in the history of the British organic movement'. Along with a group of likewise independent-minded scientists, aided and funded by progressive members of the landed aristocracy, Howard sought to limit the use of chemical fertilizers, stem soil erosion and promote the restoration of soil fertility through the methods he had pioneered in Indore.[40] Some younger British agronomists scorned his work, deeming 'his theory and practice of composting an embarrassing throwback to a long-discarded vitalism, suitable at best for the back-yard-gardener but quite out of step with modern, chemical agriculture'.[41] Nonetheless, he was awarded a knighthood, this perhaps canvassed for by the influential aristocrats who had embraced his ideas.

In 1940, Oxford University Press published Albert Howard's book *An Agricultural Testament*. Aimed at the general reader, this summed up the lessons of a lifetime of research and reflection. It is a work that is reflective, philosophical and, occasionally, polemical. The introduction lays out the philosophical principles of the book. Here Howard deplores the fact that modern agricultural science has, by and large, disregarded 'the means by which Nature manages land and conducts her water culture'.

As understood by Howard, the first of nature's principles was that monoculture was to be strictly eschewed. As he pointed out, in the world as untouched by humans, 'many species of plants and of animals live together. In the forest every form of animal life, from mammals to the simplest invertebrates, occurs. The vegetable kingdom exhibits a similar range...'

The second principle was that the soil of the forest was always protected and conserved. Thus 'the whole of the energy of sunlight is made use of by the foliage of the forest canopy and of the undergrowth. The leaves also break up the rainfall into fine spray so that it can be more easily dealt with by the litter of plant and animal remains which provide the last line of defence of the precious soil. ... The rainfall in particular is carefully conserved. A large portion is retained in the surface soil: the excess is gently transferred to the subsoil and in due course to the streams and rivers...'

The third principle was that soil fertility was maintained by natural methods. 'If we watch a piece of woodland,' wrote Howard, 'we find that a gentle accumulation of mixed vegetables and animal residues is constantly taking place on the ground and that these wastes are being converted by fungi and bacteria into humus.' He tellingly added, 'Nature has never found it necessary to design the equivalent of the spraying machine and the poison spray for the control of insect and fungous pests.'

What was true of forests was also true of other natural ecosystems. Thus 'in lakes, rivers, and the sea mixed farming is again the rule: a great variety of plants and animals are found living together: nowhere does one find monoculture'.[42]

Having outlined how nature works, Howard then contrasted agriculture as it had been traditionally practised in the Orient with agriculture as it was carried out in the modern Occident. He wrote that 'the agricultural practices of the Orient have passed the supreme test—they are almost as permanent as the primeval forest, of the prairie or of the ocean. The small-holdings of China, for example, are still maintaining a small output and there is no loss of fertility after forty centuries of management.'

Whereas the farmers of the Occident had increasingly taken to specializing in particular crops, in the Orient, noted Howard, 'mixed crops are the rule. In this respect the cultivators of the Orient have followed Nature's method as seen in the primeval forest.' Thus, where cereals were the main crop, they were always mixed with subsidiary pulses. Further, 'a balance between livestock and crops is always maintained'. He praised the Chinese who 'have for ages past recognized the importance of the urine of animals and the great value of animal wastes in the preparation of composts', noting that this was a practice Indian farmers could usefully follow too.

Howard remarked that in Western agriculture, on the other hand, 'monoculture is the rule. Almost everywhere crops are grown in pure culture.' Further, as compared to the East, there was a far greater use both of artificial manures and of mechanized instruments such as the tractor. These two methods had enabled an increase in profits and productivity. 'For the moment farming has been made to pay,' remarked Howard, before continuing, 'but there is another side to this picture. These chemicals and these machines can do nothing to keep the soil in good health. By their use the processes of growth can never be balanced by the processes of decay. All that they can accomplish is the transfer of the soil's capital to current account.' Further, 'with the spread of artificials and the exhaustion of the original supplies of humus, there has been a corresponding increase in the diseases of crops and of the animals which feed on them'.[43]

While Howard appreciated many aspects of peasant agriculture in the East, he believed that they could be improved upon further through the inputs of scientists like himself. As we have seen, apart from his work on individual crops, Howard spent many years developing a system of organic manuring capable of wide application. Four chapters of *An Agricultural Testament* were devoted to the elaboration of what he called 'the Indore Process for the manufacture of humus from vegetable and animal wastes', developed under his supervision between 1924 and 1930. He described how vegetable wastes and animal residues, combined with a substance to reduce acidity, such as powdered chalk or limestone, when placed in pits and allowed to ferment, could provide excellent humus for restoring or maintaining the fertility of the soil. He wrote with pride of how the Indore method had been used with some success in, among other places, coffee estates in East Africa, tea plantations in Ceylon and the cotton fields of central India.

In the concluding chapter of *An Agricultural Testament*, Howard reiterated the crucial importance to human civilization of soil fertility. He warned that as a result of the industrialization of agriculture 'the soils of the world are either being worn out and left in ruins, or are being slowly poisoned. All over the world our capital is being squandered.' As a consequence, 'the restoration and maintenance of soil fertility has become a universal problem'.[44]

Howard ended his book with an urgent plea for the radical reorientation of agricultural science. 'The approach to the problems of farming,' he wrote,

> must be made from the field, not the laboratory. The discovery of the things that matter is three-quarters of the battle. In this the observant farmer and labourer, who have spent their lives in close contact with Nature, can be of the greatest help to the investigator. The views of the peasantry in all countries are worthy of respect; there is always good reason for their practices; in matters like the cultivation of mixed crops they themselves are still the pioneers. Association with the farmer and the labourer will help research to abandon all false notions of prestige; all ideas of bolstering up their position by methods far too reminiscent of the esoteric priesthoods of the past.[45]

An Agricultural Testament is by far the most read and widely cited of all the works published by Albert Howard. The title of the work is intriguing. The last word has an inescapably religious ring. What was this a testament to? Perhaps to agriculture as both faith and science, agriculture considered as a way of life as well as a practice of knowledge? That is left to the reader's imagination. The book's dedication is more straightforward, less open to varying or conflicting interpretations. It was 'To Gabrielle, who is no more'.

An Agricultural Testament was published in 1940. Through the war years that followed, Albert Howard worked on a sequel, which developed and expanded upon the ideas of his earlier book, with fresh examples and a greater emphasis on human health. First published in the United Kingdom in 1945 under the title *Farming and Gardening for Health or Disease*, a revised edition appeared in the United States two years later, called *The Soil and Health*.

Under either title, the book was an extended brief on the behalf of the Indore Process of composting, a passionate plea by its inventor for its application across the world. In urging its widespread use, Howard disavowed any special interest, particularly pecuniary interest. The Indore Process, he wrote, 'involves no patents, no special materials have to be sent for, and *there is nothing secret about it*'. He warned readers against imposters who had ridden the prestige of Howard's compost campaign to market their own techniques, often patented, and 'frequently involving the purchase of inoculating cultures or plant extracts of secret manufacture, some even claiming to be based on esoteric knowledge of an advanced kind and so benefiting the health and happiness of the recipient'. Distancing himself from such 'mixture[s] of muck and magic', Howard made clear that 'the Indore Process makes no claims of this sort whatsoever. *It merely copies what goes on the floor of every wood and forest.* It has not been patented and will not be patented, because it would not be in accordance with my principles to make monetary profits out of work paid for from governmental and trust funds.'[46]

One chapter of *The Soil and Health* listed two dozen countries from where Howard had information that the Indore Process was used and known. They included the four countries of the United Kingdom, the USA, Australia, Canada, South Africa, Rhodesia, India, Malaya and West Indies, but also (outside the scope of the British Empire and the Anglosphere) several countries in Latin America. Howard mentioned several instances of the adoption of the Indore method in India itself. He wrote of a British estate owner in the Punjab, and of the chief agricultural officer in Sind, both of whom had tried it with some success on cotton farms.

By his own account, these adoptions in India were few and far between; yet Howard refused to be deterred. On a trip to the subcontinent in 1937 he had observed the problems caused by the choking of streams and ponds by the invasive water hyacinth, a plant foreign to the subcontinent. He thought it could be uprooted and turned into useful compost for farmers' fields.[47]

Howard's suggestion was taken up by a young scientist, who reported encouraging results. Now, in *The Soil and Health*, published a decade after that visit, he spoke of this experiment which demonstrated that water hyacinth made excellent compost. He believed that the annual yield of rice could be greatly increased if the composting of the water hyacinth was taken up as a mass campaign. 'No future rice famines in Bengal need be feared,' he said, 'once full use is made of the vast local supplies of water hyacinth.'[48] (The reference here was to the devastating famine that struck Bengal in 1943–44, claiming more than two million lives.)

Howard was desperately keen that his ideas, forged in India, would find fuller fruition in that land itself. 'A very promising development in compost making is now taking place in India,' he wrote. 'Although an account of the Indore Process was published in 1931, nevertheless twelve years have elapsed before any official notice was taken of the possibilities of the compost idea. The direction this is now taking will be clear from the following letter addressed to me and dated 24th August 1943 from Dr. C.N. Acharya, Chief Biochemist, Imperial Council of Agricultural Research, India.'

Howard then quoted from the letter, which told him that 'you will be interested to know that the Government of India have recently launched an all-India scheme for the preparation of compost-manure from urban refuse and have sanctioned an allotment of about 2½ lakhs of rupees for the purpose.' The scheme was to be operated by the Imperial Council of Agricultural Research; it would train officers in each province 'in the technique of compost-making from urban wastes'. The letter-writer had been placed in charge of the scheme. As he was now 'getting together all available literature relating to compost and organic manures' to share with his team in the provinces, Dr Acharya asked Howard to send copies of all his lectures and papers on the subject.[49]

No doubt Howard was touched that he had been approached by an Indian scientist working in the Agricultural Department of the Government of India. Back in the 1920s, his British colleagues in that same department had scorned his ideas; could it be that the tide of Indian agricultural science was finally changing in his favour? However, in calling this 'a very promising development', Howard was being very optimistic indeed. This seemed, on the face of it, to be a very small, almost token, attempt to promote the making of compost manure. The financial allocation was modest. The scheme only involved urban wastes, with the vast and densely populated Indian countryside falling outside its purview.

Howard ended *The Soil and Health* by an open challenge to the proponents of artificial fertilizers. One of the scientist's admirers, a Liberal peer named Baron Teviot, had urged the British government to fund and oversee a series of trials comparing the benefits of organic and artificial fertilizers respectively, in terms both of crop production and soil health. Referencing that call, Howard concluded his book with these truculent sentences:

> It is amazing that the artificial manure interests have not come forward to finance the large-scale trials Lord Teviot and his supporters have pressed for in a recent parliamentary debate. If they are sure of their ground and confident of the final results, what better and cheaper advertisement for artificials could be devised? ... Why not silence *these very tiresome and very persistent advocates of organic farming* once and for all? Refusal to join battle cannot be due to lack of money on the part of the vested interests and of the State. Is the reason for avoiding the fight to be found in another direction altogether—to the fear of the verdict of Mother Earth?[50]

The Soil and Health was published in America in 1947. Its author died in the same year. Towards the end of his life, Albert Howard had come into contact with a Pennsylvania entrepreneur named Jerome (J.I.) Rodale, who energetically took up the Englishman's ideas and became an influential proselytizer for them. He started a magazine named *Organic Farming and Gardening*, with Howard serving as a member of its editorial board. When Rodale asked Howard to write the foreword to a book of his, the teacher complimented his inexperienced acolyte's capacity for providing instructions to create composts from animal and vegetable wastes. 'What gave me most pleasure,' Howard claimed, 'was to discover that Mr. Rodale possesses that priceless quality—audacity—without which progress is never made.'[51]

Jerome Rodale regarded Howard as his guru, and the journals and books published by his eponymous press reached a wide audience. As a recent history of the Rodale Press documents, its founder 'routinely told readers and audiences the story of how discovering Sir Albert Howard's *An Agricultural Testament* inspired him to buy a farm and then grow and consume as much organic food as possible'. Testifying to a Congressional Committee in 1950, Rodale said he 'recognized Howard as the first scientist to question how food was raised'. Jerome's son and heir Robert invoked Howard almost as often as his father, most notably when assessing Rachel Carson's groundbreaking work, *Silent Spring*. In 1963, a few months after *Silent Spring* was published, he praised the book for what it said, while gently criticizing it for what it had not said. Robert Rodale faulted Carson for overlooking the damage done to the soil by chemical inputs. After citing and quoting Howard, he remarked: 'Rachel Carson here is your next book—an analysis of what commercial fertilizers are doing as far as insect and disease infestations are concerned.'[52]

One does not know whether Carson saw this review; in any case, she died shortly afterwards, of cancer. In subsequent decades, Robert Rodale carried on his father's legacy, by publishing books and magazines catering to a market of consumers concerned with matters of the environment and public health. The Rodale Press had bought the US rights of Howard's *An Agricultural Testament* from OUP, and between them father and son kept the book in print for many years. Among the Americans who thus got to know of the dissident scientist was the poet Wendell Berry, with whom we began this chapter. Berry first read Howard in the mid-1960s, when he and his wife bought a small farm. 'My reading of Howard,' he wrote many years later, 'has never stopped, for I have returned again and again to his work and his thought. I have been aware of his influence in virtually everything I have done, and I don't expect to graduate from it. That is because his way of dealing with the subject of agriculture is also a way of dealing with the subject of life in this world. His thought is systematic, coherent, and inexhaustible.'[53]

In 1990, the concept of 'organic farming' entered the official statute book, with the United States Department of Agriculture specifying national standards for the marketing of products grown on soils that used no artificial fertilizers or pesticides. As an American professor of soil science was to write some six decades after Howard's death, this scientist who had spent much of his career in India 'is regarded by most as the founder and pioneer of the organic movement'.[54]

What remains of the work of Albert and Gabrielle Howard in India itself? During their lifetime their work did have a modest influence. Mahatma Gandhi himself was aware of their ideas. In 1935, Gandhi's journal *Harijan* printed a two-part article on the methods developed by Albert Howard and his associates to convert a mixture of cow dung, farm wastes, wood ash and urine into invaluable fertilizer.[55] Later in the book we shall make the acquaintance of Gandhi's English disciple Madeleine Slade, who drew upon Howard's ideas in promoting chemical-free farming in north India in the 1940s and 1950s. Now, nine decades after he left the subcontinent, Albert Howard's name and legacy are still occasionally invoked by proponents of organic/sustainable agriculture in India, and a small press—based, appropriately, in Indore—has republished some of his books.[56]

At the same time, Howard has been done a disservice by some of his overzealous admirers. In June 2020, the activist Vandana Shiva claimed that 'Sir Albert Howard made Indian peasants his professors & brought good farming from India to Britain'.[57] This is a considerable exaggeration; for, while appreciative of the deep knowledge that peasants had of soil, climate, crop varieties, etc., the Howards both nonetheless emphasized the limitations in the cultivators' worldview. I have already spoken of their chastising Indian peasants for their unconscionable wastage of water. And at another place, the Howards went so far as to state that 'the people of rural India are for the most part uneducated, illiterate and almost incapable of thinking for themselves'.[58]

Albert and Gabrielle Howard saw agricultural renewal as a process of constructive collaboration between the scientist and the public. They certainly wanted to reform agricultural science by making it less segmentary, more interdisciplinary and transdisciplinary, making it more aware of the complexity of ecological processes and of the fragility of the web of life. They wanted scientists to be more democratic, to actively engage in conversation with farmers, and to learn to appreciate the knowledge gained by experience and transmitted over generations. At the same time, they did not unthinkingly place their faith in tradition or 'peasant wisdom' either. They were keen to incorporate the perspectives that peasants had to offer; however, rather than take this on faith, they would put it to the test of reason and practical application.

Once again, the parallels with Patrick Geddes are noticeable. Like Geddes, the Howards refused to see scientific experts as akin to an esoteric priesthood, working above and away from the ordinary citizen, while presuming to have the right to instruct, educate and chastise them. Science had to be made more democratic, its results and its recommendations flowing from an active engagement with the public. Geddes's conception of town planning rested on an ongoing engagement between the planner and the citizen. Similarly, for Albert and Gabrielle Howard, agricultural knowledge evolved through a partnership of mutual respect and understanding between researcher and farmer. However, as two scholars of their work pithily put it, this partnership was not entirely equal: rather, 'science is the arbiter, though its authority is not absolute'.[59]

In India and across the world, the name and legacy of Albert Howard are today recognized and appreciated far more readily than that of his first wife Gabrielle. This is for several reasons, and not just the Matilda Effect. For one thing, Albert wrote much more; for another, he lived far longer. Among the few writers to pay proper respect to Gabrielle's work was her sister Louise. Her book bears the title *Sir Albert Howard in India*, yet it does subtly underline the essential contributions of his first wife. Gabrielle, writes Louise, had an

> enormous capacity for patient detail and carried out a very large part of the finer minutiae of plant breeding with her own hands in the area of the Botanical Section at Pusa, at Quetta, and at Indore; with this she combined, what is rarer, a comprehensive insight into and grasp of fundamental principle. Indeed, her mind was masterly and energetic, as was shown in a smaller way in her ability to run her Indian household to perfection in the intervals of her scientific labours, to the astonishment of the ladies of the Station, who prophesied either a complete breakdown in household arrangements or at least sunstroke from so many hours spent in the field. But her chosen way of life gave her supreme happiness and her comradeship in investigation with her husband was perfect. Their combined powers of work was colossal, nor could the results of their efforts ever be disentangled, as they themselves stated to me on more than one occasion.[60]

Gabrielle Howard's scientific originality is amply demonstrated in the few works that she published singly, under her own name alone. They include an eighty-page monograph which conveyed the results of research conducted over several years on wheat cultivation in the uplands of Balochistan. Gabrielle was perhaps the first European woman to have lived in this region, and surely the first woman to have conducted scientific research there. Always harsh, arid and isolated, a hundred years later the area is known for its propensity for violence; it remains mostly outside the control of the Pakistan state and army.

Even to a non-scientific, humanistic eye—such as of this writer—the report reveals the meticulous nature of Gabrielle

Howard's research, her powers of close observation—whether describing the diversity and variety of plants, soils, farming practices and climatic conditions—and her total immersion in her chosen subject.[61]

The Wheats of Baluchistan, Khorasan and the Kurram Valley was published in 1916. Seven years later, Gabrielle Howard was elected president of the Botany section of the Indian Science Congress, the first woman to be awarded this honour. Her presidential address stressed the intimate connection between the plant and its environment, especially the soil and water regimes in which the plant and its roots are located. 'The agricultural plant physiologist,' she wrote,

> requires a vivid mental picture of the plant as a whole. It is as much a biological unit as an animal. The latter, however, is visible as an entity and acts as an entity. If we injure any portion of it, we expect reaction and disturbance of the whole. In the plant our mental conception is blurred by the fact that one of the most important structures is underground. We do not treat it as an entity, for we continually mutilate it without troubling very much about the effect on the remaining portion.

After some two decades as an agricultural scientist, Gabrielle Howard observed that the current practice among her colleagues was to conduct experiments that 'focus attention on the beginning and the end only, that is, on the conditions provided and the yield obtained. We tend to ignore the changes and processes which have been taking place in the plant. This is, in reality, a selfish and brutal method of dealing with the subject.' Gabrielle asked that 'instead of regarding it [the plant] as a machine which grinds out so much food for us', the agricultural scientist should look upon the plant 'as a living individual completing its life cycle under certain conditions'.

Another limitation of current scientific practice, Gabrielle remarked, was that it tended towards hasty generalizations. This was because it tended to 'group species together as cereals, leguminous fodders and so on, and to speak as if their requirements and physiological needs were alike'. Mistaken or misleading conclusions were drawn as to the behaviour of an entire group of plants from experiments on a single variety. She therefore urged for a greater 'recognition of the physiological individuality of species and varieties'.[62]

This is a profoundly ecological approach, emphasizing both the diversity of life forms and the interrelationships between them. The ideas animating this address to the Indian Science Congress were taken further in later works written by Gabrielle and Albert Howard, and by Albert alone. To his credit, Gabrielle's husband was fully conscious of her contributions. As Louise Howard was to write, in their years in India Gabrielle was 'not only the able housewife, the dignified hostess, and the wonderful companion, but she was also a highly trained botanist, launched on her own career of research at Cambridge, of great intellectual endowment and altogether fitted to be the comrade and inspirer of a pioneer in science, one on a level with himself, as Sir Albert never ceased to emphasize'.[63]

At the time of her death Gabrielle Howard was working on a textbook on agricultural botany for Indian students. It remained incomplete; Albert felt unable to finish it because the project 'was entirely individual to his wife and based on her ideas'. Some of her notes survived, and her sister quotes them. Here Gabrielle clearly distinguished between the aims of pure and applied science, between knowledge for its own sake and knowledge aimed at augmenting human welfare. She wrote that 'the work of the scientist who is investigating the problems of heredity and that of the plant improver, or plant breeder as he is sometimes erroneously called, are fundamentally different and call for quite different attributes and qualities'. She elaborated this distinction further, writing: 'To the geneticist the main aim is knowledge and both negative evidence and side issues may contribute to his work. But the plant improver is not paid by the State to seek negative results or follow side issues, and his quest should be knowledge, it is true, but knowledge allied with common sense and judgment; the proving to the public that science is of some use is after all very important.'[64]

Reading this, I am reminded of some remarks on science made by Mahatma Gandhi, while speaking to a group of male college students in Trivandrum in 1925. Gandhi said that he appreciated the urge that led scientists to conduct basic research, to do 'science for the sake of science'. Yet he worried that scientists and science students in India came overwhelmingly from a middle-class and upper-caste background, and hence knew only to use their minds and not their hands. His own view was that it would be 'utterly impossible for a boy to understand the secrets of science or the pleasures and the delights that scientific pursuits can give, if that boy is not prepared to use his hands, to tuck up his sleeves and labour like an ordinary labourer in the streets'. For only if one's 'hands go hand in hand with [one's] heads', could one properly place science in the service of humanity. As Gandhi put it to the students in Trivandrum:

> Unfortunately, we, who learn in colleges, forget that India lives in her villages and not in her towns. India has 7,00,000 villages and you, who receive a liberal education, are expected to take that education or the fruits of that education to the villages. How will you infect the people of the villages with your scientific knowledge? Are you then learning science in terms of the villages and will you be so handy and so practical that the knowledge

> that you derive in a college so magnificently built—and I believe equally magnificently equipped—you will be able to use for the benefits of the villagers?'[65]

Gabrielle and Albert Howard were not born or educated in India. Yet, in their work, they exemplified this 'Gandhian' approach to science better than many scientists who were, and are, Indians themselves.

CHAPTER SIX

Gandhi's Englishwoman

THE PASSIONATE ENVIRONMENTALISM OF MADELEINE/MIRA

MAHATMA GANDHI AND HIS wife Kasturba had four children. All were male. However, in the course of his life Gandhi 'adopted' two daughters, neither related to him by blood. The first was Lakshmi, whose parents, themselves from an Untouchable caste, joined Gandhi's Sabarmati ashram in 1915, when she herself was an infant. Gandhi helped supervise her education and upbringing and said that she was 'like a daughter to him'. Lakshmi and her parents remained a part of Gandhi's entourage until 1933, when she married a man chosen for her by the Mahatma.[1]

Gandhi's second (and far more famous) 'adopted' daughter was a white woman, originally bearing the name Madeleine Slade, but known as Mira (or Mira Behn[2]) after coming to India in 1926. She was then in her early thirties. Madeleine was born in 1892, with her biological father an admiral in the British Navy. She had ambitions of becoming a concert pianist. She greatly admired the music of Beethoven; it was on meeting the German composer's biographer, the French writer Romain Rolland, that she first heard of Gandhi. On reading Rolland's short (and utterly adulatory) book on Gandhi, Madeleine turned her back on music and Europe and came to live with her new hero in his ashram in Ahmedabad.

Mira is an important figure in Gandhi's life, and in his afterlife. She was part of Gandhi's inner circle from the time she arrived in India; she lived with him, she cared for him (peeling his oranges and checking his bowel movements, among other things), she travelled with him everywhere he went in India and accompanied him to the Second Round Table Conference in London in 1931. Three years later, she was sent by Gandhi to proselytize on behalf of the Indian case for political freedom in the United Kingdom and the United States. In the 1940s she was a fellow prisoner with Gandhi during his last jail term. Three decades later, by which time she had relocated to Austria, the filmmaker Richard Attenborough visited Mira several times, consulting her closely on the making of his epic film *Gandhi*, in which Mira was played by the well-known British actress Geraldine James.[3]

I have written about Mira's role in Gandhi's life at some length elsewhere, in a book on foreigners who joined the Indian freedom struggle.[4] In that work I only briefly touched on a forgotten aspect of her Indian life—her precocious environmentalism. In this chapter I wish to focus more directly on that theme. For, apart from being Gandhi's adopted daughter, apart from being an anti-colonial activist, apart from influencing a film that won eight Oscars, Madeleine/Mira wrote with insight and passion about humanity's relationship with the natural world. As we shall see, much of what she said on this subject makes for compelling reading today.

I am interested here principally in Mira's environmental writings in and about her adopted homeland. However, it is worth noting that her sensibility in this regard was nurtured well before she arrived in India. With her father often away on ship or on overseas postings, the child Madeleine spent a great deal of time in her maternal grandfather's large house in the Surrey countryside. Wandering around the grounds, she developed 'a feeling of fellowship with the trees and plants. There were some trees for which I had a special affection and some I was not very fond of, but one and all were for me personalities.'[5]

Writing many years later as 'Mirabehn', she recalled of her grandparents' estate that she 'knew every corner of the gardens, the different flowers, the vegetables, the fruit'. As a child, Mira was forbidden to pluck the flowers in the garden. She could look at them, smell them, but not pick or damage them. This restriction, she was now convinced, in fact heightened 'the admiration with which I looked at the special blooms in my grandmother's rose garden, where every plant was labelled. I studied their qualities, and the special smells associated with the different colours. If I had been allowed to tear the blossoms and do what I liked, I should never have learnt to enjoy them as I did.'

Mira was also 'taught to look at, and later on to handle, with intelligent interest', the animals in the estate. As she grew older she learned to milk the cows, groom the horses, and feed the chickens. 'I was brought up,' remembered Mira, 'to regard the teasing of animals, birds, or any live creatures, as a despicable thing. This, coupled with my own natural love of animals, led me to find in them companions, in whose joys and sorrows I shared with intimate interest and sympathy.'[6]

Mira arrived in the Sabarmati ashram in November 1925. At first she stayed as close to Gandhi as she could. Understanding how different ashram life in India was from an upper-class household in England, Gandhi wished her to slowly, gently, make herself familiar with the sights, smells and sounds of her new surroundings, and with the philosophy and practice of the Indian struggle for freedom.

For more than two years Mira was almost continuously under the same roof as Gandhi, when at Sabarmati, and in the same train carriage as him while he travelled across the subcontinent. In September 1928 Gandhi judged that finally Mira could begin to see India on her own. He sent her to north India to study the progress of one of his favourite projects, the production and promotion of homespun cotton, or khadi.

On this tour, travelling all by herself, Mira spent some time in the new imperial (and old Mughal) capital, Delhi, before venturing north, into the Kumaon Himalaya, where she had been tasked with studying the progress of khadi work. On Gandhi's birthday, 2 October, she was in the beautiful valley of Someshwar, where, as she wrote to him, 'at day break we set off for the mountain pass. It was as though nature were joining in the hymn of purest thanksgiving and joys that filled one's own head. Birds that I had never before [heard] were pouring forth the sweetest imaginable notes, heavenly scents were wafted on the air and the sky was aglow with the coming day.' After an hour of hard climbing Mira and her companions reached the top of the pass, 'and there spread out in all their glory were the snow mountains glistening in the early morning sunshine'.[7]

Mira had come to India at a time when Gandhi had temporarily abandoned the anti-colonial struggle for social and spiritual renewal. In 1929, Gandhi and the Congress Party decided to once more embrace the path of non-violent protest against the Raj. In March the Salt Satyagraha commenced, and for the next three years Gandhi was in and out of jail. Mira herself spent several brief periods in prison. Remarkably, even confined in her cell, Mira retained her interest in and love for nature. In the third week of January 1933, when she was imprisoned in one town and Gandhi was imprisoned in another, she wrote to him that

> the spirit of Spring has even touched the crows with its softening influence. There is one now, which sits in the papaya [tree] outside and utters soft croaks and would-be sweet warbles. Little singing birds now and then pass through the yard, and on their way they alight for a minute or two and tell us that Spring is there alright, outside—and my thoughts go to the river bank at the Ashram. How the little birds and squirrels must be busy all day in the grass and trees—how the water birds must be calling as they fly home in the evening to their roosting place by the well—and then, when the night has closed all in sable-stillness, how the glorious full moon will rise over the river spreading a path of gold across the water to the Ashram bank.[8]

While in prison in 1932 and 1933, Gandhi had undertaken several long fasts seeking to shame his fellow Hindus into abandoning the pernicious practice of Untouchability. After he was released from jail in August 1933, he resolved not to resume civil disobedience but to focus his attention on the uplift of the Untouchables, to whom he had given the name 'Harijans' or the children of God. He planned an all-India tour in this regard, and his adopted English daughter was chosen to accompany him.

In November 1933, shortly before the start of what was known in nationalist circles as 'the Harijan tour', Mira was with Gandhi in the town of Wardha, staying at an ashram founded and funded by Gandhi's great philanthropic benefactor Jamnalal Bajaj. In an article for Gandhi's weekly (itself now renamed *Harijan*—it had previously been called *Young India*), Mira wrote:

> The sunrise from the terrace is a perfect sight. The view stretches out over miles and miles of gently undulating country with lines of purple hills in the far distance. Long before the sun appears on the horizon, glorious rays of rosy light shoot far upon into the sky, heralding his coming. It is then that I go out across the fields and listen to the voice of Nature—the singing of the birds, the tinkling of distant cow-bells and the murmur of the morning breeze passing through the standing crops—the symphony of awakening Earth praising her Maker. And yet man thinks it preferable to live in cities and never hear God's divine music.

Living with Gandhi, Mira was more aware of the iniquities of caste than, for example, Albert and Gabrielle Howard seem to have been. In the last week of November 1933, by which time the Harijan tour had commenced, Mira wrote in Gandhi's weekly about a village named Kharangua, some seven miles from Wardha. Only one of the eleven wells was previously open to the village's Untouchables. Ashram workers had succeeded in opening five wells to Harijans, but there remained, reported Mira, the problem of divisions within the Harijans themselves. The lowest-ranking Mangs feared that Untouchable castes placed above them in the social hierarchy would not allow them access to water in these wells. Mira insisted that 'it will be the special duty of the Ashram workers to try to protect the *Mangs* in the use of the wells, which were formally opened for them as much [as] for the other Harijans'.[9]

The Harijan tour moved south, and then east. In June 1934 it reached the province of Orissa, which had a fairly substantial population of forest tribes. Here, Mira had a dream whose contours she recounted for the readers of *Harijan*. It was about a young man, a tribal who 'had never known village life' and hence knew nothing about untouchability either. One day this young man 'ventured into a "civilized" village on the edge of the forest', where, to his shock and horror, he was totally spurned by the villagers: 'He could enter in nowhere, he was refused water, he was driven from pillar to post.' In dismay the young man returned to the forest, where, as Mira's recounting of her dream continued:

> He ran and ran till he reached the depths of the wood where a brooklet was winding its way through the foliage. There he flung his arms round a mighty forest-tree and clung to it, weeping.
>
> 'Ah! Tree-brother,' he cried, 'never hast *thou* shunned me, never hast *thou* refused me shade. And thou brooklet, never hast *thou* forbidden me to drink of thy sparkling water! But those human brothers away in the village who have the same form as I—the same, just the same—*they* have spurned and reviled me. *They* have refused me shelter, they have refused me water to drink. What does this all mean? What—what—?'[10]

In the spring of 1939, Gandhi sent Mira to the North West Frontier Province to promote spinning and weaving. She would be the guest of the Khudai Khitmatgars, the organization founded and led by Gandhi's remarkable Pathan follower Khan Abdul Ghaffar Khan. Her first stop was the hill town of Abbottabad (now famous as the place where Osama Bin Laden was hiding before he was detected and killed by the US Navy Seals in May 2011). From here she proceeded into the interior, to the town of Balakot.

The first night on the road, Mira slept in the open. 'To the foot of my bed,' she noted in her diary, there was 'a velvety black mountain with the full moon just peeping over its edge, & to my left, down below, the little world of fields & farms with the huge mountains beyond gleaming mysteriously in the moonlight.' Mira got out of bed at 5 a.m. and went for a walk. She found that 'work had already begun in the fields. Treading out of corn, winnowing & ploughing are all in progress. As I was returning home the sweet summer notes of the cuckoo fell on my ear.'

After breakfast Mira and her companions set off for Balakot. On the way they passed a forest bungalow which she thought 'a possible place where Bapuji [Gandhi] might have some rest & quiet'. It was at a comfortable altitude of 3,900 feet: 'all alone in the fir woods, with peeps of the snows above & the mountain valleys below, it is certainly a very attractive spot, but water is scarce.'

The party stopped for lunch and then carried on to Balakot up the valley of the river Kumbar. The road was 'narrow & rough' as well as 'steep & twisty', and the car found it hard to negotiate the bumps and bends. Mira found the scenery absorbing though, for the road ran 'along near the right bank of the river, which is a big torrent, racing & tumbling down from the snow mountains. In its haste, as it rushes over its rocky bed, & dashes against the many twists & turns of its course, it rises into waves as formidable as the Sabarmati in flood. Here & there along its banks & shallows are great tree trunks that have got caught up on their way to the Jhelum, while others more successful pass headlong on down the centre of the stream.'

From Balakot Mira and her escorts proceeded further into the mountains. They halted at a village named Bhogarmang, which had terraced rice fields neatly laid out, as well as weaving and beekeeping. Mira was impressed by this, 'but the thing which rejoiced my heart more than anything else in this village', she wrote, 'was the living Hindu–Muslim Unity'. She found that a

'Hindu family, headed by a dear little old white-haired man, was on the sweetest terms with the young Khans who said that he had been the friend of their Father & Grandfather, & that the two communities had always lived in an atmosphere of mutual aid & consideration'. On hearing this, wrote Mira, 'the prayer which instinctively rose in my heart was "May no 'Leaders' ever reach this little village & spoil its sweet & natural life!"'

This was her last stop, and the next morning they left for Abbottabad. The last paragraph of Mira's tour diary read: 'The pity is that more use is not yet made of the beautiful air, water & scenery which India can provide, & that people still think it necessary to go abroad for their health.'[11]

In September 1939 the Second World War broke out. For three years Gandhi, with Mira occasionally acting as his emissary, sought to effect an honourable compromise with the Raj, in which the Congress would support the British war effort in exchange for a promise of independence when the conflict ended. When these talks finally failed, in August 1942 Gandhi launched his 'Quit India movement', whereupon he and his close colleagues (including Mira) were sent off to jail.

After she and her fellow Indian nationalists were released from prison, and the war itself had ended, Mira sought to realize a long-cherished dream of founding an ashram of her own. Her admiration and love for Gandhi remained undimmed, but she thought that, after two decades in India, she needed to become, in a personal and institutional sense, independent of him. Over the next decade, she established a series of ashrams in the Himalaya, where she sought to study village life with a view to making it more meaningful and sustainable.[12]

Mira was mentally and physically nourished by her move to the Himalayan foothills, which were then far more thickly wooded than they are now. 'The wild beauty of those great forests,' she wrote in her autobiography, 'and their wealth of animals and birds, stirred in me new strength. There is a vast vitality in untrammelled Nature which communicates itself to those who live with her.'[13] However, she had come here not to further a personal or mystical bond with nature but to cultivate a communal and co-operative relationship with it. In March 1946, shortly after founding her first ashram, Mira remarked that, 'having settled down to a *kisan*'s [farmer's] life for the purpose of understanding the problems of the villager, I have come to one definite conclusion, and that is that manure-making is one of the most important things we have to tackle.'

Mira was dismayed to see that 'the ordinary peasant makes no effort to make manure'. Cow dung was widely used as fuel; when it was not, it lay scattered around the place. It was not collected carefully, nor was it mixed with village waste to create a usable compost. Mira believed the production of farmyard manure to be 'a more urgent job' for a soon-to-be-independent India than setting up large factories for making chemical fertilizers. That latter path, she argued, would need a 'big outlay in capital, machinery and export'. Besides, its products would reach only a small number of villages. On the other hand, of the method she advocated she wrote that 'the materials are lying there waiting to be gathered up, the peasant with his ordinary tools can do all the work and throughout the world farm-yard manure is acknowledged as the all-round best and safest method of fertilizing the fields'. Mira instanced the widespread use of human and animal waste as manure in China, and hoped India would follow that example. The villages in China, she remarked, 'are swept clean, because everything in the way of rubbish is put into the manure pit. Here in India our villages are littered with debris from one year's end to another. All this rubbish can be turned into gold if we will use it in the right way.'[14]

India became independent of British rule on 15 August 1947. A few weeks later, Mira printed an appeal to the kisans of India's largest state, the state where she was herself now based in, Uttar Pradesh (UP). The appeal began:

> Brother Kisans,
>
> We do not treat our Mother Earth properly. She does her best to feed us all, but we do not feed her in return. How can she sustain us, her children, if we do not serve her as dutiful children should serve a revered Mother? Year after year, we plough, sow and reap harvests from the fields, but very rarely do we give any manure to the soil, and even what we give is usually half-kachcha rubbish. Just as we need well-cooked food, so does the soil need well-prepared manure.

Mira went on to explain, over five long and carefully formulated paragraphs, how to make what she called 'Kisan Compost'. She urged peasants to stop burning cow dung as fuel and to plant trees, thereby saving 'much more cattle-dung for manure'. She instructed them on how to make compost pits, in which they would place alternate layers of cow dung and household waste, sprinkled with water and covered with earth, and turned over at regular intervals.

Mira ended her appeal to the peasants of UP with these words: 'If we will take the trouble to collect all the available cattle-dung and rubbish, and treat it as I have described, we shall be able to nourish our poor famished Mother Earth, and she in return will nourish us and our starving cattle with bumper crops.'[15]

One does not know whether this appeal was translated into Hindi, or how widely it was read. Although Mira does not mention Albert Howard in this context, it is clear she had been reading his work, perhaps his book on utilizing the waste products of agriculture written with his colleague Yeshwant Wad in the early 1930s, more likely his recently published memoir *An Agricultural Testament*. (We know from other things she wrote that Mira had recommended Howard's work to Jawaharlal Nehru, for example.[16])

India, on the cusp of independence, was witnessing an active debate on how best to bring about the economic development of the countryside, where the bulk of the population resided. Intervening in this debate, Mira noted that it was intensely polarized: thus 'some people consider mechanization of agriculture the ideal goal for India, and some would not so much look at a tractor'. Mira herself advocated a 'middle path', where tractors would be used sparingly, to bring the areas of cultivable waste in north India under cultivation. Mira worried about the wholesale replacement of bullocks by the tractors, noting that bullocks were required for vital tasks such as water-lifting while also providing valuable manure. 'When we have developed village groves for fuel-wood,' she wrote, 'we do not want to find that cow-dung has been greatly reduced due to the removal of the bullock from village cultivation. On the contrary, we want to find masses of cow-dung released for the impoverished Indian soil.'[17]

In December 1947, Mira organized an 'All-India Compost Conference' in Delhi, which had social workers as well as agricultural scientists among its speakers. The conference was commended to the public by Gandhi himself. In a public meeting in Delhi, he explained the process of composting to his audience as follows: 'We have dung in plenty; there is also human faeces which can make good manure. After it is converted to compost nobody can say how it was made. If you take it in hand it has a pleasant smell, not an unpleasant one. In making compost they also mix grass, leaves and other farmyard waste with the dung and in time it is converted into very good manure.'[18]

Gandhi praised Mira's work in promoting composting for showing the way to enriching the soil, augmenting crop yields and saving India valuable foreign exchange. 'The task undertaken by Mirabehn is of immense magnitude,' he remarked. 'It will require thousands of Mirabehns. People should take up the work with zest and Government departments should be awake.'[19]

Shortly afterwards, writing in *Harijan*, Mira proudly reported Gandhi welcoming compost manure into what she called 'the Family of Constructive Activities'. She now urged the older members of this family to treat 'the new family member kindly, as being worthy of consideration'. For, as she pointed out,

> Compost will be helpful to *Khadi*, for it will grow better cotton.
> Compost will be helpful to Education, for it will teach sanitation, thrift, and the science of soils.
> Compost will be helpful to the Harijan, for it will provide a good living to the lowliest.
> Compost will be helpful to Hindu–Muslim unity, for it will bring us into useful touch with the peasants of both the communities.
> And, lastly, Compost will be helpful to all, for it will lead us from want to plenty.[20]

Mira's note on the virtues of compost manure was printed in the last issue of *Harijan* to go to press while Gandhi was alive. After he died, his adopted daughter went into several months of mourning, but eventually emerged with renewed zeal to fight on behalf of their shared ideals. She sought to implement them in her ashram in the Himalayan foothills and also wrote about them in *Harijan* as well as in mainstream newspapers such as the *Hindustan Times* (edited at the time by Gandhi's youngest son, Devadas). Mira hoped to reach Gandhian constructive workers via the former outlet and a wider middle-class Indian audience through the latter.

A year after Gandhi's death, Mira published a short but pungent article with the telling title 'Development or Destruction'. The article began, 'Development schemes are going on apace in India today. But are they all wise and far-sighted? Are they all for the good of the people?'

In her article, Mira took up three issues in particular:

First, the government programme for reclaiming so-called wastelands for cultivation. Mira believed that much of this was actually land traditionally used for cattle grazing, and that, rather than bring them under food or cash crops, they should be used for growing grasses and fodder crops. This would, she believed, be a 'far-sighted policy', which would save the cow, 'without whom man himself would perish'.

Second, she attacked the government's penchant for promoting 'huge new irrigation schemes' without thought to their social or environmental consequences. Mira drew attention to the 'disasters which have already come about as a result of the canal irrigation systems already established in U.P., Punjab, and Sind'. Here, ill-planned schemes of canal irrigation had led to large areas becoming waterlogged and going out of cultivation.

Finally, Mira deplored the haste with which the state was promoting the use of chemical fertilizers. She claimed that 'it is now an accepted fact among scientists, who have investigated the matter, that crops nourished with artificial fertilizers are inferior in quality to those nourished with compost (farmyard manure)'. Mira believed that 'soil fed with artificial fertilizers, though it gives a big yield for a few years, finally loses its strength, whereas soil fed with compost manure gets richer and richer in strength and texture'.

Mira was convinced that in these three schemes of so-called 'development', it 'was not the interests of the people which play the most influential part'. She suggested that it was Indian big business which stood to benefit most, writing that 'exploitation from within is even more dangerous than the former foreign exploitation, because it carries with it the glamour of apparent patriotism'.

Mira ended in a manner that, perhaps unconsciously, evoked Albert Howard's long-standing wish for closer collaboration between scientists and the public. Of the issues she had raised, namely, the dangers of ploughing up grasslands, of large irrigation schemes, and the introduction of artificial fertilizers, Mira remarked that 'technical experts are alive to these dangers, while individual farmers know them by experience. The knowledge and experience of both must be brought to the fore, and through it the administrators may see to it that development does not lead to destruction.'[21]

For Mira, the rapidity of ecological change and disturbance was a distinguishing feature of modern life. While ancient civilizations in North Africa and the Middle East had collapsed due to their abuse of the natural environment, she wrote in the *Hindustan Times* in June 1950, 'in those days it took centuries and centuries to reach complete destruction, but in these days of modern machinery and science, what took a thousand years or more in the past may be accomplished in a paltry hundred years today!'[22]

In common with J.C. Kumarappa, Mira Behn's primary concern was with rehabilitating the village economy of India. The two had got to know each other closely as fellow members of Gandhi's inner circle. After the Mahatma's death, Mira and Kumarappa contemplated working together on a project in central India, where, in a group of contiguous villages, they would put into practice their theories about rural renewal. This scheme came to naught; nonetheless, the two remained in correspondence through the 1950s, their letters marked by a peculiar mixture of nostalgia, hope and bitterness, as the economic policies of independent India departed ever further from Gandhi's vision.[23]

However, unlike Kumarappa, Mira expressed a spiritual affinity with nature, straight out of the European romantic tradition. She called herself a 'devotee of the great primeval Mother Earth'. As she wrote in April 1949:

> The tragedy today is that educated and moneyed classes are altogether out of touch with the vital fundamentals of existence—our Mother Earth, and the animal and vegetable population which she sustains. This world of Nature's planning is ruthlessly plundered, despoiled and disorganized by man whenever he gets the chance. By his science and machinery he may get huge returns for a time, but ultimately will come desolation. We have got to study Nature's balance, and develop our lives within her laws, if we are to survive as a physically healthy and morally decent species.[24]

In January–February 1952, India held its first general elections. The Congress won a comfortable majority, and Jawaharlal Nehru, himself a votary of rapid industrialization and mechanization, consolidated his position as prime minister. Among the minority of writers who did not share his views was his fellow former freedom-fighter, Mira. She wrote in private to Nehru about her disenchantment with the political and economic path free India was following.[25] Meanwhile, in a printed article in *Harijan*, Mira advocated a radical return to Gandhian principles. She outlined a charter of eighteen points to this effect, these including a simplification of the government machinery, a closer association of peasants and workers in the administrative process, a new electoral system emphasizing local councils rather than a national Parliament, competed for by non-party candidates, a moratorium on development schemes such as large dams and chemical farming until their benefits and costs were properly assessed, an education system based not on Western models but on Gandhi's template of 'Basic Education', etc.

Mira wrote of her utopian Gandhian charter that it was 'merely an outline'. It was drafted in her new ashram in the interior hills, in a remote part of what was once the princely state of Tehri Garhwal. 'Far away in these vast mountains,' she wrote, 'I have no one to consult but the Himalayan forests and Eternal Snows (for fundamentals indeed the best advisers), and naturally the points adumbrated here will undergo additions and embellishments when discussed and worked out in consultation with others.'[26]

Some months later, Mira published an 'Open Letter to Congress Leaders' in the *Hindustan Times*. This was in the form of a parable, an imaginary visit to the countryside accompanying a Congress minister to acquaint him with the real problems of peasants and artisans. The letter was written in the hope that the Congress would not continue to function as 'a commonplace political party' any more, but as a guide and servant to the people, as Gandhi had intended it to be. The article satirized the minister's love of cars and offices, his retinue of hangers-on, his air of appearing extremely busy and preoccupied. It ended with this plea from Mira to the unnamed, but archetypal, minister:

> If the voice of the rural masses unites in its demand for Bapu Raj, will the Congress have the courage to concede the demand? Here lies the crux of the whole question. *Is the voice of the parasitic few to count, or the voice of the productive many*? I beg you, with all the love of old friendship in my heart, to take this thought home with you and let it enter your innermost

being, from whence spring the intuitions that constitute our truest guide.[27]

Among the hallmarks of Mira's thinking was her deep appreciation of the role played by trees and forests in the economic and cultural life of rural India. Whereas most economists and agronomists focused narrowly on making the cultivated field more productive and profitable, Mira understood the intimate connections between agriculture, animal husbandry and a healthy forest cover. As she wrote in an article published in both *Harijan* and the *Hindustan Times*: 'Land, cattle and forests are so closely connected with one another, that we cannot interfere with one without dislocating the other two.'

This article went on to outline a scheme for the wiser and more sustainable use of land in India. Mira was against ongoing programmes involving the large-scale colonization, and bringing under the plough, of areas the state had erroneously classified as 'wasteland' and 'culturable waste'. Such areas were, she pointed out, being used presently for cattle grazing. She wrote that 'a good deal of land ploughed up in this manner will have to be returned to the cattle and also land for forest blocks will have to be allotted as, without cattle and without trees, India would, before long, become a desert, tractors and artificial manure accelerating the process'.[28]

Prior to Independence, Uttar Pradesh was characterized by a feudal system of landholding, with massive tracts owned by individual landlords known as zamindars. These holdings were then subdivided into tiny plots cultivated by tenants and sharecroppers. After Independence, the Congress decided that the government would take over these lands, after paying the zamindars monetary compensation, and carve them out into small plots owned directly by those who tilled them. This policy was not without merit, except that no account was taken of the fact that zamindars also owned large patches of forest. Fearing that these too would be taken over by the state, they chose to fell all the standing trees and sell them for use as timber and firewood. The zamindars would lose the lands anyway; why not, they thought, make a profit from the standing trees before the state moved in?

The savagery with which the zamindars felled their forests moved Mira to write an eloquent plea on behalf of what was being lost. She cast it as a lament for the haldu tree, an indigenous deciduous species with yellow flowers often planted near temples and with a variety of medicinal and other uses. 'The Haldu tree is no more,' she wrote, '[h]e who stood guard over the little Shiva Shrines. Every day I used to honour him in my heart. Mighty of girth, with a glorious span of countless boughs, each one gracefully curved and yet conforming in the aggregate to a perfect outline. He was indeed the king of haldus, aged some 80 to 100 years.'

This particular tree Mira had grown to love was killed when 'ruthless hands were laid on him, the itching palms of the Zamindar'. This tree and thousands like it, 'had fallen to the axe of greed'. Nor was this zamindar an exception; indeed, 'they are nearly all looting their Zamindaris as fast as they possibly can before the liquidation takes place. Lakhs upon lakhs of trees have fallen in this shameless scramble throughout India.' This, Mira sadly noted, was an ecological as much as an economic or spiritual catastrophe, for 'trees are the precious wealth of the land, giving shelter, drawing rain, and protecting the soil. It takes no time to cut them down, but it takes years and years for trees to grow.'[29]

Mira had sent a draft of the lament to Chakravarti Rajagopalachari, then serving his brief term as the last Governor General of India, and one of the very few former freedom fighters whom she felt had not entirely betrayed their shared Gandhian heritage. Rajaji (as he was known) was a politician with a literary sensibility, and Mira had in the past asked him to edit her drafts. This time he didn't, mischievously remarking: 'You will feel thankful no doubt that I did not, zamindar-like, bring my axe on any of its branches.'

Mira's lament for the fallen haldu tree reminded Rajaji of the first verse of the Ramayana, where the sage Valmiki bursts into verse at seeing a bird shot by an archer in the forest, leading to the composition of the entire epic in that same rhythm and metre. He told Mira that her prose-poem 'greatly resembles that sloka of Valmiki', which he now rendered in this translation: 'Cruel hunter! You shall have no rest or peace in your long life, for you have shot down this beautiful bird even while it was in the rapture of love and joy with its mate.'[30]

The Englishwoman's profound understanding of the place of forests in Indian life was perhaps best expressed in an article she published in the *Hindustan Times* in the summer of 1950. This was prompted by the rising concern about the growing incidence of floods in the Himalaya. Some had attributed this to deforestation in the upper catchment of the hill rivers; nuancing this interpretation, Mira pointed out that the cause was not deforestation per se, but a relatively recent change in the species composition of the Himalayan forests. This was the replacement on the mountains' southern slopes of Banj oak (*Quercus incana*) by Chil (or Chir) pine (*Pinus roxburghii*), a transformation of which she had become 'painfully aware' since coming to the hills some years ago.

To the city reader, Mira explained in some detail 'why the Banj is so much better than the Chil pine for holding back the waters of the monsoon rains'. She wrote of how, in Banj forests, there was a dense litter of fallen leaves on the ground, as well as an undergrowth of bushes, creepers and grass. This absorbed most of the rainwater, which then slowly percolated to lower altitudes, replenishing the 'beautiful sweet and cool springs' for villagers to draw upon.

On the other hand, 'the Chil pine produced just the opposite effect', since pine forests were characterized by little undergrowth. The floor was littered with pine needles which absorbed none of the rainwater. Thus, 'when the torrential rains of the monsoon beat down on these southern slopes of the Himalayas, much of the pine-needle carpet gets washed away with the water and erosion invariably takes place'.

Mira argued that Chil pine was replacing Banj oak for two reasons: the active propagation of the pine by the Forest Department since its timber and resin were commercially valuable; and the disintegration of a spirit of community, so that individual villagers lopped off oak branches in an uncoordinated manner and without a concern for the future.

Mira urged that the Forest Department and the villagers co-operate to bring back oak at the expense of pine. For, as she remarked, 'the Banj [oak] forests are the very centre of nature's economic cycle on the southern slopes of the Himalaya. To destroy them is to cut out the heart and thus bring death to the whole structure.' Her article ended with this heartfelt plea: 'The forests of the Himalaya are the Guardians of the Northern Plains, which, in their turn, are the Granary of India. Surely such guardians deserve the utmost care and attention that the Government can give them.'[31]

In 1959 Mira left India and returned to Europe. There were several reasons for this: thirty years of arduous work and travel in a tropical climate had weakened her body; the Indian state's betrayal of Gandhian principles had saddened her mind and heart; and she had rediscovered her love of Beethoven and turned to his music to restore her soul. She contemplated returning to her original homeland, England, but eventually chose to settle near Vienna, a city where Beethoven was buried and in whose woods he had walked.

Back in Europe, Mira had her autobiography (which she had written in her last years in India) published in England and the United States, and also brought out a short selection of quotes from Gandhi. She then set to work on a book on Beethoven. Meanwhile, she was reading the Western press, and following with interest the belated development of an environmental consciousness. Rachel Carson's landmark book *Silent Spring*, published in 1962, was being widely read in the Continent (translations in European languages were appearing) and scientists in Britain, the Netherlands, Germany and France were also publishing tracts about chemical contamination of the air, soil and waters. Besides, in their daily lives Europeans were confronting the pollution and habitat loss caused by a century of mostly unregulated industrialization.

In the West, there was now a burgeoning environmental movement, and Mira, resident once more in the West, was determined to contribute to it, albeit with insights garnered from her years living in the East. In Vienna, Mira subscribed to the *Guardian Weekly*, where, in September 1968, she read a report on the proceedings of a UNESCO conference held in Paris 'of Experts regarding the Biosphere'. She at once wrote a letter to the *Guardian*, introducing herself as 'the British Admiral's daughter who joined Gandhi in 1925, and remained in India for 33 years, where I was known as Mira behn', and adding that the subject of the UN Conference 'is one that has been uppermost in my mind all these years, and many a time have I pleaded with Mr. Nehru and his Ministers for less destructive development'.

To this letter—written in November 1968—Mira appended an appeal which she hoped the *Guardian Weekly* would publish. There is no sign that they did, but fortunately there is a copy in her papers. Mira praised the UN conference for focusing attention on 'the headlong destruction and pollution in which man is now blindly engaged' but urged the experts to not merely speak to and amongst themselves. The conference itself carried the wordy title: 'The Inter-Governmental Conference of Experts on the Scientific Basis for the Rational Utilisation and Conservation of Biospheric Resources', of which Mira commented, 'in simpler words protection of and co-operation with Nature's healthy balance'.

Mira suggested that the *Guardian* 'might publish a series of articles written by experts (but in easily understood language), each dealing with one particular aspect—air pollution, water pollution, destruction of vegetation etc. as also the overall psychological effects on man'. Some might argue that 'no amount of writing and talking is going to stop people from this self-destruction, and only disaster will awaken them', she said, yet she believed that 'nevertheless it is obviously the bounden duty of those who do realize what is happening, to make the truth as widely and intelligibly known as possible, and to encourage thereby constructive thinking and planning before it is too late. It is a matter in which every man, woman and child has to play a part, this planning and thinking, therefore, has to spread amongst the masses and not be left only to experts.'[32]

Apart from the *Guardian Weekly*, Mira was also reading the *International Herald Tribune* (*IHT*), published from Paris. In April 1974, she wrote to the editor of the *IHT* saying:

> I am following with deep interest, through your excellent paper, the various ideas that are being expressed concerning the Environmental Crisis, but nowhere do I find that drastic, down-to-the-roots approach which was the characteristic of Mahatma

> Gandhi's outlook. As nothing short of such an approach seems likely to bring real relief to humanity in its present predicament, I have felt obliged to express my thoughts in the enclosed article which I very much hope may appeal to you for publication. I might add that I joined Gandhi in 1925, and remained in direct personal contact with him throughout the rest of his life.[33]

The article Mira sent the *IHT* was called 'Drastic Change or Self-destruction'. Sadly, a copy does not survive, but we do have the letter Mira wrote to the editor after he had told her he could not publish what she had written. Here, she referred to an interview the paper had carried with the American environmental thinker Lewis Mumford. The letter noted that 'Mumford's ideas closely resemble mine' and ended by telling the editor that 'you will find me again taking a chance with you with some other article, because I very fully realize the value of contacting your widely spread readers'.[34]

Mira's original article was probably akin in its arguments to a typescript from the same period that does survive. This began: 'Everything had been going on merrily, and we were being told that a wonderful new world was opening up. But the wonderful new world is now proving to be a death-trap. Day after day we read in the newspapers of the deadly tide of pollution which is overtaking us—on all sides poison and ever increasing piles of waste; waste which represents reckless destruction of the Earth's natural resources.'

Mira described a typical department store with its profusion of goods, many superfluous to the necessities of human life; and then the streets of a typical Western city, 'the stream of motor traffic pouring out poisonous fumes, causing intolerable noise and jamming up the city streets'. Scenes such as these, she remarked, showed that 'we are caught in the meshes of a gigantic mechanized, money-making economy—*produce and sell, produce and sell,* on the one hand, and *buy and throw away, buy and throw away,* on the other'.

In this context of these threats to nature and human existence, Mira argued that 'we must fundamentally change our outlook and way of life. *We must simplify if we are to survive*'.

To move towards this larger ideal, she suggested that some Western government promote a small experiment which could then be scaled up to the level of a nation. 'The objective of the Experimental Area,' wrote Mira, 'would be to work out durable co-operation between Man and Nature, using science and technology wherever they can help without harming.'

Of her proposed scheme, Mira said that

> the average people of Europe and America have to be kept in mind. It is in nowise envisaged as a sectarian venture. If we are to overcome pollution, and make friends with Nature, we have all still got to join hands. We have also to bring the animals back into our lives. Man is rapidly becoming the only living creature in his environment (except for pet cats and dogs), and this is doing him incalculable harm. Not only is he becoming dehumanized by continual contact with machines, but elimination of animal-power in agriculture has, at the same time, eliminated much of our best material for ripening organic matter, without which the soil becomes impoverished.

After outlining her old objections to chemical fertilizers (rendering crops prone to disease, etc.), Mira said the newer methods of power-driven agriculture sped up work but only by discarding man and beast. 'We have got to orientate ourselves in such a way,' she wrote, 'that speed is no longer a prime objective; indeed it is high time to weigh up in all matters the advantages and disadvantages of speed.'

Mira called for a reorientation of the social and economic structure of the modern world, towards more decentralized forms of production, habitation and governance. Farmers would ideally live on their lands, not in villages that look and feel like miniature towns. Industrial units should be small, with workers living within walking distance of them. Mira accepted that, for such materials as iron and steel,

> the Experimental Area would, of course, be dependent on the modern world, but if the ideal of decentralization and minimum use of power-driven machinery could show the way to an unpolluted world which would automatically be free of industrial disputes and the spiral of rising prices and wages, it would arrest the situation of the restless, rushing, poisoned world of today.[35]

When her first effort was spurned, Mira persisted (as she had warned the editor), and was successful this time. In her papers is a three-page typescript entitled 'A Suggestion', with a line saying 'published in New York Herald Tribune, Paris, November 4 1974'. This reiterated her argument that governments should themselves create demonstration areas to show how ecological and social problems could be solved. She wrote:

> My belief is that if people could see with their own eyes functioning models of decentralized, self-sufficient and self-expressive communities, large numbers would opt for living in a similar way. This should set in motion a voluntary movement in which the right direction which, if handled carefully, could develop into a regular revolution—a revolution fostered by government, instead of the alternative of head-on clashes between government and the masses, with strikes, riots and possible civil war.

Mira thought the burden of restoring the earth's ecological integrity lay on the shoulders of the richer nations that were themselves primarily responsible for creating the problems the world now confronted. 'It is, of course, in the highly developed parts of the world, like Europe and America,' she wrote, 'where the disastrous effects of ecological disruption are already alarming the public, that these Projects would have the most powerful impact on world opinion, while, at the same time, helping to open the eyes of the developing countries who are at present all bent on imitating the "economic growth" of the industrialized world.'[36]

While following—and occasionally intervening—in Western environmental debates, Mira was yet keeping a keen (and worried) eye on what was happening back in India. Through the 1960s and 1970s she sent a steady stream of letters and articles to friends and newspaper editors in her adopted land, these largely focusing on the continuing ecological decline of the Himalayan region in which she had once lived.

In December 1967, a conference on 'Social Work in the Himalaya' was organized by the University of Delhi. Invited to participate, Mira posted the organizers a paper from Austria, where she raised five important issues concerning development strategies in the Himalaya.

The first was the potential of small irrigation schemes for meeting the water needs of Himalayan peasants. 'Much could be done (and should long ago have been attended to),' she wrote, 'by helping the villagers to tap the little springs and streams so as to conduct them into the fields and villages.'

The second, a subject she had written about in the past and would return to in the future, was the vital importance of forest conservation. 'In a sense this item should stand first,' she observed, 'for, without the forest, the mountains would become eroded, springless heights.'

The third theme was the improvement of cattle stock, for settled cultivators as well as for nomadic herdsmen. Both required good breeding bulls, and both required attention to a source of steady and sustainable fodder supply.

The fourth theme was the renewal of village industries. Mira believed that the weaving traditions of the Bhotiyas of the frontier areas had real promise; their woollen cloth, she thought, 'would sell "like hot cakes" in London's Bond Street, if left unprocessed and with still a smell of the raw wool about it, as in the Scotch tweeds'.

Finally, Mira wrote about the question of road-building in the Himalaya. After the India–China war of 1962 there was a call for all-weather tarred roads to be built all across the hills, to transport troops to the border. Mira, on the other hand, felt that motor roads were of limited benefit to the local people. She also drew attention to the ecological damage they caused, through debris being thrown by contractors down the hillsides, damaging the fields and blocking watercourses.[37]

Mira had long criticized the fascination that the Indian state had for building large dams. She believed that these projects were economically wasteful, environmentally damaging and socially unjust. In the summer of 1972, she read a newspaper report about the plight of villagers ousted by the Pong dam in Himachal Pradesh, who hadn't been provided alternative housing, schools, etc., by the government. They did not even have access to drinking water. Mira wrote about this to an old colleague, Krishna Murti Gupta, who had once worked with her in her hill ashrams. After his mentor left for Europe, Gupta established a body called the Himalaya Seva Sangh, which sought to co-ordinate social work in the hills. The report on the Pong dam, said Mira, 'shows up a thoroughly bad business for the poor Himalayan peasants who have been turned out of their homes. I wonder if your Sangh has taken up the matter. If not it is surely a thing it should investigate. It might prove to be a case suitable for true Satyagraha.'[38]

The following year, Mira sent Gupta a note about what sort of work his Himalaya Seva Sangh should focus on. She worried that those in charge of hill development were 'much too much under the influence of city people, and particularly the *Tourism Business*, which means purely and simply selling one's soul to the devil'. She was shocked that, to promote tourism in the hills, the government was contemplating constructing 'landing-spaces for aircraft, cable-ways, motor roads and the inevitable Luxury Hotels and Rest Houses'. She urged the Sangh to refocus the attention of the state on what the hill people really needed,

> such as good mule paths, small bridges for foot passengers and pack-animals, good stud bulls and rams of a suitable breed, good quality seed (not of the fancy kind requiring artificial fertilizers, pesticides and heavy irrigation), development of the wool industry and other local industries like mat and basket making from Ringal, small tanks and channels for dealing with rain water ... and above all what they need is a voice in their own affairs, and not to be dictated to by the city folks of the plains.

Mira had read that the Himalaya Seva Sangh wished to undertake programmes of afforestation. 'If this study is to be of any real value,' she told her erstwhile colleagues, 'it must be guided by some genuine, unbiased ecologist and not by the Government Forest Department which is doing untold harm to the ecological balance of the Himalayan mountains.' Mira thought the Himalaya Seva Sangh had 'a grand opportunity to show the desperate need of a new policy for the whole area', and they would do well to grasp it.[39]

Most of the India-related material in the Mira Behn papers relates to the Himalaya. However, the papers also contain a note written in October 1974, which dealt with the path of development for India as a whole. This began by deploring the country's dependence on imported oil, whose price had tripled as a consequence of the Arab–Israeli war of 1973. Mira praised the spread of windmills in Australia, which generated power for water pumps in the countryside. She urged India to get access to this windmill technology, which 'would be a start in the right direction of decentralization and self-sufficiency'. The note then moved on to her old bugbear, chemical fertilizers, the excessive use of which, in her view, 'leaves the soil more fragile year by year and in need of heavier & heavier doses of chemical fertilizer to keep it yielding'. She praised afresh the work, in India itself, of 'scientists like Sir Albert Howard who have developed and tested the value of composted organic matter'. Mira noted that in the West, 'people are becoming seriously interested in this science of the soil', and poignantly asked, 'Why cannot India's thousands of educated unemployed be drawn together in camps for quick training in this science and then take it far & wide into the villages?'

Mira concluded her note by urging the land of Gandhi to take the lead in showing a better way forward. 'The whole world,' she wrote, 'is beset by a crisis which no country can escape, not even the most powerful. ... But if India could put life back into her soil & through that back into her villages, who will decentralize power and industrialization, she could lead the way to human survival.'[40]

Because of her close connection to Gandhi, and the several long terms in prison she herself underwent, Mira was held in high personal regard by those nationalists who manned the high offices of the Indian state after the country became independent. She therefore had the confidence to write directly to Prime Minister Jawaharlal Nehru and President Rajendra Prasad, among others, about her reservations with regard to the path of centralized economic development that India had embarked upon in the 1950s. For their part, Nehru and Prasad always acknowledged her letters and responded to them with courtesy, even if they did not care to follow the advice offered therein.

Mira had great affection for Nehru's daughter, Indira Gandhi, whom she had known as a child. The affection was reciprocated. In 1971, when she was prime minister, Indira Gandhi visited Austria and called on Mira, who was then in her eightieth year. Observing her frail health and fraught economic condition, the prime minister asked the Indian embassy to take care of her medical expenses.

In 1977 the Congress Party lost the general elections and Indira Gandhi was replaced as prime minister by Morarji Desai. Mira knew Morarji too, from their days together in the freedom movement. In the winter of 1978–79 she wrote to the new prime minister about the replacement of oak by pine and the erosion and floods this had caused. Morarji replied saying that he 'share[d] your anxiety over the erosion in the Himalayas by destruction of forests', adding that he was 'very happy to see you are keeping in fine fettle turning your mind over the problems that beset the country'.

The prime minister passed on Mira's letter and concerns to the minister of Agriculture, S.S. Barnala, under whose ministry the Forest Department then lay. Briefed by his officials, the minister replied to Mira claiming that 'the Forest Departments are taking care to protect Oak wherever it exists and they are not replacing it with Chir pine. Nowhere has Chir pine been planted to replace oak.'

Mira wrote back to the minister rebutting these claims. In the five years she lived in Garhwal, she said, she 'did not see the slightest sign' of any protection the Forest Department had provided oak. On the other hand, she had seen 'many areas of pure Chir pine in the Banj zone', with the conversion actively aided by the Forest Department.[41]

With her reply, Mira attached a dozen photographs she had herself taken in the 1950s, demonstrating the replacement of oak with pine, and its environmental consequences. She sent the photos to the prime minister too, telling him: 'How good it would be if these photographs which I took 25 years ago, could at last serve the purpose for which they were meant, namely, to convince those who had the power to act, that immediate action was vitally necessary. Now, with so much Government policy being reorientated, I have every hope that the Himalayas will at last receive their due.'[42]

Morarji Desai's government did not last its full term, and in January 1980 Indira Gandhi returned as prime minister. Mira wrote her a brief message of congratulation and, after her son Sanjay died later in the year, a longer letter of condolence. She said her heart went out to Indira when she heard the news on the radio. However, she did not want to send a perfunctory telegram, 'but rather to wait & write you my deeper thoughts'. She told Indira that she was now in her eighty-eighth year, and it was fifty-five years since she joined Gandhi ('you were then a little girl'). 'What years we have been through since then!' she remarked. And now, wrote Mira, the shock of Sanjay's death 'brings us face to face with the question of the yet unknown future for India'.

Mira wrote to Indira that while she did not subscribe to any orthodox religion, 'the older one grows the more clearly one sees an all-pervading Spirit encompassing the whole of creation, and this spirit manifests itself to us through nature'. She observed that 'it is not conquest of but cooperation with Nature that can mend the [present] world situation, and how candidly Sanjay emphasized this in his call for trees, trees & even more trees. If his dynamic character could have achieved this ideal, India's landscape would have been transformed, & with that, the climate, the economy & the well-being of her people. What grander service to his memory could there be than the fulfilment of this ideal—May strength be yours to work towards [that] goal!!!'[43]

This was a warm, generous, and very delicately worded letter. As Mira surely knew, Sanjay Gandhi was a controversial figure in India, for his bullying ways, his intolerance of democratic procedure, his insistence that the government compulsorily sterilize adult men. However, writing now to the bereaved mother, Mira spoke only of what she herself found most appealing in Sanjay—his love of nature and of trees.

Indira wrote back a short but dignified reply, thanking Mira for her message while saying that 'Sanjay was so full of fun and so vibrantly alive it is difficult to realize that he isn't there any more'.[44]

A little over a year later, in October 1981, Mira wrote to Indira Gandhi about the world situation, which was 'growing worse & worse'. She hesitated to trespass on the prime minister's time, but nonetheless there was, she wrote, 'one fundamental thought I want to express while there is time'. She then offered a suggestion, incidentally one she had placed before Nehru while he was prime minister too (though she did not remind Nehru's daughter of this). I quote: 'Of all the big Schemes & Projects to place before you, the one of first priority should be: *Progressive removal of mechanization & chemical fertilizers in Agriculture.* In this lies relief to the precious soil as well as to the ever increasing unemployment & social unrest. Big Business armed with modern technology is the very devil!!'[45]

In her reply, the prime minister did not refer to the proposal for agricultural reform offered by Mira. However, she wished Mira on her impending birthday and then remarked: 'I share Europe's widespread concern over the violence that is growing.

Peace movements are heartening but I doubt if they will have much effect on Governments.'[46]

This correspondence was conducted in the second half of 1981. Mira was now eighty-nine years old. It had been more than twenty years since she left India, yet she still cared deeply for the country and worried deeply for its future. In January 1982, Mira was awarded the Padma Vibhushan, the Republic of India's second highest honour, for which she had been nominated by the prime minister herself. Since she was unable to travel to New Delhi to receive it in person, the award was bestowed on her by the Indian ambassador to Austria. Mira died in June of the same year.

In 1992, on the occasion of the birth centenary of the Englishwoman once known as Madeleine Slade, her devoted Indian associate Krishna Murti Gupta brought out a book collecting her writings and letters. He prefaced his selection with a fifty-page biographical portrait, where he noted that, 'apart from participating in the trials and tribulations of the masses and fighting for their freedom', Mira had 'won a prominent place among the early environmentalists. Her deep attachment to forests and to birds and animals and all living creatures was unique.'

Although Mira was Western by birth and upbringing, she was, as Gupta remarked, 'absolutely free from a Westerner's arrogance. At the same time, she remained unimpressed by the oriental pride that is evinced by Eastern thinkers'. Inspired by Gandhi, she had developed a universalistic outlook 'from which self and narrow-mindedness were eliminated'. Gupta himself hoped that 'her goal as well as journey will be remembered by all those who share her deep concern for man, nature and God'.[47]

I'd like to end this chapter, however, with the words of Mira herself, from a note which Gupta himself probably never saw, since I found it in a recently released collection of Gandhi's own papers. Titled 'Freedom', this note was handwritten by Mira in 1936, a year or so after she and Gandhi had moved to central India. It captures the ethical and spiritual basis of her ecological philosophy, her deep concern for humans, nature and God.

Here is the note in full:

Freedom

Come out from the world of men & houses onto the uplands of open country, & feel a vast freedom fill your soul!

Why live forever shut up physically & mentally? Walls & roofs, noise & smoke, hamper the body, while manmade problems and anxieties, quarrels & misunderstandings, set in a background of a thousand nothings, hamper the mind.

There on the hill across the fields, is the vast world of God, marching to the rhythm of His eternal Being. There the pure breeze passes over the grass whispering to the memory of the eons passed & the eons to come—softly it blows, buffeting gently, & the soul is wafted away, away, away—whither?—whither?? Yes, towards that somewhere wherever we have come, & whither we are going. Overhead great columns of clouds are passing by. The Earth breaths up her fragrance to Heaven & the benediction of Heaven is shed upon the Earth.

The elements are the rhythm of the breath of God.

There was a time when man lived in harmony with that rhythm, & until he again finds & follows it, there can be no true Freedom for him.

Mira[48]

CHAPTER SEVEN

Culture in Nature

THE FOREST ANTHROPOLOGY OF VERRIER ELWIN

IN APRIL 1931, MAHATMA Gandhi was in Bombay, having just been released from prison by the colonial state. At an inter-faith prayer meeting, he had on one side his adopted daughter Mira (formerly Madeleine Slade), and on the other a young man named Verrier Elwin, an Oxford scholar who had come to the subcontinent four years previously. This was a delicious irony; that an Indian considered by the Raj to be an 'Enemy of the British Empire' sat for his prayers flanked on either side by a person of British origin.[1]

Verrier Elwin was born in 1902, the son of a colonial bishop. His father died when he was six, and Verrier was raised by a mother committed to a particularly fanatical form of evangelical Christianity. The boy studied first at Dean Close School and then at Merton College, Oxford, where he took first-class degrees in literature and theology. Soon afterwards, he was ordained as a priest in the Church of England.

His mother hoped Verrier would become a bishop like his father. The son had other ideas. In 1927 he travelled to India to join the Christa Seva Sangh, a small sect seeking to indigenize Christianity, founded in Poona by an English priest named J.C. Winslow who admired Gandhi. The admiration was passed on to the protégé. Soon Elwin was spending time with the Mahatma in the Sabarmati ashram and writing eloquently worded tracts advancing the cause of Indian freedom.

In time, Elwin found the Christa Seva Sangh too confining for his sensibilities. In 1932, seeking to root himself even more firmly in Indian soil, he moved to a forest village in the Mandla district of the Central Provinces. For the next thirty years, he lived and worked amongst India's tribal peoples. Tribals were scorned and condescended to by urban as well as peasant society (itself dominantly Hindu), and to redress this Elwin wrote polemical pamphlets and articles in the press urging a greater respect for their culture and a safeguarding of their traditional rights in land and forests. His complete immersion in tribal culture was signified by his marriage to a Gond woman, Kosi, in 1941; when that marriage broke down, he married another tribal, Lila.

In the 1930s and 1940s Elwin ranged widely across the tribal heartland in central India, writing a series of books on the folklore, religion, art and economic life of different communities. Once an ordained priest, Elwin became a bitter critic of Christian missionaries and turned his back on his ancestral faith. A worshipful admirer of Gandhi in his early years in India, after living with the tribals he came to reject aspects of the Gandhian credo, such as its opposition to alcohol consumption and its emphasis on sexual restraint.

In 1954 Elwin moved to the northeast of India, where he served as an anthropological adviser to Nehru's government. He was assigned to a remote and unsurveyed area then known as the North-East Frontier Agency, bordering China. His work here was to study how these previously unstudied communities lived and thought, with a view to bringing them closer, emotionally and otherwise, to the Indian nation.

This chapter will focus in the main on what I have called Elwin's 'forest anthropology', his ethnographic and literary explorations of the intimate ties between tribal culture and the forest environment in which it enacted itself. However, Elwin's environmental sensibilities were manifested early, before he became an anthropologist. As a young boy, he developed a passion for the poetry of William Wordsworth. He presented a paper to his school's literary society on Wordsworth's 'nature-philosophy', attracting strong reactions from those present, pro as well as con. A classmate at Oxford remembered him as always having a copy of Wordsworth's poems in his pockets, and doubtless his enthusiasm was deepened in the classroom, where one of his teachers, H.W. Garrod, was himself a great authority on the poet.[2]

Elwin came to India in November 1927, when he was twenty-five. Three and a half years later, after having met Gandhi several times and also read his writings, he wrote an article in a Calcutta periodical comparing the English poet he had grown up with to the Indian politician he was now coming to know. As a student and admirer of both, he believed that 'on a number of points the life and outlook of these two thinkers exhibit a surprising concordance'.

Among the similarities between Gandhi and Wordsworth was that both valorized the spinning wheel, seeing it as intrinsic to peasant culture. Each thought the village the natural and normal abode of humans. Elwin quoted Wordsworth as saying that it was only in rural life that 'the passions of men are incorporated with the beautiful and permanent forms of nature'. He then reproduced two stanzas from *Song at the Feast of Brougham Castle*, of which the first (a particular favourite of his) ran:

Love had the fount in huts where poor men lie:
His daily teachers had been woods and rills.
The silence that is in the starry sky,
The sleep that is among the lonely hills.

Elwin spoke of Wordsworth's opposition to the railway planned for the Lake District, which the poet held to be a desecration of nature and of the integrity of country life. He then came to the theme of freedom, a shared passion of Gandhi's and Wordsworth's. The poet's 'naturally independent spirit', he remarked, 'was developed by the broad free spaces of his own loved Lake-land'.

'In these and other ways,' observed Elwin in conclusion, 'we see the close affinity between the great moral teacher of the English Revival and the great moral teacher of the Indian Renaissance of today.' The Englishman turning himself into an Indian saw Wordsworth as having the advantage 'in power of expression, and perhaps in the range of speculative imagination'; on the other hand, 'as a master of the art of living, as an artist who has drawn for the world an ideal picture of ennobled existence, as a practical idealist who has found it impossible to soothe the hungry millions with any poem but one, invigorating food, Gandhiji is immeasurably superior.'[3]

In his days as an Oxford scholar, Elwin had steeped himself in medieval religious history, and developed a particular fascination for the life of St Francis. Some years after he arrived in India,

Elwin wrote a slim book on the saint of Assisi, an offering 'to the great Eastern world [where] Francis is still too little known'.

This book itself remains too little known, even within Elwin's oeuvre, where his ethnographic studies and especially his autobiography, *The Tribal World of Verrier Elwin*, loom large. Yet it bears remembering today, in part because it sought determinedly to make St Francis accessible to Indians, in larger part because it may have been one of the first modern studies to present the saint as an environmentalist.

Early in his book, Elwin pointed out that by preaching to the birds, and moving to and among them, St Francis 'established a moral relationship between man and nature'.[4] This theme is developed in a chapter significantly entitled 'The Fellowship of Nature'. 'Before the time of Francis,' noted Elwin, 'Christianity did not know quite what to do with nature.' Before St Francis, 'for most people nature was a temptation either to one's senses or to one's theology'. On the other hand, St Francis experienced 'a real power of goodness stemming forth from all created things and in the virtues and actions of natural objects he saw a heavenly harmony'. He would insist 'on every part of the garden being left free so that the grass and flowers might show forth the love of Him, who is called the "flower of the field" and the "lily of the valley"'. And so 'he talked with the flowers and preached to the birds, at home in the world, for the world was at home with him'.

Elwin told the Indian reader stories of St Francis's love for all living creatures. He wrote of how one winter the priest saved bees from dying in the cold. He picked up little worms and put them in a safe place, where they would not be crushed underfoot. He hated to see animals in captivity—in Siena he freed turtle doves from a cage and made nests for them.

In his love of nature, wrote Elwin, St Francis was a true Christian. 'Christ was the Rock, and therefore he [Francis] walked over rocks and stones with a special reverence. He would not allow the brothers to cut down the whole of a tree; always the stump must remain with the chance of growing again.'[5]

Elwin noted the kinship between the ideas of St Francis and those known to Indian tradition. He spoke thus of 'the reverence for every form of life' as a characteristic of Indian saintliness, of how Indian epics admitted birds and animals into the fellowship of men. Yudhishthira refused to enter heaven without the dog that was accompanying him, Rama chose the monkey Hanuman as his retainer, and each god had an appropriate animal as their vehicle or companion. Some medieval saints had ties of deep affection with birds and animals. The seventeenth-century Marathi poet Tukaram asked that we 'embrace spiritually animals and trees'. When he disturbed a hive of bees and they settled on him, he refused to drive them off, saying, 'this body of mine is doomed to perish; let it spend itself in the service of other creatures'.

In the life of these Indian saints, as indeed of St Francis, wrote Elwin, 'the noble idea of Ahimsa [non-violence] ... blossoms into a deep and tender love for all creation, into a sense of unity with natural beauty and of kinship with its animals'.[6]

When Elwin moved to the tribal country in 1932, with him was an Indian Christian, Shamrao Hivale, who had a profound empathy with the poor and disadvantaged. The region they based themselves in was dominated by the Gond tribe. The Gonds were themselves settled agriculturists. Alongside them and in the same district lived other tribal communities such as the Pardhans, who were minstrels by profession, the Agaria, who practised a traditional form of iron-making, and the Baiga, who were swidden agriculturists.

Elwin and Hivale lived first in a village named Karanjia in the Mandla district of the Central Provinces. They established a Gond Seva Mandal, which, notwithstanding its name, sought to serve all the communities in the district, not just the Gonds. They set up a medical clinic, ran a school and mediated in social disputes. Hivale's natural penchant was to minister and serve, whereas Elwin's was to travel, read and write.

Unlike the Indo-Gangetic plains to the north, or indeed the Deccan plateau to the south, the land of the Gonds was dominated by well-wooded hills. From the first, Elwin was struck by the role played by the forests in the economic as well as cultural life of the tribals. The woods provided the Gonds, Baigas and others with fuel, fodder and medicinal plants, timber for agricultural implements and homes, and even food (in the form of tubers, roots and fruits) in times of scarcity.

The significance of the forests in tribal life is a running theme in Elwin's writings. In 1935, three years after moving to Mandla, he published a collection of Gond folk poetry. Hivale was listed as a co-author; though he helped with the research and the translation it was the literary scholar from England who wrote the scene-setting introduction. Here Elwin remarked:

> The real culture of the Gonds and Baigas is to be found in their songs and dances. Here is a poetry free of all literary convention and allusions: a poetry of earth and sky, of forest, hill and river, of the changing seasons and the varied passions of men: a poetry of love, naked and unashamed, unchecked by any inhibition or restraint. When Wordsworth says that in humble and rustic life, 'the essential passions of the heart find a better soil in which they can attain their maturity, are less under restraint and speak a plainer and more emphatic language; because in that condition of life our elementary feelings co-exist in a state of greater simplicity' he is describing exactly the poetry of the Gonds.[7]

Several of the songs in the book were accompaniments to a traditional dance form of the Gonds, known as the Karma. Elwin explained that the dance was 'filled with the breath of trees'; indeed, it 'symbolizes the bringing of green branches of the forest in the spring'. The to and fro of the dancers' movements was akin to 'the steady urge of wind coming and going among the tree tops'. One song accompanying the dance was itself 'the cry of a thousand living trees, the music of the drums is the steady beat of the moving branches'.[8]

Elwin continued:

> There can be no doubt of the intense love of the Gonds for the forest. They often stop and point out some scene of special beauty. The loneliness and grandeur of the forest intoxicates them. Their songs are full of vivid little pictures ... of forest and village scenes—bullocks returning home in the evening through a fine drizzle of rain, fish leaping about and scattering the mud in the dried bed of a stream, the lovely little red and yellow raimuntya bird hopping about the courtyard, a green parrot on a red hill, tiger's footmarks in the mud at the top of a lonely pass, dry leaves flaming in the forest fire, the bee among the blue petals of an arsi flower sipping first on one side, then on the other, the peacock spreading its fanlike tail, a dog barking at the moon and the night red with torches as the villagers come out to see what is the matter.[9]

In 1936 Elwin published *Leaves from the Jungle*, a diary of his life in the Gond country. This too spoke of the intimate bond between the tribals and nature. 'The forest-child has this one great joy,' he observed, 'that the whole world of nature is his: he is the child of the open-air, of mountains and streams, of the lonely forest-path, and of the wild rushing winds. At first he goes to the forest strapped to his mother's back as she goes to cut wood, but later he himself takes the cattle out to pasture in some glade or clearing in those thick woods...'

Growing up, the Gond child was aware that the forest had its dangers, hearing of a neighbour's cow being taken away by a panther, of another neighbour being killed by a tiger, a third being fatally bitten by a krait or cobra. Nonetheless, Elwin claimed that the Gonds did not have intimations of mortality as they went to the forest, where they were always able to savour its varied glories: 'flowers and bright colours, the sunlight on the streams, the broad sweet-smelling fields of ramtilla, the glorious orange blossoms of the palas tree, the fragrant flower of the kachnar, the ever-green sal forest.'[10]

For the Gond, the real danger held by the forests was not the deadly animals or reptiles it harboured, but the repressive state apparatus which sought to deny the tribals their customary rights of free movement, access and use. Folk memory held the tribals to be the owners of the forest, and so they had been through time, until in the late nineteenth century the British Raj constituted vast areas of woodland as state reserves and sought to strictly control its use by villagers.

Elwin found that the Forest Department and its operations were deeply resented by the tribals. When he asked a Gond what his idea of heaven was, he got this answer, 'Miles and miles of forest without any forest guards.'[11]

As a student, Elwin had studied literature both formally and informally, steeping himself in the poetry, drama and fiction of the early modern and modern periods. He had literary ambitions of his own, too. At first he hoped to make a mark as a poet and novelist. He experimented with both genres, but with modest success. It was getting to know the Gonds, whose culture and lifestyle was so different from that of his native England as well of Indian cities like Poona and Bombay, that inculcated in him an interest in anthropology. This once-amateurish discipline which had leaned towards the anecdotal was refashioning itself as a science, advocating long spells of intensive fieldwork among the communities it wished to study. Reading the works of Bronislaw Malinowski, Raymond Firth and other pioneers of this new 'scientific' social anthropology inspired Elwin to become an anthropologist himself. However, he followed the emerging intellectual trend only up to a point. He would emulate Malinowski and company by conducting empirical research, but would depart from them in conveying its results in the attractive and elegant prose that came more naturally to writers than to academics.

Travelling through Mandla District, Elwin made the acquaintance of the Baiga, a tribe of swidden agriculturists who had fallen especially foul of the colonial forest authorities. Their mode of cultivation involved clearing areas of forest in rotation, planting seeds and raising crops in one patch while leaving the others to regenerate. The burning left the land rich in manure, while the traditional rotational cycle of twelve years or more ensured that this was a sustainable form of livelihood. However, the Forest Department did not see it that way. They disparaged swidden as destructive and wasteful, and those who practised it as primitive and uncouth. Swidden cultivation was banned in most parts of the Central Provinces, except for a small area called 'Baiga Chak' where the tribe was allowed to continue with the practice.

Elwin was fascinated by the Baiga, and immersed himself in their past, present and future. He spent extended periods in Baiga Chak, while also talking to the community members who lived elsewhere and had suffered the consequences of the colonial state's ban on their customary form of cultivation. His investigations eventually led to the publication of a nine-hundred-page monograph on Baiga life, livelihood and culture.

Elwin argued that swidden cultivation (known locally as bewar) was central to the Baiga sense of identity. It defined who they were. Indeed, their origin myth had Bhagavan, or God, telling them: 'You will make your living from the earth. You will dig roots and eat them. ... You will cut down trees and burn them and sow your seed in the ashes.' They were thus commanded by God to practise swidden, and forbidden from taking to settled cultivation. For Bhagavan himself had told the first Baiga: 'You must not tear the breasts of your Mother the Earth with the plough like the Gond and Hindu.'[12]

In the course of his research, Elwin met many Baigas who had, within their lifetime, been made by the state to stop bewar, and had suffered for it. One informant told Elwin of how, after his father died, he 'cut [bewar] myself for seven years', but then 'the big sahib came from Nagpur and told us that the jungle was closed. "You must plough like the Hindus," he said.' The recollection continued with the government trying to teach them how to plough land with bullocks and cultivate crops, but failing. With no access to forests and no interest or expertise in plough agriculture, 'since then we have been slaves to the Gond cultivators'.

Another individual whose family was also subject to this ban on shifting cultivation told Elwin: 'When we cut bewar we got good crops of every kind; now we have broken the breasts of Mai Dharti [Mother Earth] and we get nothing.' A third claimed that 'it is because we commit the great sin of driving the plough that we now wear tattered clothes and have become slaves to others'. And a fourth remarked, 'When we break the belly of the earth we break our own belly and all the food falls out. By stopping bewar, the English have turned us into naked sadhus.'

Reporting these reactions, Elwin remarked that 'it is commonly believed that the present poverty of the tribe is due to their disobedience of Bhagavan's command; Mother Earth is insulted when her children tear her breasts, and now refuses to supply their needs. For this reason, their magic has decayed, the crops fail, and they are subject to the vengeance of wild beasts.'[13]

Colonial (and especially forest) officials had always been implacably opposed to bewar. Elwin quotes one late-nineteenth century writer as saying: 'The Byga is the most terrible enemy to the forests we have anywhere in the hills. Thousands of square miles of sal forests have been clean destroyed by them in the progress of their dhya [swidden] cultivation.' Elwin himself was of the view that such verdicts 'are undoubtedly exaggerated. Waste there is, but much of the waste is recouped in time.' He quoted other officials, more sympathetic to the Baiga and their way of life, who saw bewar as not necessarily destructive of forest cover. One forest official was constrained to notice 'the often wonderful regrowth of sal in all stages from seedlings to saplings to poles' in areas left fallow in the swidden cycle. This officer further observed that 'up to three years after an area has been abandoned the regrowth is scanty, but by the end of six years it is freely filling up, at the end of twelve years regeneration is usually complete'.

Elwin deplored the scapegoating of the Baiga, arguing that swidden cultivation was opposed by the colonial state because these forest areas contained timber that in the age of industrialization had valuable commercial uses. He was clear that 'axe cultivation was the despair of every forest officer' only because it competed with timber operations for territorial control of the forest. 'Among those who have served the Baiga best and loved them most,' he wrote, 'a considerable body of opinion [exists] that considers that bewar should not be regarded as quite the bogey that it has been assumed to be, that the damage it causes has been exaggerated, that given proper conditions the forest often recovers in time, and that in the case of a small tribe like the Baiga the effect on erosion and the rainfall is not a very serious danger.'[14]

Elwin thus directly took on the administration's claim that bewar destroyed the forest, a prejudice that quickly got crystallized as scientific orthodoxy. Although it was later scholars such as Harold Conklin and Clifford Geertz who more thoroughly demonstrated the ecological wisdom of swidden agriculture, Elwin had, prior to them, arrived at a not dissimilar conclusion.[15] He believed that there was no real scientific case against the stopping of shifting cultivation. And he was passionately of the view that there was a strong case for its continuance on moral and cultural grounds. He insisted that 'it is impossible to deprive primitive people of a vital part of their economy, to tear a page out of their mythology, to force them into a way of life repugnant to them by tradition, inclination, and tribal law, without irreparably injuring their life and spirit'.[16]

Colonial officials presented themselves as defenders of the forest, and the Baiga (and other tribals) as enemies of the forest. Elwin disagreed. Apart from demonstrating that in its original form bewar did not destroy forests, he also argued that in their everyday life, the Baiga had a deep understanding of, and respect for, the non-human world. He wrote that the Baiga 'claim to be able to read as an open book the great volume of Nature'. He quoted a Baiga named Mahatu as saying, 'We Baiga understand everything from trees and fruit and flowers. If we see a parrot eating a mango only in the middle, then we know there will be rain for two months but not in Bhadon (September). But if the parrot eats the whole mango, and drops the stone on the ground, then we know that there will be good rain every month.'[17]

As Elwin demonstrated, the legends, stories, poems and songs of the Baiga all displayed an intimate relationship with the natural world. 'The Baiga have the advantage of a perfect setting for their romance,' he wrote in the book's preface. 'The forest, the *madhuban*, the sweet forest, the *nandanban*, the forest of delight, is his natural home. What lover could fail to be inspired by its remoteness, the sweet smell of flowers, the murmuring of the wind in the branches of uncounted trees?'

The place of nature in tribal culture was perhaps most strikingly illustrated by folk songs set in the forest. Elwin quotes one such song, dealing with a romantic tryst, some of whose lines (in translation) run:

> GIRL: O the mango in the valley and the creeper on the hill!
> O love, come to me and I'll hide you in my dress.
> BOY: I've come to the jungle to gather leaves.
> It is in our youth that we must take delight.
> GIRL: O my love, come drink some water and enjoy me.
> As much as anyone could enjoy in all their life-time.
> BOY: I've come to the jungle to kill a porcupine.
> We'll sleep together by the mango-tree.
> Hold me so close that no one can pass between us.[18]

'No wonder the Baiga loves his forest,' wrote Elwin, 'which supplies him with food and some of the most vivid experiences of life.'[19]

The Baiga, published by John Murray in 1939, was the first of several ethnographies that Elwin wrote on individual tribal communities of central India. The others included a study of the sex life of the Muria of the princely state of Bastar, and a study of the religious beliefs of the Saora of upland Orissa. In these works, the tribal identity with nature figured, albeit in passing. 'To visit a Muria village,' wrote the anthropologist, 'is to receive a general impression of tidiness and cleanliness, careful industry that exploits to the full the gifts of Mother Earth, and a love of animals.' The tribe had an uncommon reverence for the earth, which they held to be 'the ultimate source of life and power who manifests itself in all the other deities'. In Muria cosmology, humans were 'the children of earth, fed and loved by her. She is personified in Tallur Muttal who appears frequently in legends and songs. She is one of the gods living in the ghotul [dormitory] to protect the children; she has a special concern for the success of the crops...'[20]

As for the Saora of Orissa, Elwin observed that they 'are in many respects better off than the people of the plains. They sit in the lap of Nature and she spoils them with a thousand simple gifts. ... The terraces so laboriously constructed give a rich return for the toil they demand. Free from [the] tiresome and enervating food-taboos [of caste Hindu society], the Saora has before him an abundant spread of all wild things, fruit, herbs, roots, leaves and every kind of living creature.'[21]

In a book published in 1942 on a tribe of traditional iron-smelters, the Agaria, Elwin spoke of how colonial forest laws, coupled with foreign competition, were inexorably undermining their way of life. In the Agaria heartland, British territory was interspersed with many princely states, and the book maps the desperate migrations across political frontiers of Agaria smelters thwarted at every turn by high taxation and the Forest Department. The Agaria had once revelled in their craft, 'generally delight[ing] in anything that takes them to the jungle'. Now, however, the colonial state's new laws had made these trips fraught with hazards. Even at night, the Agaria were plagued with dreams about being intercepted, abused and beaten up in the jungle by forest officials.[22]

Like the Baiga, the Saora, Muria and Agaria had enjoyed the freedom of the forest from time immemorial; like them, they reacted bitterly to the colonial state's usurpation of forests and the restrictions on traditional use that this entailed. Everywhere that Elwin went, whichever tribe he studied, he found that among all the arms of the state it was the Forest Department that was most feared and reviled. The discontent was sometimes latent and subdued; sometimes it manifested itself in open rebellion.

The anthropologist also noted the tribal opposition to colonial restrictions on traditional hunting practices. He quotes a Baiga telling him: 'Even if Government make a hundred laws that we are not to hunt, we will do it. One of us will keep the official talking, and the rest will go off to the jungle and get a good fat deer.'[23] Elwin himself recognized the necessity of wildlife conservation, once going so far as to say that 'India, of all countries, with her tradition of ahimsa and her classic love of animals, should lead the world in her preservation of the wildlife within her borders'.[24] Nonetheless, he deplored the hypocrisy with which the state viewed the matter, with Indian maharajas as well as British officials given shikar permits to hunt tigers and elephants as trophies while tribals were prevented from even shooting pigeons and partridges for the pot.

As Elwin demonstrated, state forestry and game laws represented a savage attack on the economic and cultural integrity of tribal life. Modern, instrumental attitudes to the forest rested on a legal and administrative framework that violated, at every step, the tribal's own relationship with nature. In his autobiography, the anthropologist poignantly summed up the essence of the tribal's frustration with state forestry:

> The reservation of forests, inevitable as it was, was ... a very serious blow to the tribesman. He was forbidden to practice his traditional methods of cultivation. He was ordered to remain in one village and not to wander from place to place. When he had cattle he was kept in a state of continual anxiety for fear they should stray over the boundary and render him liable to what were for him heavy fines. If he was a Forest Villager he became liable at any moment to be called to work for the Forest Department. If he lived elsewhere he was forced to obtain a licence for almost every kind of forest produce. At every turn the Forest Laws cut across his life, limiting, frustrating, destroying his self confidence. During the year 1933-34 there were 27,000 forest offences registered in the Central Provinces and Berar and probably ten times as many unwhipped of justice. It is obvious that so great a number of offences would not occur unless the forest regulations ran counter to the fundamental needs of the tribesmen. A Forest Officer once said to me: 'Our laws are of such a kind that every villager breaks one forest law every day of his life.'[25]

In 1954, after twenty years in central India, Elwin was appointed Anthropological Adviser to the administration of the North-East Frontier Agency (NEFA), a vast but thinly administered territory lying between India and China. The Indian prime minister, Jawaharlal Nehru, had read Elwin's writings, and it was at Nehru's behest that he was offered the post. The British Raj had exercised only a shadowy suzerainty over this mountainous terrain. The government of independent India sought to remedy this by seeking, albeit slowly and incrementally, to expand their footprint into NEFA.

In central India, Elwin had at first been a social worker seeking to bring health and education to the tribes. Increasingly, however, he abandoned social work for a life of research and writing. From the late 1930s he began to combine scholarship with advocacy. Alongside his books he wrote prolifically for the press, urging a greater respect for tribal culture and for tribal rights in land and forest, among the middle-class, largely Hindu, audience that read the English-language newspapers and magazines that published his writings, and from whose ranks were drawn the politicians, civil servants and lawyers in a position to influence tribal life for good and for ill.[26]

Elwin saw the move to NEFA as an exciting opportunity to put his ideas into practice. Because the region was much more isolated from the Indian mainstream than the tribal districts of central India, its communities were less touched by the disfiguring aspects of Hindu culture (such as caste and gender prejudice). They also had greater control over their natural surroundings, since the Forest Department was as yet unknown there. And now that he was no longer a freelance anthropologist but an officer of the Indian state, perhaps his recommendations would actually find their way into policy.

NEFA was populated by a variety of endogamous communities, none of whom were Hindus by faith. Some were Buddhist (reflecting the influence of the ancient kingdom of Tibet, which lay across the border, and was in 1950 annexed by Communist China), while others had their own, tribal, non-Hindu and non-Buddhist deities and forms of worship. Because so little was known about the peoples of NEFA, an anthropologist was canvassed to join the administration in an advisory, but full-time, role.

From 1954 until his death a decade later, Elwin was based in the hill town of Shillong, at the time the capital of the province of Assam. While his second wife Lila and her three children lived in Shillong, Elwin himself spent much of the year travelling through the hills and valleys of NEFA, writing a series of reports for the state about the tribes he encountered.

In 1957, Elwin published a little book called, somewhat portentously, *A Philosophy for NEFA*, which appeared in an expanded edition two years later. Each time, it carried a foreword by the prime minister himself. The second of these forewords was drafted by Elwin, although it appeared in a slightly revised form under Nehru's name. It listed five principles for administration in tribal areas:

First, that the tribals 'should develop along the lines of their own genius and we should avoid imposing anything on them' (the 'we' here connoting both non-tribal outsiders as well as the Indian state);

Second, that 'tribal rights in land and forest should be protected';

Third, that the state should endeavour to train and build up a team of administrators from a tribal background—while some technical experts would no doubt be required, 'we should avoid introducing too many outsiders into tribal territory';

Fourth, the state 'should not over-administer' tribal areas or 'overwhelm them with a multiplicity of schemes'; it should work 'through, and not in rivalry to, their own social and cultural institutions';

Fifth, the results of these official schemes should be judged not in statistical or monetary terms 'but by the quality of human character that is evolved'.[27]

Of particular interest to this book is the second of these five points, the protection of tribal rights in land and forest. In the main text of *A Philosophy for NEFA*, Elwin dealt with this question in a section called 'The Problem of the Forests'. 'I have myself recorded,' he wrote, 'the melancholy story of the effect of reservation on the Baigas of Madhya Pradesh in my book on the tribe. Nothing roused the Saoras of Orissa to such resentment as the taking from them of forests which they regarded as their own property. Of the Bhuiyas and Juangs of Bonai and Keonjhar, I wrote in a report in 1942: "It is necessary for us to appreciate the attitude of the aboriginal. To him the hills and forests are his. Again and again it was said to me, "These hills are ours; what right has anyone to interfere in our own property?"'"[28]

The situation in central India was a warning and an example. As an independent writer, Elwin could only hector and preach; now, working in the belly of the Indian state, he could, with luck, ensure that in NEFA the administration followed a more humane and sensitive path when it came to tribal rights. He claimed that 'the present forest policy in NEFA is one of exceptional liberality', with the interests of the people placed ahead of revenue generation (unlike in other parts of India). He further claimed that the new Jhum [swidden] regulations 'guarantee the rights of the tribal people over their traditional forests'. While forests in sparsely populated areas were being constituted as state reserves, elsewhere in NEFA 'the whole concept of reservation has been modified considerably by rules that existing villages falling within the proposed reserves should not be uprooted, but that sufficient land should be demarcated for their present needs as well as for their future expansion'. These were all a result of policies in the framing of which he had a part: further, 'the tribal people living in or near Reserve Forests also have the right to collect timber and minor forest produce for their customary personal use (but not for sale, barter or gift); to graze cattle; to hunt and fish freely; to collect orchids; and to keep skins, hides, tusks and horns of animals hunted in the Reserves as trophies'.[29]

Elwin worked for the NEFA administration from January 1954 until his death in February 1964. During this decade, he sought assiduously to forge a different path for tribal development. He hoped to save, in the Northeast, at least some of what had been lost by tribals in central India. That he was now an officer of the state gave him hope; that some senior Indian politicians supported him was a further source of gratification. I have already spoken of his closeness to Nehru. In the summer of 1959, the Union Home Minister Govind Ballabh Pant asked Elwin to chair a committee to advise on tribal policy for the country as a whole. Forty-three 'Special Multipurpose Tribal Blocks' had been set up in districts across India, and the committee was tasked with studying how they were faring and what could be done to improve their functioning.

Apart from Elwin, the committee included a social worker and several officials, all with experience of working in tribal areas. They travelled extensively, visiting tribal blocks in several states, taking copious notes. A year after the committee was constituted it produced a report several hundred pages long, largely drafted by the chairman and bearing the impress of his views.

In an early chapter titled 'The Fundamentals of an Approach to the Tribes', the report quoted the prime minister's foreword to Elwin's *A Philosophy for NEFA*, elaborating on each of its five postulates. Of the second point, 'tribal rights in land and forest should be protected', this report urged that tribals be granted the land they presently cultivated 'in perpetuity', and that there be an 'adjustment of forest laws to tribal conditions'.[30]

These recommendations were then fleshed out in two separate chapters. Chapter 7, 'Shifting Cultivation', began by quoting senior Indian officials, including a former Inspector General of Forests and a senior Adviser to the Planning Commission, to the effect that it was a mistake to see swidden cultivation as unscientific and destructive; rather, it should be viewed 'as an agricultural practice adopted as a reflex to the physiological character of the land'. The report suggested that, instead of banning swidden altogether (which most forest officials and agronomists wanted), it should be regulated and improved, by following a proper rotational cycle and introducing certain plants to improve soil fertility.

Elwin had, from his days with the Baigas of Mandla, believed that swidden cultivation was much more than a means of economic livelihood. As he now wrote, some two decades after he had first encountered this much misunderstood as well as unfairly demonized means of livelihood, swidden was 'as much a part of tribal culture as anything else and is a real way of life for the people'. Therefore 'we should be very careful that in our enthusiasm for bringing shifting cultivation to an end, we do not injure the people psychologically or socially'. Where modernizing economists sought to bring the tribals into the mainstream—or maelstrom—of city life, this committee, speaking here in the voice of its chief draughtsman, argued that the Indian state had 'to recognize and respect the tribal people's rights in land and forest and also their right to settle their own destinies by evolution from within and not by force imposed from outside'.[31]

Chapter 8, 'The Problem of the Forests', began by recognizing the importance of the scientific management of forests. It praised the commitment of forest officers who lived and worked in arduous conditions. However, it then stressed that

> the tribal people, who have lived for hundreds of years in the forest areas and in the past have enjoyed considerable freedom to use the wood, exploit the minor produce and hunt the animals, have an ineradicable conviction that the forest is theirs. Some of them call themselves Pashupati, the lords of the wild animals, and believe that they have a peculiar power over them. Their folktales are full of such ideas. Animals and human beings intermarry; they make ceremonial friendships with one another; they live, eat and talk together. This is, of course, much more than a mere sentiment. The forest not only satisfies a deep-rooted tribal sentiment: it provides essential food.[32]

The report argued that this clash between the imperatives of state forestry and the cultural as well as economic needs of the tribals had been intensified by 'the existence of a number of forest rules which have come down to us from British times and are not adjusted to modern conditions'. The enactment and harsh implementation of these laws had 'deeply disturbed the entire tribal economy and has introduced a psychological conflict which discourages the people from taking up development schemes with real enthusiasm'.

The report then gave some examples of the conflict playing out in the field, of how the stringent forest laws bore down heavily on the tribals' means of livelihood, by limiting access to essential materials for house construction, cultivation and local crafts. To mitigate the conflict, it made a number of suggestions, among them training to reorient forest officials so that they could 'understand the tribal point of view and thus adopt a more sympathetic attitude' towards them; the offer to the tribals of a share of the profits from commercial exploitation of forest produce (this at present was going directly and wholly to the state exchequer); the encouragement of tribal co-operative societies to make wood-based products and sell them in the market. Unless the tribal was given a direct stake, said the report, 'he cannot identify his interests with those of the forest'.[33]

In April 1960, even as this report on the functioning (as well as malfunctioning) of 'special multipurpose tribal blocks' was going to press, Elwin was asked to join a more high-powered government committee still. Chaired by the veteran nationalist U.N. Dhebar, a former president of the Congress Party, this had twelve members in all. They included several members of Parliament, among them the tribal leader Jaipal Singh, an Oxford contemporary of Elwin's.

This time, since the anthropologist was merely a member, and not chair, and because several others were influential politicians, the report that the committee produced was probably drafted by several hands rather than just one. Nonetheless, some parts of the report were unquestionably Elwin's handiwork, among them an important chapter on 'Tribals and Forest Policy', whose arguments were unmistakably his, and so also (as we shall see) was its prose.

In this chapter, Elwin, speaking through the committee, reprised five major themes of his writings over the decades. First, that for the tribes of India a healthy forest cover was crucial to survival and subsistence. It gave them food as well as 'fruits of all kinds, edible leaves, honey, nourishing roots, wild game and fish'. It provided them 'with material to build their homes and to practise their arts', it kept 'them warm with its fuel and cool with its grateful shade', and it supplemented their meagre sources of cash by providing materials to sell in the plainspeoples' bazaars.

Second, for the tribes the forests were central to their culture, their sense of self. To quote: 'Their religion leads them to believe that there are many spirits living in the trees and forests. ... Tribal folk-tales often speak about the relations of human beings and the sylvan spirits and it is striking to see how in many of the myths and legends the deep sense of identity with the forest is emphasized.'

Third, that the tribes had a sense of ownership over the forests in the traditional areas of their habitation. Since from 'times immemorial the tribal people have enjoyed freedom to use the forest', this gave them 'a conviction that remains even today deep in their hearts that the forest belongs to them'.

Fourth, that the colonial state's takeover of the forests in the late nineteenth century constituted a radical disruption of the economic and cultural life of the tribals. The commercial working of forest areas and the building of roads brought in outsiders who were in a position to exploit the tribals. Meanwhile, the 'natural desire of the forest officials to exercise even closer control over the use of forest products deeply disturbed the entire tribal economy and introduced a psychological conflict'.[34]

Fifth, the government of independent India had unfortunately continued the authoritarian policies of its colonial predecessor. The forest policy of 1952 emphasized total state control even more than the policy of 1894 which preceded it. The postcolonial state expanded its control over forests and woodland, and it began to more intensively work these areas for commercial exploitation. As a result 'the tribal who formerly regarded himself as the owner of the forests, was through a deliberate process turned into a subject and placed under the Forest Department'.[35]

State officials, both British as well as Indian, claimed that in forest areas now under their control, they had replaced the wasteful, erratic ways of the tribals with a professedly 'scientific management'. This scapegoating of the tribals, this practice of blaming the victim, was brilliantly taken apart in one paragraph of the 'Dhebar Committee report' whose prose is unmistakably Elwin's. I quote:

> There is constant propaganda that the tribals are destroying the forest. We put this complaint to some unsophisticated tribals. They countered the complaint by asking how could they destroy the forest. They owned no trucks. They hardly had even a bullock cart. The utmost that they could carry away, was a head-load of produce for sale to maintain their family and that too against a licence. The utmost that they wanted was wood to keep them warm in the winter months, to reconstruct or repair their huts and carry on their little cottage industries. Their fuel-needs for cooking, they said, were not much, because they had not much to cook. Having explained their own position they invariably turned to the amount of destruction that was taking place all around them. They reiterated how the ex-zamindars, in violation of their agreements, and the forest rules and laws, devastated vast areas of forest land right in front of officials. They also related how the contractors stray outside the contracted coupes, carry loads in

> trucks in excess of their authorised capacity and otherwise exploit both the forests and the tribals.

The Dhebar Committee's, or rather Elwin's, spirited defence of tribal rights in forests continued:

> There is a feeling amongst the tribals that all the arguments in support of preservation and development of forest are intended to refuse them their demands. They argue that when it is a question of industry, township, development work or projects of rehabilitation, all these valuable arguments are forgotten and vast tracts are placed at the disposal of outsiders who mercilessly destroy the forest wealth with or without necessity.[36]

Knowing this to be an official report, aimed at policy change, Elwin's prose then moved from its habitually polemical style to one of reconciliation and accommodation. Although it was true that the restriction of the customary rights of the tribals was 'the root cause of the delicate relations between them and the Forest Department', the committee did 'not suggest that all these complaints are justified'. Nonetheless, 'there can be no doubt that a state of tension and mutual distrust' existed. Therefore the report called for 'a partnership rather than an exclusive approach which arises from the policy enunciated in 1894 and 1952 and the manner in which it has been implemented'. If this change came about, argued Elwin on behalf of the committee, 'the tribal can easily be won over to the view that the Forest Department is not his enemy, but a friend interested in helping him'.

The Dhebar Committee's chapter on forests ended with a series of specific suggestions. These included the recruitment of tribals as forest guards, the award to tribals of plots of land controlled by the state, where they might grow trees and grasses for use and for sale, having a more liberal policy with regard to tribal access to non-timber forest produce from reserved forests, and setting up timber processing units near the forests where tribals could be gainfully employed.[37]

Tragically, none of these recommendations were given effect to in the years and decades that followed. One consequence of the continuing alienation of tribals from their forest habitat has been an insurgency fostered by Maoist revolutionaries, prompting repressive action by the state, with the tribals trapped in-between. The forests have suffered as a result of the Indian state's rejection of the anthropologist's suggestions, and the tribals have suffered too. Thousands of lives have been lost in the conflict, of policemen, revolutionaries and innocent bystanders.[38]

Elwin was a lifelong student and lover of English literature. He had assimilated vast amounts of medieval and early modern poetry. William Wordsworth was an especial favourite. However, he also kept abreast of contemporary writers, among them P.G. Wodehouse and Aldous Huxley.

After Elwin arrived in India, but before he moved to the tribal country, Huxley published an essay with the intriguing title 'Wordsworth in the Tropics'. This was based in part on a visit made by the writer to Asia in the winter of 1925–26. Accompanied by his wife, Huxley first went to India, travelling across the subcontinent, before proceeding to Burma, Malaysia and Japan. This was his first trip outside his homeland.

In the England Huxley knew and the English circles he moved in, the poetry of Wordsworth had inspired a certain form of nature worship. Those the writer called 'good Wordsworthians' believed that 'to commune with the fields and waters, the woodland and the hills, is to commune, according to our modern and northern ideas, with the visible manifestations of the "Wisdom and Spirit of the Universe"'.

Now, having spent time in hotter and less benign climes, Huxley wrote that 'the Wordsworthian who exports this pantheistic worship of Nature to the tropics is liable to have his religious convictions disturbed. Nature, under a vertical sun, and nourished by the equatorial rains, is not at all like that chaste, mild deity who presides over the *Gemüthlichkeit* [cordiality], the prettiness, the cosy sublimities of the Lake District.'

Had Wordsworth himself travelled in the tropics, he would, wrote Huxley, have been quickly disabused of his love of nature. 'Wandering in the hothouse darkness of the jungle, he would not have felt so serenely certain of those "Presences of Nature", ... which he was in the habit of worshipping on the shores of Windermere and Rydal.' For, as Huxley had witnessed in his own sojourn in Burma and Malaysia, the tropical jungle 'is marvellous, fantastic, beautiful, but it is also terrifying, it is also profoundly sinister. ... The life of those vast masses of swarming vegetation is alien to the human spirit and hostile to it.'[39]

Elwin was, as it were, a Wordsworthian who had permanently relocated to the tropics. What would he have made of Huxley's essay? Did he ever read it? Perhaps. Or perhaps not. We do know, however, that Elwin read a later work of Huxley's that returns to the arguments made in the essay of 1929. This is Huxley's 1932 book *Texts and Pretexts*, a chapter of which, entitled 'Man and Nature', is referenced in the first book that Elwin published based on his experiences of life with the tribes.

This was *Songs of the Forest*. Here Elwin quotes Huxley as writing that 'in the home counties of England, for example, Nature seems to most people, and most of the time, reassuringly human—all too human, even'. But, continues Huxley elsewhere, in tropical rather than temperate climes, 'Nature suddenly refuses to live with our life and partake of our mood. She turns round on the human spectator and gives him something utterly unlike his gift to her, reveals herself as a being either marvellously and beautifully, or else, more often, terrifyingly alien from man.'

After quoting Huxley, Elwin admits that there was 'little to remind us of Wordsworth or [John] Clare in the Gond nature-poems'. However, the Gond poetry did remind him of an earlier generation of British poets, living a couple of centuries before Wordsworth, and in a less perfectly ordered landscape. Thus 'the Elizabethan [poet] did not read his own moods into nature, but like the Gond, he wanted nature to provide an appropriate background to his emotions'.[40]

Nonetheless, poets (even Elizabethan poets) merely observed nature, whereas tribals actually lived within it. Thus, as Elwin wrote, 'The Gond lives so close to nature that he has made a family affair of it.' The Gonds were divided into many exogamous clans, these reflecting their 'special bond with the natural world. Some are named after trees, the mango, the teak, the mahua, and the members of the sept have a devotion to their particular tree, and never cut it. Others are named after animals, and have a special power over them, the tiger, the crocodile, the porcupine, the wild cat, the jungle dog.'[41]

Songs of the Forest was published in London, intended for readers who knew their Wordsworth and their Huxley too. Elwin told them that the Gonds were capable of becoming one with nature in its beauty as well as in its savagery. In their relations with nature they manifested 'a real ecstasy, even though terrifyingly alien from civilized man'.[42]

The 'civilized man' in temperate climates lived in cities, and occasionally seasoned his life with excursions to the countryside. For the English people that Huxley was writing about, nature was an episodic source of recreation, and of aesthetic pleasure. For all their professed love for woods, streams and charming landscapes, for the most part modern-day Wordsworthians lived their lives outside and apart from nature.

On the other hand, the tribes of central India whom Verrier Elwin wrote about lived in nature. The forests were the source of their economic sustenance, their culture, their sense of self. They were in or adjacent to the forest every hour of the day, every week of the year. At work and at play they saw nature in all its moods: benign, beautiful, hostile and unfathomable, these captured in their songs and stories. They were at home with nature, and nature was at home with them.

CHAPTER EIGHT

The First Hindutva Environmentalist

K.M. MUNSHI

SINCE THE 1980S, THE Government of India has had a Ministry of Environment and Forests (with Climate Change added to its title in 2014). However, in the first few decades of Indian independence, the 'environment' was not a category recognized in official nomenclature. Forestry was, except that the subject did not merit a separate ministry; it formed part of the Ministry of Food and Agriculture.

The Indian Constitution was adopted on 26 January 1950. Shortly afterwards Prime Minister Jawaharlal Nehru reconstituted his Cabinet. He appointed K.M. Munshi as the minister of food and agriculture. Munshi was a man of many parts, of multiple professions; he had been a successful lawyer in Bombay and a bestselling novelist in Gujarati while also being active in nationalist politics. Within the Congress party, he was particularly close to the deputy prime minister, Vallabhbhai Patel (a fellow Gujarati), and it must have been Patel who prevailed on Nehru to include Munshi in the Cabinet.

In May 1950—a few months after he had taken over as Union minister of food and agriculture—Munshi visited Bombay, a city where he had spent the bulk of his professional career. In this, the urbs prima of India, the country's commercial hub and the centre of its film and entertainment industry, Munshi met with a group of merchants. He told them that he had planned to introduce a new event in India's already very crowded festive calendar. This would be a week-long ceremony to celebrate trees, to be called Vana Mahotsava (literally, the Grand Festival of the Forest). 'During this week,' said the minister, 'women and children should plant trees, water them, repair to the forest and gardens and ... honour and study and worship the trees. Let those who like it revive the echoes of Vrindavan with flute and *mridanga*.'

The merchants Munshi was addressing were mostly Gujarati, mostly Hindu, and mostly Vaishnavites, bhakts or worshippers of Krishna. Hence the reference to Vrindavan, the mythical forest of tulsi plants associated with the god. Having invoked religion, Munshi went on to invoke caste as well. He had come to them, he told the merchants, as a Brahmin, and being from a lower-ranked caste they 'should be proud to give alms—at least to a Brahmin like me'. He asked each merchant to pay for the planting of fifty trees and the construction of a well in any place of their choosing—'in your compound, in your native place, in holy Banaras, in Delhi, where the Father of the Nation was cremated, or in Somnath, where there are nine square miles of land available for tree planting ... hallowed by centuries, filled with glorious memories'. The merchants and their ancestors had worshipped Krishna for two thousand years, said Munshi, yet 'the spot where

He died lies barren'. By paying for the planting of ten thousand trees there, these hopefully pious Krishna bhakts would help turn 'the sacred spot where once trod the noblest and the greatest of men' into a forest.[1]

Three weeks later, the minister of food and agriculture broadcast his plans for a national festival of forests on All India Radio. He began by announcing that the merchants of Bombay had promised to pay for the planting of 10,000 trees in Dehotsarga, the place near Somnath where, so the legend had it, Krishna had 'shuffled off this mortal coil'. Preparations were well advanced, said the minister, for similar tree-planting programmes in other sacred places, such as around the ancient Hindu temples at Tirupati, Kanchipuram and Puri. Vice chancellors of all Indian universities had been instructed to get each student to plant at least one tree apiece.

The planting of trees and forests, said Munshi, was an imperative if India had to overcome desertification, moderate the climate, and enhance its food production. However, in his own promotion of the festival he was, he confessed, prompted by something more than utilitarianism. 'I love trees so much,' remarked the minister, 'that I cannot help being a little romantic. Who can forget the loveliness of the blossoming fruit trees; the noble dignity of the venerable trees; and forests which like ancient *rishis* [sages] live but to save mankind; the richness, plenty and happiness which they bring; the joy which would be ours, if every man and woman like Parvati reared a tree with parental affection and if every village and town enveloped itself in groves of verdant beauty.'

As the reference to Shiva's wife Parvati and to programmes in temples showed, in his promotion of this new festival Munshi clothed it with a distinctively Hindu imagery, perhaps hoping thereby to stoke traditional sentiment in a modern cause. Indeed, the imagery was not just Hindu but Brahmin, as witness his saying that 'if the *Vana Mahotsava* is to be celebrated in the proper spirit, every one in India should, during the Mahotsava week, live on vegetables, fruits and tubers'.[2] For the Gujarati Brahmin, vegetarianism was a mark of ritual piety. While a majority of Hindus were meat-eaters, they were being told that if they became vegetarian for this week at least they would elevate themselves spiritually by living more like the ancient Brahmin sages who had composed Sanskrit texts in the forest.

I'll soon return to this new festival the intrepid K.M. Munshi inserted in India's ritual calendar. But first, some background about the man and his work before he became Union minister of food and agriculture, and was placed in charge of, among other things, the Forest Department that controlled some one-fifth of the country's territory.

Kanhaiyalal Maneklal Munshi was born in the Gujarati port town of Bharuch on 30 December 1887, in a comfortably well-off Brahmin family. He studied law and established a successful practice in Bombay, while at the same time being a fellow traveller of the Congress movement. He attached himself to Gandhi's lieutenant Vallabhbhai Patel, and when the Congress came to power in the Bombay Presidency in 1937 (under a scheme of limited self-government promoted by the Raj), Munshi was appointed home minister.

Alongside his law practice, Munshi had also forged a second career, as a popular novelist in his mother tongue, Gujarati. He wrote a series of bestselling historical novels, which portrayed the picture of a prosperous, self-reliant, spiritually refined and culturally sophisticated Gujarat in ancient times, its wealth and happiness destroyed by Muslim invaders. These novels, wrote one of Munshi's admiring biographers, described the 'heroism of the

[Hindu] defenders of the shrines and home of Gujarat, the mass immolation of women and the destruction and desolation that followed ... with a realism equal to that of the man on the spot'.[3]

Another reader of Munshi's novels was less enthusiastic about the ideological framework on which they rested. This was Gandhi, who believed that if Hindus rewrote the past to glorify or magnify their role in history, that was just as problematic as the Mughals or the British doing likewise. When Munshi sent Gandhi a copy of his historical novel *Prithviballabh*, he read it with interest, but also with some puzzlement. As Gandhi asked Munshi: 'Can you, as a historian, forget the whole of Muslim history? Even if you can do so, can you make the whole of India forget it? Can you reverse the flow of water and make it go upward? After the British have left, will it be possible to wipe out all the consequences of the British connection off history?'[4]

In his essays and lectures too, Munshi often spoke sorrowfully of what Muslim invaders had done to the ancient Hindu culture of India. In a talk in Kanpur in 1943 he spoke feelingly of 'the Central Asian raiders, anxious to plunder and destroy', who 'simply flung themselves on their victims thirsty for blood and booty'. India's Hindu rulers, he remarked, 'were no match for such antagonists; they were not lacking in strength, for of that they had plenty, but they were tempered by the fine feeling engendered by their culture'. The Muslims from Central Asia were followed by the Christians from Europe who came 'to trade by guile but remained to rule by force'. Munshi thus lamented of his fellow Hindus, 'We were far in advance of the world, physically, morally, mentally; but we lacked the art of organised destruction.'[5]

Munshi was convinced that, in order to become a player in world affairs, modern India had to base itself on its ancient spiritual traditions. In November 1938, while a serving minister in the Bombay government, he founded an institution for the propagation of Indian (read 'Hindu') culture called the Bharatiya

Vidya Bhavan. Initially headquartered in Bombay, the Bhavan established branches in all the cities of the subcontinent and in time in London and New York too. Munshi described the Bhavan as 'a centre in which ancient Aryan learning can be studied and where modern Indian culture will be provided with a historical background'.[6] It was, he believed, India's mission to 'recapture the spiritual leadership of the world—not merely in the realm of religion, thought and philosophy, but in life, in the affairs of the world'.[7] His Bharatiya Vidya Bhavan would, he hoped, play its part in India becoming Vishwa Guru, Teacher to the World.

Munshi's view of Hinduism was quintessentially Brahminical. Though he admired Gandhi for his leadership of the freedom movement, he was altogether untouched by Gandhi's interest in social reform. Kumarappa and Mira, who lived with Gandhi in his rural settlements, were deeply influenced by Gandhi's attacks on the practice of untouchability. Both lived for extended periods in villages themselves. Munshi, on the other hand, lived his personal and professional life among the Hindu elite of Bombay. As a student and scholar of the scriptures, and as a Brahmin himself, he thought of the past and future of India in irredeemably upper-caste terms. In this view, Brahmins, and Brahmin males more particularly, had been placed by God and nature at the pinnacle of the social hierarchy, from where it was their duty to instruct and guide those placed below.

In 1939, after the Second World War broke out, the Congress ministries resigned. Munshi now returned to his lucrative law practice, sitting out the Quit India movement of 1942. He also paid more attention to his Bharatiya Vidya Bhavan and the work it could do. In a series of programmatic essays written in the 1940s, he outlined what he saw as a civilizational alternative to the culture that then dominated the world, that of Europe. 'The basis of Westernism is materialism,' he wrote. 'It is a way of life entirely different from Indian culture, the way of our life. It is based on individual self-indulgence and collective greed, fear and hatred. It revolves round the central idea that a man is no more than his needs and passions.' 'Indian culture,' he continued, 'is a challenge to Westernism,' offering a less acquisitive and more integrated approach to life.[8]

After the Congress leaders came out of jail in 1945, and preparations for the transfer of power began, Munshi was re-inducted into the mainstream of national politics. He was sent by the home minister, Vallabhbhai Patel, as the Government of India's representative to the recalcitrant Nizam of Hyderabad. In March 1948, when Munshi was in Hyderabad, he had a long conversation with the Private Secretary to the Viceroy, who later described Munshi as 'active, purposeful and, I would guess, ambitious. He is moving up the Congress hierarchy, although lacking the particular Congress badge of honour, prison service in resistance to the Raj. This not unnaturally only enhances the vigour of his nationalism today.'[9]

After Hyderabad was merged with the Indian Union, Munshi provided some key inputs, based on his legal training, in the wording and framing of the Indian Constitution. Then, in 1950–51, he played a critical role in the restoration of Gujarat's famous Somnath temple, whose sack by Mahmud of Ghazni in the eleventh century he had vividly described in one of his novels. Once the temple restoration was complete, Munshi convened a conference of Sanskrit scholars, personally drafting a resolution declaring 'in all solemnity and faith that Sanskrit is the language of India's culture and inspiration, that it is the world's classical language and the key to a true understanding of India's cultural and spiritual greatness, and that through Sanskrit and its allied languages, particularly Pali and Prakrit, the world can realise the life of the spirit enshrined in them'.[10] Some years previously, while speaking at the holy city of Banaras, Munshi had told a crowd of university students that learning Sanskrit 'will make you a member of the great spiritual community to which the greatest men of our race belonged, and give you a capacity for universal understanding'.[11]

Munshi believed that 'India attained her solidarity and cultural vitality through Sanskrit and through Sanskrit alone has she retained them'.[12] Apart from exalting Sanskrit, an undoubtedly beautiful language with a fabulous literary heritage, Munshi also, and more controversially, exalted the caste system, whose obligations and duties had, he claimed, become 'the fortress of life' against foreign invaders.[13] Even more controversially, he praised the ancient Hindu law code, the Manu Smriti, taken apart by modern scholars for its patriarchal and casteist biases, but in Munshi's view a code of conduct that enabled 'the bulk of our people to survive the catastrophe of history as a social and cultural unit'.[14]

On 26 January 1950 the Constitution that Munshi had played a part in framing—and some of whose provisions, such as those on gender and caste, fortunately ran counter to the prescriptions of the Manu Smriti—formally came into effect. In the following month, February, Jawaharlal Nehru reorganized his Cabinet, and appointed Munshi as Union minister of food and agriculture. This was, as I have noted, most likely done at Patel's recommendation. The prime minister had little taste for Hindu revivalism, whereas his deputy prime minister had a healthy respect for Munshi's intelligence and administrative ability.

Munshi himself may have hoped to become law or education minister because of his past work in these spheres. Those posts, however, had already been filled: law by B.R. Ambedkar, the great economist, lawyer and social reformer who oversaw the drafting of the Constitution; and education by Maulana Azad, next only to

Nehru and Patel in the Congress hierarchy, a distinguished scholar of Islamic culture and a fervent advocate of Hindu–Muslim unity.

Munshi may have wanted the education or law portfolios; Nehru may have wanted to keep Munshi out of the Cabinet altogether. The allocation of the food and agriculture ministry was almost certainly a compromise brokered by Patel. Notably, Munshi himself had no previous experience or background of any kind in agriculture.

At the time, the Forest Department came under the food and agriculture minister. And so, the man who had achieved distinction in law, in literature and in politics, and who in his previous six decades on earth had shown no interest in nature or the natural world, now seized the chance to become the first Indian thinker to explicitly marry his religious faith to environmentalism.

Prior to the British conquest of India, the forests of the subcontinent had largely been under the control of peasant and tribal communities. Pre-British rulers had occasionally intervened in forest management—the Mauryans had some forest areas demarcated for raising elephants, medieval monarchs created hunting reserves for their pleasure, and in the eighteenth century the ruler of Mysore, Tipu Sultan, had designated sandalwood a royal tree. However, these interventions were minimal. It was British rule that marked a radical departure. Starting in the 1860s, the colonial government steadily took over large tracts of forest all over India and designated them as state reserves. By the end of the century, the Raj's Forest Department had emerged as far and away the subcontinent's largest landlord, controlling some 22 per cent of its territory.

The British interest in Indian forests was commercial and strategic. The timber that forests supplied was critical to the building and maintenance of the railway network—itself crucial both to trade and to the deployment of military personnel—and during the two World Wars, when wood, bamboo and other such materials were used in large quantities by the British forces in Asia and Africa. The forests of India also provided a steady stream of revenue to the imperial exchequer.[15]

On the other hand, the interest of Indian villagers in forests was linked to their livelihoods. Wood for fuel, home-building and agricultural implements; grass and leaf fodder for cattle and sheep; berries and fruit for food; bamboos for baskets and fibres for ropes; plants for medicine—these sustained the peasants, labourers, artisans and pastoralists who made up the bulk of the population of the subcontinent. Access to forests was absolutely vital to the survival of hundreds of millions of Indians. To regulate their use and check against overexploitation, many villages had informal systems of community forest management in place. Some forest areas were also set aside as sacred groves and kept wholly free of human intervention.

All this changed with the takeover of woodlands by the British Raj. The training of forest officials mandated them to treat peasants and tribals as enemies of the forest. Commerce and control, rather than ecological sustainability or the provision of rural livelihoods, was the raison d'être of forest management in India in both the colonial and postcolonial periods. Because of the disruptions they caused in the everyday life of the Indian village, the Forest Department became a most reviled arm of the colonial state. There were a series of peasant and tribal rebellions in the late nineteenth and early twentieth centuries, aimed at loosening state control over forests.[16]

This complex and troubled history was well known to the subject of our previous chapter, Verrier Elwin, who wrote so movingly about the predicament of tribals at the receiving end of colonial forest laws. It is unlikely, however, that Munshi was at all aware of how the British had taken over the forests and how they had managed them. He had lived all his life in the city; and the laws he was familiar with and dealt with as a lawyer concerned matters of urban trade, property, commerce and family life.

Munshi knew nothing about forest policy, forest law or forest life before being appointed the head of the ministry which incorporated the Forest Department. However, once he had this job, he was determined to make a mark, and make it quickly. That is why he thought up the idea of this new tree-planting festival, through which the Forest Department and the Indian villagers would together regreen the land, invoking Hindu tradition as they went.

As narrated in Chapter One, Rabindranath Tagore had started an annual tree-planting festival in his university in Santiniketan, named Briksharopan. It does not appear that Munshi knew of this precedent either. In any case, Tagore's religious heterodoxy must have grated on him; unlike the novelist, the poet did not believe that India belonged more to Hindus than to people of other faiths. Besides, Munshi set his sights far higher than Tagore; he would have this festival celebrated not merely in one university campus, but all across the land.

The first edition of Vana Mahotsava was planned for the first week of July 1950, to coincide with the onset of the monsoon. To go along with this festival he had invented, Munshi coined the slogan, 'Trees mean water, water means bread and bread is life.'

Munshi's inauguration of this tree-planting festival was consistent with his belief that 'to the Indian mind, patriotism was not merely a political sentiment as in the West; it was a sentiment charged with high emotional loyalty and deep religious devotion'.[17] In the first week of July 1950, when Vana Mahotsava was formally celebrated across the country, the minister travelled to Gujarat, where he planted a tree at the very place, Dehotsarga, where Krishna was believed to have spent his last moments on earth. After he watered the sapling he gave a speech, where he spoke of seeing visions of Krishna's brother Balaram, 'his hands on the shoulders of his wives, enjoying the voluptuous touch of the breezes flowing from the Western sea'; of his disciple, Arjuna, 'walking hand in hand with Sri Krishna'; and of 'the Lord himself sleeping under a tree'.

Three thousand and more years had passed since Krishna may have lived, yet, said Munshi, 'he lives in our hearts as no other ever did'. For 'His personality was harmonious, perfect, beautiful'. He was the 'embodiment of Indian unity, not merely the World Teacher who stood for the Moral Order, but "God Himself"'. So the minister felt specially privileged for the opportunity to plant a tree in 'these few feet of earth [which] are the holiest in the wide, wide world, for here He reclined, in the last few moments of his earthly existence'.[18]

The speech at Dehotsarga was delivered on 4 July 1950. Three days later the minister was celebrating Vana Mahotsava in the southern town of Kanchipuram, where, after planting a mango tree around the Shri Varadaraja temple, he spoke of 'the intense satisfaction' that visiting such sacred spots gave him. 'This place,' said Munshi, 'has a special attraction for me on this occasion. As the Purana says, it was always surrounded by beautiful trees...' He urged his audience to 'cultivate a sense of the holiness and nobility of trees', enumerating their attributes in an exuberant burst of lyricism. Trees, said the minister,

> have many virtues, but the greatest of them is love. Of living things, they are the most harmless. They live, but not on other living things; they feed only on the soil, the air, the light. They are strong, but never brutal in their strength. They neither rend, nor bite, nor sting. Unlike grasses, they never become weedy plagues. They give without stint—seed, acorn, timber, humus—the mainstay of our life. Their shade saves us from the Sun's

> oppression; their subtle music brings exquisite beauty to the sullen heart. Who is so ascetic as the living noble forest—so reminiscent of our forebears who built the mighty tradition of Bharat![19]

In March 1951, Munshi delivered the convocation address at the Forest Research Institute in Dehradun. This was India's premier centre of forestry research, sited in a gorgeous wooded campus on the outskirts of one of Uttar Pradesh's district towns, Dehradun. It was also where probationers of the Indian Forest Service were trained. Munshi began with patting himself on the back, for having introduced the Vana Mahotsava festival 'to arouse mass consciousness regarding the significance of trees and to revive an adoration for these silent sentinels mounting guard on Mother Earth'. Ten million trees had been planted in the inaugural edition of the festival; to the carping critics who asked, 'how many of these trees have survived?', the minister answered that they would be advised to look out for 'its cumulative effect over a series of years'. For 'it is forest-mindedness which matters in the long run, not the number of trees actually planted'.[20]

In the last week of June 1951, in preparation for the second edition of Vana Mahotsava, the minister gave a broadcast on All India Radio chastising those who had been critical of the first edition of his tree festival. Vana Mahotsava, he insisted, 'is not the product of fancy; nor is it a spectacular festival; it is the most far-reaching item in land transformation'. In his own travels around India, he said, he had found 'the thermometer registers 110 degrees in several parts of the country which were cool and richly wooded once'. The Siwaliks, the Nilgiris, the Himalaya, had all been denuded of their forest cover, leading to erosion, the formation of ravines, and the falling of water tables. Cow dung, a valuable manure, was being used as fuel since there was no wood for peasants to burn in their hearths. All this had a devastating impact on agricultural productivity.

The planting of trees and forests, argued the minister, was the only way of arresting and reversing this widespread degradation of land, soil and forests. 'If we are to survive,' said Munshi, 'our philosophy of life must be reconstructed not in words, ideas or achievements, but in terms which would replant us firmly in the earth and under the shady tree.' Therefore,

> Every one, from the humble shepherd to the President of the Republic, has to be tree-conscious. It should be accepted as a religious duty for every one to plant a tree, to water it, to preserve it, to protect it. To us Indians, this should come naturally, for the tree is sacred to us; it is associated with Vedic hymns, with the bel tree sacred to Shiva, with Shri Krishna's whole life, with the divine *tulsi* [plant] in every home, with the *pipal* [tree] which, as Bhagavad-Gita says, is God Himself.[21]

Munshi's speeches drew on his rhetorical skills, honed from decades of writing novels and arguing briefs in court. In speaking now as a minister, religious imagery, or more specifically Hindu religious imagery, came naturally to him. Ecological and economic reasons for the planting of trees and the protection of forests were not adequate or persuasive in themselves—they had to be clothed in invocations of Hindu myths and Hindu gods.

In September 1951, after a year and a half as minister of food and agriculture, Munshi gave two lectures at the country's premier institute of agricultural research. Both bore a markedly self-congratulatory tone. The first lecture spoke of how, when he took over, the ministry was merely a 'group of fragmented holdings', but now, under his leadership and direction, it had apparently become 'a compact co-operative venture'. He had accomplished this, he claimed, by formulating a five-fold scheme of land transformation as follows: first, the intensive cultivation of a targeted five million acres a year through improved seeds and better water supply; second, reclamation of a targeted one million acres a year of barren land and wasteland; third, the planting of a targeted 30 million trees a year; fourth, the development of cattle wealth by breeding a targeted six thousand pedigreed bulls a year; and fifth, the spread of the message of land transformation through extension centres and the creation of a land army.

To demonstrate the ancient origins and traditional inspiration of this modern scheme of development and transformation, Munshi helpfully provided Sanskrit terms for each of these categories and schemes, as in Bhu Parivartan for land transformation, Krishi Yoga for intensive cultivation, Punarudhara for land recalamation, Vrikhsaropan and Vana Mahotsava for afforestation, Gosamvardhan for enhancement of cattle wealth, and Bhoomi Sena for land army.[22]

The minister's second lecture at the Indian Agricultural Research Institute was more philosophical, outlining a theory of ecological history that saw Indian civilization as passing through three stages: glory, fall and renewal.

In ancient times, argued the writer-lawyer-politician, the people of India had maintained a perfect equilibrium with the natural environment. Their 'traditional art of Land Management' allowed them to capture rainwater in canals, tanks and lakes. Apparently, back then, 'every good king built a tank; every emperor built many'. Rich men of less than noble birth built tanks too; and so did ordinary villagers. Thus, 'on Bhim Ekadashi day the villagers imitated the epic hero by the collective digging of field channels; they thought it to be a religious festival, but it prevented water-logging'.

In those happy days, went on the minister, 'every village largely ate what it produced'. The cow was worshipped and cared for: 'this was a religious act; but the result was that the fields were fertilized with organic manure, and draft power and milk were supplied to the community'. Religious faith also mandated the planting and protection of trees; which in turn supplied fuel, fruit and fodder to keep the economy going.

Such was the glory; whence the fall? Here is Munshi on how the decline from grace happened:

> But the population grew fast. Religious faith which buttressed tradition was undermined. Kings neglected to build lakes; the rich, the tanks. Cows ceased to be mothers and were degraded to become animals; forests and trees were cut down; and in consequence rains became erratic, rivers were flooded or drained up, erosion spread. Cow dung was substituted for firewood for want of fuel. Men forgot collective activities; roads were neglected; fields were water-logged; lands deteriorated through over-exploitation: the equilibrium was disturbed.

Though Munshi did not care to date this decline, he implied that it had begun before colonialism. Then, 'in the British period, we began to forget our traditional arts; nor were we taught modern ways except in a few demonstration farms—museum pieces—maintained under a costly administration…'

Munshi urged modern Indians to work to restore 'the integrity of the Cycle of Life, Jiwan Chakra', which 'in its two aspects, hydrological and nutritional, is at the root of the unity of Man and Unity without which life on earth must become extinct'. Seeking to exhort and inspire his (mostly Hindu) audience, he remarked that

> This Nutritional Cycle is aptly described in the Chhandogya Upanishad:
> 'Prithivya apo rasah apamoshadhyay rasah, oshadhinam purusho rasah…'
> (That is, Water is the essence of earth, plants are the essence of waters and creatures—man is the essence of plants.)

Munshi ended his talk by saying that the expensive, state-directed methods of land reclamation and afforestation adopted by rich countries like the United States were not feasible in India. However, while material resources were scarce here, spiritual resources were inexhaustible. So, concluded the minister, India must achieve 'Land Transformation by restoring the Cycle of Life to villages one by one. The enthusiasm of the villagers themselves must be directed to the goal. This is a religious duty. An Avatar [Krishna] was needed to save the earth once; this time in India, the earth has to be saved by the labours of millions in whom He resides.'[23]

Before he became minister of food and agriculture, Munshi was well known as a novelist, a lawyer and a politician. His devotion to ancient Indian culture was also a matter of record. But this love of forests was utterly new, and, among some circles, treated with scepticism. As the then widely read *Shankar's Weekly* noted in May 1950, 'having dabbled in a diversity of fields ranging from art to archeology, Kan[hai]yalal Munshi has turned to tree-planting. ... If anybody thought that the Food Department would be the graveyard of Munshi's reputation, it must be evident that the rebuilder of Somnath has simplified the problem into a week's festivity. Indians love festivals so much that they can forget about food.'[24]

Munshi's promotion—or self-promotion—of Vana Mahotsava also attracted critical commentary in *The Current*, a popular Bombay weekly edited by the liberal anti-Communist D.F. Karaka. Educated at Oxford, where he had been the first Indian president of the Union, Karaka greatly admired Gandhi, writing a book about him with the reverential, almost hagiographic title, *Out of Dust He Made Us Into Men*. However, he disliked and distrusted Nehru, whom he saw as too soft on Communism and the Soviet Union.[25] Karaka's views on Munshi were ambivalent—while respecting his intellect and legal skills, he was put off by his sanctimonious religiosity.

I have written above of Munshi's first visit to Bombay as food and agriculture minister, and about his speech to the Indian Merchants Chamber asking businessmen to plant trees wherever they could. Among the attendees at the meeting was a reporter from Karaka's *The Current*, who later paraphrased the minister's message as follows:

> The clouds love to kiss the trees and to embrace them. They precipitate themselves like mad lovers, wherever they see a beautiful cluster of grove of trees. To get rain in plenty, therefore, all one has to do is plant and rear trees, chanted Minister Munshi as the refrain of his new song.

The *Current* reporter sarcastically remarked that if the minister 'had been a farmer, instead of a lawyer and a litterateur', he would have known that the farmer wanted not simply more rain, but rain at the right time and in the right amount. 'Will Mr Munshi enlighten us as to how his tree planting programme is going to regulate rainfall?' asked the reporter. Besides, some places, like Bombay itself, had a great deal of rain anyway. So the reporter commented: 'One wonders why he [Munshi] wants the Sethias [merchants] to plant still more trees in the grounds of their residences on Malabar Hill, which will only help in flooding Parel and Nal Bazar more frequently.'[26]

In a follow-up article, the same journalist, Thakorelal M. Desai, said that Vana Mahotsava was 'an excellent idea' which by Munshi's 'overdramatisation of it, has degenerated into a political stunt'.[27]

A few weeks later, the magazine's editor, the redoubtable Karaka, himself weighed in with an article on the subject. Karaka was astonished that Munshi, that 'brilliant, polished lawyer', that 'astute administrator', should now be 'preaching the claptrap and mumbo jumbo of Vanamahotsava'.

'What has Hindu religion got to do with the food problems of a secular state? What have Krishna and the Gopis got to do with trees?' asked Karaka of the minister. He continued:

> Unable and unwilling to tell the truth and tell India that the food shortage is due to a variety of causes which Congress is afraid to tackle, it has fallen back on the old subterfuge of confusing the Hindu mind with slogans of religious nostalgia. Mr Munshi—an adept at hair-splitting in matters of law—has deliberately split hunger into two compartments. One is heavenly intervention and the other is human abstention.
>
> Vana Mahotsava is nothing but a publicity stunt to divert the mind of the majority from reality to religion. It seeks cleverly to play on sentiment so that the need for science may not be too insistent. It seeks to remind men of the pleasing nuances of foliage so that the need for fertilizers may be forgotten. It seeks to excite [us] over trees so that no question may arise about expenditure on tractors.

Karaka remarked that instead of tackling the food crisis head on, Munshi 'quotes old Sanskrit aphorisms to appease the hunger of our people'. In any case, asked the sceptical editor, 'can't food be grown in India without Krishna and his gopis? Can't we plant trees without recourse to jaw-breaking Sanskrit names which the majority of Indians do not even understand?'[28]

Bombay was Munshi's bailiwick, the city where he had built his law practice, where he had taken his first steps in Congress politics, where he had many devoted readers of his novels. He complained to Karaka about the criticisms *The Current* had carried about him, and the editor, knowing that there was nothing like a good controversy to boost sales, asked the minister to send in a rebuttal. This Munshi did, though only a year after the original criticisms of his approach appeared.

The minister began his defence of Vana Mahotsava in *The Current* by saying:

> Man and his surroundings form an integrated whole; he exists as part of the soil and water and plants and trees of the country in which he lives. With marching civilization, however, we have destroyed forests and have upset nature's equilibrium. In our blindness we think that earth will continue to give us food even if we cut down trees on which life depends. In fact, this imbalance leads to erosion, the removal of the nutrient element in the fertile top-soil, the greatest threat to human existence.

Munshi then talked of the disappearance of forests in India in recent decades, and of how this was leading to desertification in the plains and erosions and floods in the mountains. After outlining the evidence of increasing deforestation and its consequences, Munshi revealingly remarked:

> I knew nothing of all this when I took up office [as minister of food and agriculture]. I had to study our food problem, and to my horror, I discovered that India can't grow food unless we grow trees. And in in a flash, the truth came to me:
> Trees mean water; water means bread; and bread is life.
> We had neglected this truth and we are a dying race—like the empire builders in Babylon and Egypt and Central Asia, who disappeared because their land, deprived of trees, and eroded, became deserts, incapable of sustaining life.

> I was convinced that we cannot be saved unless we become tree-minded ... What should I do I asked myself. 'Vana Mahotsava is the remedy': the answer came.

The minister ended his article by speaking of the progress made by his programme in the year since its founding. A Vana Premi Sangh (Lovers of the Forest Society) had been founded in most states. He claimed that some 41 million trees had been planted in the country since he took office. Sixty thousand of these were in a hamlet named Settimadamangalam, which was awarded the All India Jawahar Shield for the village which had planted the most trees. 'States, cities, institutions have found an echo of it [Vana Mahotsava] in their heart,' trumpeted the minister. 'I would like to know another movement which, in so short a time, brought forth such collective enthusiasm.'[29]

This article is revealing in four respects. First, though Munshi was a man of much vanity and self-regard, here he confessed that he 'knew nothing' about the subject at hand before he became the Union minister responsible for forests. Second, though Munshi was a professional writer, some of the notes for this article must have been provided by the scientists on his staff. For the sentences on deforestation and desertification paraphrase and summarize the conclusions of classic scientific works on the subject, such as George Perkins Marsh's *Man and Nature: Or, Physical Geography as Modified by Human Action* and Paul B. Sears's *Deserts on the March*, books Munshi would have been unaware of before he became minister. Third, it is notable that the minister had the prize for the best-performing village named after the prime minister, a naked piece of flattery towards a boss who had ambivalent feelings towards Munshi, and had never trusted him fully. Finally, though in his other speeches on Vana Mahotsava Munshi gave this narrative of ecological decline and ecological renewal a distinctively Hindu twist, he kept religious imagery and religious language wholly out of his article for *The Current*, perhaps because of the secular, modernist cast of mind of the editor and many of the weekly's readers too.

Munshi, we may recall, was a confidant of Vallabhbhai Patel. His undoubted intelligence and administrative abilities notwithstanding, it was his closeness to the second most powerful person in India that helped Munshi get a place in the Cabinet. However, in December 1950 Patel died, and now Nehru was pre-eminent in party and government. In the winter of 1951–52 Nehru led the Congress Party's campaign in the first general elections. After he and his party won a comfortable majority, the prime minister set about reshuffling his Cabinet. He no longer had to accommodate Patel loyalists.

Nehru had run his electoral campaign in 1952 on two principal planks: the promotion of Hindu–Muslim harmony, and the reform of Hindu personal laws so as to give equal rights to women. Both were causes dear to the prime minister, but less dear to his conservative minister of food and agriculture. So Nehru dropped Munshi from his Cabinet, but—given his past record of service—did not want to banish him from public life altogether. So he offered him the job of governor of Uttar Pradesh, a largely ornamental post with no real administrative powers. Munshi was not yet ready to return to private life in Bombay, so he agreed, joining as governor of Uttar Pradesh in May 1952.

Munshi's replacement as food and agriculture minister was Rafi Ahmad Kidwai, a left-leaning Congressman and a personal friend of Nehru. The change had been in the offing; and indeed, in the third week of March 1952, Munshi gave a speech which had all the marks of a valedictory address, delivered by a man about to demit office. This recalled all the changes in policy he had sought to bring about as minister, coining 'the phrase Land Transformation—*Bhu Parivartan* or *Bhumi Parivartan*—just to emphasize the anchorage of our movement in the soil'; the setting up of a 'Bhoomi Sena' or Land Army; 'restoring tree consciousness to the country' by having '*Vana Mahotsava* accepted as a national festival'; 'creating soil-minded[ness] among the educated', etc.

Now, in his last major speech as minister, Munshi urged Indians to restore the 'Cycle of Life' by remembering and honouring revered figures of myth and religion. He observed:

> Bhagirath was the divinely appointed master irrigator of India, bringing Ganga from God Shankar; and God Shankar's companion, Nandi, is the divine stud bull, Kamadhenu, the cow of plenty. Sita Mata—venerated throughout the country—is the daughter of the furrow; Baladeva, the lord of the plough, belongs to our pantheon. Shri Krishna, the divine cow-herd, the saviour of Govardhan, the lover of the cow, the tree and the flute, lives in every Indian heart. And *Mahavaraha*—the Divine Boar, who is God Himself—uplifted and transformed the earth. These are the names which will release springs in our unconscious, and make the Gospel of Land Transformation a vigorous cult.[30]

Before he became minister of food and agriculture, Munshi had shown no interest in the conservation of trees and forests. However, by promoting these themes instrumentally when in office he appeared to have become convinced of their importance. In his speeches as governor of Uttar Pradesh, Munshi continued to associate planting trees with acquiring spiritual merit. 'In olden days we had a loving sentiment for trees,' he said in a speech. 'We treated them as gods and goddesses. ... This sentiment we must restore, if we are to survive.'[31]

In the monsoon of 1953, when the time for the annual Vana Mahotsava arrived, Munshi chose to celebrate it at a shrine associated with Lord Krishna near the holy town of Mathura in Uttar Pradesh. This was the region where—so the legend went—Krishna had spent his boyhood and youth, playing the flute, grazing his cows, cavorting with maidens. Speaking on the occasion, Munshi recalled his participation in the original Vana Mahotsava at Dehotsarga near Somnath where Sri Krishna had left his mortal body. Now, in Vraj, where Krishna spent so much of his early life, he again described him as the presiding deity of this tree festival invented by Munshi. 'Sri Krishna loved forests,' he remarked. 'It is in Vrindavan that He pastured his cows; it is in Kadambavar that He played with the Gopis, and it was in the forest of Giriraj Govardhan that He spent his young days with His friends. Tulsi and Paryata were the favourite trees which He brought from Heaven.'

But, continued Munshi sadly, now 'Vrajbhumi, the land of forests, rivers and food in plenty is being desolated by hot winds, increasing erosion and marching desert. The Government naturally has decided ... to prevent further loss of fertility by intensive afforestation. But the efforts of Government will be of little avail, unless the people respond to this movement more enthusiastically than they have done.'

To raise the percentage of forest area to 33 per cent (as mandated by the National Forest Policy) Indians needed to plant an estimated 200 million trees. 'This can only be done,' said the minister-turned-governor, 'if tree-consciousness enters the heart of every one of us and in India everyone takes a pledge to plant and preserve a tree. The quickest remedy for this purpose is to accept tree-planting as a part of the essential duties of life. It is only if tree planting is associated with every birth, marriage and death that we can speedily achieve our objective. The whole national mind will come to associate tree-planting with great events of our life.'

'To us Indians,' said Munshi, 'the tree is sacred. It is associated with the Vedic prayers. The ancient Rishis sang: "May the gods, the waters, plants and the forest trees accept our prayers." The *bel* tree is sacred to Shiva. ... Sri Krishna's whole life is, as I stated, associated with trees. Lord Buddha got his enlightenment under the Bodhi tree.'

Then he continued, mournfully, 'But we have forgotten our heritage. We want Government to do everything which we should do ourselves. Our shrines and places of pilgrimage are bare, without trees. Just as here hundreds of thousands of pilgrims go round the Parikarama path unrelieved by any tree-shade, the whole route from Rishikesh to Badrinath by which hundreds of thousands of pilgrims go every year and which once had beautiful trees, is just treeless.'

Munshi ended his speech at Mathura with this exhortation:

> There is no greater form of worship than to plant or preserve a tree. It is the living contact between the devotee and the God. Every devotee, therefore, must at least plant one tree in the shrine which he loves most. Time and again, I have appealed to the whole country to help in restoring our sacred places to their pristine beauty ... because I felt that that was the noblest way in which religious feeling could be translated into action. ... I assure you that devotion and prayer can take no better form than that of planting a tree at the shrine we love most. I hope, therefore, that the people of Mathura and Vrindaban will make it a point to restore Vrajabhumi to its traditional beauty which lives in our hearts and that every pilgrim who comes here will plant a tree in the name of Sri Krishna and for the purpose that the land in which He was born should be as lovely as His memory.[32]

A year later, the governor of Uttar Pradesh was called upon to inaugurate an international gathering of scientists, the fourth World Forestry Congress, held at the Forest Research Institute in

Dehradun. This time the lawyer-politician adopted a resolutely secular tone in his address, in whose drafting he seems to have consulted some Indian forestry scientists.

Munshi's welcome address to the international delegates stressed the pressures on forests 'of an ever-increasing population'. An explosion of humans on earth had massively increased the demand for wood as raw material for industry and construction, had created an imbalance between land under the plough and land under forest cover, and led to increasing desertification. The solution to these varied problems was, as Munshi here defined it, 'rational land use'. He said: 'It might be that if the whole world had one Government with powers to enforce rigid forest regulations, the present forest resources, managed scientifically, would suffice for the growing needs of man. But the realization of such a state of affairs is still a dream. Forest resources, must, therefore ... be planned on a regional basis.'

In a five-page address, only one short paragraph dwelt on the cultural reasons for forest conservation, and this too in bland, unemotive, tones. The paragraph read:

> In 1950, India woke up to the danger attendant upon the denudation of its tree-growth. Tree consciousness had disappeared from the popular mind. India's culture, as you know, was born and cradled under the shade of mighty forests. Planting and protecting of trees was once part of its socio-religious traditions, which by the passage of time had all but disappeared.[33]

Note the contrast, in tenor, tone and thrust, between this address to scientists and technologists attending the World Forestry Congress, and the speeches given by Munshi to audiences of spiritually minded people. The latter looked to religion for a solution, whereas this one offered a scientific and rational programme. His long years at the bar, appearing for clients with all kinds of conflicting and contrasting briefs, had clearly prepared Munshi to play different strokes for different folks.

That said, there is no question that Munshi himself greatly preferred speaking of the importance of forests in religious rather than in scientific terms. It was then that he really warmed to the subject, his rhetorical skills finding full play, his knowledge of myth and epic effectively put in the service of human action in the present. A last example of Munshi the eloquent Hindu environmentalist is offered below.

Every year, the governor of Uttar Pradesh spent the summer months not in the state capital, Lucknow, but in the hill station of Nainital. In July 1954, the governor celebrated the fifth Vana Mahotsava by planting a magnolia tree on the promenade along the lake in Nainital. The ceremony brought back a flood of memories, which the governor later wrote up for publication; memories of how, as minister of food and agriculture with forestry as one of its charges, he had thought up the idea of this festival. In his telling, in June 1950 he was on a flight to Bombay shortly after taking over as minister, when,

> All of a sudden, trees were before me: the trees of which the Vedic rishis sang: 'May the gods, the waters, plants and the forest trees accept our prayers.' The trees of Naimisharanya under the shade of which our culture was born. The trees which gave to those who planted them the religious merit of having ten sons for each tree. The trees which Shakuntala watered daily before she took her food; trees, the new shoots of which she would not pluck lest their feelings should be hurt. The *Vat* tree which millions of women have worshipped through the ages to get the blessings of Savitri: an excellent husband, a death before he dies, and children and grandchildren. The trees and groves of Vrindavana and Nandavana.

As the aircraft made its way towards Bombay, a further flood of associations between trees and Hindu myths came to the minister's mind. These included the

> *Kalpa-Vriksha*, the wishing tree, our symbol of plenty; the *Devadaru* tree, which, when it was injured, Lord Shiva adopted as a son, and whom Parvati herself nursed; the *Bael* tree, sacred to Shiva; the *Akshayavat*, from which the sinner can jump to salvation; the *Bodhi* tree, which threw its peaceful shade over Lord Buddha when he attained Enlightenment; the *Peepul*, daily worshipped by millions as the embodiment of Brahma, Vishnu and Shiva; the *Parijataka* and *Tulsi*, so cherished by Sri Krishna and worshipped in numberless homes.

This recollection of how a new festival was added to the Hindu ritual calendar ended with these self-satisfied, self-congratulatory lines:

> And I wrote the appeal to the country to observe the Vana Mahotsava. And the country responded wonderfully. A silent chord in its heart had been touched.[34]

Munshi died in 1971 in Bombay. His legacy lives on in his novels—which still command a wide and continuing readership in Gujarat—and in the institution he founded, the Bharatiya Vidya Bhavan, which now has branches all over India, and quite a few in foreign countries too, promoting a Hindu/Sanskritic version of Indian culture to seekers of all ages and social backgrounds. Munshi also lives on, less certainly, in legal discourse, with histories of the making of the Indian Constitution occasionally nodding to his contributions.

Other major Indian thinkers—such as Gandhi, Nehru and Tagore, for example—viewed their country's past with a critical eye, seeing in ancient customs and traditions something to retain but also much to discard. Munshi's nationalism, on the other hand, had a conservative, even revanchist, tenor to it. As one of his admirers wrote on his seventy-fifth birthday, Munshi's

> love for the country was conditioned by his adoration for its past. The whole of India's history unfolded itself on the canvas of his mind and whenever he went in this vast continent, his mind flew back to its past and imbibed the glorious incidents of long ago. He always recalls to himself the historic and sacred associations of every town and city and sees through it, his motherland, in the context of what made it not merely famous but also adorable.[35]

Or as an official who worked with him when he was minister of food and agriculture remarked, Munshi 'was sustained in all his efforts by his beliefs, born out of his respect for the wisdom of the ancients and his pride in the past glories of our land'.[36]

What these admirers leave unsaid is that Munshi had an essentially Hindu, even Brahminical, understanding of India's geography and history. The sacred associations of towns and cities that he discovered were never Christian or Muslim, never Parsi, Jain or Sikh, and never Adivasi or Dalit either. As Munshi himself put it towards the end of his life, in all the decades he worked as a lawyer, novelist, politician and institution-builder, he led a parallel life of the imagination, steeped in the Hindu past of his province, Gujarat, and his country, India. I quote:

> Side by side with the real world, from 1910 up to now, I have lived in a world of my own— ... inhabited by mighty men and women of the Vedic and Epic ages—Vasishtha, Viswamitra,

> Parashurama, Agastya and Lopamundra, Krishna and Rukmini, Balarama and Uddhava. As also men and women of the golden prime of the Chalukyan era of Gujarat—Munjal, Kak, Khengar, Ranak, Manjari, Chaula, Bada Maharaj.[37]

For all his conservative tendencies, in his lifetime Munshi never explicitly identified with the Hindu Right. In the 1930s and 1940s, while retaining an uncertain position within a Congress party that under Nehru's leadership was increasingly moving leftwards, Munshi resisted the temptation to join the Hindu Mahasabha. In the late 1950s, when he finally left the Congress, Munshi joined not the explicitly Hindu-first Jana Sangh but the free market-oriented Swatantra Party.

After his death, however, Munshi became something of an inspirational figure for the ideologues of the successor party to the Jana Sangh, the Bharatiya Janata Party (BJP), and its sister organization the Rashtriya Swayamsevak Sangh (RSS). BJP leaders such as L.K. Advani and Amit Shah are said to be particularly partial to Munshi's novels, with their glorification of Hindu society and vilification of Muslim rulers. The BJP prime minister, Narendra Modi, is not known to be a reader of literature, but as a native Gujarati speaker who has spent much of his life in Gujarat, the influential, albeit fictional, renderings of history in Munshi's novels would surely have reached him at second- and third-hand.[38]

The belief system of the RSS and the BJP goes by the name of 'Hindutva'. Munshi is an acknowledged ancestor for them; his crucial role in the building of the Somnath temple is mentioned often and always approvingly. His phrase 'Vishwa Guru' is now in common currency; with the BJP in power in Delhi, its cheerleaders argue that a sufficiently Hinduized India is destined to lead the world.

I am not a man of the Hindu Right. It is the historian in me that has prompted this recovery of a now wholly forgotten part of Munshi's varied and colourful career—his phase as an environmentalist. One reason why this aspect of Munshi's work has been ignored is, in part, that like Tagore there were so many aspects to him to discuss and discover. But there may be another reason—namely, that whereas in the case of Tagore his love for, and attention towards, nature was a lifelong preoccupation, central to his way of thinking and being in this world, for Munshi it was an instrumental choice and lasted only a few years.

In recent years, as the environmental movement has spread and acquired new adherents and newer dimensions, the question of whether a person's faith can help protect or renew nature has often been discussed in the popular as well as scholarly literature. One academic paper, identifying 'religious environmentalism as a late twentieth-century phenomenon', defines it as 'a blending of environmental values derived from faith-based traditions that prompt people to work for nature conservation and sustainable models of living in the [modern] world'. The essay discusses several examples of contemporary religious environmentalism in India, as in the involvement of the traditionally vegetarian Jains in the work of the organization People for Ethical Treatment of Animals, and of devotees of the Hindu deity Krishna in the afforestation of the Vrindavan region of north India where he is said to have lived and which has many ancient shrines devoted to his worship.[39]

Strikingly, this essay, while rich and informative in itself, does not mention Munshi. Nor does a book with a long chapter entitled 'Religious Environmentalism in India', which analyses claims made by Hindutva activists today that sacred groves, sacred rivers and myths of tree and mountain worship are emblematic of how Hindus uniquely lived in harmony with the natural world.[40] The amnesia is widespread; other works which discuss contemporary Hindu/Hindutva environmentalism from both sympathetic and critical perspectives do not seem to know of what Munshi wrote on this subject many decades previously.[41]

What explains the neglect of Munshi in the now fairly widespread discussion of environmentalism with a Hindutva cast? One reason surely is that, like Indians in general, Indian environmentalists tend to be indifferent to history. Another may be that, unlike all the other individuals featured in this book, Munshi did not become an environmentalist through experience or conviction. In his work as a lawyer, novelist and politician, Munshi wrote or spoke millions of words, but I doubt whether before he became a Cabinet minister in 1950, nature or nature conservation, or forests and forestry, figured in his writings and talks at all. However, when he was appointed minister of food and agriculture, with forests under his charge, his reading of Sanskrit literature and of the epics inspired Munshi to make these connections between Hindu tradition and forest protection.

As minister, Munshi founded this new tree-planting festival, Vana Mahotsava, and energetically proselytized on its behalf. As governor of Uttar Pradesh, he liked to speak of forests and nature in religious, or Hindu, terms. However, after demitting office as governor, the subject vanished from his writings and speeches. In the last decade and a half of his life he focused principally on the cultural and literary activities of the Bharatiya Vidya Bhavan, and secondarily on his work as a member of the Swatantra Party.

Over the years, Vana Mahotsava itself became a ritual that had little tangible impact on India's forest cover. The rates of survival of saplings were very low, even in the early years. This was perhaps inevitable, because it was a top-down, state-sponsored environmentalism, and because it asked people to plant trees out of religious duty rather than practical need. And the minister who promoted it was himself only a recent and temporary convert to the cause (D.F. Karaka was perhaps not altogether mistaken in seeing Vana Mahotsava as a publicity stunt). Nonetheless, Munshi's brief foray into environmentalism is noteworthy, because of the passion and eloquence he brought to the job, and because he was the first Hindu environmentalist, the first thinker or activist in India to bring an explicitly religious dimension to the conservation and protection of nature.

CHAPTER NINE

Speaking for Nature

M. KRISHNAN AND INDIAN WILDLIFE

DESPITE THEIR VARYING BIOGRAPHICAL trajectories and their different political and philosophical orientations, the nine figures considered so far have one thing in common—that they approached nature and the environment largely from a human perspective. Tagore did write lyrically of trees, birds, rivers and mountains, but from the point of view of the aesthetic joys they provided to him, and people like him. Geddes did, in one of his forgotten Indian town plans, use the term 'biocentric' decades before it was adopted by the so-called 'Deep Ecologists', but the burden of his work was to make cities more habitable for humans. Elwin saw both beauty and mystery in the forests of central India, yet he rarely looked at them in isolation from the culture of the tribals who inhabited them. Munshi could go into raptures about the glories of the forest too, but only in so far as they contributed to the spiritual nourishment of his fellow Hindus. As for Mukerjee, Kumarappa and the Howards, the environmentalism they preached was severely pragmatic, even perhaps utilitarian. They asked that humans be respectful towards nature, and restrained in their use of natural resources, so as to ensure a dignified life for themselves and their descendants. Mira's writings on forests and rivers did occasionally exhibit a romantic (or Romantic) sensibility, but the overarching aim of her work was likewise human-centred.

The environmentalist profiled in this chapter sets himself apart from the others in this book by virtue of putting nature first, by viewing the present and the future from the perspective of the non-human world. He was an eloquent spokesman for nature, who, in the range of his experience, the quality of his prose and the directness of his thought, might be thought of as an Indian equivalent of the pioneering American wilderness advocate John Muir. If he remains far less known than Muir, this is in part because Indian nature lovers are far less historically aware than their American counterparts, and because the man himself scattered his learning and his passion in thousands of newspaper columns published in the pre-digital age, the paper they were printed on pulped soon thereafter, so that these columns could never be retrieved and read afresh. (Muir himself, cannier and sharper, made sure to leave behind a series of books for posterity.)

M. Krishnan (to give our spokesman for nature his name) was born in the southern town of Tirunelveli on 30 June 1912, the youngest of the eight children of the Tamil writer and reformer A. Madhaviah (1872–1925). Madhaviah was employed in the Salt and Abkari Department of the Government of Madras. Posted in small towns, his work involved much riding on horseback, cross-country, in search of smugglers and drug peddlers. In his spare time he read, and wrote. His vast output includes the first realistic novel published in Tamil (*Padmavathi Charithram*, 1898), an English novel published in London (*Thillai Govindan*, 1916), as well as essays, short stories, poems and skits. In about the year 1920 he took premature retirement, commuted his pension, and with the proceeds built a house in the Madras locality of Mylapore in which he installed a printing press. Madhaviah had resolved to devote the rest of his life to the production and promotion of Tamil literature, but sadly not much was left of it. He died at the age of fifty-five in the Senate House of the University of Madras, immediately after making an impassioned speech on the need to introduce Tamil (or the equivalent mother tongue) as a compulsory subject for the BA degree.

When his father died, Krishnan was studying at the Hindu High School in Madras; although not what we would term a 'prize' student, he read widely, and had developed an interest in art. Also in nature, for Mylapore in the 1920s was something of a frontier settlement, stray houses with acres of shrub and pasture in between. The area was home to a teeming bird life and the odd jackal and blackbuck as well. The environment rubbed off: at the age of eleven this son of a scholarly Brahmin had as his pet a grown mongoose.

In 1927 Krishnan joined the Presidency College in Madras, an institution which, now decayed, was then in its pomp. He appeared for the Intermediate examination and in 1931 for the BA, one of his subjects the Tamil for which his father had so vigorously fought. However, the subject he most enjoyed was Botany, taught by Professor P.F. Fyson. Fyson was a devoted field scientist who (judging from Krishnan's references to him in later life) deeply impressed the young student. He accompanied the Fysons on trips to the Nilgiri and Kodaikanal hills, learning science from the professor and discussing the techniques of watercolour painting with his wife.[1]

At the family's behest Krishnan then spent two years obtaining a law degree. He graduated in 1936, but there is no record of any subsequent briefs or court appearances. In those days the lack of an income was no bar to matrimony. Thus on 26 March 1937 Krishnan married Indumati Hasnabis from Bangalore, only fifteen, but in spirit and strength of will already a match for her husband.

The first record of any paid employment for Krishnan dates to 1937, when he published some drawings and caricatures in the now defunct *Madras Mail*. The next year he was publishing essays on book design in the low-circulation but high-prestige *Indian Affairs* and, more consequentially, nature notes in *The Statesman* and *The Hindu*, the leading English-language newspapers of Calcutta and Madras respectively. These early notes display the close observation and spare style that was to distinguish all his work.

In the early years of his marriage Krishnan irregularly held a 'regular' job—working initially with the Associated Printers, then with the Madras School of Art, and finally as the publicity officer of the local station of All India Radio. In 1942, at his family's urging and with the help of what influence they could command, Krishnan was given employment by the Maharaja of Sandur, a small princely state in the northern parts of present-day Karnataka. Employment was, it seems, a somewhat incidental consideration—the main reason for the move being that his wife's doctor had advised them to relocate to a drier place.

Krishnan was to spend eight years in Sandur—eight years under one paymaster but, true to form, in many jobs. He served successively as schoolteacher, judge, publicity officer and political secretary to the Maharaja. The work was dreary, but there was always the possibility of escape. For in his tours through Sandur the aspiring naturalist would come across the Sambar deer and the wild boar, jackals, jungle cats, porcupines and leopards. In this valley ringed by hills and forests, with fields and shrub jungle within and the Tungabhadra flowing through them, and the great ruined city of Hampi but a day's bullock-cart journey away, Krishnan could nurture his love of nature and cultural history. He raised goats, occasionally grazing them himself; bred pigeons, running an experimental pigeon-post with the state's boy scouts; and walked in the wild and among the Hampi temples, returning home to read by lantern-light the Tamil poets once patronized by the Vijayanagara kings.

Krishnan was temperamentally well suited to the informal paternalism of the princely state. He could fit in here as he would never have adjusted to the rule-bound impartiality of the administration of British India. Sandur was Krishnan's finishing school or, to vary the metaphor slightly, the laboratory where he conducted the research for his unacknowledged doctoral degree. What he learnt there was communicated in the nature essays, cultural profiles and short stories he published in the 1940s, under his own name in *The Illustrated Weekly of India* and under the nom de plume 'Z' in *The Hindu*. For years afterwards, he would embellish his articles with a fact or anecdote from his Sandur days.

In 1949, when the princely state of Sandur disappeared along with five hundred and twenty others into the Union of India, Krishnan returned to Madras, taking up residence in the tiled cottage his father had built for his press. He never took a job again, for the next forty-seven years making a precarious living as a writer and photographer. In 1950 he began a fortnightly 'Country Notebook' for *The Statesman* of Calcutta; this carried on till his death in 1996. Alert and alive, at once scientific and speculative, peppered with allusions to literature and myth, opinionated and acid in its wit, the column must rank as one of the remarkable achievements of English-language journalism in this country (or any other). While *The Statesman* was his mainstay,

Krishnan also wrote for *The Hindu*, *The Indian Express*, *The Illustrated Weekly of India*, *Shankar's Weekly*, et al., and on a staggering variety of subjects. Krishnan is known above all as a great pioneering naturalist, as he should be. But in his day he had also served notice as an art critic, a writer of fiction, a poet, a translator and a literary historian. In January 1952 he even reported for *The Statesman* on the five days of the Madras Test of that year, the match in which Vinoo Mankad took twelve wickets as India beat England for the first time. These reports were said to be 'From a Special Cricket Correspondent', a seemingly curious description more true than the newspaper knew.

Krishnan was a vegetarian who never held a rifle, a man who was exceptional in his generation for being a conservationist qua conservationist, not a shikari-turned-protector or a member of the repentant butchers' club. The finest students of India's natural history have either been Europeans, or Hindus and Christians from artisanal or labouring castes, or members of the Rajput and Muslim nobility. Europeans have been inspired to more serious study by their experience of the wild and their adherence to a post-Enlightenment scientific rationality; naturalists of plebeian background familiarized by an occupational tradition of working with animals or plants; rajas and nawabs challenged by their aristocratic lineage to move from hunting to conservation. And yet, it fell to a rasam-drinking, gun-loathing Brahmin vegetarian to become the ablest naturalist of them all.

Krishnan published close to two thousand newspaper articles in his time, a majority of them for *The Statesman*. However, I'd like to begin this exploration of his environmentalist ideas not with one of those 'Country Notebook' columns, but with a four-part essay he published in *The Illustrated Weekly of India* in February–

March 1965. The *Illustrated Weekly* was then the most popular magazine among India's influential English-speaking middle class. With barely any television then, and the internet decades in the future, this weekly periodical provided its thousands of readers with a window to their country and the world. The magazine ranged widely over the domains of politics, economics and history, with plenty of space provided for art, sports and film too. It was avidly read by civil servants, army officers, lawyers, journalists, corporate executives and homemakers.

In 1965 Krishnan was in his early fifties. He had three decades of field experience as a naturalist behind him. He had travelled to all parts of India, spending time in all its varied landscapes, whether forested or otherwise. While he knew the tiger and the elephant, he wrote as lovingly of the jackal, the ghorpad and the spotted owlet, the small, homely, unglamorous denizens of the Indian countryside. As a trained botanist, he had a deep knowledge of plants, and was a close student of bird life as well.

Krishnan's four-part series in the *Illustrated Weekly* drew on this formidable reservoir of knowledge to analyse the past, present and possible future of India's wildlife. His first article began with this lament:

> I have seen forested hills denuded, and reduced to bare, boulder-strewn slopes, within a period of four years. And over the past forty years I have observed the shady avenue and large, tree-grown compounds, the palm groves and green fields, and the mud-flats in and around Madras City gradually turn into congested housing colonies, and watched their rich bird life get impoverished. All over India, even in the remote hill-forests, such things have been happening with increasing frequency and tempo. ... Any number of instances can be cited, with circumstantial detail, of the sudden or slow conversion of jungle and scrub into barren wastes, plantations of exotics, housing colonies, roads, industrial

> centres, and Plan projects, from official records and the testimony of trustworthy people, and also from my own observation and knowledge.

Krishnan was writing this series, he said, as 'we must know how and why there has been this devastation of our great heritage of nature, to save what is left'. He spoke of the richness and diversity of Indian wildlife in ancient and medieval times, as witnessed in poetry, sculpture and hunting records of emperors. This historical evidence, he remarked, demonstrated that 'India had a fauna every bit as rich as that of any other country in the world', and that the bird life was 'superbly rich' too. Then he talked of the decimation of forests in recent decades, due to a growing population, the expansion of agriculture, commercial forestry, dams and other development projects—all of which had led to the 'general decline of the wild life, the near extinction of some species and the total extinction of the cheetah...' (Surprisingly, Krishnan did not mention hunting by colonial officials and princes as contributing to this decimation.) He also spoke of early attempts to protect endangered species, such as the Gir sanctuary for the Asiatic lion in the western state of Gujarat and the Kaziranga park for the Indian rhinoceros in the eastern state of Assam.

Unlike many other wildlife conservationists, Krishnan was as interested in plants as in animals, and keenly understood the relationship between the two. While there was some knowledge of 'the great variety and distinction of our fauna', he remarked, its 'dependence on the native flora needs to be stressed'. The 'intimate and often delicately-balanced relationship between the native plants and animals,' he added, 'is of the greatest importance in all wild life work, as has been proved over and again in so many different parts of the world'. In this context, commented the naturalist, 'the plantations of exotics by our Forest Departments, and the spread of these exotic plants by the forests being opened up, do more harm to the wildlife than is generally realized'. He then named some tree species of South American and Australian provenance that had proliferated on Indian soil—such as eucalyptus, wattle, cashew, casuarina, etc.—all promoted not on private farmland but on territory controlled by the state Forest Departments. Krishnan insisted that 'wild life can thrive only in natural forests and scrubland. We have lost too much ground, where we have not much ground, to plantations of exotics in the past 30 years.'

The naturalist argued that it was 'specially with reference to the decline in bird life that I deplore this craze for exotics...' He talked of how, in the past, indigenous species like the mahua, the banyan and the Indian laburnum were widely planted around villages and along roads, adding that these trees 'attract birds to themselves when in flower and fruit, a thing that the exotics now in vogue do not'.

Coming next to the means of protecting and renewing the wildlife that still remained, Krishnan accepted that there was a reverence for nature in some Indian spiritual traditions, and that in some places rural communities had protected the nesting sites of waterbirds. He nonetheless believed that this was 'a sentiment no longer strong in our countryside culture, and at all times it was extremely local. The fact remains that our feeling for our wild life has never risen to the level of national consciousness...' Therefore, Krishnan felt that the state had to take the lead. 'Even if an informed public feeling for our wild life could be stimulated,' he remarked, 'it can find expression for itself only through governmental agency.'

How could the Indian state best fulfil this mandate to protect India's wildlife? Among the specific suggestions made by Krishnan were: first, the expansion of the network of parks and sanctuaries under government ownership, and second, a strict prohibition on sport hunting (shikar) in these parks and sanctuaries. He asked that the state prevent other forms of disturbance and interference as well, such as poaching of small game and the grazing of domestic cattle by villagers. A third suggestion was for the state to find means to protect endangered species of the open country, such as the Great Indian Bustard and the four-horned antelope, which lived amidst farmlands and shrub where a strictly demarcated and protected sanctuary would be hard, if not impossible, to create. Finally, Krishnan urged the government to encourage natural history education in schools and colleges.

Notably, Krishnan recommended the setting up of sanctuaries oriented towards distinctive types of Indian flora in addition to distinctive types of Indian fauna. These plant sanctuaries would focus on saving and showcasing tracts of evergreen rainforest, mixed deciduous forests, scrub jungle, shola forests, etc. This, he noted, was 'a pressing need today when the natural forests are going so rapidly, and are being converted into plantations and project sites'.

'The saving of our wildlife is a race against time,' said Krishnan in conclusion. He hoped that, by means of the measures he had suggested, Indians now living 'can assure to our future generations a joy and a pride in the country's great heritage of nature, one of the most deeply satisfying things that life in India has to offer to the people'.[2]

This series on India's wildlife was occasionally wistful and elegiac, mourning what had been lost. But it was not gloomy or depressing in tone. At this stage in life, Krishnan still had faith in the intentions of the Indian government to protect the country's natural heritage, still had hope that he would himself see the fruits of purposive state action in his lifetime.

When one thinks of 'nature' or of 'wildlife' in the Indian context, two names that immediately come to mind are Jim Corbett and Salim Ali. The first, an Englishman resident in India, became famous for his stories of hunting man-eating tigers and leopards. The second, an aristocratic Muslim from Bombay, wrote many authoritative books on birds in the subcontinent. Both Corbett and Ali also vigorously advocated for the setting aside of wild areas for the protection of endangered species.[3]

Like Krishnan, neither Corbett nor Ali had advanced research degrees. Ali had a BSc from Bombay University and Corbett never went to college at all. They were self-taught and self-trained. Both focused on a particular slice of the non-human world. Corbett was associated especially with the tiger. Ali was commonly referred to as the 'Bird Man of India'. Where Krishnan differed from them was that he was an all-rounder who took equal interest in all aspects of the natural world. As Shanthi and Ashish Chandola write, Krishnan's work

> stands out as uniquely original, combining acute and systematic observation, depth of knowledge and the understanding of nature. The ultimate freelancer, Krishnan did not just write about birds, mammals, insects, and so on, but also about every aspect of natural history, even addressing issues like conservation and environment well before they had become commonplace. His mastery of English literature, exhibiting a rare charm, is evident in his writing. Such brilliance in nature writing had never been seen before or since in our part of the world.[4]

Krishnan had a well-deserved reputation as an expert on the behaviour of the tiger and the elephant, yet he was as interested in plants and trees as in spectacular animals. 'India's flora,' he wrote, 'is one of the richest in the world and definitely richer than her fauna, and no less a part of the country's wildlife. We have magnificent trees, many superb timbers, a wealth of arrestingly lovely flowering plants, and many plants remarkable for their fruits or medicinal properties—and still the flora is so seldom featured in the wildlife display of a preserve, and this is in spite of the fact that the local variations of the flora are often greater than in the fauna.' Of the publicity choices of the state Forest Departments and the conservation community, he mournfully noted that 'the lesser life and the avifauna are also remarkably versatile display material, but in our preserves such poor interpretation service as there is is preoccupied with the contrived display of a few large mammals, chief among them the man-shy and nocturnal tiger'.[5]

Writing in the early 1960s, Krishnan said to name or designate a particular area as a 'Tiger Sanctuary', as conservationists were prone to do, was misleading and inappropriate. For one thing, these areas had wild herbivores such as deer and antelope that were then being avidly hunted, and thus 'much more urgently in need of protection than the tiger'. For another, visitors to these parks were far more likely to see these other creatures than the tiger. 'Why, then,' he asked, 'call any forest area a Tiger Sanctuary, when the tiger is the most inconspicuous feature of the place?'[6]

In his attention to humdrum and unglamorous landscapes Krishnan was altogether uncharacteristic of nature conservationists in India and elsewhere. 'People who think that India is a land of tree forests outside human settlements,' he once remarked, 'know nothing about the country. A vitally geofloristic feature of India is its vast spreads of open country, arid plains and littoral scrub, tree-dotted scrub jungle, expansive herb-covered elevated plateaux, rolling hilltop pastures, and rocky hill-crests with limited xerophytic growth.'[7]

Krishnan's awareness of the wildlife potential of areas not categorized or seen—either by the state or by nature lovers—as 'forests' came in part from his childhood experience, when his father was posted in places like Ramnad and Tirunelveli, and the years he later himself spent working in Sandur, in the Deccan. He noted that areas categorized as 'wastelands' in government records once had very rich plant and animal life and could do so once again if adequately protected. Mammals such as blackbuck and the wolf flourished in the open scrub that had now come under the plough or human settlement.

In an essay written when he was in his seventies, Krishnan observed: 'Perhaps because of my boyhood interest in the open scrub and my years in the plains country, I know the plants and animals of such habitats better than most people. Such wastelands (as they are invariably termed by politicians and planners) have their own distinctive wild life which is every bit as much part of our heritage of nature as the hill forests, and much more in need of protection, because their wholesale depletion has not, apparently, caused any concern to our governmental conservation effort.'[8]

Among the non-charismatic mammals Krishnan had a special fondness for was the blackbuck. Another was the lion-tailed macaque, which he had likewise studied in the field and extensively photographed. In the 1980s, a large dam threatened to drown one of the last refuges of this latter animal, an area known as Silent Valley in Kerala. Krishnan wrote a column on why it was important to preserve this tract, for the other parts of the Western Ghats in which the macaque was once often seen had given way to fields and plantations. Silent Valley, he wrote, 'is now the only habitat where they have a fairly extensive and congenial environment'.

The naturalist argued that the case of the lion-tailed macaque demonstrated that 'it is always animals of specialized habitats, incapable of adjusting themselves to changed environments, that have the least survival potential'. He wondered how to get the point across to the decision-makers in the national capital. The lion-tailed macaque, he remarked, 'is too far away from Delhi and too little known there for any strong response; in the Delhi zoo it is housed, pitiably, in an enclosure provided with a few thorny, straggling desert trees and exotics at that (*Prosopis julifora*), to offer a denizen of the lofty, dark, evergreen forests a homely amenity!'[9]

While appreciating the need for national parks and sanctuaries, Krishnan urged that areas within cities be made hospitable for nature to flourish. 'Plant a section of every [city] park and [home] garden with native jungle trees (not forgetting a few fig trees) and thick bushes,' he wrote, 'allow creepers and the undershrub to grow, and the birds and smaller beasts will come back.' When he was a boy, he himself had 'ample opportunities for watching minor wild life in a city and in the countryside'. He wished for the present generation to be as fortunate. 'The idea that our fauna should be penned up in national parks and preserves,' he remarked, 'and that our children should visit these pens or some remote countryside for a glimpse of the great heritage of nature that is theirs, revolts me.'[10]

In 1975, Krishnan was asked by a popular magazine to write about what particularly fascinated him about Indian wildlife. He responded with a long ruminative essay, recounting his experiences with wild animals and plants over the decades. He began with elephants, encountered singly or in groups, speaking of them as 'incredibly surefooted in their movements, combining the most delicate sensibilities with terrific power, so like us in some ways and so utterly different in others, gentle and sure in their touch for all their bulk, so long and so intimately associated with our country and culture that without them I cannot envisage an India'. He then wrote with similar specificity (and sensitivity) of his experiences with the tiger, leopard, chital and blackbuck, and moved on to describing bird species which had fascinated and enchanted him, before launching into this lyrical passage on the gloriously varied vegetation of India:

> One need not be a botanist to find authentic pleasure in the wild plants, in the great, towering trees of a rain-forest, in a noble rosewood or teak tree, or in the dramatic bursting into bloom of forest flowers. Early in summer, the Indian laburnum, the red silk-cotton (what a regal canopy of crimson!) and other forest trees flower, and in November it is the turn of the lesser plants, when the vivid red-and-yellow flowers of the wild lily, *Glorioso superba*, festoon the bushes and the most gorgeous and delightfully fragrant of ground orchids, *Platanthera susanude*, is in bloom.

Krishnan ended his essay with this line: 'Yes, everything about our wildlife fascinates me. This is at once my burden and my solace.'[11]

Krishnan was once asked to speak at the Indian Institute of Science in Bangalore, perhaps the most beautiful of our university campuses. It was late February, and the avenues were set alight by the rosy trumpet tree, *Tabebuia rosea*, whose spectacular pink flowers were in blossom. At a reception after his talk, Krishnan was asked what he thought of the campus. 'Disgraceful,' he answered. 'You should uproot all those foreign trees, and plant some of our own.'[12] On another occasion, when a kinsman wrote of the death by felling of a gulmohar tree near his house, Krishnan shot back: 'Anyway, why regret the demise of a gul mohar—an exotic that litters the ground beneath with fallen, faded flowers—a vermilion strumpet from Madagascar? If you want to see a truly impressive crown of red flowers, you should see the flame-of-the forest, *Butea monosperma*, entirely our own, early in summer—3 or 4 trees close together setting the horizon ablaze.'[13]

Krishnan strongly opposed the promotion of tree species alien to India. 'I am dead against introduction of all exotics into our hospitable countrysides,' he once remarked, 'much as we may cherish them as pot-plants or in gardens—some of our finest trees have been supplanted by far less attractive exotics, out of a denationalized craze for exotics.'[14] In another column, he outlined the principles of tree planting 'in diverse denuded locations in India'. He recommended that

> the trees chosen for each location must be determined solely with regard to the nature and composition of the soil, the rainfall and elevation of the place and, of course, its indigene. No exotic tree should be selected where an Indian tree will do, and there are a great many native trees seldom considered, and perhaps even unknown, to our tree-planters. Knowledgeable regional, or even local, committees familiar with each location and the flora around it, rather than any central organization, can provide the best advice on what to plant, and where, how and when to plant it.[15]

Krishnan was particularly disappointed that the annual tree festival invented by K.M. Munshi, Vana Mahotsava, also promoted exotic species. 'Let us not plant exotics once more during future Vanamahotsavas,' he wrote in an essay of 1965. 'Let us, instead, plant a few indigenous trees that can gladden the lives of future generations and, since these trees (unlike many exotics that have a hardy youth and come up quick) need time to mature, let us devote subsequent Vanamahotsavas for the next five years not to fresh tree-planting, but to the inspection of the trees planted during the first year, so that we can know how many of them survive and how well they have been nurtured in between Vanamahotsavas. This I think will result in more trees and better-grown trees than the present procedure.'[16] His suggestion fell on deaf ears, and the state continued with its penchant for symbol over substance, with bureaucrats and politicians using the Mahotsava to plant a few 'quick-growing' exotic saplings and have a few photographs of themselves taken for public distribution.

As an ecological patriot, Krishnan was also exasperated by the widespread tendency to use European monikers for Indian animals. He was irritated by the gaur, the Indian wild oxen, commonly being referred to as a 'bison', by the sambar, the largest deer species in India, being called an 'elk', the Nilgiri tahr being termed an 'ibex', and the monitor lizard being termed an 'iguana', these being only four examples of many such mischaracterizations. For instance, India had plenty of hares, but no indigenous rabbits. Yet, noted Krishnan in dismay, 'no one ever calls a hare a hare; invariably it is miscalled "rabbit" even by those who should know better, like school-text writers and nature study teachers'. He mournfully concluded that when 'not much is done in our schools to encourage or inform the natural curiosity of children in the teeming wildlife around', perhaps 'it is better to do nothing than misinform'.[17]

Krishnan was patriotic, even xenophobic, when it came to tree and plant species, but as far as humans were concerned he was less chauvinistic, always willing to acknowledge the contributions British naturalists had made to the study of plant and animal life in the subcontinent. The attainment of independence in August 1947 had led to articles and editorials in his hometown newspaper, *The Hindu*, critically assessing the period of British rule, and largely finding it wanting for its economic exploitation and its denial of political freedoms. Krishnan was moved to write a long letter to the editor, complaining that the newspaper's commentary had 'missed the one outstanding contribution of the British servicemen to India—their contribution to our knowledge of Indian fauna and flora'.

The Hindu had accused colonial civil servants of being arrogant and patronizing towards Indians. Krishnan did not dispute this, while adding that 'it is a fact that many of them did take a genuine interest in the birds and beasts around them, and understood their ways and loved them, even if they did not mix with the people of the country'. Till the British came to India, he wrote, 'no scientific systematic study of plant and animal life was made. Within three hundred years they have made a complete survey of our fauna and flora, and ... have found the time to study and record the habits of our birds and beasts.' In this sphere, at any rate, the British 'knew and cared for India, more sincerely than we do', he said.[18]

Krishnan liked to contrast two authentically indigenous traditions of nature conservation, the traditions of Vedanthangal and of Ashoka. The first referred to a village some fifty-five miles from Madras, where custom and religious tradition had saved, for generations, breeding birds from the hunter's arrow and the shikari's shotgun; the latter to the Mauryan emperor whose edicts commanded his people to protect rare animals and plants.

Krishnan first visited Vedanthangal in the early 1950s, returning to it many times in later years. Adjoining the village was a large tank, dry during the summer, but filling up with the monsoon rains. The tank had a grove of some 300 *Barringtonia acutangular* trees, whose trunks got submerged after the rains came in September. Their crowns above the water were ideal nesting places for herons, egrets, spoonbills, storks, cormorants and other species. So, in the months after the monsoon, thousands of birds congregated on these trees. Their droppings enriched the water below, making it perfect manure for cultivation. The roosting birds were therefore highly prized by the villagers of Vedanthangal, who sought to protect them from predators of all kinds.

In a pamphlet he wrote on Vedanthangal, Krishnan spoke of the 'vivid descriptions of the birds in Sangam literature of the 2nd century AD', noting that 'from ancient times, colonies of water-birds nesting at or near villages in South India, have been protected by the resident humanity of those places, the traditional culture of the country imposing this protective duty upon the people'. As for Vedanthangal itself, he wrote that its mixed heronry was 'one of the most spectacular in India, and perhaps the most closely packed—in fact, it is its very compactness and congestion that make it so very remarkable'. The sanctuary in this village was at least a couple of hundred years old, for there was documentary evidence that in around 1790, the villagers had obtained a 'cowrie' from an official of the East India Company, 'recognizing their right to safeguard the nesting colony in their tank from those seeking to snare or shoot the birds'. This cowrie was renewed in 1858, after the Crown took over the Company's Indian territories. Shortly after Independence in 1947, the sanctuary was taken over by the government.[19]

From his experience of Vedanthangal and other such village heronries in south India, Krishnan knew that cultural traditions could be in harmony with nature. Visiting a pelicanry near Tadepallegudem in Andhra Pradesh, he wrote this was 'not something set up recently (by Governmental or other agency) but has been there for generations, and the breeding birds here have long enjoyed the protection accorded to them by the villagers—in other parts of India, too, nesting water birds have been protected by traditional rural sentiment'.[20]

However, Krishnan sensed that in an altered modern context, with rapid economic growth and human population growth as well, traditional restraint had in many cases given way to greed. In an article published in 1957 he remarked: 'I compute that within the past 30 years more live wood has been cut down, root, bole and all, than was nurtured to maturity in the past 200 years.' In the past, people in India 'planted fruit-trees and shade-trees. And nurtured them in groves and on roadsides, so that succeeding generations might enjoy the comfort and charm of their maturity and rest in their shade.' But now 'limbless and beheaded boles are depressingly common along all our roadways'. He spoke of a grove near the town of Ranipet known as the 'Nav Lakha Garden', suggesting there were once nine lakh trees planted there. A decade ago there were thousands of trees (including many fruit trees), but, wrote Krishnan sorrowfully, 'only a barren parched expanse of flat land without cover of bush or herbiage now remains; even the roots of the slaughtered trees have been extracted'.[21]

Krishnan generally saw Indians, whether living in cities or in villages, as ecologically profligate, prone to destroy rather than conserve nature. Occasionally he came across counter-examples that afforded him some fleeting pleasure. On a visit to the eastern state of Orissa he was taken to a village named Bhetnoi, whose inhabitants had protected the blackbuck that lived in the open country around. If the buck strayed into the farms, they were shooed off rather than trapped or shot.

In the Deccan, and in other places too, Krishnan had seen villagers hunt blackbuck 'ruthlessly, with snares, nets, lethal baits, and guns'. And yet 'the wonderful thing about Bhetnoi', he wrote, 'is that here, most exceptionally, the agriculturists themselves provide this strict protection the buck need, realizing that the negligible damage they do to the crops is more than compensated by the joy of having the swiftest and loveliest of all antelopes with them'.[22]

However, places like Bhetnoi were the exception that proved the rule. Krishnan was strongly of the opinion that the state had to take a leading, proactive role in effectively protecting the habitats and species that remained from the ravages of humans and their domestic animals. In an article of 1961 on 'a wild life policy for India', he argued that 'if complete freedom from human interference is assured, and the consequences of past interference are eradicated, the wildlife of any area can be definitely conserved—even such natural ecological changes as occur in the cause of time can be allowed for, if the area is sufficiently large and diversified. The only thing that our fauna and our flora need, once freedom from human interference is assured, is lebensraum' (this last word an unfortunate choice perhaps, given its other historical connotations). Having outlined what he thought was needed, Krishnan added, 'But is this ideal capable of achievement in our overpopulated country?'[23]

Krishnan believed that human beings were invariably, and almost everywhere, the principal enemy of wildlife conservation. A finely observed column on the giant squirrel, narrating in loving detail its habits and habitat, ended by asking the question, 'What enemies does it have?' Krishnan then spoke of having witnessed eagles capturing squirrels at dusk, before adding that 'its natural enemies are no threat to the future of this fecund animal. It is the denudation of all kinds of tree forests by our people and projects that poses a really serious threat to its life, and it is still hunted on the sly by many tribals who fancy its flesh.'[24]

Krishnan was appreciative of heronries protected by villagers in different parts of south India, but here too he felt that these should be converted into government sanctuaries.[25] He often complained that the Forest Department was not rigorous enough in its policing of these places from the destructive hand of man. A column of 1991 berated the central and state government for having 'failed notably to restrict human activities within wildlife preserves to the minimum needed for their efficient administration. Cattle grazing is still freely indulged in most of our preserves, and firewood collection, as also human traffic. Wildlife tourism has run riot. It is there even within the so-called core areas of national parks. Unfortunately, there is no way of telling these authorities that they should be firmer in the discharge of their obvious duties without hurting their susceptibilities in some way or other—and nothing is gained in our country by offending authority.'[26]

Krishnan's espousal of a punitive approach to nature conservation was influenced by, among other things, his intimate acquaintance with the wildlife sanctuary in the Nilgiri hills known as Mudumalai. From the mid-1950s, Krishnan began to make regular visits to the sanctuary. He liked it a lot, for its large herds of elephant and gaur, for the richness of its bird and plant life, for the diversity of landscapes it contained—'vistas on the grand scale of the Nilgiri Range, true forest panoramas, pleasant weather and perennial streams...' He sometimes moved around the park on an elephant provided by the Forest Department, at other times on foot, camera always at the ready, later writing up his field notes by the light of an oil lamp in a Forest Department guest house. 'Nowhere have I seen elephants treated more kindly than at this camp,' he remarked. Writing in 1958, he thought the Mudumalai sanctuary 'has a great future, which will be realised soon if only the feeling for wild life now so evident in the running of the sanctuary is sustained'.[27]

Some years later, Krishnan had what he termed 'one of the most depressing experiences' of his life in Mudumalai. In 1966, foot-and-mouth disease spread from domestic cattle to the wild herbivores in the sanctuary. Krishnan went to investigate, and urged the authorities that 'cattle should be banned entirely in the preserve'. His advice was not heeded, and two years later a rinderpest epidemic broke out in Mudumalai, decimating its once flourishing population of gaur.

In subsequent years the numbers of gaur in Mudumalai began to increase again, but slowly. Now, returning to the sanctuary after a gap of a dozen years, Krishnan was dismayed to find that domestic cattle were grazing freely there. The naturalist commented that he 'saw, quite clearly, how depletive cattle can be in a wild life sanctuary even apart from their being the vector of epidemics, and how damagingly they can alter the ground flora, depriving the native herbivores of their basic fodder needs'.

Reflecting on this depressing history, Krishnan ended a 'Country Life' column with this categorical statement: 'Unless cattle are effectively banned in all wild life preserves holding native herbivores, there is little point to our conservation efforts.'[28]

Krishnan's dislike of domestic cattle anywhere near protected areas was intense. It was manifested again in the late 1980s, with regard to a sanctuary in northern India, famous for its migratory birds rather than for large mammals such as the tiger and the elephant. This was the Keoladeo Ghana sanctuary in Bharatpur, formerly a hunting preserve of the local maharaja, and much visited by viceroys and their staff who sometimes shot several thousand birds in one single day. Located on a man-made wetland, and named after a Shiva temple on the premises, the area was home to large numbers of resident storks, cormorants, herons, teals, spoonbills, sandpipers, etc., as well as welcoming migratory birds including the rare Siberian crane, which arrived here in winter. Declared a sanctuary in 1971 and a National Park in 1982, it was a place much loved by birdwatchers, among them the doyen of Indian ornithology, Salim Ali, who came every year with a team from the Bombay Natural History Society (BNHS) to conduct field research in the sanctuary.

In the early 1980s, the entry of cows and buffaloes was banned in the Keoladeo Ghana sanctuary, ostensibly to help the birds flourish even better. The ban was bitterly resented by the local villagers, who had long enjoyed the right to graze their cattle in the park. There was a violent stand-off between the peasants and the police, in which several people died. The ban continued. However, by the late 1980s a significant drop in the number of migratory birds was noticed. A group of scientists from the BNHS investigated the matter and concluded that the prohibition of grazing had contributed to the decline in bird numbers. Apparently, grazing, by keeping the grass down, had allowed other plants to flourish, which migratory birds particularly relished.

With a ban in place, the profusion in particular of a species of grass from the paspalum family had choked the wetlands and deprived it of the nutrients that attracted rare birds, like the Siberian crane.

Krishnan himself had made several extended visits to the Keoladeo Ghana sanctuary in the past. Now, with the precipitous drop in numbers of migratory birds, there were suggestions afloat to permit grazing once more in the park. Krishnan wrote a column intervening in this debate, whose central paragraph read:

> I am sure the researchers of the Bombay Natural History Society (who have a camp here) would not have suggested something so short-sighted and illegal as the restoration of grazing as the only solution to the problem of the too rank growth of grasses. But their suggestion has led to others taking up the cause of the graziers with irresponsible and uninformed zeal. Last month, in the course of a railway journey (when escape was not possible) I had occasion to realize to what absurd lengths this suggestion could be carried. I was confronted by four young enthusiasts who accused me of being one of the prime movers of the ban on grazing at Bharatpur, that had led to such unfortunate consequences. I had nothing to do with the ban, but did not say so, for I am all for it.

Proponents of grazing argued that, apart from keeping the grass down, buffalo droppings were also an important nutrient in the wetland, leading to better growth of plants, fish and animals. Krishnan disputed this, arguing that the droppings of migrant birds could compensate adequately for this. While conceding that the too luxuriant growth of grass may have been a reason for the drop in numbers of migratory birds, Krishnan argued that the solution was not to allow buffaloes into the park, but to get men to selectively cut the grass before the birds came, and then again after they were gone.[29]

Krishnan's 'hands-off nature' approach was partly based on science and partly on dogma. It was true that unregulated grazing was damaging to the habitat of Bharatpur. But some amount of regulated grazing could in fact enhance the capacity of the sanctuary to attract more birds, as well as more species of birds. Contrary to what Krishnan suggested, the BNHS study had recommended that perhaps some 1500 buffaloes be allowed into the Keoladeo Ghana sanctuary, to keep the paspalum down and bring the migratory birds back to the place. It prefaced these recommendations by starkly remarking: 'The uncontrolled growth of *Paspalum distichum* as a result of the removal of buffaloes from the Park is creating an ecocatastrophe. The grass has to be contained if the Park has to be saved.' Noting that other methods such as controlled burning or cutting of the grass by hand (as Krishnan suggested) had failed, the BNHS scientists concluded that 'the only ecological viable alternative is to get the primary consumers (the buffaloes) back into the system'.[30]

One does not know whether Krishnan read this BNHS report on Bharatpur, which incidentally also contained some telling photographs, with one image of buffaloes and Siberian cranes feeding side by side juxtaposed against a grass-filled landscape utterly devoid of bird and animal life. In fact, in other habitats across India, too, studies have found that totally excluding humans and domestic animals from entering forests and sanctuaries was not necessarily in the interests of enhancing biodiversity (as Krishnan seems to have assumed). A study conducted in the Western Ghats compared three patches of forests—one totally protected from human incursions, one subject to a large degree of human interference through lopping, grazing, etc., and one subject to a modest degree of human interference. Notably, it was the last patch that contained the largest number of bird species. Large-scale degradation of forests was of course bad for birds that came there, but modest interventions in fact opened up new ecological niches for new species to come and occupy.[31]

Krishnan once ended an article on the contested concept of 'carrying capacity' with this unequivocal assertion: 'Nature, left to itself is much more capable of the diverse and delicately inter-related adjustments necessary to maintain or ultimately attain a stable balance, than when the helping hand of man sets foot in the area to aid and assist nature.'[32] This, as we have seen, was not always the case in the parks and sanctuaries of India. In making this unqualified statement, offering it as a golden rule that allowed of no exceptions, the sentimentalist was winning over the field researcher, the ideologue over the scientist.

Though the bulk of his writing was in English and for a pan-Indian audience, Krishnan also wrote a fair amount in Tamil, both essays on natural history as well as short fiction. The scholar Theodore Baskaran observes that Krishnan's writings in his native tongue 'transcended the barriers of caste-based culture and had a natural history backdrop, to do with racing pigeons, dogs, and the like'. He sought, wherever possible, to use traditional Tamil names for birds, plants and animals, and contributed entries on birds to a ten-volume Tamil encyclopaedia published in the 1950s. Three decades later, Krishnan wrote a crime novel in Tamil; this was published posthumously, with a cover illustration by the author, depicting a man with a dog of the indigenous breed known as the Kombai.[33]

Krishnan had a cultural partiality for the literature of his native Tamil Nadu. He was steeped in the poetry of the Sangam period (c. sixth century BCE to third century CE), and admired it especially for its understanding and appreciation of diverse natural landscapes. In an article in English, written for the non-Tamil, he spoke of how this verse literature rested on 'an ancient, entirely Tamilian poetic ecology', dividing the land into five categories:

Marutam—agricultural tracts and human settlement
Mullai—plains forests and woodlands
Kurinji—hill forests and montane tracts
Neital—the sea and littoral areas
Paalai—scrub and waste lands

For each category of landscape, the poets had described its fauna and flora in remarkable factual detail. Krishnan added, however, that 'if today we find that the floristic or faunal features detailed by these rules do not obtain, it is only because the Tamil country has changed so much within the last hundred years—within this period, for example, *Mullai* land has disappeared, having been converted into *Marutam* or *Paalai*'.[34]

Krishnan also had—notwithstanding all his travels and researches in other parts of India—an ecological partiality for the flora and fauna of his native south India. Thus an essay of 1958 emphatically stated that 'South India is florally the richest and most varied part of India, and faunistically as rich and more typically Indian than any other division'. He remarked that while 'the fauna of North India includes many species which are to be found in other Asian countries, or even in Europe, the mammalian wild life of the South is peculiarly Indian'. He added that among the animals 'that are exclusively South Indian (being found nowhere else in the world) are the Nilgiri Black Langur and the Lion-Tailed Macaque'. He further noted that 'the Indian elephant attains the best tusk development in South India and probably also its best size'.[35]

In the early summer of 1980 Krishnan went on a visit to the Thar desert in Rajasthan. To his pleasant surprise, he found plenty to admire in its natural life, and in particular was 'struck by the numbers and variety of the eagles and lesser raptorial birds' that he saw. His findings recalled for him the wisdom contained in the Sangam poets of the medieval era, who had identified four distinctive landscapes in the Tamil country, with a fifth residual category reserved for the arid or desert tracts whose natural characteristics did not fit in any of the other four. In Sangam poetry, further noted Krishnan, 'eagles are specified as the distinctive birds of this desert tract'. Now, after his visit to Rajasthan, and writing as 'a Tamilian steeped in the classics of my language', the naturalist 'was happy to have confirmation of the truth to nature of our old traditions so far away from home'.[36]

For all the time that Krishnan spent in large sanctuaries around India, in great parks devoted to tigers and elephants and rhinos and other spectacular species, perhaps the place whose flora and fauna he knew most intimately was his native Madras. A city with a population of about half a million in his youth had more than a million residents by the time Krishnan reached his forties, adding a further million before he had turned sixty.

In 1991, when Krishnan was just short of his eightieth birthday, and his hometown had close to four million residents, he wrote a note on the wildlife of Madras for a young ecologist he knew. This provided a magisterial survey of nature in the city past and present. It began with some paragraphs on the climate and geomorphology of the city, before moving on to the native vegetation, with Krishnan listing (with common and scientific names both) some two dozen native tree species characteristic of the terrain, and several wild shrubs too. The note then turned to the garden plants most favoured by the residents, these often not native to India, and then to what Krishnan called 'unintended exotic introductions', among them lantana, *Prosposis juliflora*, and various cactus species, which had come and established themselves in many parts of the city, as indeed they had elsewhere in India.

Krishnan came next to the mammalian fauna of Madras. 'Fifty years ago,' he wrote, 'the sunset chorus of jackals could still be heard in places on the periphery of the city'; there was even a Madras Hunt Club, complete with imported foxhounds and a Master of the Hunt. Then, the hare, the mongoose, and the civet were often seen within city limits; now, however, 'over most of Madras the only animals that can be seen are palm squirrels, rats, bandicoots, and mice'.

With the colonization of scrub and grassy areas by concrete, bird life in Madras had also declined, observed Krishnan, but not so precipitously. Herons, egrets, terns and other waterbirds were still often sighted around the Adyar river and in the Buckingham Canal, while in other parts of the city, amidst the foliage that still remained, there were many other species, these listed by Krishnan, among them doves, owls, eagles, vultures, cuckoos, etc. The note ended by speaking briefly of the extant reptilian life, of various kinds of tortoises and snakes that were still occasionally to be spotted.

Sweeping and comprehensive as it was, the note had one significant omission, acknowledged by the writer himself. While noting that Madras was on the sea, and it has the 'second-best beach in the world' (which, one wonders, did the naturalist consider the best—perhaps Cox's Bazaar in Bangladesh?), Krishnan remarked: 'Nothing can be said about the teeming marine life of this coastal environment: I am a vegetarian.'

Krishnan prefaced this extraordinarily intimate report on the wildlife of his native city with a lament: 'In Madras city it has been a longdrawn engagement between Nature and Man, and Nature has lost in the final rounds, that is, within the past 50 years to which even I have been a witness.'[37]

For some Indians, the ideals and legacy of the freedom struggle against the British constituted the principal source of the country's identity; for others, it was the Constitution of the free Republic, which came into effect on 26 January 1950, that did so. Krishnan, however, insisted that it was India's rich and unparalleled natural heritage that should provide the basis of the country's identity. He made this point repeatedly in his columns and essays. In an article of 1967, he complained that in the Constitution of India, there 'is not even any effective provision for safeguarding something so basically Indian as the flora and fauna of sanctuaries'. Suppose a government department, he wrote, wanted to fell a patch of natural mixed forests and replace it with a plantation of commercially valuable exotics of a single species, then 'if a dozen people who care for India's wildlife, horrified by the proposal, were to protest against it, all that has to be done is to get two dozen others whose Indian citizenship is beyond question, or some foreign expert who knows nothing about our flora or fauna, to support it'.[38]

A quarter of a century later, Krishnan published a two-part series in *The Statesman* on how to protect India's green cover. Written as he was approaching the age of eighty, after some six decades of studying nature and the threats to it, the series ended with this heartfelt plea:

> If only 10 per cent of our land area, representative of our much diversified wildlife, and each of adequate area, can be effectively saved from the hand of man setting foot on them, the future of our national integrity and character can be perpetuated to generations of Indians yet unborn, and provide them with an authentic Indian setting and identity and a vital interest in life that can compensate for most ills. Surely, with 90 per cent of the land at their disposal, our Governments should be able to meet the people's demands,

> but so far no Government we have had has resisted the temptation to achieve popularity at the expense of the country's entity.[39]

Krishnan returned to the theme of nature as national identity in a column published five years later, as it happened on the very day he died, 18 February 1996. The article focused on distinctively Indian wild animals like the sloth bear, the Asiatic lion, the Nilgiri tahr, the blackbuck, the lion-tailed macaque, all now threatened in various ways. It ended with this exhortative paragraph:

> Surely the future of these animals must be adequately assured right now. The snag in the way of their effective conservation seems to lie in our Constitution, evolved by men with formidable knowledge of legal and political matters, and hardly any of the unique biotic richness of India—they do not even seem to have realized that the identity of a country depended not so much on its mutable human culture as on its geomorphology, flora and fauna, its natural basis. I have never been able to understand why, when the armed forces, the postal services and the railways have the benefit of a national, Central Government administration, something of such fundamental national importance as our great biotic heritage has not been similarly taken care of. The Forest (Protection) Act of 1980 is inadequate to assure the future of this stupendous heritage.[40]

In the 1960s, as witness his four-part series in *The Illustrated Weekly of India*, Krishnan exuded a modest amount of hope that enough of India's extraordinarily rich natural heritage could be saved from the hand of man. As he grew older, his mood darkened, and turned to anger and despair. In October 1988, Krishnan heard from his nephew A. Madhavan, a member of the Indian Foreign Service now on secondment to the Prime Minister's

Office in New Delhi. The Indian Board of Wildlife, of which the naturalist had been a member in the 1960s, wanted him to once more rejoin their steering committee. Madhavan told his uncle that the government representatives on the Board 'were all fighting on the same side with you'. Krishnan was unconvinced. He had no intention of joining the body, he said, because he had absolutely no trust any more in Indian bureaucrats. He summarized a lifetime of experience in the field thus:

> Our bewilderingly varied and complex but closely integrated wildlife, which is to me so much more India than our heritage of mutable and changing religions, philosophy, literature, music, art or even regional culinary cultures, is not something one can get to know comprehensively in a lifetime. But studying what trustworthy specialists have written and by personal field studies (provided one has the needed biological background) in most regions of our vast and varied country, one does get a fair idea of it. There are possibly three or four men in India (and none outside it) who have this ecological knowledge (now it is your turn to believe me) [and] I am the best qualified of them. ... Two decades ago I thought that if I could get across the truth to these bureaucrats that the physical and biological integrity of our country (its wild flora, fauna and geomorphology) was in fact the hub and core of our national and individual identity, in this age of instant communication of alien influences, India could be saved from its predatory humanity in adequate representative preserves at least, and we would still be left with moorings in life. More fool me! ... They [the bureaucrats] now seek to 'save' the integrity of the country by concessions to its destroyers and depletors, by planting up the scrub (such a vital part of our wildlife) with exotics and by the deployment of the very artificial 'aids' they should guard against.[41]

In May 1991, a young environmentalist named Ashish Kothari wrote to Krishnan telling him of a directory of national parks and sanctuaries he had helped bring out for the Indian Institute of Public Administration in New Delhi. As the correspondence continued, Krishnan told Kothari that the 'younger generation of wildlife enthusiasts' were a 'source of vicarious solace to me'. Given his own struggles to become a naturalist when young, Krishnan found, now that he was old, 'to my delight, there are several young men who are genuinely interested in our wildlife … and find it a most vitally refreshing value in life. I know many of them. At the moment, no less than 4 young post-graduate researchers have elected me as a sort of consultant and discuss everything with me. I honestly think this great change is the one truly heartening thing I have known since, say, 1930.'

While pleased and cheered by the interest in nature and wildlife among many young people of middle-class backgrounds, Krishnan was nonetheless bitter and frustrated about the prospects for conservation itself. His letter to Kothari continued:

> But if any individual or team of wildlifers seek, over and above the joy and stimulation they find in nature and the sustenance it gives them, to contribute materially to wildlife conservation in our country, they are in for a searing disillusionment. … Neither you nor I, nor even your Institute, can make any worthwhile contribution to wildlife conservation in our country today. All our wildlife tracts are in the hands of governments and the glib conservation policy and measures proclaimed by our governments have no relation to what is actually happening.

Old and depressed as he was, with a lifetime of writing and campaigning showing no tangible results with regard to public policy, Krishnan nonetheless held out for his young correspondent the possibilities of a ray or two of light. Thus his letter to Kothari concluded:

> Who knows, the future may hold out hopes. It seems unlikely in the political climate of today, but future governments might even wake up to the realisation that their duty is not only by the people but also by the country, and that this whittling away of the biological and physical entity of the country (the *only* thing that sustains India's identity) by the populace and the government must be stopped.
>
> Perhaps you will see that day. I cannot.[42]

The library of natural history is dominated by spectacular habitats—oceans and mountains particularly—and by large and charismatic vertebrates—the whale, the lion, the tiger. Krishnan wrote, by choice, of the humdrum landscape of peninsular India, a countryside characterized by shrubs and grasses rather than grand trees or dense forests. It was his special gift to make this land come alive, to write about its apparent lack of colour in understated but wryly effective prose. That he wrote of the blackbuck in the Deccan instead of the tiger in the Himalaya is one reason why he is not as well known as Jim Corbett, a state of affairs that does not properly reflect their respective skills as writers or naturalists. While we are in the business of comparison, let me also say that Krishnan had a sharply developed visual sense unmatched by other Indian nature writers.

Krishnan never talked down to his readers, assuming in them a knowledge and range of interests equal to his own. If they had not read William Blake (and committed his poems to memory) or did not know who 'Eha' was, they could always go to the library and find out. In what I regard as Krishnan's finest period (which ran, roughly, from 1948 to 1961), the learning was carried lightly, leavened by the more-than-occasional flash of humour, this generally directed at himself. But as he grew older the tone grew more sombre. The essays were still beautifully crafted and rich in detailed information. However, they were no longer so attentive to the human or cultural context, being natural history in a more straightforward sense. Krishnan changed, so to say, with the times. If from the 1970s we find an intensity of tone and even an impatient hectoring in his essays, this was not unrelated to the rapid disappearance of forests and wildlife all over India.

I grew up reading M. Krishnan—my parents subscribed to *The Statesman*—and one of the great privileges of my life was to be asked by his family after he died to compile an anthology of his best essays and columns.[43] In making my choices for that volume my criteria were literary—that is, I chose those essays that were most readable and evocative. In revisiting Krishnan's uncollected oeuvre for this book, however, I have taken a more ecological point of view—that is, I have analysed his work and chosen my quotations from the perspective of natural processes and nature conservation.

Krishnan was a wonderful literary stylist in English and (so my sources say) in his native Tamil as well. Krishnan was also without question modern India's greatest naturalist—greater than Salim Ali and Jim Corbett and all the others in terms of the range of his knowledge and the depth of his field research. He was also modern India's most passionate and most knowledgeable spokesman for nature. In these respects he was, as I remarked in the beginning of the chapter, to this country what John Muir was to his.

Like Muir, Krishnan's work suffered from one flaw—namely, a blindness to the rights of humans less privileged than himself. Muir notoriously omitted to mention—or perhaps even to notice—that Native Americans had considered the California redwoods their home long before he, an interloper from Scotland via the Midwest ever set foot in and sought to take spiritual possession of them. Muir, albeit perhaps less notoriously, referred to domesticated sheep as 'hoofed locusts'. Likewise, in putting the rights of nature first, Krishnan often disregarded the long-standing claims of peasants and tribals who had lived in and cohabited with the forest long before the interloper from Madras via Sandur arrived with a notebook in hand and a camera slung over his shoulder. Tragically, Krishnan refused to acknowledge the colonial history of the Indian Forest Department, of how its large-scale usurpation and subsequent enclosure of forests and common land had sparked such intense, and long-standing, resentment among peasants and tribals whose survival vitally depended on access to these forests, and who had previously seen these woodlands as their own. His sole criticism of the Forest Department was that they had a partiality for exotics. In this he was altogether different from Verrier Elwin, who, because he lived with the people of the forest, was so acutely aware of how colonial and postcolonial bureaucracies had violated their rights and so grievously discriminated against them.

In their own, respective, national contexts, John Muir and Madhaviah Krishnan were both precocious in upholding and advocating for the rights of nature. Yet, in seeking to save 'untamed' and 'unspoilt' nature from the hand of man, they were also precocious in a less admirable sense—in fostering a breed of self-righteous, overbearing, indeed authoritarian conservationists, who have used the prestige of science and the power of the state to dispossess rural peoples of their traditional rights in many parts of Asia, Africa and the Americas.

I would like to end, however, on a more appreciative note, with a story told by Krishnan's only child, who himself spent much of his professional life in the outdoors, albeit as an officer of the Indian Forest Service rather than an itinerant freelancer.

Krishnan got chicken pox in middle age, and this made him prone to periodic bouts of delirium for the rest of his life. During one such bout, he was confined to his bed, and from there he called out to his son and said to him, quietly but clearly: 'Trees ... not close ... grass ... shrubs ... breeze ... smell of rain ... Sambar and gaur ... that is India.'[44]

Epilogue

A Partially Usable Past?

ENVIRONMENTAL HISTORIANS ARE ESPECIALLY prone to what is known as 'presentism', drawing lessons from their researches into the past for how humans should conduct themselves in the present and the future. In the preface to his pioneering history of ecological thought, Donald Worster writes: 'The study of the earth's household of life has opened not one but many doors. My intention here is to ask: Who opened them? Why? What has been seen? Seeking answers to these questions may better prepare us to choose which doors we will want to open in the future.' The first writer whom Worster's book profiles is the eighteenth-century English naturalist Gilbert White. Visiting White's village, Selbourne, and seeing a thousand-year-old yew tree casting its shade over a similarly ancient church, the historian ventured to hope that 'mankind everywhere—even in the face of an uprooting technology—can work out a lasting harmony with the natural world'. Three hundred pages later, after having outlined the early-twentieth-century biologist Aldo Leopold's move from a utilitarian to a nature-centred ethic of conservation, the historian speculated that 'perhaps ... a quasi-religious conversion ... will be needed to open men's eyes to the "oneness" in or beyond nature'.[1]

Historians who write about environmentalism are also prone to 'patriotism', to seeing events, processes and individuals in their country as offering models for the rest of the world to adopt and follow. Once again, American historians have been in the lead, though historians of other nations have not been slow to follow. In his 'new history of German environmentalism', Frank Uekötter argues that 'it is rewarding to approach Germany as a kind of laboratory for the future: what does the German case say about [global] environmentalism in the twenty-first century?'[2] Likewise, in his history of Norwegian environmentalism, Peder Anker explains how thinkers from his small, remote, scantily populated and altogether unglamorous country shaped global debates in the twentieth century, by coining such influential frameworks as 'sustainable development' and 'deep ecology'. This salutary environmental influence of Norway on countries far more populous and politically important than itself demonstrated for the historian the 'power of the periphery'.[3]

I must plead guilty to these dual sins of presentism and patriotism myself. My most famous—or notorious—piece of environmental writing was an essay I published in 1989, attacking American environmentalism for its single-minded focus on wilderness preservation and its separation from the everyday lives and struggles of ordinary folk. I focused in particular on self-styled 'Deep Ecologists', whose lofty invocation of a 'biocentric ethic' which was allegedly superior to a shallow anthropocentricism masked their own privileged position in American and global society. It led them to ignore the deep inequalities between and within human nations, which posed a greater challenge to environmental sustainability than a supposedly flawed moral philosophy adhered to by activists other than themselves. Rather than export their environmental ideas overseas, I argued, these Americans would be well advised to import ideas from contemporary Indian movements like Chipko and long-dead Indian thinkers like Mahatma Gandhi.[4]

The essay has been reprinted in more than a dozen anthologies, a sign not necessarily of its scholarship but more likely of its ability to provoke—and shock. It is now more than three decades since I wrote that polemic. The tone in this book is far less hortatory. It is constructed as a work of intellectual history, an exploration of the thought of ten individuals who are no longer alive. This is an exercise in reconstruction, not prescription. Nonetheless, given its theme, the book shall also, willy-nilly, be seen as a contribution to the conversation about the human present and the human future. For, we are all—almost all—environmentalists now. With every unanticipated drought, cyclone, flood or forest fire, the number of climate change sceptics further declines. The awareness of the crisis that confronts us is particularly acute among the young, the majority of whose lifespan still lies ahead of them. I must therefore ask, and at least tentatively answer, the question: Can the readers of this book find in its rendition of past environmentalisms some ways to inform and enrich the environmentalisms of the present?

In the prologue, I spoke of the Euro-American bias in the literature on environmentalism. Some writers in the North Atlantic world have sought to compensate for this bias by a redemptive search for an 'indigenous' or 'non-Western' perspective on nature. In her introduction to a special *Granta* issue on climate change, the British writer Isabella Tree remarks, 'Of course, many societies in the world have lived in harmony with nature for millennia. Indigenous societies can teach us about sustainability and the fundamental importance of forging a closer, more respectful relationship with nature ... The knowledge is already out there. We just have to listen.'[5]

While well intentioned, this approach is extremely problematic. For one thing, it rests on a tendentious dichotomy between modernity, allegedly always exploitative towards nature, and tradition, apparently always respectful towards nature. It presents non-Western societies as unchanging, 'for millennia', even. Above all, it is highly non-specific. From its mystical affirmation of indigenous societies in harmony with nature we learn nothing of how to evolve more sustainable forms of living in the contemporary world.

On the other hand, from the ten environmental thinkers profiled in this book we may learn things that are more concrete, and, as it were, more actionable in the present. The poems, plays, songs and novels of Rabindranath Tagore may be read (or heard) principally for their literary or affective qualities. His educational ideas, however, have an enduringly practical component. 'Environmental education' is now formally part of the school curriculum in India, its inclusion belatedly prompted by the climate change debate. That Tagore was, in this respect, a true pioneer—and not merely in the Indian context—is confirmed by an essay published in 2007 by the Canadian novelist Margaret Atwood. Here, Atwood observes, 'One of the reasons people are afraid of forests is that—especially if they've grown up in cities—they aren't familiar with them. The value of early education is being increasingly recognized, as witness the growth of "outdoor classrooms" in Britain, where it's been found that children actually learn better when they're not in a closed-classroom environment. Young children have a natural interest in nature, if they aren't discouraged by adults. (How many outdoor classrooms do we have in Canada? None at the moment. Though we do have summer camps.)'[6]

Canada is far away from Bengal, and Tagore himself is long dead, and—at least outside India—little read anymore. It thus bears stating that, a century or so prior to Atwood's lament, Tagore was building on the 'natural interest' that young children have in nature, nurturing it through classrooms open to the sky and surrounded by trees, flowers, butterflies and birds.

Tagore may also have been one of the first writers to recognize the damaging *ecological*—as distinct from political or economic—effects of Western imperialism. As he wrote in 1917, the political civilization of Europe was 'carnivorous and cannibalistic in its tendencies, it feeds upon the resources of other peoples and tries to swallow their whole future'.[7] Europe grew prosperous in part because of what it could extract from its colonies in Asia and Africa; the United States because the white colonists found a resource-rich, sparsely populated continent which—by means fair and foul—they made their own. Tagore's great contemporary Mahatma Gandhi had claimed that to 'make India like England and America is to find some other races and places of the earth for exploitation'. As it appeared that the Western nations had already 'divided all the known races outside Europe for exploitation and there are no new worlds to discover', he pointedly asked, 'What can be the fate of India trying to ape the West?'[8]

Gandhi's disciple, J.C. Kumarappa, insisted that India must not try to ape the West. The urban-industrial model of development that Europe and America had adopted was, he argued, wholly unsuited to India. Rather, this country must build its economic future on its agrarian foundations. To be sure, Kumarappa did not romanticize traditional peasant society. He clearly saw its fault lines of caste and class, the relative inefficiency of its traditional technologies. He strove strenuously to work with villagers in overcoming these obstacles and help build what he called an 'economy of permanence', the title of a book he published in 1945.

Kumarappa died in 1960. A decade later, a British economist of German extraction wrote an article titled 'The Economics of Permanence'. Three years later still, its author, E.F. Schumacher, published his book *Small Is Beautiful*. Here he quotes Kumarappa in passing, referring to him as the 'Indian philosopher and economist'.[9] Schumacher had visited India in the late 1950s; though he did not meet Kumarappa, he did speak with several other followers of Gandhi, who must have introduced him to Kumarappa's work. Schumacher also came to develop a considerable admiration for Gandhi himself.[10]

First published in 1973—the year the Chipko movement began—*Small Is Beautiful* has since deservedly become a classic of environmental literature. The article which preceded it remains much less known. Although Schumacher's essay borrows the title of a book by Kumarappa without acknowledgement, I think the Indian would have enthusiastically endorsed these words from it:

> The Economics of Permanence implies a profound re-orientation of science and technology, which have to open their doors to Wisdom ... Scientific or technological 'solutions' which poison the environment or degrade the social structure and man himself, are of no benefit, no matter how brilliantly conceived or how great their superficial attraction. Ever bigger machines, entailing ever bigger concentrations of economic power and exerting ever greater violence against the environment do not represent progress: they are a denial of Wisdom. Wisdom demands a new orientation of science and technology towards the organic, the gentle, the non-violent, the elegant and beautiful.[11]

These last sentences have an uncanny resonance with the ideas of Albert Howard, and indeed Howard was a major (if largely unacknowledged) influence on the author of *Small Is Beautiful*.[12] It was he and his wife Gabrielle who, some four decades before Schumacher's call, started reorienting their own science towards the organic, the term here understood in a deeply ecological rather than merely metaphorical sense. It was his experiences working with peasants in India which convinced Howard that—as he put it in his book *The Soil and Health*, 'the slow poisoning of the life of the soil by artificial manures is one of the greatest calamities that has befallen agriculture and mankind'.[13]

The author of *An Agricultural Testament* would surely have been dismayed by the ways in which so many Indian and Chinese farmers have gone Occidental, abandoning mixed cropping for monocultures and organic manure for chemical fertilizers. He may have taken some consolation, however, in the fact that in some parts of the Occident, farmers are turning away from mechanized and chemicalized forms of agriculture. Howard's influence on the Rodales and the organic farming movement in the United States has been noted in an earlier chapter. On the other side of the globe, in Australia, we now find a thriving farmers' movement which eschews the use of chemicals altogether, seeking to nourish soils, maintain biodiversity and offer better nutrition by natural means. A practitioner and theorist of this movement says it is inspired by 'a group of early-twentieth-century thinkers in organic agriculture, including Albert Howard ... who had learned from a culture of Indian subcontinental agriculture...'[14]

Globally, Albert Howard is recognized as, to quote a recent book, 'the main founder of organic farming'.[15] I believe he should share that honour with his first wife Gabrielle, whose status as a woman and tragic early death prevented her from being accorded the intellectual and professional distinction she surely deserved.

The work of the Howards acquires increasing salience in the context of growing criticisms of the forms of industrial agriculture that have so dominated the modern world over the past hundred years. These methods, once so productive and profitable, may have finally run up against the limits of nature. In the United States, the bastion of chemical farming, the accumulating evidence of groundwater depletion, river pollution, soil erosion and dependence on fossil-fuel-based inputs has raised serious questions about the sustainability of the agricultural model practised in regions such as California and the Corn Belt of the Midwest.[16]

While they lived, Albert and Gabrielle Howard challenged the conventional agricultural science of their times. Largely ignored then, they have finally found a receptive audience, if more among activist practitioners than professional scientists per se. They would surely have found some vindication in 'save the soil' campaigns now visible around the world, which stress the importance of humus, and recognize—as the Howards did—the significance of maintaining soil health and fertility. The attention that the Howards paid to peasant knowledge resonates with contemporary scholarship, which seeks to understand rather than dismiss out of hand non-modern systems of information and classification.[17]

The other individuals featured in this book can all be made to speak to the present too. Radhakamal Mukerjee's integrative approach to knowledge and research challenges university scholars in India and elsewhere to reach beyond their disciplinary silos. M. Krishnan's holistic approach to biodiversity conservation challenges the narrow-minded focus on the protection of large species such as the lion, the tiger and the elephant. The work of Mira and Verrier Elwin can, and should, inspire the state machinery to more actively involve peasants and tribals in the management of forests and other common property resources. And Patrick Geddes's ideas on ecological town planning remain of compelling relevance to countries in Asia and Africa, which are witnessing a rapid shift of their population from the countryside to the city. As the sociologist Indira Munshi writes, 'the way cities have been planned in India ... at the cost of trees, coastlines, rivers, water bodies, hills and forests, as well as [of] old urban villages, neighbourhoods, public places, street corners, community settlements, iconic houses, cafes, theatres, bazaars, one cannot but recognise the value of Geddes' approach to urban development'.[18]

Apart from presentism and patriotism, a third trait many environmental historians are prone to is 'partisanship'. This may take one of two forms: individual or ideological, which sometimes overlap. The biographer of John Muir might suggest that his ideas are especially relevant or pertinent to the present because Muir is, after all, the author's chosen subject; or else because the writer is a partisan of the wilderness movement and thus prone to favour those who worked in that particular vein in the past. On the other hand, historians who believe that technological solutions are more important than moral change might underplay the importance of Muir and elevate that of some more scientifically minded individual instead.

This book, however, is a group portrait, that features ten thinkers whose intellectual and ideological trajectories were very diverse. They present before us many varieties of environmentalism, not just one. Though some chapters are longer than others, this should not be taken as any indication of the relative importance of their subjects, or of the relative interest this historian has in them. All ten wrote with insight about environmental matters, albeit in very different ways. Individual readers will doubtless have their own preferences, liking some chapters more than others, finding some of these dead thinkers more alive than others. I have not sought in any conscious way to aid them in making their choices.

As noted in the introduction, when I began working on this book in the 1990s, I hoped it might provide an intellectual genealogy for the 'livelihood' environmentalism of that time, represented by grassroots struggles like Chipko which wished to restore local control over water, forests and other gifts of nature in pursuit of a sustainable path of decentralized development. However, the book is being published when the pre-eminent environmental challenge is that of climate change. India itself is under grave threat from global warming, as witness the alarming shrinking of the Himalayan glaciers and the rapid increase in heatwaves and the excess mortality they have caused. As a recent article in the *Economist* warns, 'year by year, parts of the poor and crowded Indo-Gangetic Plain will become increasingly unlivable for days or weeks on end. Even the most capable government would struggle to prevent that leading to catastrophe. And India's, much less Pakistan's, is not the most capable.'[19]

However, even if climate change did not exist, India would still be an environmental disaster zone. Its cities have the highest rates of air pollution in the world. Many of its rivers are biologically dead, killed by untreated industrial effluents and domestic sewage. Its underground aquifers are depleting rapidly. The chemical contamination of its soils is extremely high. Its forests are degraded and made much less biodiverse by invasive weeds of exotic origin. These varied forms of environmental abuse exact a horrific economic and social cost, adversely affecting the livelihood options and health status of hundreds of millions of human beings.[20]

Sadly, even tragically, the political leadership in India has largely disregarded these multiple forms of environmental degradation and their human consequences. Back in the 1980s, grassroots environmental initiatives such as Chipko had enabled a series of progressive policy measures to be put in place. In recent decades those safeguards have been steadily dismantled. Regimes led by both the Congress and the Bharatiya Janata Party have granted a free licence to coal and petroleum extraction and other industries that devastate landscapes as well as human communities. Perhaps no government has so actively promoted destructive practices as that led by Narendra Modi, who became prime minister in 2014. The environmental scholar Rohan D'Souza has documented the Modi government's easing of environmental clearances for polluting industries and its 'watering down of operating norms for coal tar processing, sand mining, and paper pulp industries'.

By 2018, writes D'Souza, 'the slash and burn attitude of gutting and weakening existing environmental institutions, laws and norms was extended to forests, coasts, wildlife, air, and even waste management'.[21]

In 2014, India ranked 155 out of 178 countries assessed by the Environmental Performance Index. By 2022 it ranked at the very bottom, 180 out of 180.[22] This degradation has been enabled by an antiquated economic ideology which adheres to the mistaken and out-of-date belief that only rich nations need to behave responsibly towards nature. Free market ideologues savagely attack Indian environmentalists as backward-looking, going so far as to speak of 'the fundamentalist and irrationalist nature of the ecology movement'.[23] Their views are amplified by politicians in power, who insist that 'in a developing country, environment standards laid down by developed countries can't be taken as the thumb rule'.[24]

In fact, for reasons outlined already, densely populated countries with fragile ecologies need to be even more responsible regarding how they use nature and natural resources. No coal mine in India comes up in a vacuum; to establish it requires the destruction of large areas of forests and the displacement of thousands of forest-dependent people. In forest and farm, village and city, with regard to the use of water and the health of the soil, Indians need to act more wisely and prudently if they are to assure for themselves a safe and sustainable future.

It is not as if by reading the ten thinkers here we might automatically reset India on the path to that future. Nonetheless, their ideas and example might inspire more Indians to work creatively and constructively towards that end. I hope therefore that my compatriots will read this book; and perhaps some citizens of other countries too. The lineages of Indian environmentalism outlined in these pages can, I think, enrich transnational debates in three ways in particular. First, they might help focus sharper attention on the question of sustainable lifestyles. One powerful strand in the climate change debate puts much faith in new technologies, arguing that the environmental crisis shall be solved by new energy sources such as solar, hydrogen, and wind, by moving from cars fuelled by petrol to those run on electric batteries, by carbon capture and geo-engineering. A recent book, published under the telling title *Climate Capitalism* and endorsed by some of the world's top tech billionaires, itemizes such innovations while confidently proclaiming that humans can 'tackle climate change within the world's dominant economic system {namely, capitalism] and ensure that the wheels of progress don't come to a halt...'[25]

Innovations in the field of renewable energy are to be welcomed. But surely lifestyles matter too. The epigraph to this book has Mahatma Gandhi prophesying in 1928 that if Indians took to European forms of production and consumption, they would strip the world bare like locusts. The thinkers featured here were not so crisp or epigrammatic, yet the burden of much of their work was to provide evidence to sustain Gandhi's claim.

A leading American environmental historian has remarked that 'restraint [is] a decidedly un-American idea'.[26] Alas, with the globalization of the consumer society, restraint is no longer an idea much welcomed in other parts of the world either. Like their American counterparts, Indian and Chinese billionaires wish to see climate change arrested without giving up their private planes, their private yachts, their magnificent houses strewn across multiple continents. These lifestyles are seen as aspirational by those below them in the status hierarchy, who may never own a yacht or a home in another country but still desire to sample the pleasures of foreign travel, and of cuisine, clothes and cars sourced from all parts of the world, regardless of the cumulative consequences of their consumption choices for humans less fortunate than them or humans yet unborn, let alone for species other than their own or for the earth as a whole.

The protagonists of this book would be decidedly sceptical of the Pollyannaish boosterism of the technological utopians of the present, who see the world from their screen or from an aeroplane high above. They would be more appreciative of the ground-level view of ethnographic field researchers such as Julie Livingston, who coined the term 'self-devouring growth' to refer to 'the ways that the super-organism of human beings is consuming itself'. Such a model of growth, writes Livingston, is 'predicated on uninhibited consumption', whose mantra of 'grow the economy, grow a business, grow a market, grow, grow, GROW!' is 'so powerful that it obscures the destruction it portends'.

Livingston takes as her illustrative case study the small African nation of Botswana, which has been hailed as a rare postcolonial success story, for its impressive rates of economic growth, good roads and telecommunications, decent education and healthcare, and well-tended nature preserves. Yet, as the anthropologist demonstrates, this 'growth' has come about through intensive diamond mining and commercial beef production that has led to acute water scarcity, soil degradation, etc., raising questions about how long this prosperity can continue.

Julie Livingston eviscerates a 'facile evolutionary model' whose 'implicit aim is to take Botswana or Honduras or Cambodia and, through economic growth, create infrastructure and consumption like there is in Canada or Australia. ... And yet, these developed economies that are the aspiration are the prime engines of a kind of voraciousness that is leading us off a cliff.' As Livingston further observes:

> Food, water, movement. All are necessary to humans and other vital forms of life. All are complex relationships rather than resources that exist in isolation. Recognizing as much is necessary

> to understanding the difference between growth that is healthy and growth that is self-devouring. The animated ecology is not a bank from which humans compete to extract. It is a living manifestation of myriad, ongoing historical relationships. … What happens if we eviscerate the animated ecology? What use are our ancestors in such a world? What use will we be when we become those ancestors?[27]

Julie Livingston's book carries the subtitle 'A Planetary Parable as Told from Southern Africa'. Her book's arguments bear, unconsciously but tellingly, a striking resonance with the extra-planetary parable offered by Rabindranath Tagore almost a hundred years previously, of a new race being born on the moon, 'that began to greedily devour its surroundings'.[28]

In 1922, Tagore presciently remarked that 'Mother Earth had enough for the healthy appetite of her children and something extra for rare cases of abnormality. But she has not nearly sufficient for the sudden growth of a whole world of spoiled and pampered children.'[29] Two and a half decades later, and almost certainly without having read his words, Mira similarly warned about the ecological destruction that human greed coupled with technological arrogance might bring about. As she wrote in 1949, 'This world of Nature's planning is ruthlessly plundered, despoiled and disorganized by man whenever he gets the chance. By his science and machinery, he may get huge returns for a time, but ultimately will come desolation. We have got to study Nature's balance, and develop our lives within her laws, if we are to survive as a physically healthy and morally decent species.'[30]

The protagonists of this book thus drew early and sharp attention to the ideas, institutions and technologies required to facilitate sustainable lifestyles. Second, the writers and scholars featured here help us think more meaningfully about the links between the deepening of democracy and environmental sustainability. Several of our exemplars advocated vigorously for political decentralization, for the strengthening of community control over natural resources. They included J.C. Kumarappa and Mira Behn, who, following Mahatma Gandhi, had a natural suspicion of bestowing too much power in a centralized state. They focused instead on revitalizing local communities, seeking to make them more responsible in their stewardship of nature.

In parallel to Kumarappa and Mira, but independently of them, Radhakamal Mukerjee had begun to document the importance of common property resources in agrarian life. He argued that community control of forests, pasture and water, once vigorous and active, had decayed and atrophied under British colonial rule. He hoped that after Independence these community traditions could be revived—instead, the state gave itself ever greater powers over these resources. The only presumed alternative to state control was that of unleashing the market, by handing over forests, minerals, etc., to private entrepreneurs.

In the first half of the twentieth century, economists the world over divided themselves into two rival camps—those who saw the state as the main driver of economic growth, as against those who wished to accord that role to the market. That the community constituted a third, and potentially complementary, pole was considered by virtually no Indian economist except Radhakamal Mukerjee. Then, in the 1980s, six decades after Mukerjee first wrote on the subject, the economist N.S. Jodha began to empirically document the role of common property resources in sustaining rural livelihoods. Jodha's work was taken note of among environmental activists, but largely ignored by professional Indian economists, who still would not look beyond the dichotomy of state versus market.[31]

In 2009, Elinor Ostrom was awarded the Nobel Prize in economics for her work on common property resources. The prize citation in part read:

> It was long unanimously held among economists that natural resources that were collectively used by their users would be over-exploited and destroyed in the long-term. Elinor Ostrom disproved this idea by conducting field studies on how people in small, local communities manage shared natural resources, such as pastures, fishing waters, and forests. She showed that when natural resources are jointly used by their users, in time, rules are established for how these are to be cared for and used in a way that is both economically and ecologically sustainable.[32]

The committee that awarded Ostrom her (justly deserved) prize had not of course heard of Radhakamal Mukerjee, to whose researches of the 1920s and 1930s this description—'when natural resources are jointly used by their users, in time, rules are established for how these are to be cared for and used in a way that is both economically and ecologically sustainable'—also applies. In India today, the work of Mukerjee—and Jodha, and Ostrom—remains entirely relevant. The Indian state remains largely reluctant to cede control over woodlands—unless it be to mining companies that finance politicians and political parties—but where it has, this devolution has led to a remarkable flourishing of community forestry that has had salutary environmental as well as social effects.

One such experiment is in the tribal district of Gadchiroli in Maharashtra, where several dozen villages have been allocated their own 'community forests'. Visiting Gadchiroli some years ago, I spent a day in forests once controlled by the state, but now managed by tribal communities. The landscape was beautiful and diverse; rich in bird, insect and plant life, and with multiple species of flowering trees in coexistence (in contrast to the monocultural stands of pine, teak or eucalyptus so beloved of the state Forest Department). We passed young villagers on their way to voluntary guard duty; saw the remains of stone quarries, now happily shut down; and came across two little lakes deep in the forest, visually very attractive while yielding fish, a vital source of protein.

Unlike the Forest Department, which likes to clear-fell trees for sale, tribal villagers prefer to sustainably harvest non-timber forest products (NTFPs) such as tendu leaves, bamboo, amla, and mahua flowers. Focusing on NTFPs rather than timber had provided a steady stream of income to the local economy while, at the same time, forestalling environmental degradation. The renewal of the village economy had also led to a stream of reverse migration, with tribal youths returning from the city to their villages to avail of the dignified and sustainable livelihood that had now been made possible.[33]

The success of the Gadchiroli experiment would have delighted many of the individuals featured in this book, perhaps Elwin, Kumarappa and Mira most especially, though Tagore and Mukerjee would surely have appreciated it too. This emphatic demonstration of how decentralized democracy aids environmental renewal should have prompted its wider replication across the tribal forest belt of central India. It hasn't, largely because that would undermine the strong nexus between politicians, contractors and mining operators. Nor is the Gadchiroli case relevant only to the countryside. In cities and towns, too, encouraging the creation of community spaces, whether these take the shape of parks, gardens or water bodies, can greatly enhance the environmental and social quality of urban life.[34]

Several of our exemplars asked for greater democracy in decision-making; others for greater democracy in the creation and dissemination of knowledge. I think in particular of Albert and Gabrielle Howard, in the sphere of rural development, and of Patrick Geddes, in the realm of urban planning. Unlike other agricultural scientists, the Howards fashioned their science in active collaboration with the peasants who were its presumed beneficiaries; unlike other planners, Geddes associated ordinary citizens with both the diagnostic process and with the crafting of the recommendations themselves.

Finally, and perhaps most importantly, the thinkers featured in this book might offer some ballast to the strand in the environmental movement that pays greater attention to questions of social justice—whether justice within a nation, or between nations, or between generations. I think here of American environmentalism, where, despite the challenge of the environmental justice movement, the exaltation of wilderness remains the dominant and perhaps even hegemonic motif. Consider in this connection a recent book by the prominent historian Douglas Brinkley. Close to nine hundred pages in print, it is a largely celebratory, and often triumphalist, account of American environmentalism, focusing on wilderness protection and the promulgation of laws promoting it enacted by successive presidents.

Brinkley's book shows no awareness of different articulations of environmentalism in the rest of the world, not even in Britain or Europe. And it scarcely touches environmental justice questions within the United States itself. There is no acknowledgement at all of America's disproportionate contribution to global warming. Brinkley's main focus is on the decades of the 1960s and 1970s, and he charts the growth of environmental consciousness in these years without so much as mentioning that this was simultaneously a time of rapid industrialization and the expansion of a consumer society whose ecological footprint embraced, and often damaged, the landscapes and peoples of many countries other than the United States.

Remarkably, Brinkley's book even fails to mention the landmark *Limits to Growth* report, produced by an American university in 1972. Ironically, the book's narrow thematic focus is bruited as its strength: so, as the author writes, 'What hopefully will be instructive about reading *Silent Spring Revolution* is learning how grassroots citizens *demanded* an American life replete with birdsong, sweet waters, fresh air, and green pastures aplenty.' He adds, 'In some small way, I hope this book illuminates how an engaged citizenry can bring America's natural beauty back from the brink. ... If nothing else, I hope *Silent Spring Revolution* helps readers reconnect with America's public lands and freshwater resources: our lakes, mountains, rivers, seashores, islands, deserts, marshes, and woods...'[35]

One might usefully contrast Brinkley's approach with that of other, if somewhat less widely read, perspectives on American environmentalism. In her book on African American environmental thought, Kimberley Smith writes that while in the dominant tradition 'pristine nature or wilderness—the natural world as it exists independent of human manipulation—is the central value, and humans' duty lies in preserving untouched nature as far as possible', on the other hand, in the black tradition, humans 'are to be active, creative, co-equal partners in giving meaning to and redeeming the natural world'.[36] In the same vein, in reflecting on her experiences compiling an anthology of four centuries of African American nature poetry, Camille Dungy remarks that 'the history of African Americans in this country complicates their ability and/or desire to write of a rapturous idealized connection to the natural world'. The contributors to her book, writes Dungy, 'do not fall in line with the praise school of nature poetry'; rather, they 'mix their visions of landscapes and animals into investigations of history, economics, resource extraction, and other very human and deeply perilous concerns.'[37]

What about the individuals featured in the present book? Here, J.C. Kumarappa and M. Krishnan mark two ends of the spectrum; the former with a severely practical approach to life that left little time for the joyous or even aesthetic contemplation of nature; the latter immersed in nature, celebrating all its myriad forms, whether small and unglamorous or large and spectacular, while tending to see humans as unwelcome intruders and interlopers. As for K.M. Munshi, he wished to instrumentalize nature for a religious cause. The other seven all fall squarely in the camp endorsed by Dungy: that is to say, their writings, and their way of thinking more broadly, blended an appreciation of nature and natural beauty with a sharp awareness of how political systems, social structures, and the dynamics of economic and technological change have created deep inequalities between and within nations while simultaneously leading to severe and possibly irreversible environmental degradation.

I have spoken of Radhakamal Mukerjee's prescience with regard to common property resources. I must here note his prescience with regard to environmental philosophy as well. In the 1980s, the American radical Murray Bookchin began fashioning a way of thinking he called 'social ecology'. Bookchin saw his theory as an alternative both to the movement called 'Deep Ecology', which privileged nature protection above all else and had little interest in inequalities within human society; and to orthodox Marxism, which recognized no natural limits to economic growth, dismissing environmentalism as a mere bourgeois fad, a distraction from the class struggle.[38]

When canvassing for the term 'social ecology', Bookchin had no knowledge that an Indian thinker had coined the same phrase many years previously, even using it as the title of a book published in 1942. Mukerjee was at once a sociologist among the ecologists, and an ecologist among the sociologists. Unlike the pure ecologists of his time, he was strongly invested in the promotion of social justice. Unlike the conventional sociologists of the time, he was deeply engaged in the study of nature and natural processes. This interest in the natural world separated him not just from professional sociologists but from progressive intellectuals, more broadly speaking. Mukerjee saw himself as a man of the Left; but unlike Indian Marxist intellectuals, he understood and was fully aware of the ecological challenges posed by unbridled industrialization.

Patrick Geddes owed his interest in social justice to his acquaintance with (non-Marxist) socialist movements in nineteenth-century Europe. Albert and Gabrielle Howard were not 'political' in this sense, yet, like Geddes, they were strongly committed to making their science accessible and available to the socially disadvantaged sections of society. As for Rabindranath Tagore, his progressivism stemmed from a crisis of conscience, from being a wealthy landlord who had belatedly become aware of the pitiful living conditions of his tenants. Verrier Elwin's empathy for the tribals stemmed from not dissimilar sources; as an Englishman in a colonial context, as an Oxford scholar living with illiterate folk, and as a radical Christian with a partiality for St Francis, he felt obliged to stand with the powerless against the powerful.

In the last month of Gandhi's life, a young Indian asked him what ideals he should follow. It was the Mahatma's day of silence, so he wrote out a note which read: 'I will give you a talisman. Whenever you are in doubt, or when the self becomes too much with you, apply the following test. Recall the face of the poorest and the weakest man whom you may have seen, and ask yourself, if the step you contemplate is going to be of any use to him. Will he gain anything by it? Will it restore him to a control over his own life and destiny?'[39]

Gandhi was using the gendered language of the time—of course by 'man' he meant 'man or woman', while 'he/him' also stood for 'she/her'. That noted, this was a talisman that was admirably followed by the direct disciples of Gandhi featured in this book—J.C. Kumarappa and Mira Behn. Yet it was also a talisman that would have resonated with Rabindranath Tagore and Verrier Elwin—who both knew Gandhi well without being in any sense his 'followers'—and with Patrick Geddes, who met

Gandhi briefly once and corresponded with him. It would surely have appealed as well to Radhakamal Mukerjee and to Albert and Gabrielle Howard, who never met Gandhi but were aware of his work. What distinguishes these eight individuals from most other public-spirited individuals of their time is this—that while being committed to the pursuit of social justice, they simultaneously displayed a precocious awareness of the impossibility of replicating, across the globe, models of resource-intensive, capital-intensive industrialization followed by countries such as the United States and the Soviet Union.

Consider again, and in full, the epigraph to this book:

> God forbid that India should ever take to industrialization after the manner of the West. The economic imperialism of a single tiny island kingdom is today keeping the world in chains. If an entire nation of 300 million took to similar economic exploitation, it would strip the world bare like locusts.[40]

While the last phrase is particularly striking, to understand its full import it must be read alongside a phrase that appears in the first sentence. India would strip the world bare like locusts if it 'took to industrialization after the manner of the West'. Not took to industrialization per se. Gandhi's talisman recognized that India was disfigured by its mass poverty; and his other writings and activities (such as the promotion of village industries) demonstrate that he was not opposed to, indeed actively welcomed, changes in economic and technological practices that would eliminate poverty, illiteracy and ill health.

Gandhi was frequently caricatured as anti-modern. Indian environmentalists are often dismissed as 'anti-development'. In fact, what they, as well as their precursors celebrated in this book, were arguing, is that because of India's demographic size and ecological diversity, it had to forge a model of development that did not mimic that of the West. Central to this argument was the historical fact of imperialism. Europe and Europeans had grown wealthy through their political control of vast territories in Asia and Africa and by colonizing and peopling even vaster territories in the Americas and Oceania. Indians, coming late to the game, would have no access to new territories or their resources.

Gandhi had merely an intuitive understanding of the global unsustainability of Western forms of production and consumption. Writers like Tagore, scholars like Elwin and Mukerjee, scientists like Geddes and the Howards, and grassroots activists like Mira and Kumarappa came to similar conclusions through empirical research or field experience. They studied this particular terrain much more thoroughly than Gandhi (who had other preoccupations, such as leading India's quest for political freedom, seeking to end caste prejudice and promoting inter-religious harmony). They provided rich documentation of the ways in which the abuse of nature was damaging the prospects of human life. Based on what they saw and what they observed, they, much more fully than Gandhi ever could, elaborated on why India had to find its own path to sustainability. As Radhakamal Mukerjee so succinctly put it, 'in a new country [like America] man can with impunity disobey the order of nature, mainly because of the large margin and variety of nature's reserve; but, when man has become established in his adopted region [as in India], his security and well-being will be found to rest on maintaining the balance and rhythm in the organic nature that forms his environment'.[41]

Mukerjee's warnings are still entirely relevant to his homeland, yet they might also find resonance in the other countries of the so-called Global South, likewise characterized by high population densities, fragile ecologies, and ambitious—sometimes overambitious—plans for industrialization and urbanization.

Eight of the ten individuals in this book can properly be characterized as 'social ecologists', as seeking to address injustice within human society while simultaneously seeking to mitigate or reverse environmental degradation. The exceptions are K.M. Munshi and M. Krishnan, who were each noteworthy for other reasons—the first for opportunistically marrying environmentalism to Hinduism, the latter for practising an ecumenical form of wilderness conservation. Krishnan may have been distinctive in the Indian tradition in speaking *for* rather than *with* nature; nonetheless, unlike most wildlife enthusiasts of his time and ours, he went beyond a concern with the tiger and the elephant by urging the protection of small mammals, birds, reptiles, plants, trees, shrub forests, grasslands and wetlands.

As noted in Chapter Nine, Krishnan once advocated the setting apart of one-tenth of India's land area and keeping it free of human interference. His proposals sound positively modest when compared with what is now demanded by what we may characterize as the 'Nature First and Foremost' strand of global environmentalism. This has now gone so far as to press for the setting aside of half of the earth as areas fully and rigorously protected from human activity. The idea was originally put forward by the American biologist E.O. Wilson,[42] and has since gained influential and vocal supporters among Western, and especially American, environmentalists.

Fortunately, this grandiose scheme has not gone unopposed. Scholars have argued that it shall put in place a punitive and authoritarian system of conservation, which would further marginalize the rural and tribal communities who have contributed least to our environmental predicament. At the same time, it would do little to address the destructive forms of resource extraction which would still prevail in the other half of the earth. As an essay co-authored by fifteen scholars from around the world observes, 'the only logical conclusion of the Half-Earth proposal would be injustice on a large scale without effectively addressing the actual roots of the ecological crisis'. Indeed, 'cutting inequality in half would do more for conservation than attempting to protect half of the Earth from humanity'.[43]

These critics of the superficially seductive (but ultimately disastrous) 'Half Earth' scheme would find a ringing endorsement from the older lineages of environmentalism studied in this book. Respect for nature and respect for human dignity: it was these inseparably intertwined ideals that animated the work of the individuals featured here. They worked and wished for a future that was less environmentally destructive as well as less socially unjust. They thus anticipated, by many decades, recent calls to forge 'a politics that finds a way to merge, or at least hold together, certain questions that we have called ecological and others that we have called humanitarian, questions of conservation and questions of justice.'[44]

In rehabilitating these forgotten pioneers, I do not wish to suggest that in their work one can find specific solutions to all the environmental problems of the present. While it was Patrick Geddes who coined that memorable phrase 'carboniferous capitalism', these individuals all mostly wrote before the arrival of the age of private motorized transport, which, in India as elsewhere, has so radically reshaped the natural environment and patterns of human life. Nor, writing largely when India's population was much smaller and much less urbanized than it is, and its agriculture and hence its soils much less toxic, could they have anticipated the water crisis that engulfs so much of the country today.[45]

Their limitations noted, let me insist that these environmentalists who lived well before climate change became visible, are nonetheless worthy of attention and respect in an age so dominated by it. They worked in many socio-ecological domains: the wild, the forest, the farm, the village, the city. They came from different disciplinary and intellectual backgrounds. Their heterogeneous legacies refute simple-minded dichotomies that posit modernity versus tradition, science versus activism, East versus West, nature versus humanity. My compatriot Shiv Visvanathan likes to say that India has long been the home of innovative trends in social thought, the field that has formed a glorious compost of ideas drawn from all ages and all parts of the world. I offer in this book a compost of environmentalism and environmentalists—in the hope that it may (organically and cleanly) fertilize our minds, and with luck, our air, water, fields, forests and factories too.

Acknowledgements

MORE THAN FORTY YEARS ago, when I was a doctoral student in search of a dissertation topic, Jayanta Bandyopadhyay and Shiv Visvanathan suggested that I work on the emerging environmental movement in India. I remain deeply grateful to them for introducing me to key readings, and for helping provide a framework to study human interactions with nature.

Not long after I met Jayanta and Shiv, I was introduced to the ecologist Madhav Gadgil. Madhav and I collaborated on two books in the 1990s and have continued to be in close touch since. His work ethic, his deep engagement with field research and his instinctively interdisciplinary approach have been inspirational, though doubtless I have fallen short of his standards in these respects.

My research on Indian environmentalism has brought me in contact with hundreds of scholars, scientists and activists, whom I have met and spoken with in field and forest, mountain and coast, seminar room and university canteen. Of them I may be permitted to single out a few: the activists and institution-builders Ashish

Kothari, Dunu Roy and S.R. Hiremath, the historians Shekhar Pathak and Arupjyoti Saikia, the sociologists Nandini Sundar and Amita Baviskar, the ecologists M.D. Subash Chandran, Raman Sukumar, Kartik Shanker, Harini Nagendra, Ravi Chellam and T.R. Shankar Raman, the intrepid journalists Chitrangada Choudhury, Hridayesh Joshi and Kalpana Sharma, and the heterodox economists John Kurien and Sharachchandra Lele. Their writings have inspired and educated me, and so have my conversations with them. And I owe an enormous and absolutely irredeemable debt to the late Krishna Raj, who allowed me to use the columns of the *Economic and Political Weekly* to try out all sorts of ideas, uncooked, half-baked, and just occasionally passably plausible, on environmentalism in India and the world.

This book is written by an Indian shaped in the first instance by Indian scholarship. Yet it is also an engagement with scholars elsewhere, and particularly in the United States. Absolutely formative to my work on environmentalism in a comparative context were eighteen months I spent at Yale University, shortly after completing my doctorate in Kolkata. My mind was opened and enriched, my presumptions questioned and challenged by the vibrant intellectual community at what was then called the School of Forestry and Environmental Studies. I remember with particular warmth Bill Burch, Timothy Weiskel, Bill Cronon and Joe Miller among my faculty colleagues, and Mike Bell, Julia Falconer, Joel Seton, Jeff Campbell and Nancy Sheehan among my students.

While living in the States I also made the acquaintance of scholars at other American universities, whose work on environmental history and sociology provided stimulating leads for me to follow. They included Michael Adas of Rutgers University, Louise Fortmann and Carolyn Merchant at the University of California at Berkeley and Donald Worster, then at Brandeis University. Like my former colleagues at Yale, I think that were these scholars to read this book, they may see echoes in its pages of our conversations of times past.

As I mention in the Introduction, the research for this book commenced in Yale's Sterling Memorial Library, where I first came across the writings of Radhakamal Mukerjee and J.C. Kumarappa. Other libraries and archives which I have raided for manuscripts, reports, letters and books include the Ratan Tata Library of the Delhi School of Economics; the National Library in Kolkata; the Nehru Memorial Museum and Library in New Delhi; the British Library in London; the Doe Library of the University of California at Berkeley; the Green Library at Stanford University; and the National Library of Scotland in Edinburgh. I must also acknowledge two wonderful booksellers, K.K.S. Murthy of Select Books in Bangalore, and Vijay Kumar Jain of Prabhu Book Service in Gurgaon, for providing me rare pamphlets and out-of-print books authored by the individuals I write about here.

I have, over the years, taught courses or run seminars on the history of environmentalism at universities around the world. They include Yale, of course, but also Stanford University, Oslo University and the Indian Institute of Science. These courses/seminars allowed me to formulate my ideas with greater clarity, while the participants provided a stream of suggestions that I have sought to take account of. Most recently, my association with Krea University has introduced me to a cohort of brilliant young intellectuals who constitute, as it were, the 'third generation' of environmental scholarship in India. Speaking with and listening to them has been a vital stimulus in nudging this project towards completion.

It was, as already noted, Krishna Raj's *EPW* where the earliest results of my research on Indian environmental ideas were reported. They were then outlined in somewhat more substantial form as the Radhakrishnan Lectures, hosted by All Souls College in Oxford in the year 2010. In April 2023, I presented an updated version of my research at the University of Pennsylvania, at a public lecture organized by the Center for the Advanced Study of India. I am thankful to my hosts at All Souls and UPenn, and for the comments from the audience in both places, for helping me refine my arguments.

Though focused on environmentalism in India, this book carries further a conversation begun many years ago with scholars in the United States. It is therefore appropriate that it has had the benefit of being commented on, in manuscript form, by four of the finest environmental scholars living in that country. Three are historians, all American by birth and upbringing—John McNeill, Paul Suter and Aaron Sachs. The fourth is a literary scholar originally from South Africa—Rob Nixon. Aaron, John, Paul and Rob have all been extraordinarily generous with their time as well as penetratingly insightful with their comments. Each helped improve both the framing of the book as well as the narrative flow of individual chapters.

Speaking for Nature was read in draft by my old friend, the historian David Gilmour, who helped clean up the prose and correct some errors. Swati Ganguly provided key inputs and advice for the chapter on Rabindranath Tagore, and A.R. Vasavi did likewise for the chapter on the Howards. I am also grateful to two anonymous readers who commented on a draft at the request of Yale University Press.

Finally, I would like to thank my two editors, Jennifer Banks at Yale and Udayan Mitra at HarperCollins India, for their critical advice and steadfast support in the making and fulfilment of this project. As with my previous books, Cara Jones and Rogers, Coleridge and White have helped find the most suitable home(s) for it.

Notes

Introduction: Shades of Green

1 E.P. Thompson, 'The Nehru Tradition', in *Writing by Candlelight* (London: The Merlin Press, 1980), p. 148.

Thompson's essay was written in 1978, shortly after an extended visit to India. He had never been to the country before, yet had a long association with it. His father, E.J. Thompson, had taught for many years in Bengal, written the first scholarly biography of Rabindranath Tagore, and befriended Mahatma Gandhi and Jawaharlal Nehru. The celebrated author of *The Making of the English Working Class* had grown up on stories about the vitality of Indian life—and now his own conversations in India had confirmed them.

2 Lester Thurow, *The Zero-Sum Society: Distribution and the Possibilities for Change* (New York: Basic Books, 1980), pp. 104–05, emphasis added.

3 For an overview, see Madhav Gadgil and Ramachandra Guha, *Ecology and Equity: The Use and Abuse of Nature in Contemporary India* (London: Routledge, 1995). Cf also the pioneering early Citizens'

Reports on the state of the Indian environment produced by New Delhi's Centre for Science and Environment in 1982 and 1985 respectively.

4 Ramachandra Guha, *The Unquiet Woods: Ecological Change and Peasant Resistance in the Himalaya* (first published in 1989: third edition Ranikhet: Permanent Black, 2009); Ramachandra Guha and Joan Martinez-Alier, *Varieties of Environmentalism: Essays North and South* (London: Earthscan, 1998).

5 Cf Paul Suter, 'The World with Us: The State of American Environmental History', *Journal of American History*, Volume 100, Number 1, 2013. Over the years, the American Society for Environmental History's (ASEH) flagship journal, *Environmental History*, has published a series of essays on the development of the field in different territories. See, for example, Michael Bess, Marc Cioc and James Sievert, 'Environmental History Writing in Southern Europe', *Environmental History*, Volume 5, Number 4, 2000; Marc Cioc, Björn-Ola Linnér and Matt Osborn, 'Environmental History Writing in Northern Europe', *Environmental History*, Volume 5, Number 3, 2000; Mark Carey, 'Latin American Environmental History: Current Trends, Interdisciplinary Insights, and Future Directions', *Environmental History*, Volume 14, Number 2, 2009.

To demonstrate how quintessentially American the field is, consider these remarks from a scholar reflecting on how he was appointed editor of *Environmental History*: 'When John Opie approached me in 1991 to ask me to pinch-hit for him as editor of *Environmental History Review* while he was on sabbatical, neither of us imagined that he'd end up being Wally Pipp and I'd do a lame imitation of Lou Gehrig.' (Hal Rothman, 'A Decade in the Saddle: Confessions of a Recalcitrant Editor', *Environmental History*, Volume 7, Number 1, 2002, p. 9.) Here was a baseball metaphor being used naturally and unselfconsciously, though—unlike football, hockey, golf, tennis, rugby and even cricket, baseball is an American rather than global sport.

6 Alfred Crosby, 'The Past and Present of Environmental History', *The American Historical Review*, Volume 100, Number 4, 1995, p. 1186.

7 The important early histories of American environmentalism include Roderick Nash, *Wilderness and the American Mind* (New Haven: Yale University Press, 1967); Donald Worster, *Nature's Economy: The Roots of Ecology* (San Francisco: Sierra Club Books, 1977); Stephen Fox, *The American Conservation Movement: John Muir and His Legacy* (Madison: University of Wisconsin Press, 1981); Curt Meine, *Aldo Leopold: His Life and Work* (Madison: University of Wisconsin Press, 1988). Many more books have followed in their wake, adding new insights, information and points of departure. There is also a very large periodical literature on the subject.

8 On England, see Jan Marsh, *Back to the Land: The Pastoral Impulse in England, from 1800 to 1914* (London: Quartet Books, 1982); Keith Thomas, *Man and Nature: A History of the Modern Sensibility* (New York: Pantheon, 1982); Jonathan Bate, *Romantic Ecology: Wordsworth and the Environmental Movement* (London: Routledge, 1991); and Harriet Ritvo, *The Dawn of Green: Manchester, Thirlmere, and Modern Environmentalism* (Chicago: University of Chicago Press, 2009); on Germany, see Raymond H. Dominick III, *The Environmental Movement in Germany: Prophets and Pioneers, 1871–1971* (Bloomington: Indiana University Press, 1992), and Frank Uekötter, *Greenest Nation? A New History of German Environmentalism* (Cambridge, Mass.: MIT Press, 2014); on France, see Michael Bess, *The Light-Green Society: Ecological and Technological Modernity in France, 1960–2000* (Chicago: University of Chicago Press, 2003), especially Chapter Three, 'The Prehistory of Ecological Awareness'; on Norway, see Peder Anker. *The Power of the Periphery: How Norway Became an Environmental Pioneer for the World* (Cambridge: Cambridge University Press, 2020). For a pan-European treatment, see Simon Schama, *Landscape and Memory* (New York: Alfred A. Knopf, 1995). I am referring here to select literature in English only; there are of course many more books on these themes published in French, Spanish, German, Dutch, Italian, etc.

Unlike the countries of Western Europe, Soviet Russia did not have an environmental 'movement' per se, since citizens' movements and street protests were not feasible in a totalitarian state. Nonetheless, there were individual thinkers and the odd (if scrupulously non-political) civic group who focused on nature conservation. They have been treated in two fine works by the American historian Douglas Weiner: *Models of Nature: Ecology, Conservation, and Cultural Revolution in Soviet Russia* (Bloomington: Indiana University Press, 1988); and *A Little Corner of Freedom: Russian Nature Protection from Stalin to Gorbachev* (Berkeley: University of California Press, 1999).

Also of note is a remarkable article by the Brazilian scholar José Augusto Padua, which argues that the first modern environmentalist may have been a Brazilian magistrate named José Gregório Moraes Navarro, who, following a savage attack on forests by Portuguese colonists in search of gold and precious stones, criticized the miners for 'destroy[ing] the land in order to retrieve from its bowels those treasures that were more agreeable to their ambitions'. Navarro remarked that 'of all the elements that God created for His glory, and for the use of man, certainly none is more worthy of contemplation than the Earth, the common Mother of all creatures. She still gives us the same protection that she offered to those born in the beginning of the world. ... She will always be, until the end of the world, as she was in the beginning ... despite the ungratefulness of men, who seem to work continuously to destroy and annihilate her natural productions, and to consume and weaken her primitive substance.'

Padua writes that Navarro was one of at least thirty-eight Brazilian commentators, who, between the years 1786 and 1888, 'wrote regularly' about 'the socially negative consequences of the destruction of the natural environment'. His essay quotes some of the others, who appear to have been as wise and far-seeing as Navarro. See José Augusto Padua, '"Annihilating Natural Productions": Nature's Economy, Colonial Crisis and the Origins of Brazilian Political Environmentalism (1786–1810)', *Environment and History*, Volume 6, Number 2, 2000, quoted remarks on pp. 259, 255–56, 260.

9 On Marsh, see David Lowenthal, *George Perkins Marsh: Prophet of Conservation* (Seattle: University of Washington Press, 2000—this is the

revised version of a book first published under a different title in 1958); on Pinchot, Char Miller, *Gifford Pinchot and the Making of Modern Environmentalism* (Washington, DC: Island Press, 2001). Also valuable is the classic early work of Samuel P. Hays, *Conservation and the Gospel of Efficiency: The Progressive Conservation Movement, 1890–1920* (Cambridge, Mass.: Harvard University Press, 1959).

10 See Bill McKibben, 'Introduction', in *American Earth: Environmental Writing Since Thoreau* (New York: Library of America, 2008), pp. xxii–xxiii, xxvi–xxvii, emphasis added.

11 The phrase is that of Andrea Wulf. See her essay 'The Forgotten Father of Environmentalism', *The Atlantic Monthly*, December 2015, https://www.theatlantic.com/science/archive/2015/12/the-forgotten-father-of-environmentalism/421434/ (accessed on 23 June 2023); also Andrea Wulf, *The Invention of Nature: Alexander Humboldt's New World* (New York: Alfred A. Knopf, 2015).

12 Richard Grove, *Green Imperialism: Colonial Expansion, Tropical Island Edens and the Origins of Environmentalism*, 1600–1860 (Cambridge: Cambridge University Press, 1996); J.M. Powell, *Environmental Management in Australia, 1788–1914* (Melbourne: Oxford University Press, 1976).

13 Ellen Griffith Spears, *Rethinking the American Environmental Movement Post-1945* (New York: Routledge, 2020), pp. 3–4 and passim.

14 Kimberley K. Smith, *African American Environmental Thought: Foundations* (Lawrence: University Press of Kansas, 2007).

15 Eric Hobsbawm, *The Age of Extremes: The Short Twentieth Century, 1914–1991* (first published in 1994: reprint London: Abacus, 1995), p. 496.

16 Cf Susanna B. Hecht and Alexander Cockburn, *The Fate of the Forests: Developers, Destroyers, and Defenders of the Amazon* (London: Verso, 1989).

17 See, for example, Karen Armstrong, *Sacred Nature: How We Can Recover Our Bond with the Natural World* (London: The Bodley Head, 2022).

18 The first quote is from J.R. McNeill, 'The State of the Field of Environmental History', *The Annual Review of Environment and Resources*, 2010, p. 362. The second is from J.R. McNeill, *Something New Under the Sun: An Environmental History of the Twentieth-Century World* (New York: W.W. Norton, 2000), p. xxiii. McNeill's book provides a detailed, fact-filled account of the ways in which global ecology was disturbed by humans in the twentieth century as a result of, among other things, increases in the production and use of coal, oil and chemical fertilizers, and through new forms of transport and machinery that altered the earth's surface biologically, chemically and physically, the process intensified and aided along by the massive increases in human population, which grew from 1.2 billion in 1850 to 6 billion in 2000.

Also worth consulting is a later co-authored work by this historian: J.R. McNeill and Peter Engelke, *The Great Acceleration: An Environmental History of the Anthropocene since 1945* (Cambridge, Mass.: Harvard University Press, 2014).

19 On traditional systems of water conservation in India, the work of Anupam Mishra is particularly noteworthy. Most of his writing is in Hindi; however, one tract has been translated into English as *The Radiant Raindrops of Rajasthan* and is available at https://www.arvindguptatoys.com/arvindgupta/anupam.pdf (accessed on 23 June 2023).

20 Cf the essay 'The Indian Road to Sustainability', in Ramachandra Guha, *How Much Should a Person Consume? Environmentalism in India and the United States* (Berkeley: University of California Press, 2006).

21 Ramachandra Guha, 'Prehistory of Indian Environmentalism: Intellectual Traditions', *Economic and Political Weekly*, 4–11 January 1992.

22 A.P. Thornton, *For the File on Empire: Essays and Reviews* (London: Macmillan, 1969), p. vii.

23 For a recent materialist environmental history of India, see Sumit Guha, *Ecologies of Empire in South Asia* (Seattle: University of Washington Press, 2023).

24 McNeill, *Something New Under the Sun*, p. 337.
25 Paul Warde, *The Invention of Sustainability: Nature and Destiny, c. 1500–1870* (Cambridge: Cambridge University Press, 2018), p. 5.
26 Rob Nixon, *Slow Violence and the Environmentalism of the Poor* (Cambridge, Mass.: Harvard University Press, 2013), p. 25.
27 Such a book may consider including, among others, the Bengali novelist Bibhutibhushan Bandyopadhyay, the Kumauni poet Gauri Dutt Pande, the Malayalam poet Sugathakumari, and the Kannada poet, novelist and public intellectual K.V. Puttappa 'Kuvempu'.
28 Warde, *The Invention of Sustainability*, p. 3.
29 Anil Agarwal, 'Beyond Pretty Trees and Tigers: The Role of Ecological Destruction in the Emerging Pattern of Poverty and People's Protests', *ICSSR Newsletter*, Volume 15, Number 1, 1984 (available now at https://archive.org/details/beyond-pretty-trees-and-tigers-anil-agarwal/page/1/mode/2up). Cf also Anil Agarwal, 'Human-Nature Interactions in a Third World Country', *The Environmentalist*, Volume 6, Number 3, 1986.
30 Callum Roberts, 'Shifting Baselines', *Granta*, number 153, Autumn 2020, p. 20.

Chapter One: The Myriad-Minded Environmentalist

1 Krishna Datta and Andrew Robinson, *Rabindranath Tagore: The Myriad-minded Man* (London: Bloomsbury, 1997).
2 In 1961, on the occasion of Tagore's birth centenary, the Indian Academy of Letters published a compendious volume on his life and work. Among the sixty contributors to the volume were Tagore's great compatriots Jawaharlal Nehru and Sarvepalli Radhakrishnan (then Prime Minister and Vice President of India respectively), the linguist Suniti Kumar Chatterjee and the novelist Mulk Raj Anand. From outside India we had the American poet Robert Frost, the Italian scholar Giuseppe Tucci, the Argentinian writer Victoria Ocampo, the Alsatian doctor and philosopher Albert Schweitzer. There were essays on Tagore

and music, Tagore and art, Tagore and children, Tagore and education, an array of personal reminiscences, etc., but nothing at all on Tagore and nature (nor even on Tagore and landscape, or Tagore and the forest). See *Rabindranath Tagore: A Centenary Volume, 1861–1961* (New Delhi: Sahitya Akademi, 1961).

3 Rabindranath Tagore, *My Reminiscences* (first edition London: Macmillan and Co., 1917; fourth reprint 1921), pp. 4–5.

4 Ibid., pp. 10–13, 22.

5 Tagore, *My Reminiscences*, pp. 226–27.

6 Quoted in G.D. Khanolkar, *The Lute and the Plough: A Life of Rabindranath Tagore*, translated from the Marathi by Thomas Gay (Bombay: The Book Centre Private Ltd, 1963), p. 94.

7 Quoted in Aseem Shrivastava, 'An Ecology of the Spirit: Rabindranath's Experience of Nature', in Sukanta Chaudhuri, editor, *The Cambridge Companion to Tagore* (Cambridge: Cambridge University Press, 2020), p. 326.

8 Tagore, *My Reminiscences*, pp. 91–94.

9 Ibid., p. 163.

10 Rabindranath Tagore, *A Visit to Japan*, translated from the Bengali by Shakuntala Rao Sastri (New York: East West Institute, 1961), pp. 19–21.

11 Ibid., pp. 26–27.

12 Tagore to Pratima Devi, 30 August 1927, in *Letters from Java: Rabindranath Tagore's Tour of South-East Asia 1927*, translated by Indiradevi Chaudhurani and Supriya Roy (Kolkata: Visva-Bharati, 2010), p. 31.

13 Tagore to Rathindranath Tagore, 7 September 1927, in Ibid., p. 84.

14 Tagore, *A Visit to Japan*, pp. 19–21.

15 Niharranjan Ray, *An Artist in Life: A Commentary on the Life and Works of Rabindranath Tagore* (Trivandrum: University of Kerala, 1967), pp. 112–14.

16 See Fakrul Alam, 'Rabindranath Tagore and Eco-Consciousness', in Fakrul Alam, *Rabindranath Tagore and National Identity Formation*

in Bangladesh: Essays and Reviews (Dhaka: Bangla Academy, 2012), p. 175.

17 See C.F. Andrews, 'An Evening with Rabindra', *The Modern Review*, August 1912, reprinted in Bimalendu Dutta (editor), *Tagore Abroad* (Calcutta: Papyrus, 2001), pp. 129–30.

18 Ray, *An Artist in Life*, pp. 217–18.

19 See V.S. Naravane, 'Tree Worship in India', *Illustrated Weekly of India*, 1 September 1957.

20 Rabindranath Tagore, 'Sadhana' (1914), in Sisir Kumar Das (editor), *The English Writings of Rabindranath Tagore: Volume Two: Poems, Stories, Essays* (New Delhi: Sahitya Akademi, 1996), pp. 281–83.

21 'The Message of the Forest' (1919), in Sisir Kumar Das (editor), *The English Writings of Rabindranath Tagore: Volume Three: A Miscellany* (New Delhi: Sahitya Akademi, 1996), p. 386.

22 'The Religion of the Forest' (1922), reprinted in Das (editor), *The English Writings of Rabindranath Tagore: Volume Two*, p. 512.

23 Cf Irawati Karve, *Yuganta: The End of an Epoch* (Poona: Sangam Books, 1974).

24 On the influence of the Upanishads on Tagore, see Debarati Bandyopadhyay, *Rabindranath Tagore: A Life of Intimacy with Nature* (New Delhi: Rupa, 2019), pp. 48ff.

25 K.R. Kripalani, 'The Poet as Educationist', *The Visvabharati Quarterly*, Tagore Centenary Number, Volume 26, Numbers 3 and 4, 1961, pp. 180ff.

26 Tagore, *Letters from Java*, pp. 154, 156–57.

27 See Swati Ganguly, *Tagore's University: A History of Visva-Bharati, 1921–1961* (Ranikhet: Permanent Black, 2022).

28 Khanolkar, *The Lute and the Plough*, pp. 300–01, 331.

29 Quoted in Uma Dasgupta, *A History of Sriniketan: Rabindranath Tagore's Pioneering Work in Rural Reconstruction* (New Delhi: Niyogi Books, 2022), p. 75.

30 Amit Ray, 'Rabindranath Tagore's Vision of Ecological Harmony', typescript, Department of Humanities and Social Sciences, Indian Institute of Technology, Kanpur, c. 1990.

31 This discussion draws on Sumana Roy, *How I Became a Tree* (New Delhi: Aleph Book Company, 2017), especially pp. 85–90.

32 In his own memoirs, Tagore's son, Rathindranath, wrote perceptively about his father's profound attachment to the countryside of eastern Bengal, where he spent some of his happiest days. Tagore loved the river Padma, wrote poems in praise of its grandeur and beauty, and named his houseboat after it. The son says of his father that 'there is no doubt that his first and deepest love was for the country of mellow green fields with their clusters of bamboo shoots swaying gently in the south breeze and hiding villages in their midst, of majestic rivers with their stretches of gleaming white sand—the haunts of myriads of wild ducks, as well as of homely rivulets with sweet-sounding names, meandering in and out through peaceful villages hugging their banks. Such associations had entered deeper into his life than the parched and barren wastes that surrounded him at Santiniketan, the choice of his later years. The river Padma and its sandbanks, Shelidah and its fishermen and minstrels and its fields of golden yellow mustard blossoms, the houseboat with its plucky boatman, Tapsi, and its grey-bearded cook, Phatik, must have haunted him in his old age and made him feel homesick for all that he missed at Santiniketan.' See Rathindranath Tagore, *On the Edges of Time* (Bombay: Orient Longman, 1958), pp. 39–40. One supposes the trees and shrubs Tagore helped plant in Santiniketan made him less homesick.

33 Shrivastava, 'An Ecology of the Spirit', pp. 330–31.

34 Letter of 9 August 1894, quoted in Bandyopadhyay, *Rabindranath Tagore: A Life of Intimacy with Nature*, p. xxv.

35 Raymond Williams, *The Country and the City* (1973; reprint London: Vintage, 2016), p. 64.

36 Rabindranath Tagore, 'The History and Ideals of Sriniketan' (1939), quoted in Uma Dasgupta, 'Redeeming the Indian Village: Rabindranath

Tagore and the Sriniketan Experiment', in Shubhra Chakrabarti and Utsa Patnaik (editors), *Agrarian and Other Histories: Essays for Binay Bhushan Chaudhuri* (New Delhi: Tulika, 2017), p. 202.

37 See Khanolkar, *The Lute and the Plough*, pp. 183–85.

38 'Personal Reminiscences', in Leonard K. Elmhirst, *Poet and Plowman* (Calcutta: Visva-Bharati, 1975), pp. 15–16.

39 Cf Leonard Elmhirst, 'Rabindranath Tagore and Sriniketan', *The Visvabharati Quarterly*, Tagore Centenary Number, Volume 26, Numbers 3 and 4, 1961.

40 'Personal Reminiscences', in Leonard K. Elmhirst, *Poet and Plowman*, pp. 18, 21.

41 Elmhirst, 'Rabindranath Tagore and Sriniketan', p. 213.

42 Tagore, *A Visit to Japan*, pp. 19–21.

43 Rabindranath Tagore, *Nationalism* (first published in 1917; reprint New Delhi: Penguin Books India, 2009), p. 57.

44 See http://www.worldjute.com/ about_jute/juthist.html#:~:text=Period%20from%201855&text=The%20first%20jute%20mill%20was,were%20operating%20with%20950%20looms (accessed on 19 February 2022).

45 Tagore, *My Reminiscences*, pp. 208–09.

46 'The Modern Age', in Rabindranath Tagore, *Creative Unity* (first published 1922; reprint London: Macmillan, 1926), pp. 115–16.

47 For more on the British nature poets of the eighteenth and nineteenth centuries, see Jonathan Bate, *Romantic Ecology*, as well as Ramachandra Guha, *Environmentalism: A Global History* (New York: Longmans, 2000), Chapter 2.

48 Tagore, *Nationalism*, pp. 8–9.

49 Ibid., pp. 17–18.

50 Ibid., pp. 31–32. Sadly, these fond hopes were to be shattered as, in later decades, Japan itself went down the route of conquest and the acquisition of colonies, leading to a deep disillusionment in Tagore about a culture and nation he had once loved and admired. See the essay 'Travelling with Tagore', in Ramachandra Guha, *Democrats and*

Dissenters (second edition New Delhi: Penguin Random House India, 2017).

51 See 'The Robbery of the Soil', in *Poet and Plowman*, pp. 34, 38–39.

52 Ibid., p. 37.

53 Ray, *An Artist in Life*, pp. 218–19.

54 Khanolkar, *The Lute and the Plough*, p. v.

Chapter Two: Ecological Sociologist

1 T.N. Madan, *Sociological Traditions: Methods and Perspectives in the Sociology of India (*New Delhi: Sage, 2011), p. 145.

2 'Mukerjee' is how he normally spelt his own surname, though it was often rendered in print as Mukherjee, or even Mookerji or Mookerjee, these alternate renderings even prefixing articles or books written by him.

3 Radhakamal Mukerjee, *India: The Dawn of a New Era (An Autobiography)* (New Delhi: Radha Publishers, 1987), pp. 41–42.

4 Ibid., pp. 42–43. The echoes with Rabindranath Tagore's memories of his childhood, the banyan in the home and the great river nearby, may not be accidental. Mukerjee had surely grown up reading Tagore's writings in their shared mother tongue, Bengali.

5 Ibid., p. 58. Cf Sumit Sarkar, *The Swadeshi Movement in Bengal, 1903–1908* (first published in 1973; second edition Ranikhet: Permanent Black, 2011).

6 Mukerjee, *India*, p. 68.

7 These paragraphs are based on Ibid., pp. 95–97.

8 Patrick Geddes, 'Introduction' in Radhakamal Mukerjee, *The Foundation of Indian Economics* (London: Longmans, Green and Co, 1916), pp. ix–xi, Mukerjee himself (Ibid., pp. 3–4) referred to Indian village communities as 'the most complete and contented in the world'.

9 Ibid., pp. 328–29.

10 Ibid., Book IV, Chapters I and II.

11 Ibid., pp. 448–49.

12 Ibid., pp. 18–19.

13 Radhakamal Mukerjee, *Principles of Comparative Economics*, Volume II (London: P.S. King and Son Ltd, 1922), pp. 3–4.

14 Ibid., p. 72.

15 Ibid., p. 245.

16 Ibid., pp. 19–20.

17 Ibid., pp. 47–48.

18 Ibid., pp. 148–49.

19 Mukerjee, *Principles of Comparative Economics*, Volume II, p. 189.

20 Ibid., pp. 324–26.

21 Radhakamal Mukerjee, *The Rural Economy of India* (Longmans, Green and Co. Ltd, 1926), pp. vii, 1.

22 Ibid., p. 147.

23 Ibid., pp. 156–58.

The Japanese occupation of Korea also had a harsh and brutal side, particularly with regard to how the colonizers treated the colonized, though this seems to have escaped Mukerjee. The historian Paul Suter further informs me that recent scholarship presents a somewhat less flattering picture of Japan's forest legacy in Korea.

On the history of forestry in Japan itself, see Conrad Totman, *The Green Archipelago: Forestry in Pre-Industrial Japan* (Berkeley: University of California Press, 1989).

24 Ibid., pp. 161–62. See also Radhakamal Mukerjee, 'Our Crime against Trees, Grasses and Rivers', *The Modern Review*, November 1930.

25 The classic works are those of Harold Conklin. See his essays 'An Ethno-ecological Approach to Shifting Agriculture', *Transactions of the New York Academy of Sciences*, Series 2, Volume 17, Number 2, 1954; and 'The Study of Shifting Cultivation', *Current Anthropology*, Volume 2, Number 1, 1961.

26 Radhakamal Mukerjee, 'The Misconception about the Indian Agrarian System', *The Modern Review*, September 1923, pp. 287–88. Cf also idem, 'The Contrast between Socialism and Eastern Communalism', *The*

Modern Review, October 1921; idem, 'The Web of Indian Communal Democracy', *The Modern Review*, December 1923.

27 Radhakamal Mukerjee, *Borderlands of Economics* (London: George Allen and Unwin Ltd., 1925), pp. 227–28.

28 On Mukerjee's integrative approach to the social sciences, and how it was abandoned by later generations of economists, see Manuel Gottlieb, 'Mukerjee: Economics Becomes Social Science', *Journal of Economic Issues*, Volume 5, Number 4, 1971.

29 Cf Martin Bulmer, *The Chicago School of Sociology* (Chicago: The University of Chicago Press, 1984).

30 Cf Donald Worster, *Nature's Economy: A History of Ecological Ideas* (second edition New York: Cambridge University Press, 1994).

31 Radhakamal Mukerjee, 'An Ecological Approach to Sociology', *Sociological Review*, Volume 22, Number 4, 1930, pp 281ff.

32 Radhakamal Mukerjee, 'The Regional Balance of Man', *American Journal of Sociology*, Volume 36, Number 3, November 1930, pp. 455–60.

33 Radhakamal Mukerjee. 'The Broken Balance of Population, Land and Water', *Indian Journal of Economics*, Volume 14, Issue 154, 1934, reprinted in J. Krishnamurty (editor), *Towards Development Economics: Indian Contributions, 1900–1945* (New Delhi: Oxford University Press, 2009), pp. 159–67.

34 Mukerjee, *India: The Dawn of an Era*, pp. 160–65. See also Mukerjee's essay, 'The Concentration of Population in Eastern Bengal', *The Indian Journal of Economics*, October 1928.

35 See report in *Bombay Chronicle*, 16 October 1937. 'Provincial Autonomy' refers to the scheme of limited self-government under which Congress governments had come to power in seven out of nine provinces of British India.

36 Radhakamal Mukerjee, 'A Preface to Planning', in Radhakamal Mukerjee and H.L. Dey (editors), *Economic Problems of Modern India, Volume II* (London: Macmillan, 1941), esp. pp. x–xv. 'Brajabhumi' is the area around the temple towns of Vrindavan and Mathura, reputed

to be the places where the Hindu god Krishna, a cowherd by his caste occupation, lived and flourished.

37 Radhakamal Mukerjee, *Planning the Countryside* (first published in 1946; second edition Bombay: Hind Kitabs Ltd, 1950), pp. 9, 10.

38 Ibid., pp. 79, 81.

39 Ibid., pp. 87–90. Whether the Maharaja of Gwalior ever read this report is not known. In the event, the erosion of the ravines of Bhind and Morena lay unchecked; with the desperate poverty that ensued spawning a cycle of violence and banditry that was to plague these districts for decades to come.

40 Ibid., pp. 95–97.

41 Radhakamal Mukerjee, *An Economist Looks at Pakistan* (Bombay: Hind Kitabs, 1944), pp. 20–22 and passim.

42 George B. Tindall, 'The Significance of Howard W. Odum to Southern History: A Preliminary Estimate' in *The Journal of Southern History*, Vol. 24, No. 3, 1958, quoted passage on p. 298.

43 Radhakamal Mukerjee, *Regional Sociology* (New York: The Century Company, 1926), pp. 45–46.

44 Ibid., pp. 167–68, etc. In 1937 Mukerjee and Odum finally met in person when the Indian travelled to the United States.

45 Radhakamal Mukerjee, *The Regional Balance of Man: An Ecological Theory of Population* (Madras: University of Madras, 1938), being based on the Sir William Meyer Foundation Lectures, delivered at the University in 1935–36), pp. 2–3.

46 See Mukerjee, *The Regional Balance of Man*, p. 296.

47 Ibid., pp. 306, 304.

48 Ibid., p. 36.

49 Radhakamal Mukerjee, *Social Ecology* (London: Longmans, Green and Company, 1942), pp. 336–37.

50 I have listed only a selection of Radhakamal Mukerjee's books in English. He also wrote many popular and scholarly articles, and also published fairly widely in his mother tongue, Bengali.

51 Lewis Mumford to Patrick Geddes, 31 March 1925, in Ms. 10575, Patrick Geddes Papers, National Library of Scotland, Edinburgh.

52 See Ramachandra Guha, 'Lewis Mumford: The Forgotten American Environmentalist', *Capitalism, Nature, Socialism*, Volume 2, Number 3, 1991.

53 Radhakamal Mukerjee, 'The Social Philosophy of Rabindranath Tagore', *The Visvabharati Quarterly*, Tagore Centenary Number, Volume 26, Numbers 3 and 4, 1961.

54 Radhakamal Mukerjee, *The Changing Face of Bengal: A Study in Riverine Economy* (Calcutta: University of Calcutta, 1938), p. 17.

These sentiments were ahead of their time, though one word was emphatically of its time—the use of the male pronoun to denote humans as a whole.

Chapter Three: Gandhi's Economist

1 J.C. Kumarappa to Gandhi, 22 May 1929, in Subject File No. 5, Kumarappa Papers, Nehru Memorial Museum and Library, New Delhi (hereafter NMML).

2 See Ramachandra Guha, *Gandhi: The Years that Changed the World, 1915–1948* (New York: Alfred A. Knopf, 2018), pp. 177–78.

3 Letter of 21 November 1928, in Subject File No. 1, J.C. Kumarappa Papers, NMML.

4 Venu Madhav Govindu and Deepak Malghan, *The Web of Freedom: J.C. Kumarappa and Gandhi's Quest for Economic Justice* (New Delhi: Oxford University Press, 2016), p. 36.

5 D.B. Kalelkar to J.C. Kumarappa, 2 June 1929; Kumarappa to Kalelkar, 4 June 1929, both in Subject File No. 5, Kumarappa Papers, NMML. Also Govindu and Malghan, *The Web of Freedom*, pp. 38–39.

6 Letter dated Lucknow, 8 June 1929, in Subject File No. 5, Kumarappa Papers, NMML.

7 D.B. Kalelkar, 'Prefatory Note', in J.C. Kumarappa, editor and compiler, *A Survey of Matar Taluka* (Ahmedabad: Gujarat Vidyapeeth, 1931), p. vii.

8 *A Survey of Matar Taluka*, p. 94.
9 Ibid., pp. 14–15, 99–102.
10 Ibid., pp. 38–42, 127.
11 Ibid., pp. 16, 136.
12 Ibid., pp. 24, 35, 37.
13 Ibid., pp. 116–18.
14 Ibid., pp. 119–21.
15 Ibid., p. 8.
16 Ibid., p. 131. A maund is a unit of weight equivalent to about 37 kg.
17 Ibid., pp. 131–32.
18 Ibid., pp. 140–41.
19 Ibid., pp. 143–44.
20 See the letters reproduced in S.K. George and G. Ramachandran, editors, *The Economics of Peace: The Cause and the Man* (Wardha: Gram Udyog Vibhag, 1952), pp. 55–63. Cf also M.A. Thomas, 'J.C. Kumarappa—The Good Christian', in *Kumarappa Centenary Souvenir—1992* (Bangalore: J.C. Kumrappa Birth Centenary Committee, Karnataka, 1992) pp. 12–13.

On the Christian core of Kumarappa's thought, see also S. Victus, *A Study on Religion and Social Philosophy of Dr J.C. Kumarappa*, unpublished PhD thesis, Tamilnadu Theological Seminary, Madurai, May 2000.

21 This account of the formation of the AIVIA draws on M. Vinaik, *The Gandhian Crusader: A Biography of J.C. Kumarappa* (Gandhigram: Gandhigram Trust, 1987) Chapter 4.
22 See Vinaik, *The Gandhian Crusader*, pp. 105–09.
23 J.C. Kumarappa, 'Intelligent Buying', *Bombay Chronicle*, 26 September 1941; idem, 'Women and Village Industries', *Bombay Chronicle*, 2 October 1941.
24 J.C. Kumarappa, 'Scientific Use of Natural Resources', in George and Ramachandran (editors), *The Economics of Peace*, pp. 113–14. Cf also J.C. Kumarappa, 'What is Progress?', *Harijan*, 13 April 1947.
25 J. C. Kumarappa, 'A Noble Lead', *Harijan*, 4 May 1947.

26 See K.R. Subbaraman, 'Kumarappaji—The Great Teacher'. in *Kumarappa Centenary Souvenir—1992*, p. 20.

27 J.C. Kumarappa, 'Rural Development', *Harijan*, 23 November 1947.

28 This discussion is based on J.C. Kumarappa, *Why the Village Movement?* (Second edition Rajahmundry: Hindusthan Publishing Corporation, 1938).

29 Kumarappa, *Why the Village Movement?*, pp. 27–28.

30 See *A Survey of Matar Taluka*, pp. 36–38, 46–47, 117.

31 J.C. Kumarappa, *The Economy of Permanence*, second edition (Wardha: All India Village Industries Association, 1948), Part II, p. 55.

32 J.C. Kumarappa, 'What is Progress?', *Harijan*, 13 April 1947.

33 J. C. Kumarappa, *The Gandhian Economy and Other Essays* (Wardha: All India Village Industries Association, 1948), p. 10.

34 J.C. Kumarappa, *Gandhian Economic Thought* (Bombay: Vora and Co., 1951), pp. 14–15.

35 See, in this connection, the book by his brother, Bharatan Kumarappa: *Capitalism, Socialism or Villagism?* (first published in 1946: reprint Varanasi: Sarva Seva Sangh, 1965).

36 'The Cow Economy', *Gram Udyog Patrika* (hereafter GUP) October 1947, in G. Bandhu, editor, *Back to Basics: A J.C. Kumarappa Reader* (Udhagamandalam: Odyssey, 2001), pp. 110–11.

37 J.C. Kumarappa, 'His Majesty's Opposition', *Harijan*, 1 February 1948.

38 M.K. Gandhi, 'Draft Constitution of Congress', *Collected Works of Mahatma Gandhi* (New Delhi: Publications Division, 1958–1994—hereafter CWMG), Volume 90, pp. 326–28.

39 Quoted in George and Ramachandran (editors), *The Economics of Peace,* pp. 27–28.

40 Mahadev Desai, quoted in Narayan Desai, *Bliss Was It to be Young with Gandhi* (Bombay: Bharatiya Vidya Bhavan, 1988), p. 26.

41 Labaya Kumar Chaudhury to J.C. Kumarappa, 6 October 1947; Kumarappa to Labaya Kumar Chaudhury, 6 November 1947, both in File No. 15, J.C. Kumarappa Papers, NMML.

42 Letter of 2 July 1948, Kumarappa Papers, NMML.

43 'Bullock Carts Not Allowed', GUP, September 1951, in G. Bandhu, editor, *Back to Basics*, pp 283–85.

Kumarappa's clash with Nehru about his means of transport became the stuff of legend. A decade after the incident, a fellow Gandhian recalled 'the day when Dr. Kumarappa called to represent the villages at New Delhi, rode in a bullock cart to the office of the Prime Minister. Would [that] we had a film of that event! One can picture the strange sightI A man in his immaculate khadi proceeding to meet an old comrade in the struggle for freedom but halted as he drew near his destination because bullock carts were not allowed at the capital! Then how was the peasant to meet his servant? It took a dramatist like Kumarappa to bring home to each one of us how easily we lost contact with our own people when we get power.'

See R.R. Keithahn, writing in *Dr J.C. Kumarappa: A Brief Tribute* (Madras: Kumarappa Publications, 1959—issued on the occasion of his sixty-ninth birthday), pp. 7–8. In truth, Kumarappa had ridden in a horse-driven tonga, though he did threaten to come in a bullock-cart the next day.

44 J.C. Kumarappa, 'Some Thoughts on the Plan', GUP, August 1951, in G. Bandhu (editor), *Back to Basics*, pp. 126–29.

45 'Our Guides', GUP, December 1953, in in G. Bandhu (editor), *Back to Basics*, pp. 133–35.

46 J.C. Kumarappa, 'The Reorganisation of States and Riverine Valley Planning', unpublished typescript, c. November 1955, in G. Bandhu (editor), *Back to Basics,* pp. 198–200.

47 Cf Hallam Tennyson, *India's Walking Saint: The Story of Vinoba Bhave* (New York: Doubleday, 1955).

48 J.C. Kumarappa, 'The Sarva Seva Sangh: A Scheme for an Agricultural Research and Experimental Centre', typescript dated 8 March 1951, in File No. 25, J.C. Kumarappa Papers, NMML.

49 See document entitled 'Pannai Ashram, Seldoh: Development Report from Its Foundation—17/5/51 to 31/5/53', in File No. 25, J.C. Kumarappa Papers, NMML.

50 Kumarappa to Bhave, 27 April 1955, in File No. 31, J.C. Kumarappa Papers, NMML. Cf also J.C. Kumarappa, 'Ends and Means in Bhoodan', *Harijan*, 11 June 1955.

51 Bhave to Kumarappa, 14 May 1955 (in Hindi), in Ibid.

52 Kumarappa to Bhave, 22 May 1955, in Ibid.

53 G. Ramachandran, 'The Man Kumarappa' (c. 1952), in K.C.R. Raja, editor, *Thoughts and Talks of G. Ramachandran* (Gandhigram: G. Ramachandran 60th Birthday Committee, 1964), p. 30.

54 See J.C. Kumarappa, *A Peep Behind the Iron Curtain (Life in the Soviet Union and in Peoples' China* (T. Kallupatti: Published by the author, 1956), p. 107.

55 J.C. Kumarappa to G. Ramachandran, letters of 10 October and 17 October 1951, in Subject File No. 23, Kumarappa Papers, NMML.

56 J.C. Kumarappa, *Report on Agriculture and Cottage and Small Scale Industries in Japan*, thirty-eight-page pamphlet, publisher unknown, c. 1952, quotes from pp. 6, 11, 36–37.

57 Newsletter No. 4, *International Economic Conference*, April 1952, in Subject File No. 23, Kumarappa Papers.

58 J.C. Kumarappa, *A Peep Behind the Iron Curtain: Life in the Soviet Union and in Peoples' China* (T. Kallupatti: Published by the author, 1956), pp. 16–17 and passim.

59 S.K. Dey to J.C. Kumarappa, 7 July 1952; Kumarappa to Dey, 21 August 1952, Kumarappa Papers, NMML.

60 Dey to Kumarappa, 15 December 1955, in Ibid.

61 Dey to Kumarappa, 5 January 1956, in Ibid.

62 J.C. Kumarappa, *Report on Rural Development Work in Madurai District* (1956), unpublished copy in the Kumarappa Papers.

63 Kumarappa to Dey, 22 October 1956, Kumarappa Papers.

64 Dey to Kumarappa, 21 November 1956, in Ibid.

65 As reported in *The Hindu*, 2 February 1960.

66 M. Sivaramakrishnan, 'The late Dr. J.C. Kumarappa', typescript in Subject File No. 37, Kumarappa Papers.

67 See M. Vinaik, *J.C. Kumarappa and the Quest for World Peace* (Ahmedabad: Navajivan Publishing House, 1956), p. 151.

68 At long last, and not a moment too soon, J.C. Kumarappa is being rediscovered by contemporary scholars. The Indian scientists Venu Govindu and Deepak Malghan have published a fine intellectual biography, entitled *The Web of Freedom*, from which I have drawn upon in my own account. The American Gandhian, Mark Lindley, has published a study of Kumarappa's economic ideas: *J.C. Kumarappa: Mahatma Gandhi's Economist* (Mumbai: Popular Prakashan, 2007). Cf also Chaitra Rediker, *Gandhian Engagement with Capital: Perspectives of J.C. Kumarappa* (New Delhi: Sage Publications India, 2019).

Chapter Four: Scottish Internationalist

1 See Sian Reynolds, 'After Dreyfus and before the Entente: Patrick Geddes's Cultural Diplomacy at the Paris Exhibition of 1900', in Martyn Cornick and Ceri Crossley, *Problems in French History* (New York: Palgrave, 2000), pp. 149–67.

2 Tribute by Patrick Geddes in S.K. Radcliffe, et. al., *Margaret Noble (Sister Nivedita)* (London: Sherratt and Hughes, 1913), p. 12f.

3 See The Sister Nivedita (Margaret E. Noble), *The Web of Indian Life* (London: Longmans, Green and Co., 1904).

4 Patrick Geddes, *On Universities in Europe and in India, And a Needed Type of Research Institute, Geographical and Social: Five Letters to an Indian Friend* (Madras: Mount Road, 1903), p. 9.

5 Quoted in Philip Mairet, *Pioneer of Sociology: The Life and Letters of Patrick Geddes* (London: Lund Humphries, 1957), p. 17.

6 Quoted in Mairet, *Pioneer of Sociology*, p. 61.

7 Geddes, 'Life and Its Science' (1895), reprinted in *Edinburgh Review*, Summer 1992, pp. 24–30. Here, by arguing that humans have an innate identification with nature, Geddes is anticipating, almost by a century, the American biologist E.O. Wilson's idea of 'biophilia'. See Wilson,

Biophilia: The Human Bond with Other Species (Cambridge, Mass.: Harvard University Press, 1986).

8 See Patrick Geddes, 'Nature Study and Geographical Education', *The Scottish Geographical Magazine*, October 1902, pp. 528, 534.

9 Murdo Macdonald, 'Patrick Geddes—Educator, Ecologist, Visual Thinker', *Edinburgh Review*, Summer 1992, pp. 114–19. See also Murdo Macdonald, *Patrick Geddes's Intellectual Origins* (Edinburgh: Edinburgh University Press, 2020).

10 Patrick Geddes, 'The Civic Survey of Edinburgh', in *Transactions of the Town Planning Conference, London, 10–15 October 1910* (London: The Royal Institute of British Architects, 1911), pp. 537–74.

11 Patrick Geddes, *Cities in Evolution: An Introduction to the Town Planning Movement and to the Study of Civics* (London: William and Norgate, 1915), pp. 92–93.

12 Geddes to Barrington, 25 July 1914, in Ms. 10514, Patrick Geddes Papers, National Library of Scotland, Edinburgh.

13 Quoted in Mairet, *Pioneer of Sociology*, p. 157.

14 Patrick Geddes to E.B. Havell, 26 August 1915, Mss. Eur. D. 730/1, Asia, Pacific and Africa Collections, British Library, London (hereafter APAC/BL).

15 Quoted in Mairet, *Pioneer of Sociology*, pp. 159, 164.

16 Patrick Geddes to C.H. Roberts, 4 December 1917, Mss. Eur. F. 170/25, APAC/BL. Roberts was a Liberal member of Parliament who had served as Under Secretary of State for India.

17 See Jacqueline Tyrwhitt (editor), *Patrick Geddes in India* (London: Lund Humphries, 1947), pp. 57–58.

18 Patrick Geddes, *Reports on Replanning of Six Towns in Bombay Presidency* (1915; reprint Bombay: Government Central Press, 1965), p. 3.

19 *Patrick Geddes in India*, p. 91.

20 See Geddes, *Cities in Evolution*, pp. 51–52.

21 *Patrick Geddes in India*, p. 15.

22 Patrick Geddes, *Town Planning Towards City Development* (first published in 1918: reprint New Delhi: Vitastaa Publishing Ltd, 2016), Part I, p. xxvi.

23 Geddes, *Reports on Replanning of Six Towns in Bombay Presidency*, pp. 10–11.

24 Patrick Geddes, 'Town Planning in Lahore: A Report to the Municipal Council' (1917), reprinted in Marshall Stanley, editor, *Patrick Geddes, Spokesman for Man and Environment* (New Brunswick: Rutgers University Press, 1972), pp. 383–449 (quote from pp. 394–95).

25 See *Patrick Geddes in India*, p. 22.

26 Patrick Geddes, *Report on Town Planning, Dacca* (Calcutta: Bengal Secretariat Book Depot, 1917), p. 14.

27 Cf Philip Boardman, *Patrick Geddes: Maker of the Future* (Chapel Hill: University of North Carolina Press, 1944), pp. 346–47.

28 Geddes, *Reports on Replanning of Six Towns in Bombay Presidency*, p. 13.

29 Ibid., pp. 24–25.

30 Geddes, *Town Planning Towards City Development*, Part I, p. 4.

31 Ibid., pp. 44, 43.

32 Ibid., pp. 38–39.

33 Ibid., p. 52. A lac (or lakh) equals one hundred thousand.

34 Ibid., pp. 150–52.

35 Ibid., pp. 113–16.

36 Ibid., pp. 130–33.

37 Ibid., Part II, p. 233.

38 Geddes's hope that small cities would be the harbingers of a richer, more socially fulfilling and more ecologically responsible future, was eloquently expressed in his report on Nadiad, where he wrote: 'So here—nowhere better than in Nadiad—may be created the very type of that decentralised and semi-rural garden city which is the best hope of the future; best for the health of individuals and of the race, and even best for quality of civilisation also. For history abundantly shows that in arts and crafts, in thought and in religion, in character and personality,

in initiative and action … the small cities are constantly surpassing the great.' Geddes, *Reports on Replanning of Six Towns in Bombay Presidency*, p. 15.

39 Patrick Geddes, *Town Planning in Balrampur: A Report to the Honourable the Maharaj Bahadur* (Lucknow: Murray's London Printing Press, 1917), pp. 44–45.

40 Ibid., p. 15.

41 Ibid., p. 62.

42 Quoted in Robert Stephens, *Ahmedabad Walls: A Circumambulation with Patrick Geddes*, unpublished monograph, c. 2020, p. 69.

43 Quoted in Indra Munshi, *Patrick Geddes's Contribution to Sociology and Urban Planning* (London: Routledge, 2022), p. 63.

44 See Bose to Geddes, letters of 11 February, 6 March and 25 June 1918, in Ms. 10576, Patrick Geddes Papers, National Library of Scotland, Edinburgh.

45 Frank G. Novak, Jr. (editor), *Lewis Mumford and Patrick Geddes: The Correspondence* (New York: Routledge, 1995), pp. 50–51.

46 Pheroze Bharucha, obituary of Geddes in *Journal of the University of Bombay*, 1932, p. 227.

47 Letter of 15 April 1922, in Novak, Jr. (editor), *Lewis Mumford & Patrick Geddes*, p. 127.

48 Cf Diwan Jarmani Dass, *Maharaja* (first published 1969, reprint New Delhi: Penguin India, 2019).

49 Geddes to H.H. the Maharaja of Patiala, 15 September 1922, in Ms. 10516, Patrick Geddes Papers, National Library of Scotland, Edinburgh.

50 Patrick Geddes to Dewan of Patiala, 21 September 1922, in ibid.

51 Geddes to Mumford, 20 December 1922, in Novak, Jr. editor, *Lewis Mumford & Patrick Geddes*, p. 147.

52 Cf Helen Meller, 'Urbanisation and the Introduction of Modern Town Planning in India, 1910–1925' in K.N. Chaudhuri and C.J. Dewey (eds), *Economy and Society: Essays in Indian Economic and Social History* (New Delhi: Oxford University Press, 1979), especially pp. 342–45.

53 Geddes, *Cities in Evolution*, pp. 210–11.

54 Geddes, *Report on Town Planning, Dacca*, p. 17, emphasis in original.

55 Ibid., p. 2.

56 Geddes, *Town Planning in Balrampur*, p. 3.

57 Geddes, *Report on City Development*, Part I, p. 23.

58 Shiv Visvanathan, 'Ancestors and Epigones', *Seminar*, February 1987.

59 Cf Geddes to Bhagwandas, 3 October 1916; Geddes to M.M. Malaviya, c. November 1916; both in Ms. 10515, Patrick Geddes Papers, National Library of Scotland, Edinburgh.

60 Letter of 9 May 1922, in Bashabi Fraser, editor, *The Tagore-Geddes Correspondence* (Kolkata: Visva-Bharati, 2004), pp. 63–64.

61 J.C. Bose to Patrick Geddes, letters of 8 January 1920 and 18 May 1921, in Ms. 10576, Patrick Geddes Papers, National Library of Scotland, Edinburgh.

The admiration between Geddes and Bose was entirely mutual, the Scottish planner even going so far as to publish an adulatory short biography of the Indian scientist. See Patrick Geddes, *The Life and Work of Sir Jagadis C. Bose* (London: Longmans, Green, and Co., 1920).

Chapter Five: Dissenting Scientists

1 Wendell Berry, *The Unsettling of America: Culture and Agriculture* (San Francisco, Sierra Club Books, 1977), pp. 46, 142.

Wendell Berry's admiration for Albert Howard is enduring. Forty years after mentioning it in *The Unsettling of America*, he chose Howard's *An Agricultural Testament* as one of his '6 favourite books about environmental protection'. See https://theweek.com/articles/543707/wendell-berrys-6-favorite-books-about-environmental-protection. And in an interview from 2013 he described Howard's work as 'the scientific bedrock of organic agriculture'. See https://ourworld.unu.edu/en/nature-as-an-ally-an-interview-with-wendell-berry (accessed on 9 August 2022).

2 Wes Jackson, Wendell Berry and Bruce Colman, editors, *Meeting the Expectations of the Land* (San Francisco: North Point Press, 1984).

3 See Gregory A. Barton, *The Global History of Organic Farming* (Oxford: Oxford University Press, 2018), pp. 50–51.

4 See Bill Palmer, 'Ida Freund: Teacher, Educator, Feminist and Chemistry Textbook Writer', undated, available on http://tir.ipsitransactions.org/2007/July/Paper%2012.pdf (accessed on 12 September 2023).

5 See https://www.newbotaniststwo.uk/gabrielle-matthaei%20 (accessed on 9 September 2023).

6 Quoted in Louise E. Howard, *Sir Albert Howard in India* (London: Faber and Faber, 1953), pp. 38–39.

7 Barton, *The Global History of Organic Farming*, p. 69.

8 Ibid., pp. 94–95.

9 Louise E. Howard, *Sir Albert Howard in India*, pp. 50f.

10 Ibid., p. 15.

11 Ibid., pp. 57–59.

12 Howard, *Wheat in India*, quoted in Ibid., pp. 227–28.

13 Ibid., p. 90.

14 See the discussion of Brayne's life and work in Clive Dewey, *Anglo-Indian Attitudes: The Mind of the Indian Civil Service* (London: Hambledon Press, 1993).

15 Alyssa M. Kinker and Thomas F. Gieryn, *Composting as Practice and Technology: The Deployment of Scientific Authority in Indian Agriculture*, unpublished typescript, c. mid-1990s, in the author's possession. Quotes from pp. 5, 9, 25.

Howard is also the subject of a chapter in Thomas Gieryn's book, *Cultural Boundaries of Science: Credibility on the Line* (Chicago: The University of Chicago Press, 1998).

16 Bret Wallach, *Losing Asia: Modernization and the Culture of Development* (Baltimore: The Johns Hopkins University Press, 1996), p. 113.

17 Gabrielle L.C. Howard (editor), *The Improvement of Fodder and Foage in India: Papers Read before a Joint Session of the Sections of Agriculture and Botany*, Indian Science Congress, 1923 (Calcutta: Government Press, 1923).

18 Albert Howard and Gabrielle L.C. Howard, *The Saving of Irrigation Water in Wheat Growing* (Calcutta: Government Press, 1921), pp. 1, 9–10 and passim.

19 Howard, quoted in Kinker and Gieryn, *Composting as Practice and Technology*, pp. 19–20.

20 Louise E. Howard, *Sir Albert Howard in India*, p. 40.

21 Albert Howard, 'Introduction', to J. Rodale, *Pay Dirt: Farming and Gardening with Composts* (New York: Devin-Adair, 1947), accessible at https://journeytoforever.org/farm_library/howard_whole.html.

22 Louise E. Howard, *Sir Albert Howard in India*, p. 49.

23 Albert Howard, *Crop Production in India: A Critical Survey of its Problems* (London: Oxford University Press, 1924), p. 28.

24 Ibid., p. 186, emphasis in original.

25 Cf Worster, *Nature's Economy*, p. 234f.

26 J.E. Weaver, review of Albert Howard, 'Crop Production in India: A Critical Survey of its Problems', *Ecology*, Volume 8, Number 2, 1927, pp. 267–68.

27 Albert Howard and Gabrielle L.C. Howard, *The Development of Indian Agriculture* (Bombay: Oxford University Press, 1927), p. iii.

28 Ibid., pp. 13–15.

29 Ibid., p. 49.

30 Ibid., pp. 51–52.

31 Ibid., pp. 60–61.

32 Ibid., p. 67.

33 F.H. King, *Farmers of Forty Centuries: Or Permanent Agriculture in China, Korea and Japan* (first published in 1911, reprint London: Jonathan Cape, 1917), available at https://archive.org/details/in.ernet.dli.2015.224405/page/n1/mode/2up.

34 Albert Howard and Yeshwant D. Wad, *The Waste Products of Agriculture: Their Utilization as Humus* (London: Oxford University Press, 1931), especially Chapters 4 and 5. A printed copy of this book was unavailable to me in Bangalore; I therefore relied on a version up on the Web (at https://journeytoforever.org/farm_library/HowardWPA/

WPAtoc.html). Howard summarized the arguments of this monograph in a lecture he delivered to the Royal Society of Arts. See Howard, 'The Waste Products of Agriculture: Their Utilization as Humus', *Journal of the Royal Society of Arts*, Volume 82, No. 4229, December 1933.

35 Howard and Wad, *The Waste Products of Agriculture*, Preface.

36 Kinker and Gieryn, *Composting as Practice and Technology*, pp. 2–3.

37 Albert Howard, *The Soil and Health* (first published 1947, reprint Lexington: The University Press of Kentucky, 2006), pp. 245–46.

38 Cf Albert Howard, 'An Experiment in the Management of Indian Labour', *International Labour Review*, Volume 18, 1931, reprinted as Appendix D in Howard and Wad, *The Waste Products of Agriculture*.

39 Yeshwant D. Wad, 'The Work at Indore', first published in *Organic Gardening Magazine*, Volume 13, Number 8, September 1948 (Sir Albert Howard Memorial Issue), also available at https://journeytoforever.org/farm_library/howard_memorial.html.

40 See, for more details, Philip Conford, 'The Alchemy of Waste: The Impact of Asian Farming on the British Organic Movement', *Rural History*, Volume 6, Number 1, 1995.

41 Kinker and Gieryn, *Composting as Practice and Technology*, p. 32.

42 Albert Howard, *An Agricultural Testament* (first published by Oxford University Press in 1943, reprint: Rodale Press, 1976), pp. 1–5.

43 Ibid., pp. 9–21.

44 Ibid. p. 219.

45 Ibid., pp. 221–22.

46 Albert Howard, *The Soil and Health* (first published 1947, reprint Lexington: The University Press of Kentucky, 2006), p. 212, emphases in original.

47 See Barton, *The Global History of Organic Farming*, pp. 105–06.

48 Howard, *The Soil and Health*, p. 125.

49 Ibid., pp. 236–37.

50 Ibid., p. 253, emphasis in original.

51 Quoted in Andrew N. Case, *The Organic Profit: Rodale and the Making of Marketplace Environmentalism* (Seattle: University of Washington Press, 2018), pp. 40–41.

52 Case, *The Organic Profit*, pp. 17–18, 36, 129–30.

53 Wendell Berry, 'Introduction', in Howard, *The Soil and Health* (2006 edition), p. viii.

54 J. Heckman, 'A History of Organic Farming: Transitions from Sir Albert Howard's "War in the Soil" to USDA National Organic Program', *Renewable Agriculture and Food Systems*, Volume 21, Number 3, 2006, p. 144.

55 'Compost Manure', *Harijan*, issues of 17 and 24 August 1935.

56 Personal communication from A.R. Vasavi, 7 November 2022. The press in Indore that continues to publish the Howards' books is called Banyan Tree. See www.banyantreebookstore.com.

57 See https://twitter.com/drvandanashiva/status/1275695548729786369.

58 *The Development of Indian Agriculture*, p. 22.

59 Kinker and Gieryn, p. 17.

60 Ibid., pp. 21–22.

61 Gabrielle L.C. Howard, *The Wheats of Baluchistan, Khorasan and the Kurram Valley*, Memoirs of the Department of Agriculture in India, Botanical Series, Volume VIII, No. I (Calcutta: Thacker, Spink and Co., 1916), p. 4 and passim.

62 Gabrielle L.C. Howard, 'The Role of Plant Physiology in Agriculture', *The Agricultural Journal of India*, Volume xviii, Part ii, 1923 (Presidential Address, Section of Botany, Indian Science Congress), quoted remarks from pp. 213, 210, 217.

63 Louise E. Howard, *Sir Albert Howard in India*, p. 21.

64 Ibid., pp. 245–46.

65 'Speech in Reply to Students' Address, Trivandrum', 13 March 1925, in *CWMG*, Volume 26, pp. 299–303.

Chapter Six: Gandhi's Englishwoman

1 See Nandini Oza, 'Laxmi, Mahatma Gandhi's daughter, albeit adopted', in http://nandinikoza.blogspot.com/2015/11/laxmi-mahatma-gandhis-daughter-albeit.html.

2 'Behn' is Gujarati and Hindi for 'sister'.

3 See Richard Attenborough, *In Search of Gandhi* (London: The Bodley Head, 1982), pp. 152–53.

4 Ramachandra Guha, *Rebels against the Raj: Western Fighters for India's Freedom* (London: William Collins, 2022).

5 Madeleine Slade, *The Spirit's Pilgrimage* (New York: Coward-McCann, Inc., 1960), p. 12.

6 Mirabehn, 'The Blessings of Discipline', *Harijan*, 30 November 1947.

7 Mira to Gandhi, 14 October 1928, in Tridip Suhrud and Thomas Weber, editors, *Beloved Bapu: The Gandhi–Mirabehn Correspondence* (Hyderabad: Orient Blackswan, 2014), pp. 120–21.

8 Mira to Gandhi, 16 January 1933, S.N. 20048, Sabarmati Ashram Archives, Ahmedabad. Also in *Beloved Bapu*, p. 341.

9 Mira, 'Wells Opened in Wardha Tahsil', *Harijan*, 24 November 1933.

10 Mira, 'Landscapes', *Harijan*, 8 June 1934.

11 Mira, undated diary entry, c. April 1939, in Correspondence File No. 31, M.K. Gandhi Papers, 1st and 2nd Instalments, NMML.

12 Mira's work with peasants in the Himalayan foothills and her (mostly unsuccessful) efforts to get them to adopt more nature-friendly techniques of farming, animal husbandry, etc. are described in detail in Bidisha Mallik, *Legends in Gandhian Social Activism: Mira Behn and Salara Behn: Addressing Environmental Issues by Dissolving Gender and Colonial Barriers* (Cham, Switzerland: Springer, 2002), Chapter 5 and *passim*.

13 Slade, *The Spirit's Pilgrimage*, p. 277.

14 Mirabehn, 'From Rubbish to Gold', *Harijan*, 10 March 1946.

15 *Harijan*, 23 November 1947.

16 See *Harijan*, 24 April 1949; Guha, *Rebels against the Raj*, p. 301.

17 Mirabehn, 'Tractors v. Bullocks', *Harijan*, 29 September 1946.

18 *CWMG*, Volume 90, p. 264.

19 'Compost Manure', *CWMG*, Volume 90, pp. 269–71.

20 Mirabehn, 'The New Family member', *Harijan*, 1 February 1948.

21 Mirabehn, 'Development or Destruction?', *Harijan*, 23 January 1949.

22 See Krishna Murti Gupta, editor, *Mira Behn: Gandhiji's Daughter Disciple: Birth Centenary Volume* (hereafter *Mira Behn Birth Centenary Volume*, New Delhi: Himalaya Seva Sangh), pp. 147–48.

23 See the correspondence between Mira and Kumarappa in the J.C. Kumarappa Papers, NMML.

24 Mirabehn, 'Startling Facts—II', *Harijan*, 24 April 1949.

25 See the correspondence in *Mira Behn Birth Centenary Volume*, pp. 213–15.

26 Mirabehn, 'Straight from the Heart: A Question and a Suggestion', *Harijan*, 12 April 1952.

27 Mirabehn, 'An Open Letter to Congress Leaders', *Hindustan Times*, 9 July 1952, emphasis in original.

28 Mira, 'Land for the Cow', *Harijan*, 16 August 1952 (originally published in the *Hindustan Times*, 11 July 1952).

29 Mira Behn, 'Itching Palms', typescript, c. mid-October 1949, in Mira Behn Papers, Himalaya Seva Sangh, New Delhi (hereafter Mira Behn Papers).

30 Rajaji to Mira, 19 October 1949, C. Rajagopalachari Papers, NMML. It appears that Mira's lament for the haldu tree was published both in the *Hindustan Times* of New Delhi and the *Amrita Bazar Patrika* of Calcutta.

31 'Something Wrong in the Himalayas', article of June 1950, reprinted in *Mira Behn Birth Centenary Volume*, pp. 145–47.

32 Madeleine Slade to the Editor, *Guardian Weekly*, 20 November 1968., in Mira Behn Papers,

33 Letter from Madeleine Slade to the Editor of the *International Herald Tribune* (IHT), Paris, 11 April 1974, in Mira Behn Papers.

34 Letter to IHT editor, signed Mira Behn/Madeleine Slade, dated 26 April 1974, in Mira Behn Papers.

35 Unpublished article by Mira entitled 'Simplify and Survive', eight-page typescript, c. 1974, in Mira Behn Papers, emphases in original.

36 Copy in Ibid.

37 Mira, 'The Himalayan Frontier', a paper written for a seminar on 'Social Work in the Himalaya', organized by the Delhi School of Social Work, University of Delhi, December 1967, in *Birth Centenary Volume*, pp. 159–62.

38 Mira to Krishna Murti Gupta, 28 May 1972, in Mira Behn Papers.

39 Mirabehn, 'Note on My Feelings about the Himalaya', two-page note, undated, c. 1973, in Mira Behn Papers.

40 Seven-page handwritten note, untitled, dated 22 October 1974, in Mira Behn Papers.

41 See the correspondence in *Birth Centenary Volume*, pp. 288–92.

42 Mira to Morarji Desai, 29 January 1979, in Mira Behn Papers.

43 Mira to Indira Gandhi, 6 July 1980, four-page handwritten letter, in Ibid.

44 Indira Gandhi to Mira, 18 August 1980, in Ibid.

45 Mira to Indira Gandhi, 7 October 1981, emphasis in original, in Ibid.

46 Indira Gandhi to Mira, 18 November 1981, in Ibid.

47 Krishna Murti Gupta, 'Mira Behn', in *Birth Centenary Volume*, p. 49. This was a fine and moving tribute. Otherwise too I owe Krishna Murti Gupta much, for, apart from drawing upon the Birth Centenary Volume he edited, I have also had access to a trove of materials by or about Mira he collected but did not publish, which I found, long after Gupta's own passing, in a cupboard of the Himalaya Seva Sangh in New Delhi.

48 Mira, 'Freedom', a handwritten note, c. April/May 1936, in Correspondence File No. 31, M.K. Gandhi Papers, 1st and 2nd Instalments, NMML.

Chapter Seven: Culture in Nature

1 Verrier Elwin, 'A Darshan of Bapu', *The CSS Review*, Volume 1, Number 4, June 1931.

2 Ramachandra Guha, *Savaging the Civilized: Verrier Elwin, His Tribals, and India* (New Delhi: Oxford University Press, 1999), pp. 11, 15–16; interview with F.W. Dillistone, May 1991.

3 Verrier Elwin, 'Mahatma Gandhi and William Wordsworth', *Modern Review*, February 1931.

4 Verrier Elwin, *St. Francis of Assisi* (Madras: Christian Literature Society of India, 1933), p. 45.

5 Ibid., pp. 99–100.

6 Ibid., p. 97. Elwin was basing his account not on St. Francis's own writings, but on the hagiographies written in the decades and centuries after his death. For an analysis of how this image of St. Francis as a nature lover was constructed by his early followers, see Lisa J. Kiser, 'The Garden of St. Francis: Plants, Landscape and Economy in Thirteenth-Century Italy', *Environmental History*, Volume 8, Number 2, 2003.

7 Shamrao Hivale and Verrier Elwin, *Songs of the Forest: The Folk Poetry of the Gonds* (London: George Allen and Unwin, 1935), p. 33.

8 *Songs of the Forest*, pp. 33–34.

9 Ibid., pp. 40–41.

10 Verrier Elwin, *Leaves from the Jungle: Life in a Gond Village* (London: John Murray, 1936), pp. 28–29.

11 Ibid., p. 22.

12 Verrier Elwin, *The Baiga* (London: John Murray, 1939), pp. 106–07.

13 Ibid., pp. 150–51, 165, 375, 107.

14 Ibid., pp. 124–29.

15 See Harold Conklin, 'An Ethno-Ecological Approach to Shifting Cultivation' (1954), reprinted in Andrew Vayda (ed), *Environment and Cultural Behaviour* (Garden City, NY: Anchor Books, 1969); Clifford Geertz, *Agricultural Involution* (Berkeley: University of California Press, 1963).

16 Elwin, *The Baiga*, p. 131.

17 Ibid., p. 65.

18 Ibid., p. 256.

19 Ibid., p. 260.

20 Verrier Elwin, *The Muria and their Ghotul* (Bombay: Oxford University Press, 1947), pp. 23, 181–82.

21 Verrier Elwin, *The Religion of an Indian Tribe* (Bombay: Oxford University Press, 1955), p. 58.

22 Verrier Elwin, *The Agaria* (Calcutta: Oxford University Press, 1942), pp. 121–22, 267–68, etc.

23 Elwin, *The Baiga*, p. 51.

24 Typescript entitled 'Rhino Reserve' (undated) in File No. ATA/Misc/1 (Serial No. 107), Verrier Elwin Papers, NMML.

25 Verrier Elwin, *The Tribal World of Verrier Elwin: An Autobiography* (Oxford: Oxford University Press, 1964), p. 115.

26 For more details, see Guha, *Savaging the Civilized*, Chapters VI to VIII.

27 Jawaharlal Nehru, 'Foreword to the Second Edition', in Verrier Elwin, *A Philosophy for NEFA* (second edition: Shillong, Government of Assam), p. xiii. For evidence that Elwin helped draft Nehru's foreword, see Guha, *Savaging the Civilized*, pp. 257–59.

28 Elwin, *A Philosophy for NEFA*, p. 66.

29 Elwin, *A Philosophy for NEFA*, pp. 67–69.

30 *Report of the Committee on Special Multipurpose Tribal Blocks* (New Delhi: Ministry of Home Affairs, 1960), pp. 15–16.

31 Ibid., pp. 55–56.

32 Ibid., p. 57.

33 Ibid., pp. 57, 63–65, 67.

34 *Report of the Scheduled Areas and Scheduled Tribes Commission, Volume I* (Delhi: Government of India Press, 1961), p. 125.

35 Ibid., p. 129.

36 Ibid., p. 131.

37 Ibid., pp. 135–37.

38 Cf Nandini Sundar, *The Burning Forest: India's War in Bastar* (New Delhi: Juggernaut, 2016).

39 Aldous Huxley, 'Wordsworth in the Tropics', in *Do What You Will: Twelve Essays* (first published in 1929, reprint London: Chatto and Windus,1956), pp. 113–14.

40 *Songs of the Forest*, pp. 35–36.

41 Ibid., p. 37.

42 Ibid., p 38.

Chapter Eight: The First Hindutva Environmentalist

1 'Freedom from Foreign Bread', in K.M. Munshi, *The Gospel of the Dirty Hand, and Other Speeches on the Policy and Programme of Land Transformation* (New Delhi: The Publications Division, 1952), pp. 9–10.

2 'The Vana Mahotsava', in Munshi, *The Gospel of the Dirty Hand*, pp. 11–13.

3 V.B. Kulkarni, *K.M. Munshi* (New Delhi: The Publications Division), p. 242.

4 Gandhi to K.M. Munshi, 2 November 1945, CWMG, Volume 82, p. 9. For a recent assessment of Munshi as a writer of historical fiction, see Rita Kothari and Abhijit Kothari, 'Past Continuous: K.M. Munshi, Gujarat and the Patan Trilogy', *Economic and Political Weekly*, 1 May 2021.

5 'Vikramaditya: A Living Flame', in K.M. Munshi, *Our Greatest Need and Other Addresses* (Bombay: Bharatiya Vidya Bhavan, 1953), pp 15-18. Cf also the analysis of Munshi's writings in Manu Bhagvan, 'The Hindutva Underground: Hindu Nationalism and the Indian National Congress in Late Colonial and Early Post-colonial India', *Economic and Political Weekly*, 13 September 2008.

6 Kulkarni, *K.M. Munshi*, pp. 254–55.

7 See K.M. Munshi, *Views and Vistas* (Bombay: Bharatiya Vidya Bhavan, 1965), p. 125.

8 K.M. Munshi, *The Creative Art of Life* (Bombay: Bharatiya Vidya Bhavan, 1965), pp 18-20.

9 Alan Campbell-Johnson, *Misson with Mountbatten* (New York: E.P. Dutton and Co, Inc., 1953), p. 294.

10 Munshi, *The Creative Art of Life*, p. 218.

11 'The Culture-Crisis in India', in Munshi, *Our Greatest Need and Other Addresses*, p. 35.

12 'Sanskrit Through the Ages', in Munshi, *Our Greatest Need and Other Addresses*, p. 191.

13 See 'Social Foundations of Indian Culture', in Munshi, *Our Greatest Need and Other Addresses*, pp. 56–57.

14 'Manu Smriti', in Munshi, *Views and Vistas*, pp. 153–54.

15 See Ramachandra Guha, 'Forestry in British and Post-British India: A Historical Analysis', *Economic and Political Weekly*, in two parts, issues of 29 October and 5–12 November 1983.

16 Cf Ramachandra Guha and Madhav Gadgil, 'State Forestry and Social Conflict in British India', *Past and Present*, number 123, May 1989.

17 See Munshi, *Views and Vistas*, p. 24.

18 'A Holy Spot', in Munshi, *The Gospel of the Dirty Hand*, pp. 14–15.

19 'Trees have Many Virtues', in Munshi, *The Gospel of the Dirty Hand*, pp. 16–17.

20 'Sentinels of Culture', in K.M. Munshi, *Our Greatest Need and Other Addresses* (Bombay: Bharatiya Vidya Bhavan, 1953), pp. 77–78. My father and maternal grandfather were most likely in the audience when the minister spoke; in 1951 both were scientists working in the Forest Research Institute.

21 'Safeguarding the Future by Planting Trees', in Munshi, *The Gospel of the Dirty Hand*, pp. 106–08.

22 'Replanting our Life's Philosophy', in Munshi, *The Gospel of the Dirty Hand*, pp. 115–16.

23 'A Philosophy and a Faith', in Munshi, *The Gospel of the Dirty Hand*, pp. 119–22, 126.

24 *Shankar's Weekly*, 2 May 1950.

25 Cf D.F. Karaka, *Nehru: The Lotus Eater of Kashmir* (London: Derek Verschoyle, 1953).

26 Thakorelal M. Desai, '"So Plant More Trees", says Munshi', *The Current*, 7 June 1950.

27 See *The Current*, 12 July 1950.

28 D.F. Karaka, 'Off My Chest', *The Current*, 19 July 1950.

29 K.M. Munshi, 'The Meaning of Vana Mahotsava', *The Current*, 26 September 1951.

30 'The Gospel of the Dirty Hand', in Munshi, *The Gospel of the Dirty Hand*, pp. 181–84.

31 'Trees', in Munshi, *Views and Vistas*, pp. 240–41.

32 The quotations in the preceding paragraphs are from 'Address by Sri. K.M. Munshi, Governor of Uttar Pradesh, on the occasion of Vraj Vana Mahotsava at Giriraj Govardhan near Mathura on August 31, 1953', printed copy in K.M. Munshi Papers, NMML.

33 'Welcome Address by K.M. Munshi, Governor of Uttar Pradesh, at the Fourth World Forestry Congress, Dehra Dun', 11 December 1954, printed copy in Munshi Papers. My father and grandfather would most likely have attended this Munshi speech at the FRI too. I was myself born in the same campus, but only in 1958.

34 See K.M. Munshi, *The Wolf Boy and Other Kulapati's Letters* (Bombay: Bharatiya Vidya Bhavan, 1956), pp. 60–61.

35 P. Sankaranarayanan, 'Many-Sided Munshi', in *Munshi at Seventy-Five: Volume of articles on the various facets of Dr. K. M. Munshi by his contemporaries* (Bombay: Dr. K. M. Munshi's 76th Birthday Celebrations Committee, 1962), p. 13.

36 'Minister of Food and Agriculture', chapter written by 'an old associate in the Food Ministry', in J.H. Dave, C.L. Gheewala, A.C. Bose, R.P. Aiyar and A.K. Majumdar, editors, *Munshi: His Art and Work: Volume II: Fifty Years of Politics* (Shri Munshi Seventieth Birthday Citizens' Celebrations Committee, 1957), p. 317.

37 'Dr Munshi's Reply to Felicitations', in *Munshi at Seventy-Five*, p. 176.

38 See Shvetal Vyas Pare, 'Writing Fiction, Living History: Kanhaiyalal Munshi's Historical Trilogy', *Modern Asian Studies*, Volume 48, Number 3, 2014, pp. 600–01; Vinay Sitapati, *Jugalbandi: The BJP Before Modi* (New Delhi: Penguin, 2020), p. 124.

39 K. Sivaramakrishnan, 'Ethics of Nature in Indian Environmental History', *Modern Asian Studies*, Volume 49, Number 4, 2015.

40 Emma Tomalin, *Biodivinity and Biodiversity: The Limits to Religious Environmentalism* (London: Routledge, 2009).

41 See, among other works, O.P. Dwivedi and B.N. Tiwari, 'Environmental Protection in the Hindu Religion', in. O.P. Dwivedi, editor, *World Religions and the Environment* (New Delhi: Gitanjali Publishing House, 1989); Banwari, *Pancavati: Indian Approach to Environment*, translated from Hindi by Asha Vohra (Delhi: Shri Vinayaka Publications, 1992); and Mukul Sharma, *Green and Saffron: Hindu Nationalism and Indian Environmental Politics* (Ranikhet: Permanent Black, 2012), in all of which there is no mention of Munshi.

Chapter Nine: Speaking for Nature

1 These paragraphs draw on an unpublished memoir written by Krishnan and shared with me by his nephew, A. Madhavan.

2 M. Krishnan, 'Wild Life—I: The Past; II: The Near Past; III: The Present; IV: The Future', *The Illustrated Weekly of India*, (hereafter IWI), 21 and 28 February and 7 and 14 March 1965.

3 There are many biographies of Jim Corbett, among which my personal favourite is Martin Booth, *Carpet Sahib: A Life of Jim Corbett* (London: Constable and Co., 1986). Salim Ali has not yet been the subject of a proper biography. However, he did write a delightful autobiography—*The Fall of a Sparrow* (New Delhi: Oxford University Press, 1988), which describes his work in rich detail.

4 'Introduction', in M. Krishnan, *Birds and Birdsong*, edited by Shanthi and Ashish Chandola (New Delhi: Aleph, 2012), p. 13.

5 M. Krishnan, 'Wildlife Tourism', *The Sunday Statesman* (hereafter TSS), 6 December 1981.

6 M. Krishnan, 'A Tiger Sanctuary', TSS, 15 September 1963.

7 M. Krishnan, 'Trees for the Countryside', TSS, 13 September 1987.

8 M. Krishnan, 'The Wild Life of Wastelands', TSS, 23 June 1985.

9 M. Krishnan, 'Spirit of Silent Valley', TSS, 15 June 1980. Silent Valley was finally saved through the combination of a popular social movement led by the Kerala Sastra Sahitya Parishad, a critical report by a group of scientists, and the personal intervention of Prime Minister Indira

Gandhi. See Darryl D' Monte, *Temples or Tombs? Industry versus Environment: Three Controversies* (New Delhi: Centre for Science and Environment, 1985).

10 M. Krishnan, 'Non-Reclamation', TSS, 7 March 1954.

11 See M. Krishnan, *My Native Land: Essays on Nature*, edited by S. Theodore Baskaran and A. Rangarajan (Mumbai: Indus Source Books, 2019), pp. 234–40.

12 Personal communication from Professor Madhav Gadgil, who was present on the occasion.

13 From a letter written in the 1980s to A. Madhavan, shared with me by the recipient.

14 M. Krishnan, 'The Day–Flowering Cactus', TSS, 13 May 1984.

15 M. Krishnan, 'Trees for the Countryside', TSS, 13 September 1987.

16 M. Krishnan, 'Down South', IWI, 7 October 1965.

17 M. Krishnan, 'Unnatural Natural History', *The Hindu*, 20 February 1955.

18 M. Krishnan, 'Englishmen's Interest in Natural History', *The Hindu*, 17 August 1947.

19 M. Krishnan, *Vedanthangal: Water-Bird Sanctuary* (first published 1960, revised edition Madras: Government of Tamil Nadu, 1986), pp. 11, 22–23, etc.

20 M. Krishnan, 'Focus on the Fauna', IWI, 4 September 1966.

21 M. Krishnan, 'A Lament for Lost Wood', *The Hindu*, 21 July 1957.

22 M. Krishnan, 'The Blackbuck of Bhetnoi', TSS, 8 September 1974.

23 M. Krishnan, 'A Wild Life Policy for India', TSS, 12 March 1961.

24 M. Krishnan, 'Giant Squirrels', TSS, 20 September 1992.

25 Cf M. Krishnan, 'Nesting Grey Pelicans', TSS, 3 January 1985.

26 M. Krishnan, 'Eating Night and Day', TSS, 13 January 1991.

27 M. Krishnan, 'The Mudumalai Sanctuary', *The Hindu*, 27 April 1958.

28 M. Krishnan, 'Cattle Grazing in Sanctuaries', TSS, 17 February 1985.

29 M. Krishnan, 'Grazing in the Ghana', TSS, 4 January 1987.

30 V.S. Vijayan, *Keoladeo National Park Ecology Study, 1980–1990: Final Report* (Bombay: Bombay Natural History Society, 1991), quotes from pp. 301–02.

31 Cf R.J.R. Daniels, Madhav Gadgil and N.V. Joshi, 'Impact of Human Extraction on Tropical Humid Forests in the Western Ghats, Uttara Kannada, South India', *Journal of Applied Ecology*, Volume 32, Number 4, 1995.

32 M. Krishnan, 'Carrying Capacity', TSS, 11 October 1981. Cf also M. Krishnan, 'The Wild Life (Protection) Act of 1972: A Critical Appraisal', *Economic and Political Weekly*, 17 March 1973.

33 S. Theodore Baskaran, 'The Tamil Writings of M. Krishnan', *Blackbuck,* Volume 16, Number 1.

34 M. Krishnan, 'Rural Themes in Indian Writing: Tamil', IWI, 18 August 1963.

35 M. Krishnan, 'The Fauna and Flora of South India', TSS, 19 June 1958. Cf also M. Krishnan, 'South India Offers the Best of Wildlife in the World', *Deccan Herald*, 20 August 1967.

36 M. Krishnan, 'Eagles in the Desert', TSS, 13 July 1980.

37 M. Krishnan, 'The Wildlife of Madras City: A Note for Kartik Shankar (sic)', c. November 1991, copy in the possession of Kartik Shanker. This note was reprinted in *Current Conservation*, Volume 8, Number 1, 2014.

38 M. Krishnan, 'Down South', IWI, 16 April 1967.

39 M. Krishnan, 'The Green Cover', in two parts, TSS, 5 and 19 May 1991.

40 M. Krishnan, 'Exclusively Indian', TSS, 18 February 1996.

41 M. Krishnan to A. Madhavan, 30 October 1988, copy in my possession.

42 M. Krishnan to Ashish Kothari, 18 June 1991, letter in the possession of Ashish Kothari.

43 Ramachandra Guha, editor, *Nature's Spokesman: M. Krishnan and Indian Wildlife* (New Delhi: Oxford University Press, 2000).

44 M. Harikrishnan, 'Krishnan as I Knew Him', in *Birds and Birdsong*, p. 302.

Epilogue: A Partially Usable Past?

1 Donald Worster, *Nature's Economy* (1986 edition), pp. xi, 5, 338. Apart fom being presentist, Worster's book is also marked by ideological fervour, with the historian as partisan praising those thinkers of the past who embraced what he sees as an authentically 'biocentric' perspective on nature, while disparaging those who took a more human-centred approach.

2 Frank Uekötter, *The Greenest Nation?*, p. 23.

3 Peder Anker, *The Power of the Periphery*, pp. 4–5, 75–87, etc.

4 Ramachandra Guha, 'Radical American Environmentalism and Wilderness Preservation: A Third World Critique', *Environmental Ethics*, Volume 11, Number 1, Spring 1989.

5 Isabella Tree, 'Introduction', in *Granta*, Number 153, Autumn 2020, p. 11.

6 Margaret Atwood, *Burning Questions: Essays and Occasional Pieces, 2004–2021* (London: Chatto and Windus, 2022), p. 76.

7 Tagore, *Nationalism*, pp. 8–9.

8 'The Same Old Argument', *Young India*, 7 October 1926, in CWMG, Volume 31, p. 478f.

9 E.F. Schumacher, *Small Is Beautiful: A Study of Economics as if People Mattered* (first published in 1973, reprint London: Abacus, 1975), p. 46.

10 See Barbara Wood, *Alias Papa: Life of Fritz Schumacher* (London: Jonathan Cape, 1984).

11 E.F. Schumacher, 'The Economics of Permanence', *Resurgence*, Volume 3, Number 1, May/June 1970.

12 The influence of Howard on Schumacher is documented in Gregory Barton, *The Global History of Organic Farming*, p. 160f.

13 Howard, *The Soil and Health*, p. 253.

14 Charles Massy, 'The Ard, the Ant and the Anthropocene', *Granta*, Number 153, Autumn 2020, pp. 35–36 and passim.

15 Barton, *The Global History of Organic Farming*, p. 2.

16 See Tom Philpott, *Perilous Bounty: The Looming Collapse of American Farming and How We Can Prevent it* (New York: Bloomsbury Publishing, 2020).

17 This account of the contemporaneity of the Howards' work owes a great deal to conversations with the sociologist A.R. Vasavi.

18 Munshi, *Patrick Geddes's Contribution to Sociology and Urban Planning*, p. 146.

19 Cf 'Global Warming is Killing Indians and Pakistanis', https://www.economist.com/asia/2023/04/02/global-warming-is-killing-indians-and-pakistanis (accessed on 3 April 2023).

20 For a valuable overview of the environmental challenges India faces today, see Usha Alexander, 'The Overshoot Story: India's Approach to Global Warming Cannot Mirror the West', *The Caravan*, June 2023 (also accessible at https://caravanmagazine.in/books/india-approach-global-warming).

On the economic costs of environmental degradation in India, see Muthukumara Mani, editor, *Greening India's Growth: Costs, Valuations, and Trade-Offs* (New Delhi: Routledge, 2013).

21 Rohan D'Souza, 'Environmental History of South Asia in the Time of Hindutva', *Environmental History*, Volume 27, Number 4, 2022, pp 628-29 and passim.

22 See https://www.clearias.com/environmental-performance-index/, accessed on 9 September 2023.

23 Gurcharan Das, writing in *The Times of India*, 6 March 2011.

24 Praful Patel, then minister of civil aviation, quoted in *The Times of India*, 13 October 2010.

25 Akshat Rathi, *Climate Capitalism: Winning the Race to Zero Emissions* (London: John Murray, 2023), p. 8.

26 Hal K. Rothman, *Saving the Planet: The American Response to the Environment in the Twentieth Century* (Chicago: Ivan R. Dee, 2000), p. 192.

27 Julie Livingston, *Self-Devouring Growth: A Planetary Parable as Told from Southern Africa* (Durham, N.C.: Duke University Press, 2019), quoted remarks from pp. 1, 5, 8, 125–26.

28 Tagore, 'The Robbery of the Soil', in *Poet and Plowman*, p. 34.

29 Ibid., pp. 38–39.

30 Mirabehn, 'Startling Facts—II', *Harijan*, 24 April 1949.

31 Jodha's essays of the 1980s and 1990s are collected in his book *Life on the Edge: Sustaining Agriculture and Community Resources in Fragile Environments* (New Delhi: Oxford University Press, 2001).

32 See https://www.nobelprize.org/prizes/economic-sciences/2009/ostrom/facts/ (accessed on 31 December 2023).

33 For a book-length study of these community forestry initiatives, see Milind Bokil, *Village Republic: The Story of Mendha-Lekha* (Hyderabad: Orient Blackswan, forthcoming).

34 Cf Harini Nagendra, *Nature in the City: Bengaluru in the Past, Present and Future* (New Delhi: Oxford University Press, 2016).

35 Douglas Brinkley, *Silent Spring Revolution: John F. Kennedy, Rachel Carson, Lyndon Johnson, Richard Nixon and the Great Environmental Awakening* (New York: HarperCollins, 2022), quotes from pp. xxviii, xxix, emphasis in original.

36 Smith, *African American Environmental Thought*, p. 9.

37 Camille T. Dungy, 'Is All Writing Environmental Writing', *The Georgia Review*, Fall/Winter 2018, available online at https://thegeorgiareview.com/posts/is-all-writing-environmental-writing/ (accessed on 11 November 2023).

38 Cf Murray Bookchin, 'What Is Social Ecology?' (1993), in https://theanarchistlibrary.org/library/murray-bookchin-what-is-social-ecology (accessed on 1 January 2024).

39 See CWMG, Volume 89, p. 125.

40 'Discussion with a Capitalist', *Young India*, 20 December 1928, in CWMG, Volume 38, p. 243.

41 Radhakamal Mukerjee, *The Regional Balance of Man: An Ecological Theory of Population* (Madras: University of Madras, 1938), being based on the Sir William Meyer Foundation Lectures, delivered at the University in 1935-36), pp. 2–3.

42 See E.O. Wilson, *Half Earth: Our Planet's Fight for Life* (New York: Liveright, 2016).

43 See Bram Büscher, Robert Fletcher, et al., 'Half Earth or Whole Earth? Radical Ideas for Conservation, and their Implications', *Oryx,* Volume 51, Number 3, 2017, pp 407-10. Cf also Sharachchandra Lele, 'From Wildlife-ism to Ecosystem-service-ism to a Broader Environmentalism', *Conservation*, Volume 48, Number 1, 2020.

44 Jedediah Purdy, *After Nature: A Politics for the Anthropocene* (Cambridge, Mass.: Harvard University Press, 2015), p. 6.

45 See, for example, this report: https://indianexpress.com/article/india/india-heading-towards-groundwater-depletion-tipping-point-warns-un-report-9001338/ (accessed on 26 November 2023).

Index

About the Author

Ramachandra Guha was born and raised in the Himalayan foothills. He studied in Delhi and Kolkata, and has lived for many years in Bengaluru. His books include a pioneering environmental history, *The Unquiet Woods*, a landmark history of the Republic, *India after Gandhi*, and an authoritative two-volume biography of Mahatma Gandhi, each of which was chosen by the *New York Times* as a Notable Book of the Year. His books and essays have been translated into more than twenty languages.

Ramachandra Guha has taught at Stanford and Oslo, held the Phillippe Roman Chair at the London School of Economics, and served as the Satish Dhawan Visiting Professor at the Indian Institute of Science. He is currently Distinguished University Professor at Krea University. Guha's awards include the Leopold-Hidy Prize of the American Society of Environmental History, the Howard Milton Prize of the British Society for Sports History, the Elizabeth Longford Prize for Historical Biography, the Sahitya Akademi Award, and the Fukuoka Prize for contributions to Asian studies. He is the recipient of an honorary doctorate in the humanities from Yale University.

HarperCollins *Publishers* India

At HarperCollins India, we believe in telling the best stories and finding the widest readership for our books in every format possible. We started publishing in 1992; a great deal has changed since then, but what has remained constant is the passion with which our authors write their books, the love with which readers receive them, and the sheer joy and excitement that we as publishers feel in being a part of the publishing process.

Over the years, we've had the pleasure of publishing some of the finest writing from the subcontinent and around the world, including several award-winning titles and some of the biggest bestsellers in India's publishing history. But nothing has meant more to us than the fact that millions of people have read the books we published, and that somewhere, a book of ours might have made a difference.

As we look to the future, we go back to that one word—a word which has been a driving force for us all these years.

Read.

Harper Collins · 4th · HARPER FICTION · HARPER NON-FICTION · HARPER BUSINESS · HarperCollins *Children's Books*

HARPER DESIGN · Harper Sport · HARPER PERENNIAL · HARPER VANTAGE · हार्पर हिन्दी